THE KINGDOMS OF ISRAEL AND JUDAH IN THE EIGHTH AND SEVENTH CENTURIES B.C.E.

Biblical Encyclopedia
Leo G. Perdue, Series Editor

An English Translation of Biblische Enzyklopädie
Walter Dietrich and Wolfgang Stegemann, Editors

Volume 5

The Kingdoms of Israel and Judah in
the Eighth and Seventh Centuries B.C.E.

THE KINGDOMS OF ISRAEL AND JUDAH IN THE EIGHTH AND SEVENTH CENTURIES B.C.E.

by

Antoon Schoors

Translated by Michael Lesley

Society of Biblical Literature
Atlanta

THE KINGDOMS OF ISRAEL AND JUDAH IN THE EIGHTH AND SEVENTH CENTURIES B.C.E.

Copyright © 2013 by the Society of Biblical Literature

A translation of Die Königreiche Israel und Juda im 8. und 7. Jahrhundert v. Chr. (1998), published under license from © W. Kohlhammer GmbH Stuttgart.

All rights reserved. No part of this work may be reproduced or transmitted in any form or by any means, electronic or mechanical, including photocopying and recording, or by means of any information storage or retrieval system, except as may be expressly permitted by the 1976 Copyright Act or in writing from the publisher. Requests for permission should be addressed in writing to the Rights and Permissions Office, Society of Biblical Literature, 825 Houston Mill Road, Atlanta, GA 30329 USA.

Library of Congress Cataloging-in-Publication Data

Schoors, A. (Antoon), author.
 [Königreiche Israel und Juda im 8. und 7. Jahrhundert v. Chr. English]
 The Kingdoms of Israel and Judah in the eighth and seventh centuries B.C.E. / by Antoon Schoors ; translated by Michael Lesley.
  p. cm. — (Society of Biblical Literature biblical encyclopedia series ; no. 5)
 Includes bibliographical references and indexes.
 ISBN: 978-1-58983-264-0 (paper binding : alk. paper) — ISBN 978-1-58983-671-6 (electronic format) — ISBN 978-1-58983-764-5 (hardcover binding : alk. paper)
 1. Jews—History—To 586 B.C. 2. Bible. O.T. Kings, 2nd. XV,8–XXI,26—History of Biblical events. 3. Bible. O.T. Chronicles, 2nd. XXVII–XXXIII—History of Biblical events. 4. Judaism—History. I. Title.
 DS121.6.S3613 2013
 222'.54095—dc23   2013004008

Printed on acid-free, recycled paper conforming to
ANSI/NISO Z39.48-1992 (R1997) and ISO 9706:1994
standards for paper permanence.

Contents

Foreword ix
Timeline x
Abbreviations xi
Map: Palestine in the Iron Age xv
Acknowledgments for Figures xvi

I. The Biblical Depiction of the Period 1
    I.1.   Presentation 1
    I.1.1.   The Kings of Israel and the Fall of Samaria 1
    I.1.2.   The Kings of Judah 3
    I.1.3.   The Prophets 8
    I.1.4.   Further Literary Activity 10
    I.2.   Analysis...10
    I.2.1.   2 Kings 15:8–21:26 10
    I.2.1.1.   The Kings of Northern Israel 11
    I.2.1.2.   The Kings of Judah 14
    I.2.1.3.   The Deuteronomistic Image of the Era 27
    I.2.2.   2 Chronicles 27–33..31
    I.2.2.1.   The Kings of Judah 32
    I.2.2.2.   The Chronicler's Image of the Era 43
    I.2.3.   The Prophets 45
    I.2.3.1.   Hosea...45
    I.2.3.2.   Isaiah 49
    I.2.3.2.1. Analysis of Texts from Isaiah with Historical Information.......50
    I.2.3.2.2. Outcome 62
    I.2.3.3.   Micah 64
    I.2.4.   Further Biblical Sources 65

II. The History of the Era..67
    II.1.   Sources..67
    II.1.1.   Literary Sources...67
    II.1.2.   Inscriptions 68
    II.2.   Archaeological Discoveries..73

	II.3.	Economic and Social History 88
	II.3.1.	Economy 88
	II.3.2.	Society 93
	II.3.3.	Institutions 97
	II.4.	Political History 100
	II.4.1.	The Assyrian Crisis 101
	II.4.2.	The Syro-Ephraimitic War and the End of the Kingdom of Israel 102
	II.4.3.	Judah under Hezekiah 104
	II.4.4.	Judah under Manasseh and Amon 106
	II.5.	Religious History 108
	II.5.1.	Assyrian Religion 108
	II.5.2.	Hezekiah's Reform 110
	II.5.3.	The Prophets 111
III.	The Literature of the Era 121
	III.1.	Genres 121
	III.1.1.	Prophetic Genres 121
	III.1.2.	The Covenant Code 132
	III.1.3.	Ur-Deuteronomy 136
	III.1.4.	Wisdom Literature: The Proverbs of Solomon 140
	III.2.	Works 149
	III.2.1.	Prophetic Works 149
	III.2.1.1.	Amos 154
	III.2.1.2.	Hosea 161
	III.2.1.3.	Isaiah 167
	III.2.1.4.	Micah 175
	III.2.1.5.	Nahum 180
	III.2.2.	The Covenant Code 183
	III.2.3.	Ur-Deuteronomy 188
	III.2.4.	Early Royal and Prophetic Narratives 197
	III.2.5.	Early Forms of the Patriarchal History 203
	III.2.6.	Collections of Proverbs in the Book of Proverbs ... 210
	III.2.7.	Conclusion 214
IV.	The Theological Significance of the Era 217
	IV.1.	The Prophets 217
	IV.1.1.	Theological Significance of the Prophets 217
	IV.1.2.	Relationship with God 219
	IV.1.2.1.	Monotheism 224
	IV.1.3.	Cult 227

IV.1.4.	Law and Justice: The Ethics of the Prophets	230
IV.1.5.	Politics	236
IV.1.6.	Judgment and Conversion	238
IV.1.7.	History, Eschatology, and Messianism	244
IV.1.7.1.	Conception of History	244
IV.1.7.2.	Eschatology and Messianism	245
IV.1.7.2.1.	Zion according to Isaiah	247
IV.1.7.2.2.	The Messianism of Isaiah and Micah	248
IV.2.	The Laws	251
IV.2.1.	Law and Prophets	251
IV.2.2.	The Religious and Ethical Message of the Laws	253
IV.3.	Narrative Literature	255
IV.3.1.	The Early Kingship Narratives	255
IV.3.2.	The History of the Patriarchs	256
IV.4.	Proverbs	257
IV.4.1.	Prophecy and Wisdom	257
IV.4.2.	The Theology of Proverbs	258
IV.5.	The Importance of Prophetic Theology for Our Time	261

Index of Names 267
Index of Authors 271
Index of Subjects 277
Index of Biblical References 280

Foreword

The editor of this series, Prof. Dr. Walter Dietrich, was of great assistance in the realization of this work with his critical notes and suggestions. I owe special thanks to him, as well as to Dr. Stefan Wälchli and Licentiate Alois Greiler for their careful proofreading and linguistic revisions of my German text.

This book is dedicated with love to my children, Miriam and Johan, who, along with their mother, suffered a bit *"from the Assyrian crisis."*

Lubbeek, June 1997   Antoon Schoors

Timeline

Nearly all the sketches of ancient Near Eastern chronology differ from one another, even the ones in the individual volumes of the Biblical Encyclopedia series. The dates in this volume take the following timetables as a basis.

Judah	Israel	Assyria	Egypt
Jotham (?–742)	Zechariah and Shallum (745)		
	Menahem (745–736)		
		Tiglath-pileser III (744–727)	
Ahaz (742–727)			
	Pekahiah (736–735)		
	Pekah (735–732)		
	Hoshea (732–723)		
Hezekiah (727–698)		Shalmaneser V (727–722)	
	fall of Samaria (722)	Sargon II (722–705)	Shabaka (712–698)
		Merodach-Baladan (Babylon; 721–710; 703)	
		Sennacherib (705–681)	
Sennacherib's campaign (701)			Shebitku (698–690)
Manasseh (697–642)			Taharqa (690–671)
		Esarhaddon (680–669)	
		Ashurbanipal (668–627)	
Amon (642–640)			

Abbreviations

AB	Anchor Bible
ABRL	Anchor Bible Reference Library
AcOr	*Acta orientalia*
AJSL	*American Journal of Semitic Languages and Literatures*
ANET	*Ancient Near Eastern Texts Relating to the Old Testament.* Edited by James B. Pritchard. 3rd ed. Princeton, N.J.: Princeton University Press, 1969.
AOAT	Alter Orient und Altes Testament
AOT	*Altorientalische Texte zum Alten Testament.* Edited by Hugo Gressmann. 2nd ed. Berlin: de Gruyter, 1926.
ASTI	*Annual of the Swedish Theological Institute*
ATD	Das Alte Testament Deutsch
ATDan	Acta theologica danica
AUSS	*Andrews Univesity Seminary Studies*
BA	Biblical Archaeologist
BASOR	*Bulletin of the American Schools of Oriental Research*
BBB	Bonner biblische Beiträge
BBET	Beiträge zur biblischen Exegese und Theologie
BEATAJ	Beiträge zur Erforschung des Alten Testaments und des antiken Judentum
BETL	Bibliotheca ephemeridum theologicarum lovaniensium
BEvT	Beiträge zur evangelischen Theologie
Bib	*Biblica*
BibLeb	*Bibel und Leben*
BKAT	Biblischer Kommentar. Altes Testament
BN	*Biblische Notizen*
BO	*Bibliotheca orientalis*
BWANT	Beiträge zur Wissenschaft vom Alten und Neuen Testament
BZ	*Biblische Zeitschrift*
BZAW	Beihefte zur Zeitschrift fur die alttestamentliche Wissenschaft
CAT	Commentaire de l'Ancien Testament
CBQ	*Catholic Biblical Quarterly*

CBQMS	Catholic Biblical Quarterly Monograph Series
ConBOT	Coniectanea biblica: Old Testament Series
DBS	*Dictionnaire de la Bible: Supplément*. Edited by Louis Pirot and André Robert. Paris: Letouzey et Ané, 1928–.
EBib	Etudes bibliques
EdF	Erträge der Forschung
ErIsr	*Eretz-Israel*
EÜ	Einheitsübersetzung
EurHS	Europäische Hochschulschriften
EvT	*Evangelische Theologie*
FAT	Forschungen zum Alten Testament
FOTL	Forms of the Old Testament Literature
FRLANT	Forschungen zur Religion und Literatur des Alten und Neuen Testaments
FzB	Forschung zur Bibel
GAT	Grundrisse zum Alten Testament
HALOT	Ludwig Köhler and Walter Baumgartner. *The Hebrew and Aramaic Lexicon of the Old Testament*. Rev. by Walter Baumgartner and J. J. Stamm. Translated and edited under the supervision of M. E. J. Richardson. 5 vols. Leiden: Brill, 1994–2000.
HAR	*Hebrew Annual Review*
HAT	Handbuch zum Alten Testament
HKAT	Handkommentar zum Alten Testament
HUCA	*Hebrew Union College Annual*
IB	*The Interpreter's Bible*. Edited by G. A. Buttrick et al. 12 vols. Nashville: Abingdon, 1953–1957.
ICC	International Critical Commentary
IEJ	*Israel Exploration Journal*
Int	*Interpretation*
JAOS	*Journal of the American Oriental Society*
JBL	*Journal of Biblical Literature*
JETS	*Journal of the Evangelical Theological Society*
JNES	*Journal of Near Eastern Studies*
JNSL	*Journal of Northwest Semitic Languages*
JSem	*Journal of Semitics*
JSOT	*Journal for the Study of the Old Testament*
JSOTSup	Journal for the Study of the Old Testament Supplement Series
KAI	*Kanaanäische und aramäische Inschriften*. Edited by Herbert Donner and Wolfgang Rollig. 2nd ed. Wiesbaden: Harrassowitz, 1962–1964.

KAT	Kommentar zum Alten Testament
KHC	Kurzer Handcommentar zum Alten Testament
LTK	*Lexikon für Theologie und Kirche*
MdB	Le Monde de la Bible
NCB	New Century Bible
NEchtB	Neue Echter Bibel
NedTT	*Nederlands theologisch tijdschrift*
NICOT	New International Commentary on the Old Testament
NKZ	*Neue kirchliche Zeitschrift*
OBO	Orbis biblicus et orientalis
OIP	Oriental Institute Publications
OLP	*Orientalia lovaniensia periodica*
OrAnt	*Oriens Antiquus*
OTL	Old Testament Library
OTM	Old Testament Message
OTS	*Oudtestamentische Studien*
POT	De Prediking van het Oude Testament
RB	*Revue biblique*
RevScRel	*Revue des sciences religieuses*
RHPR	*Revue d'histoire et de philosophie religieuses*
SBLDS	Society of Biblical Literature Dissertation Series
SBLMS	Society of Biblical Literature Monograph Series
SBS	Stuttgarter Bibelstudien
ScEs	*Science et Esprit*
ScrHier	*Scripta Hierosolymitana*
SJOT	*Scandinavian Journal of the Old Testament*
SEÅ	*Svensk exegetisk årsbok*
SHANE	Studies in the History of the Ancient Near East
ST	*Studia theologica*
TAJ	*Tel Aviv Journal of the Institute of Archaeology*
TGI	Textbuch zur Geschichte Israels. Edited by Kurt Galling. 2nd ed. Tübingen: Mohr Siebeck, 1968.
ThB	Theologische Bücherei
ThWAT	*Theologisches Wörterbuch zum Alten Testament.* Edited by G. J. Botterweck and H. Ringgren. Stuttgart: Kohlhammer, 1970–.
TLZ	*Theologische Literaturzeitung*
TOTC	Tyndale Old Testament Commentaries
TP	*Theologie und Philosophie*
TRE	*Theologische Realenzyklopädie.* Edited by Gerhard Krause and Gerhard Müller. 36 vols. Berlin: de Gruyter, 1976–2004.

TRu	*Theologische Rundschau*
TTZ	*Trierer theologische Zeitschrift*
TUAT	*Texte aus der Umwelt des Alten Testaments.* Edited by Otto Kaiser. 3 vols.; Gütersloh: Mohn, 1982–1997.
TZ	*Theologische Zeitschrift*
UF	*Ugarit-Forschungen*
VD	*Verbum domini*
VF	*Verkündigung und Forschung*
VT	*Vetus Testamentum*
VTSup	Supplements to Vetus Testamentum
WBC	Word Biblical Commentary
WMANT	Wissenschaftliche Monographien zum Alten und Neuen Testament
ZAW	*Zeitschrift für die alttestamentliche Wissenschaft*
ZBK	Zürcher Bibelkommentare
ZDMG	*Zeitschrift der Deutschen Morgenländischen Gesellschaft*
ZDPV	*Zeitschrift des Deutschen Palästina-Vereins*
ZTK	*Zeitschrift fur Theologie und Kirche*

Palestine in the Iron Age

Acknowledgments for Figures

Fig. 1. After Yohanan Aharoni, *Beer-Sheba I: Excavations at Tel Beer-Sheba, 1969–1971 Seasons* (Tel Aviv: University Institute of Archaeology, 1973), 71.

Figs. 2 and 10. © Trustees of the British Museum.

Figs. 3, 4, 6, 7, and 8. After Helga Weippert, *Palästina in vorhellenistischer Zeit* (Handbuch der Archäologie, Vorderasien 2.1; Munich: Beck 1988), (3) 590; (4) 592; (6) 602; (7) 630; (8) pl. 19.

Fig. 5. After Volkmar Fritz, "Die eisenzeitliche Stadt auf dem Tell es-Seba' im Negev," *Antike Welt* 9.4 (1978): 28.

Fig. 9. From David Ussishkin, *The Conquest of Lachish by Sennacherib* (Tel Aviv: Institute of Archaeology, 1982), 88–89. Drawing by Judith Dekel.

I. The Biblical Depiction of the Period

I.1. Presentation

I.1.1. The Kings of Israel and the Fall of Samaria

The history of the kings of (northern) Israel is recounted only in 2 Kings because the Chronicler, the redactor of the books of Chronicles, writes as little as possible about the kingdom of Israel. Although the reign of Jeroboam II had been both long and economically and politically successful, the biblical author of Kings still strongly condemned it. After Jeroboam's reign, the dynasty of Jehu came to an end. Jeroboam's son Zechariah reigned in Samaria for only six months before he was killed by a conspirator named Shallum, who became king in his place. The author of Kings accuses Zechariah and his ancestors of the sins of Jeroboam I (2 Kgs 15:8–10). The end of the dynasty is explained as having been the fulfillment of the word of the Lord to Jehu: "your sons of the fourth generation shall sit on the throne of Israel" (2 Kgs 10:30).

Zechariah's successor, Shallum, reigned only one month and was then himself a victim of usurpation, by Menahem of Tirzah. The Bible refers to a bloody incident during this revolution: Menahem conquered Tirzah, and because the people did not open the gates for him, he killed all the residents of the town and, in the massacre, cut open the wombs of all pregnant women (2 Kgs 15:13–16).

Menahem reigned for ten years and he, too, did not abstain from the sins of Jeroboam. During his reign, Pul (Tiglath-pileser III), king of Assyria, entered the land, and Menahem paid him tribute of a thousand talents silver, "so that he might help him confirm his hold on the royal power" (2 Kgs 15:19). To afford this heavy tribute he was forced to impose a tax of fifty silver shekels of silver on the prosperous men (2 Kgs 15:20). His son Pekahiah succeeded him and reigned for two years. His throne was also usurped, by his adjutant

(שליש), Pekah son of Remaliah, who, with the help of the Gileadites, killed Pekahiah at his palace in Samaria (2 Kgs 15:23–25).

Pekah reigned for twenty years. During his reign, the Assyrian king Tiglath-pileser advanced on Ijon, Abel-beth-maacah, Janoah, Kedesh, Hazor, Gilead, and Galilee, conquered them, and carried off their inhabitants to Assyria (2 Kgs 15:27–29). Second Kings 16:7–9 recounts that King Ahaz of Judah appealed to Tiglath-pileser for aid against the kings of Damascus and Israel, which led to the fall of Damascus. The biblical narrator does not mention any connection between this conflict and the conquest of the aforementioned cities and districts.

Pekah also was usurped and killed by Hoshea, son of Elah, who became king in his place (2 Kgs 15:30). Hoshea reigned for nine years, and the author of the biblical history stresses that, although he did what displeased the Lord, he did not do it to the same extent as his predecessors. Shalmaneser of Ashur challenged him, and Hoshea became his vassal. Later, however, Hoshea participated in a conspiracy against the Assyrian king, which is clear both in his negotiations with the Egyptian king So and in his cessation of tribute payments. The Assyrians arrested him, invaded the whole land, and went to Samaria, to which they laid siege for three years. The city was conquered and the Israelites were taken to Assyria, where they were settled in Halah, on the Habor River, and in the cities of the Medes (2 Kgs 17:1–5; 18:9–11). According to Isa 8:1–14, the prophet had predicted the destruction of Damascus and Samaria.

This was the end of Israel's kingdom. Reflecting on the end of the northern kingdom, the author of Kings offers a long list of sins that were supposed to have led to the destruction. The supposedly primary sin was the religious schism (1 Kgs 12:26–33), a sin mentioned alongside each king of Israel as well as in 2 Kgs 17:21–22. While the two calves in particular are mentioned (2 Kgs 17:16; cf. 1 Kgs 12:28), a list of other sins is added to it: the kings built high places for themselves and erected pillars and sacred poles (מצבות ואשרים); they made graven images; they prayed to the whole host of heaven, the astral bodies, and served Baal. They put their sons and daughters through fire and practiced fortune-telling and magic. The prophets of YHWH had warned them, but they did not want to hear. "They would not listen but were stubborn, as their ancestors had been, who did not believe in the Lord their God. They despised his statutes and his covenant that he made with their ancestors, and the warnings that he gave them" (2 Kgs 17:7–23, here vv. 14–15). The passage ends: "So Israel was exiled from their own land to Assyria until this day" (v. 23).

After the deportation of the residents of Samaria, the king of Assyria brought people from Babylon, Cuthah, Avva, Hamath, and Sepharvaim to settle in the cities of Samaria in place of the Israelites. Ezra 4:2, 9–10 tells of

I. THE BIBLICAL DEPICTION OF THE PERIOD

more people from Erech, Babylon, and Susa who were sent off to Samaria by Kings Esar-haddon and Osnappar (Ashurbanipal). The perpetuation of the YHWH cult in the pagan surroundings is explained with a short story (2 Kgs 17:25–28): the new settlers did not show devotion to YHWH, so he sent lions among them, killing many of them. Hearing of this, the Assyrian king commanded that one of the deported priests be returned to teach the colonists how to worship the local God. The priest settled in Bethel and instructed the colonists in accordance with the king's orders. The colonists, however, worshiped their own gods alongside YHWH, whose names the author recorded: Succot-benoth (Babylon), Nergal (Cuth), Ashima (Hamath), Nibhaz and Tartak (Avva), Adrammelech and Anammelech (Sepharvaim). He then explains in detail that these customs were against the law to which YHWH had bound the Israelites with his covenant (2 Kgs 17:24–41).

I.1.2. The Kings of Judah

After Azariah's (Uzziah's) long reign, his son **Jotham** became king of Judah. He reigned for sixteen years, although neither 2 Kings nor 2 Chronicles clarifies whether this includes the years of Uzziah's illness (2 Kgs 15:5; 2 Chr 26:21). He did as YHWH ordered, but the high places did not disappear. He appears to have built prodigiously: in 2 Kgs 15:35 we read that he built the upper gate of the temple and in 2 Chr 27:3–4 that he did much building on the wall of Ophel, that he built cities in the mountains of Judah, and that he erected forts and towers in the wooded hills. Further, 2 Chronicles reports that he waged war on the Ammonites and defeated them; it also states that the Ammonites presented him a tribute of a hundred talents of silver, ten thousand cors of wheat, and ten thousand cors of barley for three years. Does this mean that his supremacy over Ammon lasted only three years? According to 2 Kgs 15:37 the attacks on Judah by Rezin, king of Aram (Damascus), and Pekah, king of Israel, which led to the so-called Syro-Ephraimitic war, began during Jotham's reign.

Jotham's son **Ahaz** succeeded his father and the Bible judges him very negatively: he followed the ways of the kings of Israel, meaning that he cast images of Baals, made offerings in the valley of the son of Hinnom, made his sons pass through fire, and sacrificed and burned incense at the high places and under every green tree (2 Kgs 16:2–4; 2 Chr 28:1–4).

The Bible's accounts of the Syro-Ephraimitic war are not uniform. According to 2 Kgs 16:5, Rezin and Pekah besieged Ahaz but were unable to overcome him. Second Chronicles 28:5–8, however, relates that the Arameans defeated him and took a great number of captives to Damascus and that Pekah, too, dealt him a great blow: the Chronicler states that Pekah killed 120,000 men in one day; that the Israelites took 200,000 women, sons and daughters from Judah, captive; and that they took a vast amount of booty. In Samaria, however, a prophet of YHWH by the name of Oded approached the returning army and convinced the leader of the Ephraimites (northern Israelites) to set free the captives and return the loot. The Chronicler concludes: "they brought them to their kindred at Jericho, the city of palm trees" (2 Chr 28:15). Second Kings 16:6 also reports that Rezin of Damascus expelled the Judeans from Elath, which the Edomites occupied thereafter. As for the involvement of non Syro-Ephraimitic neighbors in this conflict, here too the Chronicler gives much greater detail: the Edomites invaded Judah, besieged it, and took captives, while the Philistines invaded the cities in the Shephelah and the Judean Negev and captured the cities of Beth-Shemesh, Aijalon, Gederoth, Soco, Timna and Gimzo, where they established themselves (2 Chr 28:17–18).

King Ahaz turned to the Assyrian king Tiglath-pileser for help with the message: "I am your servant and your son" (2 Kgs 16:7). This meant that he declared himself a vassal of Tiglath-pileser, which he demonstrated by sending him homage of silver and gold from the temple and the royal treasury. The Assyrian king answered his request and went to war against Damascus, captured it, and deported its inhabitants to Kir. The Chronicler sees this episode in an entirely negative light: Tiglath-pileser did come to Ahaz, but rather than giving any aid he only caused Ahaz distress. Ahaz robbed the temple, the royal palace, and the upper classes and gave everything to the Assyrian king—but to no avail. In the Chronicler's depiction, Ahaz's homage is portrayed as robbery.

In the midst of the Syro-Ephraimitic war, the prophet Isaiah intervened. Isaiah 7 recounts that the prophet had been sent to the king because he and the people were panicked about the Syro-Ephraimitic threat. In Isaiah's speech to the king we learn that the allies wanted to make Tabeal king in Jerusalem. Tabeal, which means something like "good for nothing," is probably a tendentious reading of a name that originally read Tabe'el (טבאל), "God is good." On the basis of the name, one can assume that its bearer was Aramean. In his encounter with Ahaz, Isaiah tried to give the king courage, and it is in this context that he gave the famous Immanuel prophecy: "Look, the young woman is with child and shall bear a son, and shall name him Immanuel [God is with us] for before the child knows how to refuse the evil and choose the good, the land from whose two kings you are in dread will be deserted" (Isa 7:14–16). As in 8:1–4, the prophet predicts the destruction of the kingdoms of Damascus and Syria.

Ahaz's contract of vassalage with Tiglath-pileser was not without religious consequences. According to 2 Kgs 16:10–13, when Ahaz went to Tiglath-pileser in Damascus, he saw an altar, the image and description of which he

I. THE BIBLICAL DEPICTION OF THE PERIOD

sent to the priest Uriah to reproduce. After he returned from Damascus, the king consecrated the altar by offering sacrifices on it. The Chronicler, however, accuses Ahaz of sacrificing to the gods of Damascus. The account in Chronicles continues, stating that Ahaz destroyed the vessels of the temple, shut its gates, set up altars in every corner of Jerusalem, and set up high places in every city of Judah to make offerings to other gods (2 Chr 28:23–25). Second Kings offers a few more details: Ahaz cut off the frames of the stands and removed the laver from them, and he removed the sea from the bronze oxen and put it on a pediment of stone. He also removed the covered Sabbath passage and the entrance to the temple reserved for the king. The editor of Kings writes: "He did this because of the king of Assyria" (2 Kgs 16:17–18). After his death, according to 2 Kgs 16:20, Ahaz was buried with his fathers in the city of David, although according to 2 Chr 28:27 he was interred inside Jerusalem and therefore not in the tombs of the kings of Judah.

Hezekiah became king of Judah in the third year of Hoshea of Israel. He was twenty-five years old at the time and he reigned for twenty-nine years. He is judged entirely positively in 2 Kings: "He did what was right in the sight of the Lord just as his ancestor David had done" (2 Kgs 18:3). He abolished the high places, destroyed the pillars, eradicated the *ʾăšērîm* (NRSV: sacred poles), and destroyed Nehushtan, the bronze serpent that Moses had made and to which, until that time, the Israelites had still brought incense offerings (2 Kgs 18:4).

In the exegetical literature these actions are known as Hezekiah's reform. The Chronicler deals with this reform in much greater detail, dedicating three entire chapters to it (2 Chr 29–31). Already in the first month of his reign Hezekiah opened the gates of the temple that had been closed and commanded the priests and Levites to purify the temple. The priests brought everything impure that they found inside the temple into the temple courtyard. From there the Levites took over, carrying them off to the Kidron Valley. The work was completed in sixteen days. When it was done, the king offered sacrifices with great solemnity in an impressive atonement ritual, after which the normal cult would resume. It began with celebratory ritual: seventy cattle, one hundred rams, and two hundred lambs were given as a burnt offering, after which six hundred cattle and three thousand sheep were offered as a consecrated offering. "Thus the service of the house of the lord was restored" (2 Chr 29:35). Afterward they celebrated the Passover festival and the festival of unleavened bread. Not only were the Judeans invited but also all of the Israelites "from Dan to Beersheba." Though all Judeans came to the festival, only a few men from Asher, Manasseh, and Zebulun came to Jerusalem. The festival was celebrated with great joy for seven days, the Levites taking part especially enthusiastically. When it was to end, the whole congregation decided to celebrate seven days more. "There was great joy in Jerusalem, for since the time of Solomon son of King David of Israel there had been nothing like this in Jerusalem" (2 Chr 30:26). Only after this does the Chronicler describe the destruction of the high places, the *maṣṣēbôt*, and the *'ăšērîm* referred to in 2 Kgs 18:4.

According to Chronicles, Hezekiah also divided the priests and Levites according to their offices. He ordered that the contributions that were due to the priests and Levites (the firstfruits and the tithes) be given, and he had storerooms prepared in the temple to which the contributions, the tithes, and the consecrated things could be brought. He then saw to it that all the priests and Levites received their share, including those who did not live in Jerusalem.

According to the author of Kings, as a result of Hezekiah's reforms, YHWH was with him and he was politically successful. He broke away from the king of Assyria and beat the Philistines all the way to Gaza. In the sixth year of his reign, Samaria was conquered by the Assyrians, but it was not until the fourteenth year that King Sennacherib threatened Judah. Hezekiah submitted immediately and was forced to pay three hundred silver talents and thirty gold talents. To pay this he had to turn over all the silver in the temple and in the palace treasury. He even stripped down the doors and doorposts that had been covered with metal and gave it all to the Assyrian king (2 Kgs 18:7-16). This does not seem to have satisfied Sennacherib, however, and he sent a delegation accompanied by a great army from Lachish to Jerusalem. From the words of the Rabshakeh (meaning the cup-bearer who led the delegation) it is clear that Judah and Assyria were still in a state of war. The Assyrian delegate alludes to an alliance with Egypt (vv. 19-21), against which the prophet Isaiah had also raised sharp protest: "Alas for those who go down to Egypt for help" (Isa 30:1-7; 31:1-3). The Rabshakeh also alludes to Hezekiah's reforms: "But if you say to me, 'We rely on the Lord our God,' is it not he whose high places and altars Hezekiah has removed?" (v. 22). This was all part of a long speech that the delegate gave with the intention of terrifying the people who were seated on the wall (2 Kgs 18:19-36).

When King Hezekiah heard this, he turned to the prophet Isaiah with a plea to pray "for the remnant that is left." The prophet answered with a short oracle of salvation: "Do not be afraid.... I myself will put a spirit in him [the king of Assyria], so that he shall hear a rumor and return to his own land; I will cause him to fall by the sword in his own land" (2 Kgs 19:1-7). Isaiah 10:5-15 contains a threat against Assyria's presumptuousness, which might have been made in response to these circumstances. In the meantime Sennacherib had pulled out of Lachish and was fighting against Libnah, where he heard that Tirhakah, the king of Egypt (who, being of Ethiopian heritage, is called the king of Cush in the Bible), had advanced against him. In response, he again sent a messenger to Hezekiah with a message mocking YHWH. This was a written communication, expressly called a letter in 2 Chr 32:17, which Hezekiah laid out in the temple before YHWH, accompanied by a prayer for deliverance (2 Kgs 19:18–19). In answer to his plea he received a prophecy from Isaiah in the form of a satirical song threatening Sennacherib, ending with a promise to Hezekiah that concludes: "He shall not come into this city. For I will defend this city to save it, for my own sake and for the sake of my servant David" (2 Kgs 19:20–34). That same night YHWH's angel set out and killed 185,000 men in the Assyrian camp. Sennacherib departed and returned to his country, where he would later be killed by his sons Adrammelech and Sharezer. He was succeeded by Essar-haddon.

Isaiah 36–37 has the same story as that found in 2 Kgs 18:13–19:37, with a few unimportant differences; 2 Chr 32:1–23 also tells the story of the war with Sennacherib, though in a much shorter form. It does, however, mention Hezekiah's military preparations, which are absent from 2 Kings: they blocked all the springs and the brook that flowed through the middle of the land (LXX: city). Hezekiah improved the defenses of the city with high towers and a second wall; he strengthened the Millo and increased the arsenal of weapons (vv. 3–5). Besides these preparations, he also exhorted the people to trust in YHWH's help (vv. 7–8). The account in 2 Chronicles, however, seems to know of only one embassy from Sennacherib to Hezekiah. The Chronicler ends his account with the statement that from that time on Hezekiah was highly regarded in the eyes of all nations.

The Bible also states that Hezekiah had been gravely ill. The prophet Isaiah came to tell him he was going to die, but after the king prayed to God, the prophet promised healing. Here, through Isaiah, the king received a sign from God: the shadow on the sundial moved ten steps backwards, the same ten that it had just advanced up the steps to the upper chamber built by Ahaz. After being treated with a salve made of figs, the king was healthy again (2 Kgs 20:1–11). According to Isa 38:9–20, after his recovery Hezekiah composed a hymn about his illness. All of this seems to have taken place during the siege of Jerusalem, as YHWH says through Isaiah: "I will deliver you and this city out of the hand of the king of Assyria; I will defend this city" (Isa 38:6). Second Chronicles gives only a very short account of Hezekiah's illness; of the unusual features in the story, only the miraculous sign is mentioned. The Chronicler does state, however, that Hezekiah showed no thankfulness for the favor he had received and was arrogant; thus wrath came against him and against Judah and Jerusalem. Hezekiah then humbled himself along with the citizens of Jerusalem, however, and YHWH's wrath did not come upon them as long as Hezekiah lived. Indeed, Hezekiah instead became very wealthy (2 Chr 32:24–29).

The episode of Hezekiah's arrogance seems to be the Chronicler's version of the story of Merodach-baladan's embassy. The king of Babylon sent letters and gifts to Hezekiah, who responded by showing the ambassadors his entire treasury. He erred in doing so, though, and Isaiah prophesied the future plundering of Jerusalem and the deportation of some of his sons. Hezekiah praised the words of Isaiah, thinking to himself "Why not, if there will be peace and security in my days?" (2 Kgs 20:12–19; Isa 39).

At the conclusion of Hezekiah's history, both 2 Kings and 2 Chronicles recount that he closed the upper outlet of the waters of Gihon and led them down to the west, to the city of David (2 Kgs 20:20; 2 Chr 32:30). The Chronicler refers to the visions of the prophet Isaiah and the Book of the Kings of Judah and Israel as having been the sources for the history of Hezekiah.

In 2 Kgs 21, Hezekiah's successor **Manasseh** is given only an endless list of sins: high places, *maṣṣēbôt* and *'ăšērôt*, altars to the whole host of heaven, child sacrifice, soothsaying, and augury. He spilled innocent blood "until he had filled Jerusalem from one end to another" (v. 16). Unnamed prophets threatened him with the destruction of Jerusalem and the delivery of the people into the hand of the enemies (vv. 10–15). The same charges are raised in 2 Chr 33:1–20, which adds that Manasseh was captured by the Assyrians and taken to Babylon. He had a conversion while there, and God took pity on him and allowed him to return as king of Jerusalem, where he repealed all his heretical measures. The people still offered sacrifices at the high places, however, but now only to the God YHWH. Manasseh also built an outer wall for the city of David in the valley west of Gihon and put commanders in all the fortified cities of Judah. At the end of the account of Manasseh, the Chronicler cites the words of Hozai (LXX: the seers) as a source of "his prayer, and how God received his entreaty, all his sin and his faithlessness, the sites on which he built high places and set up the sacred poles and the images, before he humbled himself."

Manasseh's son and successor **Amon** followed the path his father had taken previously, abandoning YHWH and worshiping idols. His servants conspired against him and killed him, but the people of the land (עם הארץ) killed all those who had conspired against Amon and made his son Josiah king in his place (2 Kgs 21:19–24; 2 Chr 33:21–25).

I.1.3. The Prophets

During this period some of the most important prophets in Israel's history were active. The words of Hosea are dated synchronously with the reigns of Kings Uzziah, Jotham, Ahaz, Hezekiah of Judah, and Jeroboam of Israel

I. THE BIBLICAL DEPICTION OF THE PERIOD

(Hos 1:1). Isaiah is matched with the reigns of the same Judean kings (Isa 1:1), while Micah prophesied during the reigns of Kings Jotham, Ahaz, and Hezekiah. For the most part, individual statements of the prophets are not dated any more precisely, nor are they given in connection with any specific historical context. Not a word of the prophet **Hosea** is historically situated, though all of his words are directed to northern Israel. Only a few short lines deal with Judah, and these only incidentally (Hos 1:7; 4:15; 5:5; 6:11; 12:3). There are allusions to political affairs in his statements—the fickle foreign policy of the kings of Israel, for example (7:8–12; 12:1–2). Hosea also speaks of his marriage, to which he accords prophetic significance, comparing it to the relationship between YHWH and his people (Hos 1–3). The main theme in Hosea's prophetic message is God's love, which his people underestimate. Hosea directs his words first and foremost to the ruling class, the kings and the priests who were leading the people into ruin. He condemns injustice, but, more than Amos, he emphasizes religious unfaithfulness and idolatrous worship in which YHWH was put on the same level as Baal. The prophet is convinced that God's judgment and punishment are inevitable. Just as surely, however, it would not be the end; God punishes only in order to save. This is the meaning of the command to love an unfaithful woman anew (Hos 3): even when he punishes, God still loves his people and will always take them back.

Isaiah has already been mentioned in relation to the Syro-Ephraimitic war and Sennacherib's campaign. His prophetic calling (Isa 6) is dated to the year of the death of King Uzziah. Outside of these, almost none of the prophet's other statements are dated in the book that bears his name. The oracle against the Philistines (14:28–32) is dated to the year of Ahaz's death. It is also recounted that, at the same time as King Sargon of Assyria's field commander was besieging Ashdod, Isaiah was wandering three years naked and barefoot. This was a symbolic prophetic act symbolizing the coming defeat (captivity) of the Egyptians, done in order to prevent an alliance between the Judeans and the Egyptians (Isa 20). Isaiah's words are not generally organized chronologically, but they do evince a certain thematic organization. Chapters 1–12 contain only statements about Judah and Jerusalem and are organized as a prologue (Isa 1), a collection of prophecies about Zion (Isa 2–5), and the so-called Immanuel Book (Isa 6–12). In the Zion prophecies social injustice is condemned repeatedly, just as it was by Amos and Hosea. Chapters 13–23 contain a series of oracles about foreign peoples, followed by the so-called Isaiah Apocalypse (Isa 24–27), a poetic impression of God's final judgment, a description broken up by prayers. Chapters 28–33 contain a series of oracles about Judah that are preceded by an oracle against Samaria (28:1–6). Here, too, there are warnings against an alliance with Egypt (30:1–6; 31:1–3). Chapter 34 announces God's judgment against the nations, especially against

10   ISRAEL AND JUDAH IN THE EIGHTH-SEVENTH CENTURIES

Edom, whereupon Isa 35 describes the salvation and glorious future of Jerusalem.

No statements in the book of **Micah** are dated or are connected with any historical context. The prophet alternately preached threat and promise. His words of judgment condemned religious offenses but above all unfair social conditions, injustice, and the oppression of the humble person by the rich and by creditors, merchants, judges, and the like. This theme is also prominent in the prophecies of Amos, Hosea, and Isaiah. Social injustice in many forms seems to have been characteristic of this time, and as we go along we will attempt to get a better understanding of it.

I.1.4. Further Literary Activity

According to biblical tradition, this era also saw literary activity in the genre of wisdom literature. Proverbs 25–29 is presented as a collection of "Proverbs of Solomon that the officials of King Hezekiah of Judah copied" (25:1).

I.2. Analysis

I.2.1. 2 Kings 15:8–21:26

Brettler, Marc Zvi. "Ideology, History and Theology in 2 Kings xvii 7–23," *VT* 39 (1989): 268–82. **Dietrich**, Walter. *Prophetie und Geschichte: Eine redaktionsgeschichtliche Untersuchung zum deuteronomistischen Geschichtswerk* (FRLANT 108; Göttingen: Vandenhoeck & Ruprecht, 1972). **Hardmeier**, Christof. "Umrisse eines vordeuteronomistischen Annalenwerks der Zidkijazeit," *VT* 40 (1990): 165–84. **Hoffmann**, Hans Detlef. *Reform und Reformen: Untersuchungen zu einem Grundthema der deuteronomistischen Geschichtsschreibung* (ATANT 66; Zurich: Theologischer Verlag, 1980), 127–39. **McKenzie**, Steven L. *The Trouble with Kings: The Composition of the Book of Kings in the Deuteronomistic History* (VTSup 42; Leiden: Brill, 1991). **Nelson**, Richard D. *The Double Redaction of the Deuteronomistic History* (JSOTSup 18; Sheffield: JSOT Press, 1981). **Noth**, Martin. *The Deuteronomistic History* (1943; JSOTSup 15; Sheffield: JSOT Press, 1991). **Provan**, Iain W. *Hezekiah and the Books of Kings: A Contribution to the Debate about the Composition of the Deuteronomistic History* (BZAW 172; Berlin: de Gruyter, 1988). **Weippert**, Helga. "Die 'deuteronomistischen' Beurteilungen der Könige von Israel und Juda und das Problem der Redaktion der Königsbücher," *Bib* 53 (1972): 301–39. **Winckler**, Hugo. *Alttestamentliche Untersuchungen* (Leipzig: Pfeiffer, 1892), 1–54.

The two books of Kings are neither annals in which historical facts were written down shortly after they occurred, nor are they a single work written by one author as a distinct piece. It is now commonly accepted that these books had a long and occasionally complicated redaction history. In a pioneering work, Martin Noth called the final form of these books part of the Deuteronomistic History (Dtr), a larger work that included the books of Joshua, Judges, Samuel, and Kings. Noth's work was an analysis of its structure, construction, and character. According to his theory, the Deuteronomistic redactor based his history of the Israelite and Judean kings on the oft-cited Annals of the Kings of Israel/Judah (ספר דברי הימים למלכי ישראל/יהודה). These sources contained a chronological framework and synchronisms, but the general assessments of the kings come from the Deuteronomistic redactor. Other studies have sought to prove that not just one redactor had been active during or after the exile, but that there was a Deuteronomistic school or tradition already redacting in preexilic times. More common, though, is the hypothesis of a Deuteronomistic redactor during Josiah's lifetime followed by a later, exilic redaction. This view is found mostly in English literary-critical works, though it is not uncommon in the German-speaking world. There is no consensus on this question, though, as the preexilic redaction might be non-Deuteronomistic (that is, pre-Deuteronomistic), like the aforementioned chronological framework. More promising are the attempts of literary critics to differentiate between a first, fundamental redaction of the history (DtrG or DtrH)[1], later expansions from a prophetically minded redactor (DtrP), and a redaction inspired by Deuteronomic law (DtrN). Literary-critical differentiation between sources and later redactional revisions makes it easier to get a better sense of the historical events through source criticism and also helps the scholar get a clearer sense of the way later redactors viewed this era.

I.2.1.1 The Kings of Northern Israel

There are only very short reports about the kings Zechariah, Shallum, Menahem, Pekahiah, and Pekah, all of which have the same structure (2 Kgs 15:8–31):

	Introduction	Judgment	Events	Concluding Note	Death + Succession
Zechariah	15:8	15:9	15:10	15:11–12	(15:10)
Shallum	15:13		15:14, 16	15:15	(15:14)

---

1. In this work a differentiation will be made between DtrG and DtrH: DtrG means the entire Deuteronomic History, while DtrH indicates a first redactional layer, which was later expanded in DtrP and DtrN.

Menahem	15:17	15:18	15:19–20	15:21–22	←15:22
Pekahiah	15:23	15:24	15:25	15:26	(15:25)
Pekah	15:27	15:28	15:29–30	15:31	(15:30)

This structure shows that the whole section was tightly organized by the Deuteronomistic Historian. The formulaic introductions include the synchronisms with the kings of Judah and the length of reign of the respective Israelite kings. Christof Hardmeier has plausibly suggested that the redactor used pre-Deuteronomistic annals from Zedekiah's time (598–587). Such annals would have been standardized works that would have given Kings its basic framework: its chronology, regnal dates, and concluding notices. The authors of these annals also wrote stereotyped summaries of the events that were important to them as they looked back at earlier kings. These annals might indirectly connect to the Annals of the Kings of Israel/Judah; if so, this would preclude the need to imagine a first, late-preexilic version of the Deuteronomistic History (see Hardmeier, "Umrisse"). Although the Deuteronomistic redactor used some sort of annals, there are still many inconsistencies, such as those between regnal synchronisms and years of reign: for example, while 2 Kgs 15:30 situates the plot against Hoshea in the twentieth year of Jotham of Judah, according to verse 33 Jotham reigned only sixteen years.

The judgments about the kings are entirely Deuteronomistic and stereotypical: "He did what was evil in the sight of the Lord; he did not depart from all the sins of Jeroboam son of Nebat, which he caused Israel to sin." This judgment is also given to the early kings of Israel. The judgment is in keeping with the views of the author toward the history of the kings of northern Israel and tells us nothing about the individual kings. Further on we will return to these judgment formulas and compare them to judgment formulas referring to other kings. The references to the aforementioned Annals of the Kings of Israel/Judah found in the conclusions of the accounts are also stereotyped and were probably borrowed from the annals book. The only addition comes in 15:12, which emphasizes the fulfillment of a prophecy about Jehu (10:30); here the Deuteronomistic Historian refers to his own concluding reflection which he added to the history of Jehu in 10:28–33.

Menahem was the only northern Israelite king to die a natural death, and he was succeeded on the throne by his son (15:22). All other kings of the northern kingdom were killed by usurpers. The accounts of these usurpations and other events must have been taken from some source, most likely the aforementioned annals (15:10, 14, 16, 19–20, 25, 29–30). The adverb "then" (אז) in 15:16 seems to suggest an annals entry, as in 1 Kgs 3:16. Not all the details were correctly transferred, however, and since it is not very likely that Menahem had been on an expedition to Tifsah (Tapsake on the Euphrates), the name should probably be read "Tappuah" (so LXX^L; cf. Karl Elliger, *ZDPV* 53 [1930]: 292–93). Otherwise, there are no inner-textual reasons to doubt the historical veracity of the information.

The account about Hoshea (2 Kgs 17:1–6) deviates from the tight schema, with only the introduction (17:1) being similar to the previous accounts. Following that is a judgment that reads somewhat differently: "He did what was evil in the sight of the Lord, yet not like the kings of Israel who were before him" (17:2). The event section (17:3–6) gives a brief report of Shalmaneser's campaign, Hoshea's conspiracy against him, Hoshea's imprisonment, the siege of Samaria, its capture, and the deportation of the Israelites to Assyria.

The report of the capture of Samaria (vv. 5–6) is also found in the account of Hezekiah (18:9–11). Literary critics are not in agreement as to the original home of this account. There is no reference to the Annals of the Kings of Israel, and obviously there is no mention of a successor. Instead, as mentioned earlier, the Deuteronomistic History concludes with a long reflection about the end of the northern kingdom (17:7–23), which is entirely Deuteronomistic in both content and style. Walter Dietrich distinguishes multiple strata in this parenetic summary of Israel's history: vv. 7–11, 20: DtrG (= our DtrH); vv. 12–19: DtrN; vv. 21–23: RedP (redactor of the prophetic texts). According to Noth, too, vv. 21–23 come from a later addition (*Deuteronomistic History*, 115 n. 2). In contrast, however, Hans Detlef Hoffmann defends the unity of this pericope, which he calls the "final supporting pillar" of the Deuteronomistic cultic historiography of the northern kingdom that began with 1 Kgs 12:26–32 (*Reform*, 127–33). However, the belief that the break from the Davidic dynasty caused Israel's downfall is not found anywhere else in the Deuteronomistic History; instead the division is portrayed as having been desired by God. Hoffmann's focus only on cultic sins is therefore clearly too one-sided. Moreover, verse 23 interprets prophecy differently than verse 13: the prophets are portrayed as Deuteronomic preachers, while in the former they are seen as prophets of doom. The DtrN stratum can be dated after the conquest of Jerusalem, because verses 13 and 19–20 include the downfall of Jerusalem.

Incidentally, verses 16–17 are largely parallel to 2 Kgs 21:3, 6, both of which list Manasseh's sins: each version states that they (the Israelites or Manasseh) made a sacred pole (אשרה), worshiped the whole host of heaven, and served Baal; they made their sons and daughters pass through fire and practiced soothsaying and augury; they did what displeased the Lord and incensed him. These parallels show that the end of the southern kingdom is interpreted alongside that of the northern one, ahead of the narrative about it (cf. Hoffmann, 133; Dietrich, 45).

The Deuteronomistic reflection in 2 Kgs 17:7–23 breaks the connection between verses 6 and 24. The latter verse reports on those the king of Assyria settled in the cities of Samaria in place of the Israelites. Just as with 17:6, most of verses 17:24, 29–31 might have come from annals. In verse 29, however, the reference to the shrines of the high places is taken from 1 Kgs 12:31–13:34, Jeroboam's erection of the shrines of the high places. The account in verses 24 and 29–31 is combined with a cultic history local to Bethel (17:25–28). Finally, appended to all of this is a remark about the cultic situation in the former kingdom of Israel (vv. 32–34a). The entirety of 2 Kgs 17:24–41 is likely a later addition intended—perhaps in the spirit of Ezra—to exclude the inhabitants of Samaria from the pure community of the returning Judean exiles. Verses 34b–40 include a further addition, perceptible in the repetition of verses 33–34a in verse 41, which intends to communicate to the Israelites even more clearly its judgment on the new inhabitants of the region.[2]

I.2.1.2. The Kings of Judah

Camp, Ludger. *Hiskija und Hiskijabild: Analyse und Interpretation von 2 Kön 18–20* (Münsteraner theologische Abhandlungen 9; Altenberge: Telos, 1990). **Childs**, Brevard S. *Isaiah and the Assyrian Crisis* (SBT 2/3; London: SCM, 1967). **Clements**, R. E. *Isaiah and the Deliverance of Jerusalem: A Study of the Interpretation of Prophecy in the Old Testament* (JSOTSup 13; Sheffield: Department of Biblical Studies, 1980). **Gonçalves**, Francolino J. *L'expédition de Sennacherib en Palestine dans la littérature hébraïque anciennne* (Publications de l'Institut orientaliste de Louvain 34; Louvain-la-Neuve: Université catholique de Louvain, Institut orientaliste, 1986). **Haag**, H. "La campagne de Sennacherib contre Jérusalem en 701," *RB* 58 (1951): 348–59. **Hardmeier**, Christof. *Prophetie im Streit vor dem Untergang Judas: Erzählkommunikative Studien zur Entstehungssituation der Jesaja- und Jeremiaerzählungen in II Reg 18–20 und Jer 37–40* (BZAW 187; Berlin: de Gruyter, 1990). **Irvine**, Stuart A. *Isaiah, Ahaz, and the Syro-Ephraimitic Crisis* (SBLDS 123; Atlanta: Scholars Press, 1990). **Kooij**, Arie van der. "Das assyrische Heer vor den Mauern Jerusalems im Jahr 701 v.Chr.," *ZDPV* 102 (1986): 93–109. **Leeuwen**, Cornelis van. "Sanchérib devant Jérusalem," *OTS* 14 (1965): 245–72. **Spieckermann**, Hermann. *Juda unter Assur in der Sargonidenzeit* (FRLANT 129; Göttingen: Vandenhoeck & Ruprecht, 1982). **Tadmor**, Hayim, and Mordechai **Cogan**. "Ahaz and Tiglath-Pileser in the Book of Kings: Historiographic Considerations," *Bib* 60 (1979): 491–508. **Vogt**, Ernst. *Der Aufstand Hiskias und die Belagerung Jerusalems 701 v.Chr.* (AnBib 106; Rome: Biblical Institute Press, 1986). **Wildberger**, Hans. *Isaiah 28–39* (trans. Thomas H. Trapp; CC; Minneapolis: Fortress, 2002).

---

2. Richard D. Nelson also believes that vv. 34b–40 were the work of a second "exilic editor" (pp. 63–65).

I. THE BIBLICAL DEPICTION OF THE PERIOD

The accounts of the Judean kings Jotham, Ahaz, Hezekiah, Manasseh, and Amon are parallel in structure, though the scope varies greatly depending on the king (2 Kgs 15–16; 18–21).

	Introduction	Judgment	Events	Concluding Note
Jotham	15:32–33	15:34–35a	15:35b, 37	15:36, 38
Ahaz	16:1–2a	16:2b–4	16:5–18	16:19–20
Hezekiah	18:1–2	18:3–7	18:8–20:19	20:20–21
Manasseh	21:1	21:2	21:3–16	21:17–18
Amon	21:19	21:20–22	21:23–24	21:25–26

The account of **Jotham** (2 Kgs 15:32–38) is constructed similarly to the accounts of the kings of northern Israel. Here, too, the introductory formula (vv. 32–33) and the concluding note (vv. 36, 38) could be ascribed to the pre-Deuteronomistic annals.[3] The Deuteronomistic assessment of Jotham differs from those of the northern Israelite kings: "He did what was right in the sight of the Lord, just as his father Uzziah had done" (v. 34). This positive judgment, however, is somewhat qualified in the next verse: "Nevertheless the high places [במות] were not removed; the people still sacrificed and made offerings on the high places." This positive assessment, including the qualification, is strictly formulaic (cf. 1 Kgs 22:43–44; 2 Kgs 12:3–4; 14:3–4; 15:3–4). According to Helga Weippert, this formula is from a pre-Deuteronomistic redaction, while Iain W. Provan ascribes it to a preexilic deuteronomistic layer (Weippert, "Die 'deuteronomistischen' Beurteilungen," 334–37; Provan, *Hezekiah*, 171). In our three-part division of DtrG, it belongs to DtrH, a redacted stratum that can best be dated to the beginning of the exile (Dietrich, *Prophetie*, 139–48). Verse 35b mentions a building project on the Jerusalem temple by Jotham. The Deuteronomist could have taken this detail about the temple, of interest only to him, from an extensive list, as seen in the parallel account in 2 Chr 27:3–5 (see Hoffmann, *Reform*, 126). The concluding note includes an odd piece of information about the Syro-Ephraimite war (v. 37)—that it had already begun during Jotham's reign. Presumably this is historically incorrect, though, and

---

3. In contrast to the accounts referring to the kings of northern Israel, those referring to the Judean kings also include the year of the king's ascent to power and the name of his mother (see 2 Kgs 15:2, 33; 18:2; 21:1, 19). The Judean sources that were used by the author of the annals book were evidently designed differently than those of northern Israel.

it is not clear why the Deuteronomist ascribes the beginning of the war to Jotham's time (Noth, *Deuteronomistic History*, 114).

The account about **Ahaz** is much more detailed (2 Kgs 16). In v. 2b the negative assessment of him is expanded into a catalogue of his sins (vv. 3–4). The assessment is introduced with a general characterization of the king in which his conduct is seen as connected to that of the kings of northern Israel (v. 3a; cf. 2 Kgs 8:18, 27, about Joram and Ahaziah). This note might have been found by the Deuteronomistic redactor in some source, where it perhaps had more political implications than religious ones; this is clearly the case with 8:18, 27, in which the relationship by marriage with Ahab's house is mentioned specifically (see Irvine, *Isaiah, Ahaz*, 77). Verse 3b, which refers to child sacrifice, does not conform to the standard outline of judgments about kings in DtrH. This judgment might have been taken from the story of Manasseh by a later Deuteronomistic redactor (21:2, 6) to contrast Ahaz and Hezekiah in a manner similar to the contrast between Manasseh and Josiah made in DtrH.

Second Kings 16:5–18 includes an account of the Syro-Ephraimitic war (vv. 5–9) and another account of the Damascene altar (vv. 10–18). The section is interspersed throughout with references to the Assyrian king (vv. 7, 8, 9, 10, 18)—this section could well have the phrase "Alliances and Their Consequences" as an epigraph. Historical source material is used in the first section on the war, though the exact source is difficult to identify, since the passage looks like a redactor's summary (Dtr or P?). Nevertheless, there is no reason to doubt the historical veracity of the accounts of the events, including the conquest of Elath by Edom (v. 6; the Masoretic reading "Aram" should be corrected to Edom throughout the verse, except the expression "King of Aram"). The particle אז, "then," and the time designation בעת ההיא, "at that time," introduce references to archival sources or annals and have no strict chronological value. In putting verses 5 and 6 next to each other, the Deuteronomistic redaction facilitated some of the corruption in the text: "Edom" was changed to "Aram," and the name "Rezin" was inserted. There had been no Aramean intervention in the war between the Edomite king and Ahaz, and the capture of Elath did not coincide with the siege of Jerusalem by Rezin and Pekah. By inserting this account here, the Deuteronomistic redactor meant to portray the war, and the loss of Edom, as punishment for the sins of Ahaz (Tadmor and Cogan, "Ahaz and Tiglath-Pileser," 496–97).

Second Kings 16:10–18 describes the cultic consequences of Ahaz's submission to Tiglath-pileser, which included the erection of a new altar as well as changes to the cultic implements and to the temple. Two short scenes between Ahaz and the priest Uriah (vv. 10–11 and 15–16) frame a central scene (vv. 12–14) that recounts the king's dedication of the new altar. In this central scene the author mentions the four types of sacrifices, arranged as a list in fixed sac-

I. THE BIBLICAL DEPICTION OF THE PERIOD 17

rificial order: עלה, burnt offering; מנחה, grain offering; נסך, drink offering; and שלמים, peace offerings (v. 13). In an in-depth analysis, Rolf Rendtorff showed that these terms originated in P terminology. He also convincingly demonstrated that the text in verse 15 "shows traces of editing very similar to those of the priestly sacrifice texts" (*Studien zur Geschichte des Opfers im Alten Testament* [WMANT 24; Neukirchen-Vluyn: Neukirchener, 1967], 47–49). Because of this, Hoffmann is convinced that the account of Ahaz's actions concerning the temple cult presupposes the language and cultic system of postexilic P literature and therefore cannot be ascribed to the Deuteronomist. Thus, 2 Kgs 16:10–18 would be a post-Deuteronomistic insertion (Hoffmann, *Reform*, 139–45). Verses 17–18, pertaining to construction, need not necessarily have the same origin and could be based on reliable historical information. Notably, these verses play no role in Hoffmann's argument for P origin. He is therefore mistaken in including verses 17–18 along with the preceding verses. He may be correct regarding verses 10–15, though, so the historicity of this section is still debatable. At the same time, a number of details point to preexilic conditions in the temple, such as the king's unrestricted power over the temple and the priesthood and the cultic regulations established by Ahaz. The preexilic context of this section is clear in comparison with later priestly cultic regulations (e.g., only one daily burnt offering [עולה] and no חטאת, sin offering). The section shows no polemical character either, although it is possible that the Deuteronomistic redactor intended the list of events themselves to be polemical (cf. Spieckermann, *Juda unter Assur*, 365–66).

The account of **Hezekiah** (2 Kgs 18–20) is even more detailed than that of Ahaz. The introduction and concluding note (18:1–2; 20:20–21) correspond exactly to those used for the kings of Judah. In the concluding note, the construction of the pool and the conduit (the pool and tunnel of Siloam) are mentioned among the "rest of the deeds" (the formula ויתר דברי ... הנם כתובים בספר מלכי, "and the rest of the deeds of X ... they are written in the books of the annals of the kings of Y; cf., e.g., 2 Kgs 15:6, 11, 15 with 2 Kgs 20:20). The assessment (18:3–8) views him entirely positively.

It is obvious that these verses are Deuteronomistic, but is their redaction entirely uniform? If there was a preexilic Deuteronomistic redaction (which, in my opinion, is not entirely out of the question), verse 3 would belong to it ("He did what was right in the sight of the Lord just as his ancestor David had done" [Weippert, "Die 'deuteronomistischen' Beurteilungen," 332–33]). The comparison with David, however, is connected to even more material (vv. 7–8), showing a singular correspondence between Hezekiah and David: about David and Hezekiah alone it is said that YHWH was with them (1 Sam 16:18 and passim), that they had success (השׂכיל; 1 Sam 18:5 and passim), and that they beat the Philistines (נכה hiphil; 1 Sam 18:27 and passim; cf. Provan,

Hezekiah, 116–17), making Hezekiah—not the later Josiah—the new David. In verses 7–8 the Deuteronomistic redactor uses source material, as he does in the note in verse 4a pertaining to the high places.

Like a leitmotif, the same thing is always repeated about the former kings: "only the high places did not disappear" (לֹא־סָרוּ; 1 Kgs 3:3; 15:14; 22:44; 2 Kgs 12:4; 14:4; 15:4, 35). Here, finally, the sequence ends: הוּא הֵסִיר אֶת־הַבָּמוֹת, "he abolished the high places." This marks 2 Kgs 18:4a as the end of the "high places" motif in the preexilic Deuteronomistic stratum (Provan, *Hezekiah*, 85). Verse 4b, however, is a later reworking of this note, as can be seen in its relation to 1 Kgs 14:22–24 and 2 Kgs 17:7–17. The *wĕ-qatal* וְשִׁבַּר, "and he broke," marks the beginning of the later addition. Finally, 18:5 also belongs to the preexilic Deuteronomistic layer. The end of the high places motif and the comparison to David is capped off in 18:5b: "there was no one like him among all the kings of Judah after him." This could hardly have been written after Josiah's reign, about whom the same is said in 2 Kgs 23:5. To summarize, 18:3–4a, 5, and 7–8 may be part of a preexilic layer, while 18:4b, and perhaps 18:6, too, should be ascribed to a later Deuteronomistic redaction. Nevertheless, this does not exclude the possibility that the concrete information in 18:4b (Nehushtan) and 8 (war against the Philistines) might be taken from historically reliable sources.

We encountered previously the short version of the capture of Samaria (18:9–11) in 2 Kgs 17:5–6 and have also dealt with the question of its original placement, whether here or there (see p. 13). Noth is probably correct when he claims that the account originated in Judean sources:

> These events are summarized in the section on the reign of the Judaean king of that time, Hezekiah (2 Kgs 18.9–11). The Judaean annals of the kings would doubtless have treated these events because of their prime importance for Judah and they would have been reported in the 'Books of the Chronicles of the Kings' which was in the course of compilation. However, Dtr. has anticipated this report, almost word for word, as early as 2 Kgs 17.5–6—the section on the reign of Hoshea had to deal with the end of the state of Israel. (*Deuteronomistic History*, 106)

Hardmeier reconstructs the pre-Deuteronomistic annals as follows: 17:1, 3–5; 18:1–2, 8, 10aβ, 11, 13b–16. The Deuteronomist would then have drawn 17:6 out of 18:10aβ–11, while the narrator's opening of the story in 18:9–10aα is an adaptation of 17:5. The theological motivation behind 18:12 is clearly a Deuteronomistic commentary on the capture of Samaria, and the section as a whole (vv. 9–12) was included to contrast with the fates of Hezekiah and Jerusalem. "The group of DtrG authors created the redactional composition 18:1–12 for the purpose of expressing their own version of the account, most noticeably in verses 3–7 and 12" (Hardmeier, *Prophetie*, 115).

I. THE BIBLICAL DEPICTION OF THE PERIOD

The greater portion of the account about Hezekiah pertains to Sennacherib's campaign, which ends with the deliverance of Jerusalem, Hezekiah's illness and recovery, and Merodach-Baladan's embassy (2 Kgs 18:13–20:19). Isaiah 36–39 is entirely parallel to this account and, with the exception of 2 Kgs 18:14–16 and Hezekiah's song in Isa 38:9–20, the differences between these two versions are minimal. Most interpreters consider the accounts to be a duplicate transmission and agree that 2 Kings is the original home of this account. This is clearly evident in the beginning of the account of Sennacherib's invasion, in which Isa 36:1, the parallel to 2 Kgs 18:13, lost the continuation of the introduction found in 2 Kgs 18:14–16. Moreover, the account fits much better into the context of the book of Kings than into Isaiah. This does not mean that the redactor of the book of Kings composed these stories himself, though; rather, he found their primitive form in Isaiah legends.

Most scholars consider the pericope 2 Kgs 18:13–16 to be the original account because it agrees substantially with Assyrian accounts, as we will see further on. Attached to this section, they believe, was a later "legendary" story. The pericope begins with a date—"the fourteenth year of King Hezekiah"—whose word order is unusual for the book of Kings (עשרה שנה בארבע). Based on other biblical verses with similar wording, Ludger Camp is inclined to ascribe the figure to DtrN (*Hiskija*, 96–97). With the aid of a computerized concordance, however, Hardmeier concluded that the manner of dating found here is complementary to dating with ordinal numbers found, for example, in verse 9. This is one indication among others that 18:9–10a is the beginning of the narrative in 18:13ff. Verses 13b–16 were then incorporated as a quote into the story of the threat to Jerusalem and its deliverance (Hardmeier, *Prophetie*, 116–17). In these verses the narrator probably offers a reliable account of the events of Sennacherib's campaign to Palestine, which he took from the Annals of the Kings of Judah. Camp also believes that verses 9 and 13 belong to the same redaction, in his view DtrN. According to Hardmeier, however, the narrative is earlier than the composition of DtrG.

Camp sums up the redaction-critical result for 18:1–16 and 20:20–21 as follows:

> Verses 18:1, 2, 4*, 7b, 8*, 13b–16*; 20:21 are believed to be traditional, and are probably taken from the "Journals of the Kings of Judah" referred to in 20:20. These verses do not amount to a consistent base text that DtrH simply adopted, however. Rather, DtrH excerpted his sources to paint a theologically-colored image of Hezekiah's reign. Beyond the compilation, the author's creative hand is limited to verses 18:3 and 18:4*. The remaining verses can be ascribed to DtrN: 18:5–7a, 9–12, 13a. (*Hiskija*, 106)

This is an adequate summary, though Iain W. Provan dates the redaction of 18:5–7 earlier than Camp's DtrN, attributing it to a preexilic redaction. In exegetical literature, 18:13–16 and 18:17–19:37 are differentiated as narrative A and narrative B. Since the work of Bernhard Stade the consensus has been that narrative B consists of two separate narratives combined into one, which he divides as follows: B^1 = 18:13, 17–19, 9a, and B^2 = 19:9b–37 (*ZAW* 6 [1886]: 172–83). This structure was refined by Brevard Childs (who also proposed the shorthand B^1 and B^2): B^1 = 18:17–19:9a, 36–37, and B^2 = 19:9b–35. Contra Stade, it is clear that 18:13 belongs to narrative A, while 18:17–18 is indisputably the beginning of the B narrative. To make the whole comprehensible in this context, 18:1–16 is necessarily presupposed. The original introduction to the B^1 narrative must have disappeared, meanwhile, when 18:1–16 was worked into these verses (Camp, *Hiskija*, 159).

The Rabshakeh's first speech in B^1 (18:19–25) is built around a base text that might include 18:19a, 20a, 23–24a, which was later reworked theologically in 18:19b, 20b, 21, 24b, 25. Many authors believe that 18:22 fits poorly in its surroundings; according to Camp, the note in this verse about Hezekiah's cultic reforms is an adaptation of 18:4. The use of בטח in the sense of "trusting in the Lord" would refer to 18:5, so that 18:22 might come from DtrN (*Hiskija*, 115). There is general agreement on the secondary character of this verse, and it is indeed possible that it originates from DtrN. Verses 26–27 also belong to the base text. In the Rabshakeh's second speech in B^1 (18:28–32), 18:31–32a—the logical continuation of the first speech—also belong to the textual foundation. Verses 28–30a (30b seems to have been inserted secondarily, in reference to 19:10b) belong to the redaction that we saw in 18:19b, 20, 21, 24b, 25. "Characteristic of these redactions is the insertion of the theologically significant terms בטח *rely* (7x) and נצל *deliver* (3x) into the Rabshake's speech" (Camp, *Hiskija*, 166). The base of the pericope in which Hezekiah sends his emissaries to Isaiah (19:1–7) includes 19:1abα, 2, 5–7, while 19:1bβ, 3–4 were edited with an eye to B^2. Second Kings 19:8–9a, 36–37 also belong to the base layer of this story, since without these verses it would have no ending, and these verses correspond exactly to Isaiah's promise in 19:7. In summary, the base of 18:17–19:9a, 36–37 is reconstructed as 18:17–19a, 20a, 23–24a, 26–28, 31–32a, 36–37; 19:1abα, 2, 5–9a, 36–37. While there is no historically reliable source material beyond some theological themes in the Rabshakeh's speech, the narrative account is entirely possible. To clarify this complicated redaction-critical situation, what follows is the text of the B^1 narrative differentiated by layer (base text; *theological reworking*; **DtrN**; secondary addition):

> [18:17]The king of Assyria sent the Tartan, the Rabsaris, and the Rabshakeh with a great army from Lachish to King Hezekiah at Jerusalem. They went up

and came to Jerusalem. When they arrived, they came and stood by the conduit of the upper pool, which is on the highway to the Fuller's Field. [18]When they called for the king, there came out to them Eliakim son of Hilkiah, who was in charge of the palace, and Shebnah the secretary, and Joah son of Asaph, the recorder. [19]The Rabshakeh said to them, "Say to Hezekiah: *Thus says the great king, the king of Assyria: On what do you base this confidence of yours?* [20]*Do you think that mere words are strategy and power for war? On whom do you now rely, that you have rebelled against me?* [21]*See, you are relying now on Egypt, that broken reed of a staff, which will pierce the hand of anyone who leas on it. Such is Pharaoh king of Egypt to all who rely on him.* [22]**But if you say to me, 'we rely on the Lord our God,' is it not he whose high places and altars Hezekiah has removed, saying to Judah and to Jerusalem, 'You shall worship before this altar in Jerusalem'?** [23]Come now, make a wager with my master the king of Assyria: I will give you two thousand horses, if you are able on your part to set riders on them. [24]*How can you repulse a single captain among the least of my master's servants, when you rely on Egypt for chariots and for horsemen?* [25]*Moreover, is it without the Lord that I have come up against this place to destroy it? The Lord said to me, Go up against this land, and destroy it.*" [26]Then Eliakim son of Hilkiah, and Shebnah and Joah said to the Rabshakeh, "Please speak to your servants in the Aramaic language, for we understand it; do not speak to us in the language of Judah within the hearing of the people who are on the wall." [27]But the Rabshakeh said to them, "Has my master sent me to speak these words to your master and to you, and not to the people sitting on the wall, who are doomed with you to eat their own dung and drink their own urine?" [28]*Then the Rabshakeh stood and called out in a loud voice in the language of Judah,* "Hear the word of the great king, the king of Assyria! [29]*Thus says the king:* 'Do not let Hezekiah deceive you, for he will not be able to deliver you out of my hand. [30]Do not let Hezekiah make you rely on the Lord by saying, The Lord will surely deliver us, <u>and this city will not be given into the hand of the king of Assyria</u>.' [31] Do not listen to Hezekiah; for thus says the king of Assyria: 'Make your peace with me and come out to me; then every one of you will eat from your own vine and your own fig tree, and drink water from your own cistern, [32]*until I come and take you away to a land like your own land, a land of grain and wine, a land of bread and vineyard, a land of olive oil and honey, that you may live and not die. Do not listen to Hezekiah when he misleads you by saying, The Lord will deliver us.* [33]*Has any of the gods of the nations ever delivered its land out of the hand of the king of Assyria?* [34]*Where are the gods of Hamath and Arpad? Where are the gods of Sepharvaim, Hena, and Ivvah? Have they delivered Samaria out of my hand?* [35]*Who among all the gods of the countries have delivered their countries out of my hand, that the Lord should deliver Jerusalem out of my hand?*'" [36]But the people were silent and answered him not a word, for the king's command was, "Do not answer him." [37]Then Eliakim son of Hilkiah, who was in charge of the palace, and

Shebna the secretary, and Joah son of Asaph, the recorder, came to Hezekiah with their clothes torn and told him the words of the Rabshakeh.

^{19:1}When King Hezekiah heard it, he tore his clothes, covered himself with sackcloth, *and went into the house of the Lord.* ²And he sent Eliakim, who was in charge of the palace, and Shebna the secretary, and the senior priests, covered with sackcloth, to the prophet Isaiah son of Amoz. ³*They said to him, "Thus says Hezekiah, This day is a day of distress, of rebuke, and of disgrace; children have come to the birth, and there is no strength to bring them forth. It may be that the Lord your God heard all the words of the Rabshakeh, whom his master the king of Assyria has sent to mock the living God, and will rebuke the words that the Lord your God has heard; therefore lift up your prayer for the remnant that is left."* ⁵When the servants of King Hezekiah came to Isaiah, ⁶Isaiah said to them, "Say to your master, 'Thus says the Lord: Do not be afraid because of the words that you have heard, with which the servants of the king of Assyria have reviled me. ⁷I myself will put a spirit in him, so that he shall hear a rumor and return to his own land; I will cause him to fall by the sword in his own land.'"

⁸ The Rabshakeh returned, and found the king of Assyria fighting against Libnah; for he had heard that the king had left Lachish. ⁹ When the king heard concerning King Tirhakah of Ethiopia, "See, he has set out to fight against you," he sent messengers again to Hezekiah, saying, ³⁶Then King Sennacherib of Assyria left, went home, and lived at Nineveh. ³⁷As he was worshiping in the house of his god Nisroch, his sons Adrammelech and Sharezer killed him with the sword, and they escaped into the land of Ararat. His son Esar-haddon succeeded him.

Finally, quoting Camp, it could be said that:

> The oldest form of the narrative available to us is already *theologically-infused history*. In this history the relationship between YHWH and Judah is unproblematic. Precisely this lack of a deep break between the two sides, the work of the Deuteronomists, means it is probable that B^1 was formulated before 587, most likely at a time when the Assyrian vassalhood was no longer known and the Babylonian one was not yet known, but while "Assyria" was still a term in use, around the "last two decades before the fall of Nineveh (612)" (So Würthwein, ATD 11/2 [1984], 424)." (*Hiskija,* 170)

Arie van der Kooij sees the B^2 narrative (2 Kgs 19:9b–35, 36aβ) as "supplying coherence to the text, which does not stand without the continuation in 19:36. B^2 was therefore intended *from the outset* as a supplement, not as its own independent text" ("Das assyrische Heer," 108). This assumption goes against exegetical consensus, which holds that the narrative was originally an independent work. Nevertheless, Ernst Vogt (*Der Aufstand Hiskias,* 46) and

Francolino J. Gonçalves also hold that the B² narrative is entirely dependent on B¹. Gonçalves takes 19:10aβb to be literarily dependent on 18:29–30, and since 19:10 cannot be separated from 19:11–13, which in turn cannot be separated from the rest of the narrative, the entirety of B² is therefore dependent on B¹. B² is based both on B¹ and on an anti-Assyrian edition of the book of Isaiah, the former dating to the middle of the seventh century and the latter to the time of Josiah. On the other hand, the closest parallels in phrasing and subject matter can be found in the earliest strata of Deuteronomy (Deut 4; 27–31), Deutero-Isaiah, and in Deuteronomistic literature. Thus, the B² narrative would have been written by an exilic author. However, contrary to the opinion of van der Kooij, B², notwithstanding its dependence on B¹, originally stood on its own (van der Kooij, "Das assyrische Heer," 478–80). This view is not far from the aforementioned consensus, and it also fits the literary evidence.

The beginning of the B² narrative is missing, and the introductory word וישב, to be translated as "again," stems from the joining of B¹ and B². Sennacherib's embassy in 19:10–13 shows parallels to the Rabshakeh's second speech in B¹ (18:28–35), though it is much shorter and contains different content: rather than dealing with political or military issues, it is concerned only with the God of Israel. The place names in 19:12aβb were added later. Camp rightly says this about Hezekiah's prayer (vv. 14–19): "The literary- and theological-historical position of B² is especially clear in Hezekiah's prayer: the theologoumena of the uniqueness of YHWH, YHWH as creator of the world, and the recognition of the singular importance of YHWH for the nations all express a theology marked by the catastrophe and are similar to Deutero-Isaiah, that is, to the Deuteronomium" (*Hiskija*, 198) (cf. Deut 4:35, 39; Isa 43:10–11; 44:6–8, 24; 45:5–7; passim). Verse 14bβ seems to be a redactional insertion.

Among Isaiah's words (19:20–34) 19:21–31 are believed to be an insertion, and within these, 19:29–31 are considered secondary to 19:21–28. The satirical song about the king of Assyria (19:21–28) was written in imitation of Isa 14 and shows a connection to Deutero-Isaiah. It "clearly hints at the context enough" (Kaiser, ATD 18 [1973], 312; cf. 19:22–23 with 18:33–35; 19:4, 6, 10–13, 16; 19:25 with 18:13; 19:28 with 19:33). It can be assumed, therefore, that the poet knew the narrative and that the song was not taken from elsewhere. Isaiah closes with the words נאום־יהוה, "thus says YHWH." It is clear that 19:34, "for I will defend this city to save it, for my own sake and for the sake of my servant David," is an addition, which recent scholarship takes to be Deuteronomistic (e.g., Wildberger; Würthwein). Other authors, such as Gonçalves, omit 19:33 from Isaiah's oracle (*L'expédition*, 453). If v. 34 is considered a later addition, 19:35 would also be one. This is the position of authors such as R. E. Clements, Ernst Würthwein, Ernst Vogt, and Ludger Camp: "The goal of

B² is Sennacherib's departure, announced in 19:33 and occurring in 19:36aβ. This shows that the destruction of the Assyrian army (19:35) was a later, more dramatic addition to the description of the deliverance of Jerusalem" (Camp, *Hiskija*, 209). In sum, the base stratum of B² can be reconstructed as follows: 19:9b–12aα, 13–14abα, 16–18ab*, 19–20, 32–33, 36aβ; redactional editing is found in 19:12aβb, 14bb, 18b, 21–31, 34–35.

In contrast to other literary critics, Hardmeier examines the origins of this text in relation to the author's perspective on the Assyrian threat and the deliverance of Jerusalem (the ABBJ narrative [*Assyrischen Bedrohung und Befreiung Jerusalems*], approximately the same as B¹), which he believes to be the first place historical exegesis should concentrate to understand the whole section. In his view, the point of the ABBJ narrative is not to give an account of military history but to tell the story of a specific threat against Jerusalem of blasphemous propaganda speeches from the Assyrian enemy. Second Kings 18:14–16 are part of the base of the story, which means that they did not originate from a separate source (A) written by a different hand from that of 18:17ff. and inserted before it. Second Kings 19:9–36 is considered to be a secondary interpretation of the ABBJ narrative. Hardmeier writes: "The thematic history in the ABBJ narrative is informed by a combination of experiences and problems relevant to the overall situation *contemporary* to the composition of the narrative, not the historical events of 701" (*Prophetie*, 167). He sees such a combination of experiences and problems in the sudden interruption of the siege of Jerusalem in 588, and he believes that the ABBJ narrative is a "counter-prophecy" of sorts that tried to use the guise of a "historical" narrative to sway King Zedekiah against Jeremiah and his council (cf. Jer 37–38). Hardmeier calls the reinterpretation of the story in 19:9–36 a narrative Zion theology from an exilic perspective, as he explains in this enlightening passage:

> What we have is an exilic expression of Zion-theology's hope of deliverance, one which led to a devastating political self-deception in Jerusalem before 587, and eventually to cataclysmic destruction....
>
> It is remarkable that a theology that had failed so catastrophically and had been proven so corrupt in light of the events of 587 could continue to be transmitted, rather than that the ABBJ-narrative—biased and propagandizing against Ezekiel and Jeremiah—would simply disappear into oblivion, for instance. It persisted thanks to the new focus of the work, found in 19:9bff., for which the ABBJ narrative was an inalienable precondition. It is possible that the new focus came about only because in the situation of the exile, the reception of the ABBJ narrative had changed radically: what had been written as a biased historical-fictional narrative in 588 had become de-fictionalized, because it was read as a primary source from Hezekiah's time. With its new identity as a theological-historical narrative of a miraculous deliver-

ance, the story was then accepted as historical and included in DtrG as part of the historical tradition of the Assyrian crisis from 701, and so it remained until the present day (!). (*Prophetie*, 432–33)

Hardmeier believes that the exilic authors of DtrG were strongly influenced by this sharp opposition against Ezekiel and Jeremiah, and thus by the biased rejection of the prophecy of disaster (*Prophetie*, 467). This provocative analysis is quite interesting and may be at least partially correct. In my opinion, however, it does not prove either that narrative A is not independent of B, or that it is not close to the historical events.

Second Kings 20:1–19 recounts Hezekiah's illness and recovery (vv. 1–11) and Merodach-baladan's embassy (vv. 12–19). It is clear that 20:8–11 is supplementary, as Hezekiah's plea for a sign comes too late. Nor is 20:1–7 entirely unified. The account of the healing in 20:1, 3b, 7 has been reworked as follows: 20:2–3a, 5abα, 6aα are probably attributable to DtrN; 20:5bβ seems to be a later addition intended to link 20:1–7 to 20:8–11. Verse 6b is a duplication of 19:34, but as the primary text is more likely 19:34, 20:6aβb should be attributed to a late or post-Deuteronomic redaction. Second Kings 20:8–11 (which is, as noted, supplementary to 20:1–7) might also be late or post-Deuteronomic.

With Camp it can be stated that "as in B², in 20:5bβ, 8–11* Isaiah is valorized after the fact with the addition of a sign of God's validation. Later these verses were reworked again to make the miracle even more miraculous (20:9bβ, 10abα). 20:6aβb and 20:11b are signs of a process of ongoing literary realignment" (*Hiskija*, 236). The insertion in 20:8–11 probably occurred under chronistic influence. In Isa 38:1–8 the narrative found in 2 Kgs 20:1–11 is smoothed out and expanded with the addition of Hezekiah's psalm (Isa 38:9–20), inserted between verses 8 and 21. Verse 22 must have been added later in an effort to bring the section in line with 2 Kgs 20:8.

The formula בעת ההיא, "at that time," in 20:12 connects the narratives of Hezekiah's illness with Merodach-baladan's embassy (20:12–19; 12b is a literary link to the previous story). It is generally accepted that 20:12a, 13 contain reliable information about Hezekiah's relations with Babylon, which the narrator may have taken from an annals entry. The current form of the narrative concludes in a dialogue between Hezekiah and Isaiah, which clearly ends with the formula "says the Lord" (v. 17); accordingly, the original narrative ended with the threat in 20:17. Hans Wildberger believes that this threat shows definite marks of the historical Isaiah. Perhaps the prophet actually did announce that the treasures of Jerusalem would be taken away, though to Ashur, not Babel, and the narrative might therefore have originated soon after 701. The reformulation of 20:6, however, would belong to the years after Jerusalem had been sacked by Nebuchadnezzar, while 20:18–19 might not have been added until the time of Persian rule (Wildberger, *Isaiah*, 3:473). This theory, dating the origin of the threat to Isaiah's time, is not convincing, however. The formula הנה ימים באים, "days are coming," betrays late linguistic usage and probably comes from the Deuteronomistic redaction of the prophetic books. Thus the mention of Babel can also be retained. It could be argued that the text that was transmitted in 20:12a and that verses 13–17 were reworked in 20:18–19. The base text can probably be ascribed to DtrP, which also follows from its context of prophecy/fulfillment (2 Kgs 24:13 DtrP). The additional verses, 20:18–19, are kinder to Hezekiah and can probably be ascribed to DtrN. According to Hardmeier, the scene in 20:12–19 was an epilogue to the ABBJ narrative; the legend of Hezekiah's illness can be ascribed to a later, exilic editor.

Following a classic Deuteronomistic introduction (v. 1) in the account of **Manasseh** (2 Kgs 21:1–18), there is a completely negative assessment of him: "He did what was evil in the sight of the Lord, following the abominable practices of the nations that the Lord drove out before the People of Israel" (v. 2). Helga Weippert dates this assessment formula to the reign of King Jehoahaz (609 B.C.E.) ("Die 'deuteronomistischen' Beurteilungen," 332), though in this hypothesis the section would still remain in the DtrH period. The concluding notice (vv. 17–18), which probably contains reliable information in v. 18, can also be ascribed to the same stratum. A Deuteronomistic redaction is also clearly visible in the "events" section of the account (21:3–16). This account offers a sort of negative background for Josiah's reforms: 21:3a sets up 23:8, just as 23:4 is prepared for in 21:3b; 23:12 in 21:5, and 23:6a in 21:7a. "This shows," according to Walter Dietrich, "that the author of vv. 3, 5, 7a composed the kings formulas, and therefore the Book of Kings in general" (*Prophetie*, 33). This author is a Deuteronomist—DtrH to be precise—to whom we already ascribed 21:1–2 and 17–18, and there is no reason to assume that 21:6 does not also come from him. The purpose of 21:15–16 is to provide an explanation for the fall of Judah: not only is Manasseh guilty but the people are too. These two verses may be assigned to DtrN. Dietrich showed that 21:7b–9 also come from DtrN, which can be seen in the train of thought and the terminology found in these verses (*Prophetie*, 31). Embedded in this Deuteronomistic context is a threat by "the servants of the Lord, the prophets" (vv. 10–14), a speech that should be ascribed to DtrP. In conclusion, we can say that the base stratum—by DtrH—includes 21:1–3, 5–7a, 17–18, into which DtrP inserted his prophetic warning (vv. 10–14) and which DtrN then surrounded with his commentary (vv. 7b–9 and 15–16). But the references in 21:5 and 7a to the "altars to the whole host of heaven" and the Asherahs existed already before DtrH, and so they contain older information about the cultic practices from Manasseh's time that probably came from contemporary records (Spieckermann, *Juda unter Assur*, 164–66). The charge that Manasseh spilled innocent blood (v. 16) might also come from historical information. Based on 2 Kgs 21, though, it is still difficult to get a precise historical picture of the political and religious state under Manasseh.

The account about **Amon** is very short (2 Kgs 21:19–26). After the Deuteronomistic introduction (21:19) and the Deuteronomistic judgment (21:20–22) comes an account of the conspiracy by his servants and their subsequent punishment by the people of the land (21:23–24) that might have been taken from annals. The account ends with the Deuteronomistic concluding note (21:25–26).

I.2.1.3. The Deuteronomistic Image of the Era

In his standard work on the Deuteronomistic work (Dtr), Martin Noth claimed that Dtr included entries from chronicles only from a very specific viewpoint. "The history of the kings of Israel has been drastically shortened because Dtr. regards it as nothing but a rapid progression towards the annihilation which took place a mere two centuries after Solomon's death" (*Deuteronomistic History*, 102). In other words, the Dtr chose only the facts from the historical sources that illustrated his image of the time of kings. He took somewhat more from the Annals of the Kings of Judah, though, most notably statements referring to the temple in Jerusalem. With respect to the period under consideration, these are 2 Kgs 15:35b and 16:7–18; 18:4b as well as 18:13–16, which refers to the tribute given to Sennacherib at the expense of the temple and palace treasuries. In addition to the chronological framework, Dtr also took from these journals important details about the succession of the Judean kings, including, for instance, the account of the murder of Amon and the appointment of Josiah in 2 Kgs 21:23–24. "In his history of the monarchical period Dtr. has made extensive use of stories about the prophets. The prophets, 'men of God', appear chiefly as opponents to the kings and surely Dtr. meant them to be understood in this way" (Noth, *Deuteronomistic History*, 107). In just this way the Isaiah narratives were available to him.

The selection of material shows a few important themes of the Deuteronomistic redaction: an interest in the temple, which is plainly connected to their sense of the importance of cultic reform. The special role given to the prophets can be seen in the incorporation of the Isaiah narratives (2 Kgs 18:17–20:19) into the Deuteronomistic historical work, a move that can clearly be ascribed to DtrP. The typical interests of the Deuteronomist are found above all in the redactional pieces such as the judgment formulas. Judgment about the kings of northern Israel is extremely negative and is very stereotypical, as mentioned earlier: not one of them is said to have abandoned Jeroboam's sins. "The sin of Jeroboam" was not the separation of Israel from the Davidic dynasty, however; in 1 Kgs 14:8 God says to Jeroboam, "I tore the kingdom away from the house of David to give it to you"; YHWH himself wanted the division. From the Deuteronomist's standpoint, the sins of Jeroboam were related only to cultic centralization: he set up golden calves in Bethel and Dan against the temple in Jerusalem: "he made priests for the high places from among all the people.... this matter became the sin of the house of Jeroboam" (1 Kgs 13:33–34). The Deuteronomist even interpolates a threat into the end of the Ahijah narrative, in which the prophet Ahijah looks ahead to the end of northern Israel and sees as its cause the sins of Jeroboam: "he will give Israel up because of the sins of Jeroboam, which he sinned and which he caused Israel to commit" (1 Kgs 14:16).

The span of Jeroboam's sins stretches all the way to the destruction of Samaria, and the Israelite kings of the Assyrian period are an integral part of this unfavorable history. Only Shallum escapes judgment, which plainly corresponds to the brevity of his reign of one single month. The judgment of Hoshea is somewhat milder than for the other kings, though no specific reason for this is given (2 Kgs 17:2). According to Hoffmann,

> the theological interests of the Dtr are hiding underneath it all: a king's individual fortune is always in *continuity* with his predecessors, to make it clear that disaster does not occur because of the transgression of any one person—not even the last one before the catastrophe—but that the sins of the fathers, the sins of the whole dynasty, and the sins of the whole people, of all of the generations, led to the Lord's judgment. (*Reform*, 86)

This negative assessment of Israelite history is given detailed treatment particularly in the admonitory reflection on the destruction of northern Israel (2 Kgs 17:7–23). The older, DtrH stratum (vv. 7–11, 20) refers only to cultic sins, such as the worship of other gods, the construction of high places, the erection of pillars and sacred poles on every high hill and under every green tree, and making offerings at all high places. Here, too, the examples of the kings in particular are mentioned (v. 8). In the DtrN stratum Israel is accused of further sins: they cast images for themselves, worshiped the whole host of heaven, and served Baal; they made their children pass through fire; and they practiced divination and augury. As mentioned earlier, this list is largely parallel to the list of Manasseh's sins in 2 Kgs 21:3, 6, and the parallels show that here Judah's end is anticipated alongside that of Israel. In this stratum, Judah's history and fate are explicitly associated with Israel's: "Judah also did not keep the commandments of the Lord their God but walked in the customs that Israel had introduced" (v. 19; cf. v. 13). The guilt of Israel and Judah is all the greater because YHWH had warned them through the prophets, depicted in this redactional stratum as Deuteronomic preachers: "Turn from your evil ways and keep my commandments and my statutes, in accordance with all the law that I commanded your ancestors and that I sent to you by my servants the prophets" (v. 13). In 21:21–23, which can be ascribed to DtrP, a different image of the prophets is given: the prophets heralded the catastrophe. There are exact parallels to earlier prophetic speeches, such as 1 Kgs 14:7–11 (v. 8: קרע מבית דוד, "tore the kingdom away from the house of David"), 2 Kgs 9:7 ("my servants the prophets"), and 1 Kgs 16:2; 21:22 (חטא hiphil, "to cause to sin"). Here, therefore, the split of the northern kingdom from the House of David is, finally, the start of northern Israel's original sin (v. 21). The cultic sins that Jeroboam caused the Israelites to commit are not listed here in all their particulars.

The assessment of the Judean kings is not as uniform. While Jotham and Hezekiah did what was pleasing to YHWH, Ahaz, Manasseh, and Amon are judged negatively in every respect. As mentioned earlier, the positive assessment of Jotham is somewhat qualified, however, while the assessment of Hezekiah is unequivocally positive. This wholly positive assessment, which also played a decisive role in his "victory" against Sennacherib, was due to his cultic reforms. Judgment of other kings was based on their cultic measures, too, or, rather, on their errors vis-à-vis the norms as the redactors knew them to be. Hoffmann aptly characterized the depiction of Ahaz's cultic sins, his sacrifice of children and his intensive worship at the high places:

> The account of the cultic conditions under Ahaz summarized in 2 Kgs 16:3–4 is exclusively the product of the dtr cultic critics. They may not have had any special sources, reports, or oral records; all the details were contextual, systematic conclusions. This increasingly negative image of Ahaz was intentionally created as a *negative foil* to Hezekiah's upcoming reforms. (*Reform*, 141)

According to Hoffmann, the Deuteronomistic account of Hezekiah's cultic reform was an elaborate, fictitious scenario created using only few and faint traces from the tradition (Nehushtan; 18:4). His reform marked a high point in the cultic history, not so much because of its scope as because of the particular importance attached to it, underscored in the assessment formulas. Clearly toward the end of the history of Judah the assessments of the individual kings become increasingly more extreme, with starkly contrasted characters alternating in an increasingly rapid succession. Of all the textual or traditional material available to the author, only the Isaiah legends would have offered a possible starting point for an entirely positive assessment of the king. The Deuteronomist took the image of the exemplary, pious king from these legends and interpreted it to correspond with ideal image of the cult. The "high places" formula is inverted for Hezekiah to give it a positive spin for the first time (2 Kgs 18:4). The positive assessment is bolstered by the contrasting examples on either side of the account: Ahaz's worship at the high places preceding it (2 Kgs 16:4), and Manasseh's resumption of it after (2 Kgs 21:13). This literary technique is not all that reveals the cultic centralization under Hezekiah to have been a Deuteronomistic fiction. The centralization sits very well with the overall Deuteronomistic cultic historiography and the systemic conformity inherent in it. With this in mind, Hoffmann makes the striking historical conclusion that "[t]here was no Hezekian cultic reform" (*Reform*, 154–55). I believe that he is correct: the account of Hezekiah's cultic reforms (2 Kgs 18:4) is so general and written entirely in stock Deuteronomistic phrasing that it informs us only about Deuteronomistic cultic ideology, not about roughly historical events. As we saw earlier, the comment about Hezekiah's cultic reform in the Rabshakeh's speech (18:22) should also be ascribed to a Deuteronomistic revision; if not, it belongs to the ABBJ narrative, where, according to Hardmeier, it was developed out of an analogy with Josiah's reform. At any rate, the speech is not a verbatim repetition of the Assyrian's words.

DtrH took the story of the removal of one ancient cultic symbol (Nehushtan) and created out of it the story of a cultic centralization, complete with the eradication of the high places, pillars, and sacred poles, all in accordance with the basic Deuteronomic requirements; thus, Hezekiah "did what was right in the sight of the Lord just as his ancestor David had done" (18:3). The rescue of Jerusalem from Sennacherib's threat confirmed Hezekiah's righteousness for DtrH. DtrP, meanwhile, had a somewhat less positive attitude toward Hezekiah: his reception of Merodach-Baladan's embassy led the prophet Isaiah to predict the looting of Jerusalem (20:17). DtrN returns to a friendlier attitude toward Hezekiah: in 19:34–35 he links Zion theology—God's unconditional faithfulness to Zion—with the Davidic promise. In 20:1–7 the deliverance of Jerusalem is seen in relation to Hezekiah's illness and healing: his healing is ascribed to his sincere repentance before YHWH (v. 3), thus assimilating both Torah theology and Zion theology. The distinction between the unconditional promise and the requirement of faithfulness brings up the possibility of a double DtrN-stratum (cf. Camp, *Hiskija*, 304–17).

The completely negative assessments of Manasseh and Amon—found both in the judgment formula and in the accounts of the events of their reigns—is entirely attributable to Deuteronomistic redaction or redactions. In the verbatim repetition of 21:16 in 24:4, "for the innocent blood that he had shed, for he had filled Jerusalem with innocent blood," the section about Manasseh becomes the real key to the downfall of Judah (cf. Hoffmann, *Reform*, 157). This is clear already in the prophetic threat of 21:10–15, however, and in the previously mentioned connections between a number of verses in Manasseh's event section with verses in the account of Josiah. It is therefore difficult to assess the historical reliability of Manasseh's account with any precision. Hoffmann believes that the Deuteronomistic account in 2 Kgs 21 probably correctly describes the essential features of the cultic situation of the period, notwithstanding its schematization and typical exaggeration (*Reform*, 165). This is only a conjecture, however, and if Hezekiah did not in fact introduce any real cultic reforms it can be assumed that the cultic situation under Manasseh would have remained substantially the same. Hoffmann admits this implicitly when he writes that "Manasseh's prominent *position* in the cultic history exists only because the Dtr wanted to use his reign as a negative foil for the subsequent Josian reforms. His son *Amon*, who was Josiah's immediate predecessor (and father), only reigned for two years, and as such was a rather less suitable figure to contrast with Josiah. Dtr refrained from describing Amon's cultic policies in detail, therefore, and noted him only briefly, stressing his retention of his father's cultic policies unchanged" (*Reform*, 166). Spieckermann summed up the literary situation nicely, stating that DtrH focused his attention on carefully setting up the stage for the Josian reforms, a slant that was still highlighted by DtrN (*Juda unter Assur,* 196–97).

I.2.2. 2 Chronicles 27–33

Ackroyd, Peter R. "The Death of Hezekiah—a Pointer to the Future?" in *Mélanges bibliques et orientaux en l'honneur de M. Henri Cazelles* (ed. A. Caquot and M. Delcor; AOAT 212; Kevelaer: Butzon & Bercker, 1981), 222–25. **Ahlström**, Gösta W. *Royal Administration and National Religion in Ancient Palestine* (SHANE 1; Leiden: Brill, 1982), 75–81. **Benzinger**, Immanuel. *Die Bücher der Chronik* (KHC 20; Tübingen: J. C. B. Mohr, 1901). **Born**, A. van den. *Kronieken* (De Boeken van het Oude Testament 5; Roermond: Romen, 1960). **Delcor**, Mathias. "Le récit de la célébration de la Pâque au temps d'Ezéchias d'après 2 Chr 30 et ses problèmes," in *Studien zum Opfer und Kult im Alten Testament* (ed. Adrian Schenker; FAT 3; Tübingen: J. C. B. Mohr, 1992), 93–105. **Dillard**, Raymond B. *2 Chronicles* (WBC 15; Waco: Word, 1987). **Ehrlich**, E. L. "Der Aufenthalt des Königs Manasse in Babylon," *TZ* 21 (1965): 281–86. **Haag**, H. "Das Mazzenfest des Hiskia," in *Wort und Geschichte: Festschrift für Karl Elliger zum 70. Geburtstag* (ed. Hartmut Gese and Hans Peter Rüger; AOAT 18; Kevelaer: Butzon & Bercker, 1973), 87–94. **Japhet**, Sara. *I and II Chronicles: A Commentary* (OTL; Louisville: Westminster John Knox, 1993). **Michaéli**, Frank. *Les livres des Chroniques* (CAT 16; Neuchâtel: Delachaux et Niestlé, 1967). **Moriarty**, F. L. "The Chronicler's Account of Hezekiah's Reform," *CBQ* 27 (1965): 399–406. **Meyers**, Jacob M. *II Chronicles: Translation and Notes* (AB 13; Garden City, N.Y.: Doubleday, 1965). **Noth**, Martin. *The Chronicler's History* (1943; trans. H. G. M. Williamson; JSOTSup 50; Sheffield: JSOT Press, 1987). **Rudolph**, Wilhelm. *Chronikbücher* (HAT 21; Tübingen: Mohr Siebeck, 1955). **Welch**, Adam C. *The Work of the Chronicler: Its Pur-

pose and Its Date (Schweich Lectures 1938; London: Oxford University Press, 1939). **Welten**, Peter. *Geschichte und Geschichtsdarstellung in den Chronikbüchern* (WMANT 42; Neukirchen-Vluyn: Neukirchener, 1973). **Willi**, Thomas. *Die Chronik als Auslegung: Untersuchungen zur literarischen Gestaltung der historischen Überlieferung Israels* (FRLANT 106; Göttingen: Vandenhoeck & Ruprecht, 1972). **Williamson**, H. G. M. *1 and 2 Chronicles* (NCB; Grand Rapids: Eerdmans, 1982).

I.2.2.1. The Kings of Judah

The historical reliability of Chronicles is hotly disputed in exegetical literature. Bernhard Stade, for instance, writes that any information found in these books not found in Kings is historically worthless (*Geschichte des Volkes Israel* [2 vols.; Berlin: Grote, 1887–1888], 1:81–84). At the same time, many scholars are convinced that the Chronicler (Chr) had another source, or several other sources beyond Samuel–Kings, as it would make little sense for him to have invented so many details. It therefore seems appropriate for us to examine these texts literary critically.

The accounts in 2 Chronicles of the Judean kings Jotham, Ahaz, Hezekiah, Manasseh, and Amon are structured exactly as they are in 2 Kings (2 Chr 27–33).

	Introduction	Judgment	Events	Concluding Note
Jotham	27:1	27:2	27:3–6	27:7–9
Ahaz	28:1a	28:1b–4	28:5–25	28:26–27
Hezekiah	29:1	29:2	29:3–32:31	32:32–33
Manasseh	33:1	33:2	33:3–17	33:18–20
Amon	33:21	33:22–23	33:24–25	

The introductory formulas are taken, almost entirely unchanged, from the parallel texts in 2 Kings, omitting only the synchronisms with the kings of northern Israel. The assessment of **Jotham** (2 Chr 27:2) also includes 2 Kgs 15:34, though without the note that the cultic high places did not disappear, replacing it instead with the comment that Jotham did not invade YHWH's temple. The latter remark is connected to the Chronicler's previous account, which pertains to a sacrilegious act performed by Uzziah in the temple (2 Chr 26:16–20). Undoubtedly the Chronicler means to emphasize the difference between Jotham and his sinful father. From time to time the Chronicler omits references to the cultic high places (2 Chr 24:2//2 Kgs 12:4; 2 Chr 25:2//2 Kgs

14:4; 2 Chr 26:4//2 Kgs 15:4), always in passages that offer a positive image of a king's reign. In v. 2 the note is replaced with a euphemistic comment: "the people still followed corrupt practices" (v. 2b).

The comment in 2 Chr 27:3b-4 on the quote from 2 Kgs 15:35b about Jotham's construction does not show clear signs of the use of an exact source, and it might instead originate from a chronistic image of what the appropriate armament ought to have been. Martin Noth states: "It seems, therefore, that Chr. had available to him an ancient source in which he found various items concerning the defensive building work undertaken by the kings of Judah. On the basis of this, he seems to have developed his own presentation of the royal armaments which he applied primarily to his favourite characters in the history of the kings of Judah" (*Chronicler's History*, 59; cf. Williamson, *Chronicles*, 342). Peter Welten, who studied precisely this question, also holds that 27:3b-4 came from the Chronicler's "construction" motif and are not based on any particular source (*Geschichte*, 28-29). According to Noth, a note in 27:5 concerning a war with the Ammonites must have come from an ancient written source (*Chronicler's History*, 60). This is not entirely certain, however, and it is impossible to prove the historicity of this campaign (Judah did not border Ammon). Welten remarks that the Chronicler's language, in particular in the short note in 27:6 about the war and the colossal tribute, shows that no older source had been used in this section. This note is more likely part of the "tribute payment" motif than an actual account of a war, so there is probably no historical source about a war to be found here. According to Welten, reference to the Ammonites in this section can be understood in light of postexilic conditions, a period when the Ammonites were known to be among Judah's enemies (as in Nehemiah, for example, in the construction of the wall; cf. Neh 2:19; Welten, *Geschichte*, 164-66). Verse 6 is a clear statement of the doctrine from Chronicles of direct retribution, which finds expression in the relation between power and obedience to God. The Chronicler omitted the note about Rezin and Pekah's campaign against Jotham (2 Kgs 15:37), because it is not compatible with the positive statement expressed in 2 Chr 27:6. The concluding note follows 2 Kgs 15:36, 38 and includes a repetition of verse 1, which also might be a stray gloss, a variant of 28:1 that reads twenty-five years instead of twenty.

In 28:1b-4 the Chronicler adopts the negative assessment of **Ahaz** from 2 Kgs 16:2b-4. In 28:2b-3a, however, he adds that Ahaz allowed cast images for the Baals to be made and that he gave offerings in the valley of the son of Hinnom. This comment is closely associated with child sacrifice (cf. 33:6; Jer 7:31). The events section is significantly longer in Chronicles than in Kings. To do so the Chronicler either created a whole tale out of 2 Kgs 16:5 or supplemented 2 Kings with material from a northern Israelite source (2 Chr 28:5–

8); whatever the case, its historicity appears doubtful. The section treats the Aramean and Israelite attacks as two separate campaigns, and it changes the report in Kings of Ahaz's victory (or at least his non-loss) into a great defeat, a defeat brought about with YHWH's help. Here again is an expression of the doctrine of direct retribution. The names in verse 7 could hardly have been invented, but the numbers of those killed in battle or taken prisoner are undoubtedly exaggerated.

The pericope about the prophet Oded is not found in 2 Kings. According to Noth, Oded is a character invented entirely by the Chronicler. This is suggested by the fact that in the cases of prophets whose names were not handed down to him, the Chronicler fashioned names out of the stem עדד, which means something like "interpret oracles" (cf. Iddo [2 Chr 9:29; 12:15; 13:22], Oded [2 Chr 15:1]; see Noth, *Chronicler's History*, 53 and n. 13, 79–80). Other authors believe that 2 Chr 28:9–15 was not invented by the Chronicler but represents traditions that the Chronicler adopted and then heavily reworked (e.g., Rudolph, *Chronikbücher*, 289; Williamson, *Chronicles*, 346). This insertion was intended to show that Ahaz was even worse than the northern Israelites. It may also have been inserted because of the Chronicler's particular interest in prophetic figures. It is worth noting that in 28:12–15 the noun שביה is used four times to mean "captivity/captives," while elsewhere in Chronicles the same meaning is expressed with the form שבי (6:37–38; 28:17; 29:9), which may point to use of a source. The names mentioned in verse 12 and the specification of Jericho as the city to which the captives were brought (v. 15) are both details that give the impression of their having been taken from a source and not of having been invented (see Williamson, *Chronicles*, 347; also §III.2.4 below). Nevertheless, no certainty can be reached on this. Whatever the case, the military clash with the northern kingdom becomes the singular theme of the account in Chronicles in contrast with the version in 2 Kings, and the reference to the two hundred thousand captives and their return shows the particular importance it had in the chronistic view of Judean–northern Israelite relations (Welten, *Geschichte*, 174).

According to 2 Kgs 16:7, Ahaz called for Tiglath-pileser's aid because of the attack by the Syro-Ephraimitic coalition, while in 2 Chr 28:16–19 it was because of attacks by the Edomites and Philistines. Noth believes that the report of the cities taken by the Philistines from Ahaz does not sound like an invention of the Chronicler and must therefore have been taken from an older written source (*Chronicler's History*, 60). As we will see below, Assyrian texts refer to a war between the Philistines and Tiglath-pileser in Philistia (*ana Pilišta*; *ANET*, 274, and letters found in Nimrud), though this does not prove that the Philistines attacked Judah. Because of the Chronicler's bias toward exaggerating Ahaz's failures, and because of the uncertainty surrounding the Chronicler's sources, F. J. Gonçalves is very suspicious of this account in 2 Chronicles (*L'expédition*, 16 n. 69). The story of a war with the Edomites probably pertains to the same event as in 2 Kgs 16:6, but it appears as if the text in 2 Kings prompted the Chronicler to take the war with the Edomites in the south and connect it to a war with the Phlistines in the Shephelah and the Negev, such that Judah would have been besieged from all sides (Welten, *Geschichte*, 174). The assertion that YHWH humiliated Judah is another expression of the Chronicler's theology of direct retribution. In contrast with the note in 2 Kgs 16:9, in 2 Chr 28:20 Tiglath-pileser comes not as a helper but as an oppressor. Assyrian sources state that Ahaz had to pay tribute, yet there is no mention of a raid or an attack, though Assyrian texts readily recount attacks on Damascus, northern Israel, and Gaza. Second Chronicles 28:21 reworks 2 Kgs 16:8, while 2 Chr 28:22–25 is a drastic reworking of 2 Kgs 16:10–18: the adoption of an Aramean altar in 2 Kgs 16:10–13 becomes in Chronicles wholesale apostasy. In the same vein, Chronicles describes the construction projects and changes to temple implements as fundamentally anti-Yahwistic actions (vv. 24–25). Given what follows in Hezekiah's narrative, this is to be understood as a closure of the temple. The concluding note (vv. 26–27) alters 2 Kgs 16:9-10 in an important detail: like Jehoram (21:20), Joash (24:25), and Uzziah (26:23), Ahaz was also not buried in the tombs of the kings of Israel (as the Chronicler calls them) or the city of David.

As in 2 Kings, the most detailed account in 2 Chronicles is **Hezekiah**'s (2 Chr 29–32). The emphasis is entirely different, though: after a nearly identical introduction and assessment (29:1–2) there is a detailed narrative of the cleaning and reopening of the temple (29:3–36), the celebration of the Passover festival (2 Chr 30) and subsequent cultic reforms (31:1), as well as the new organization of priests and Levites (31:2–31). In contrast, Sennacherib's invasion is recounted only briefly (32:1–23), Hezekiah's illness is given just three verses (32:24–26), and the embassy from Babylon one single verse (32:31). "The laconic note about Hezekiah's cultic measures (2 Kgs 18:4) gave Chr. the opportunity to introduce a very long description of them. Its basic orientation was modelled on Josiah's reform; like that reform it concluded with a Passover celebration and its aim was again to show how one ought to visualize the measures taken by the king (2 Chron. 29.3-31.21)" (Noth, *Chronicler's History*, 79).

Literarily, these stories give at once a pompous and chaotic impression. This has led many scholars who differentiate between various sources, redactions, and later expansions to doubt the literary unity of these accounts (Welch, *Chronicler*, 103–7). According to Thomas Willi, 29:12–15 is secondary and "29:25–30, 34–35a may have been added, while the editing of the double Passover celebration (the feast of mazza and the feast of gladness) appears to extend through verses 30:16b, 17b, 21b–22. In chapter 31 verses 12b–19 might also be excluded" (*Die Chronik*, 199–200). In 31:2, everything pertaining to the Levites should also be deleted. In Willi's opinion, the original Chronicler knows priests only as cult officials and Levites only as "ark bearers" (*Die Chronik*, 196–97). Other exegetes, however, defend the literary unity of the narrative (Rudolph, *Chronikbücher*, 293–94; Williamson, *Chronicles*, 352–56). Whatever the case, it is impossible to prove that the Chronicler used a historical source. One can surely agree with Rudolph when he says, "Inasmuch as he [the Chronicler] heavily exaggerated [Ahaz's] abuses, the gravest historical misgivings also surround his account of their abolition, which is an immense expansion of 2 Kgs 18:4" (*Chronikbücher*, 293). Here, too, the Chronicler fleshed out the historical narrative in lively, vivid detail above and beyond his possible *Vorlage* by expanding the scene in light of the world and institutions from his own period. He added details about date and time that give the impression of being entirely fabricated. "It would certainly be a mistake to assume that Chr. had a particular source for a single one of these time indicators, for they are simply a matter of Chr.'s literary habit" (Noth, *Chronicler's History*, 79). Hezekiah's speech to the Levites about the importance of purifying the temple (29:6–11) and his letter to the inhabitants of northern Israel (30:6–9) were formulated in the style of the Levitical sermons of his time (Noth, *Chronicler's History*, 80). Additionally, the list of the Levites' names (29:12–14) connecting the singers and the Levites reflects a postexilic setting and has no relation to Hezekiah's time. Peter Ackroyd points out that concern for the protection and holiness of the temple equipment was an important theme in the postexilic community ("The Temple Vessels," in *Studies in the Religion of Ancient Israel* [VTSup 23; Leiden: Brill, 1972], 166–81).

The historicity of the account of the Passover festival (2 Chr 30) is subject to serious doubt (e.g., Benzinger, *Die Bücher*, 123). This celebration is generally viewed as anachronistic, since the celebration of Passover at a central shrine seems to have been an innovation of Josiah's Deuteronomistic reform (2 Kgs 23:22). The Chronicler described the festival and the purification of the temple in great detail, intending to present Hezekiah as a prototype of Josiah and as a new Solomon. The strong emphasis on the state of impurity and the difficulties of the travelers ("the people had not assembled in Jerusalem"; v. 3) can be explained in light of living conditions after the exile and the problems of the Diaspora. Furthermore, the Chronicler's interest in the relationship of the residents of Samaria and the Galilee with the kingdom and the cult of Jerusalem appears when he has Hezekiah invite not only Ephraim and Manasseh, but "all of Israel from Beersheba to Dan" to the Passover (v. 5)—and then has many members of the Samarian and Galilean tribes accept this invitation (vv. 10–11, 18, 25). Incidentally, the Chronicler seems to set the beginning of Hezekiah's reign sometime after the destruction of Samaria (721), which poses chronological difficulties, since the best date for the beginning of Hezekiah's rule is 727.

Other exegetes, in contrast, hold the opposite opinion: the Chronicler reports that the festival was delayed by one month, that it was attended by people who were ritually impure (v. 18), and that the festival was lengthened by a week—all of which would have been deviations from "orthodox" practice. According to these scholars, these deviations prove the authenticity of the account: if the Chronicler was entirely inventing his account, he would not have created a "heterodox" celebration but would instead have come up with an appropriate observance of a ritually prepared group, in the first month (cf. Moriarty, *Chronicler's Account*, 404–6; Dillard, *2 Chronicles*, 240–41). This argument is not entirely unassailable, however, inasmuch as the delay corresponds exactly to the regulations of late P law, such as in Num 9:9–11. The decree to celebrate the Passover in Jerusalem is Deuteronomic (Deut 16:5), and could hardly have been applied before Josiah's time. The only problem remaining is the participation of impure Israelites in the celebration, which, according to established laws, is not permitted and which, according to Lev 15:31, can result in death. It is not out of the question, however, that the Chronicler was rejecting an overly intolerant interpretation of the purity laws. It is not the fault of the king that many of the people gathered had not purified themselves, after all. Indeed, this gives the king the opportunity to pray for them and to bring about their "healing" (רפא; v. 20), just as YHWH had promised Solomon (2 Chr 7:14). In other words, the cultic "irregularity" had a thematic function as part of the Chronicler's depiction of Hezekiah as a new Solomon.

According to H. Haag, who distinguishes four separate layers in the narrative—a source (1aα, bα, 6aα, bα, 13a, 18a, bβ, 20–21a, 26b–27), the Chronicler (1aβ, 6aβ, bα–11, 13 [in the second month], 19), a second editor (2, 4–5, 12, 14–15aα, bα, 16–17, 21b–26a), and harmonizations—the source included only the festival of Mazzah, while the Passover celebration entered with the second editor, in imitation of the Josian account (Haag, "Das Mazzenfest"). In H. G. M. Williamson's assessment, too, the author used a source that gave an account of a festival of unleavened bread under Hezekiah that was not yet connected to the Passover. The source was reworked to such an extent, however, that it is no longer possible to reconstruct it (*Chronicles*, 365). In summary, the essential historicity of the Passover festival under Hezekiah cannot be discounted with certainty. But since the literary characteristics and ideology of the account are so markedly chronistic and fit so well into the scheme of Chronicles, at least some doubt is cast on its historicity. Whatever the case, the narrative recounts not simply what occurred but what the Chronicler believed to be important.

The brief account in 2 Chr 31:1 of the campaign against cultic high places is dependent on 2 Kgs 18:4, though it omits mention of Nehushtan (who had already been removed during the purification of the temple in 29:16) and adds the areas of Benjamin, Ephraim, and Manasseh to the campaign. The campaign thus grew, expanding to include the northern kingdom, in imitation of the Josian account (2 Chr 34:6–7; cf. Benzinger, *Die Bücher*, 124). The narrative that follows, on the reorganization of the priests and Levites (31:2–19), is shaped entirely around the presentation of Hezekiah as the new Solomon (8:14) and the new David (1 Chr 23–26), notwithstanding the possible use of a source. Strikingly, too, P law (Num 28–29 in v. 3; Num 18:8–24 in v. 5) is in force here. The Chronicler presents an idealized picture of the people's considerable contribution to support the priests and Levites, in order to set a good example for his contemporary readers (cf. Neh 12:44–47; 13:10–13). According to v. 4, the contributions of the people were intended to allow the priests and the Levites to dedicate themselves entirely to YHWH's law: this chronistic assertion may reflect the growing importance of the study of the law in the postexilic period (Williamson, *Chronicles*, 374). The section as a whole ends (vv. 20–21) with a eulogy for Hezekiah that may have been inspired by 2 Kgs 18:5–7a.

While the Chronicler expanded 2 Kgs 18:4 in 2 Chr 29–31, in 2 Chr 32 he took the detailed account of Sennacherib's invasion from 2 Kgs 18:13–21:21 and condensed it. This is all the more striking since this chapter contains around ten verses of extra material (32:2–8, 23). This separate story (32:1–8) begins with an echo of 2 Kgs 18:13, where the deliverance of Jerusalem is seen as a reward for Hezekiah's loyalty (אמת) and the cities of Judah are not actually conquered. In other words, this section entirely ignores the fact that Sennacherib's invasion was the greatest catastrophe for Judah since the kingdoms split. This is the price that the Chronicler has to pay for his doctrine of direct retribution. The Chronicler may have used a separate source relating to Hezekiah's activities, but, given his interest in defensive construction and armaments in general, he might have made up his own image (Noth, *Chronicler's History*, 59). As we will see below, the Chronicler probably had reliable information about the construction of the Siloam Tunnel, which he used especially in 32:2–4. At the same time, 32:5–6a display the characteristic features of the chronistic "construction" motif, including a connection between construction and an assertion of the king's increasing power. Thus, it may not be unjustified to assume that he had no source but simply created this latter note independently (Welten, *Geschichte*, 31). As Raymond B. Dillard commented, this sort of construction is an indication in Chronicles of divine blessings granted to faithful kings (*2 Chronicles*, 256). It is possible that the note may indeed be reliable, however, as Isa 22:9b–11 also mentions considerable work done on the water supply, as well as important construction on the fortifications. Further on we will consider the possible archaeological evidence for these events.

Hezekiah's speech (vv. 7–8) is a summary of YHWH-war ideology composed of expressions found also elsewhere in the Bible (Hos 10:25; Deut 31:6; 2 Kgs 6:16; Isa 31:3; Jer 17:5). The Chronicler did not use the short account in 2 Kgs 18:14–16—an account presumed to come from archival sources or annals and therefore presumed to be historically reliable—because it was entirely at odds with his positive image of Hezekiah. Verses 9–23 should be interpreted as parallel to 2 Kgs 18:17–19:37. The differences between these two versions are so great, however, that scholars as early as I. Benzinger already stated that the chronistic version was not literarily or terminologically dependent on Kings. Similarly, A. van den Born considers it improbable that the Chronicler had the original form of the account in 2 Kings (Benzinger, *Die Bücher*, 126; cf. van den Born, *Kronieken*, 219). Haag gives a possible explanation of the literary process: the Chronicler was directly dependent on a narrative that was part of an Isaiah cycle, while the redactor of 2 Kings had two accounts that were developed out of that narrative ("Das Mazzenfest," 351–52). It is also possible, however, to interpret the chronistic rendering as a midrashic revision of the Deuteronomistic version of 2 Kings, as Childs did. Although much shorter, Chronicles contains the essential parts of the Deuteronomistic version. The Chronicler sought a midrashic solution for the uneven or unclear portions of 2 Kings. In 2 Kgs 19:14, for instance, Hezekiah receives a letter that had not been previously mentioned; 2 Chr 32:17, however, relates that Sennacherib wrote a letter and then briefly summarizes its malicious content. The Chronicler brought his own interpretation to bear on the account above all in order to show Hezekiah in the most favorable light, omitting all its political and military parts. In the speech of the Assyrian king's servant, the arguments are entirely theological, just as they are in the summary of the letter. The theme of blasphemy is further developed: the Assyrians speak out against God (v. 16), mock YHWH (v. 17), and, worst of all, "they spoke of the God of Jerusalem as if he were like the gods of the peoples of the earth, which are the work of human hands" (v. 19). Moreover, the central theme is explicitly more about the deliverance of the people than the deliverance of Jerusalem (vv. 13–15), which might reflect a postexilic concern. The account of Isaiah's intervention (2 Kgs 19:1–34) is condensed into one verse, 2 Chr 32:20. This implies that the prophet no longer had the same important role as in 2 Kings, and that he was no longer the messenger of deliverance (cf. Childs, *Isaiah and the Assyrian Crisis*, 105–11). After the abrupt end of the narrative in 32:21, the Chronicler adds a final reflection in praise of the king.

The Chronicler summarizes the account of Hezekiah's illness and healing (2 Kgs 20:1–11) in 2 Chr 32:24. After this Chronicles briefly alludes to the embassy of Merodach-Baladan (v. 25; cf. 2 Kgs 20:12–18) and to Hezekiah's selfish answer to Isaiah, which is interpreted as the king's having humbled himself. The note about Hezekiah's wealth (vv. 27–29) also is taken from the account of the Babylonian embassy (cf. 2 Kgs 20:13). The enumeration of the riches is more detailed than in 2 Kings, though, which again highlights YHWH's blessings on Hezekiah. Quite abruptly after this comes the statement about the Siloam Tunnel (v. 30). According to Noth, it captures the essential features of the tunnel so precisely that it could only have come from very precise knowledge about it. He continues:

> It is therefore not possible that it was made up from the short and very ambiguous statement of Dtr. in the concluding notice about Hezekiah in 2 Kgs 20.20. One might, of course, consider the possibility that Chr. here had local knowledge of Jerusalem and used this in order to present the vague note in Dtr. in a more detailed and accurate manner. In fact, however, this is quite out of the question. Not only has he erratically inserted his account into the middle of his abbreviating and divergent version of 2 Kgs 20.12–19, but in 2 Chron. 32.3f. he has in addition already made some mention of the topic using partly the same wording but in a way which shows all too clearly that he himself was far removed from any such local knowledge. It follows that 2 Chron. 32.30 must be a word-for-word citation from some source otherwise unknown to us. (Noth, *Chronicler's History*, 57)

Based on the nonchronistic use of language, Welten (*Geschichte*, 39) also assumes that the Chronicler probably used an older account. After this note, the Babylonian embassy is mentioned specifically (2 Chr 32:31). According to Chronicles, the embassy came to inquire about the sign that had appeared in the land. As for the Deuteronomistic condemnation of Hezekiah's overly friendly reception of the embassy, all that remains is a test from God of the Judean king's attitude. Thus, in 32:21–31 the Chronicler "midrashically" reworked the Deuteronomistic account of the embassy.

The concluding note (32:32–33) follows that of 2 Kgs 20:20–21, though the Chronicler expanded it somewhat and named as a source not only the Book of the Kings of Judah and Israel but also the vision of the prophet Isaiah. The Chronicler must have been familiar with the editorial superscription of the book of Isaiah (1:1) and refers to that book in its contemporary form, which may have been quite similar to the final form (*contra* Dillard, *2 Chronicles*, 260, who understands the vision of the prophet Isaiah as a section of the Annals of the Kings of Judah and Israel). In 32:33 the Chronicler adds information about Hezekiah's burial, on the ascent to the tombs of David's descendants, and the honor accorded him by the inhabitants of Jerusalem. This honor is part of the high estimation the Chronicler had for

I. THE BIBLICAL DEPICTION OF THE PERIOD 41

this devout king. According to Ackroyd, Hezekiah is being idealized, and the Chronicler paints a quasi-messianic image of him that may have fed later Jewish speculation about Hezekiah as a potential messianic figure (Ackroyd, "Death of Hezekiah," 222–25). It is hard to imagine that the Chronicler took the detail about the grave from an outside source. More likely, the Chronicler invented it, attempting to give Hezekiah a privileged place in the higher section of the tombs.

The beginning of the account about **Manasseh** (2 Chr 33:1–9) is much the same as the one in the Deuteronomistic source, minus a few unimportant details (2 Kgs 21:1–9). The image, however, is somewhat darker. Baal and Asherah are introduced in the plural, which better reflects the reality of the cult; the single son that Manasseh passed through fire is now many sons, and soothsaying and augury increased (כשׁף is added to עונן and נחשׁ). The Chronicler mentions only briefly the prophetic threat in 2 Kgs 21:10–15, which is lexically similar to the end of 2 Kgs 21:1–9: "The LORD spoke to Manasseh and to his people, but they gave no heed" (33:10). On the other hand, the account of Manasseh's imprisonment and conversion (33:11–13) is unique to Chronicles. Many authors are of the opinion that the imprisonment may indeed be historical (e.g., Benzinger, *Die Bücher*, 128–29; Rudolph, *Chronikbücher*, 315–17; Michaéli, *Les livres*, 236–37): Assyrian texts of Esarhaddon and Ashurbanipal mention Manasseh as a vassal, and on a clay prism Esarhaddon claims that on a trip to Egypt he summoned Manasseh along with other kings from Hatti (Canaan) to his presence (see *ANET*, 291, 294; *AOT*, 357). These texts, however, do not mention imprisonment.

One would expect that a vassal would be called to Ashur and not Babylon. It has been pointed out, however, that, after that fall of the Babylonian king Shamash-shuma-ukin, Ashurbanipal also reigned in Babylon (though the aforementioned texts say nothing about this). We therefore find ourselves with the paradox that, while Shamash-shuma-ukin's rebellion offers the best historical context for the imprisonment of Manasseh, Assyrian texts mention an encounter between Manasseh and Esarhaddon or Ashurbanipal only under very different circumstances. The historicity of Manasseh's conversion is generally doubted and is considered to have been a theological supposition on the part of the Chronicler to justify the king's long reign. Jeremiah 15:4 does not seem to know about any conversion by Manasseh: "I will make them a horror to all the kingdoms of the earth because of what King Manasseh son of Hezekiah of Judah did in Jerusalem."

In sum, Manasseh met Assyrian kings (under duress?), but there is no evidence in the sources for his imprisonment, nor is it historically documented. Instead it is more likely part of an "imprisonment–conversion–return" pattern imagined by the Chronicler, probably with the model of the Babylonian exile in mind. This would also help explain why he was imprisoned in Babylon, rather than Ashur (cf. Williamson, *Chronicles*, 389).

After Manasseh's return from captivity, 2 Chr 33:14a gives a report of his construction projects. This section also is unique to Chronicles and is, according to Noth, based on historical sources (*Chronicler's History*, 59). Other authors also defend the historicity of the material: these fortifications were not a defense against the Assyrians but were erected at Assyrian behest against the Egyptians (Meyers, *II Chronicles*, 199; Ehrlich, "Der Aufenthalt," 282; Michaéli, *Les livres*, 236–37; Dillard, *2 Chronicles*, 269). On the other hand, Welten points out that 33:14a contains a number of terms otherwise found only in late strata of the Old Testament (חיצון, "outer"; מערבה, "westward") and that this statement thus comes from the "building" motif, used in the part of the king's reign judged to be positive. In Welten's opinion the specific place names in 33:14 have no significance other than to ascribe to Manasseh construction around the city, perhaps of an outer retaining wall. The whole should be understood as an extensive repair. He concludes as follows: "not only verbal observations but also historical-archaeological interpretation advanced here clearly demonstrate that this section comes straight from the Chr's own world" (Welten, *Geschichte*, 33). After the construction comes an account of a cultic reform (33:15–17) that stands in glaring contradiction to 2 Kgs 21; 23:4–6, 12, 26; 24:3; and Jer 15:4. "These statements are the necessary consequence of Manasseh's alleged conversion," a postulate of the doctrine of direct retribution (Benzinger, *Die Bücher*, 129). Gösta W. Ahlström ("Royal Administration") is of the opinion that the account in 2 Chr 33:14–17 could not have been entirely invented, and it is clear that Manasseh rebuilt and strengthened Jerusalem's defenses, restored the garrisons in other fortified cities, and at the same time carried out a reorganization of the cult. The goal of these measures was to incorporate into his kingdom the regions lost during Hezekiah's reign.

The concluding note in 2 Chr 33:18–20 is taken from 2 Kgs 21:17–18, though it is aligned to fit the supplementary material discussed above. Regarding Manasseh's prayer and the words of the seer spoken to him in YHWH's name, the Chronicler refers the reader to the Annals of the Kings of Israel. A few LXX manuscripts preserve an apocryphal "Prayer of Manasseh," which, in light of verse 18, was probably composed in Greek in roughly the second or first century B.C.E., or perhaps even in the early Christian period (Otto Eissfeldt, *The Old Testament: An Introduction* [1934; New York: Harper & Row, 1965], 588). In verse 19, however, a collection called דברי חוזי is mentioned as a source. It is unclear whether the name is that of an otherwise unknown prophet Hozai or a corrupt form of the word חוזים, "seers" (pl.; cf. LXX ὁρώντων), or חוזיו, "his seers," in other words, "the words/history of Hozai/the (his) seers." According to William M. Schniedewind, verse 19 is an independent composition of the Chronicler, while for the "words of the kings of Israel" (דברי מלכי ישראל; not the Book of the Kings of Judah and Israel, as with other kings) he was dependent on a source (Schniedewind, *VT* 41 [1991]: 455–61). Willi believes that the allusion to the "Kings' Book" is in keeping with the Deuteronomistic citations from annals, while in a verse of his own composition the Chronicler points to the writings of anonymous prophets as his primary source (*Die Chronik*, 239–40).

In his account of **Amon** (2 Chr 33:21–25), the Chronicler generally follows his source, 2 Kgs 21:19–26. The most important difference is in verse 23, in which the author uses Manasseh's conversion—which he himself added—to reflect Amon in a negative light: "He did not humble himself before the Lord, as his father Manasseh had humbled himself, but this Amon incurred more and more guilt."

I.2.2.2. The Chronicler's Image of the Era

First let us briefly assess the Chronicler as historian. As Welten says, the Chronicler's account of history is based largely on the two books of Kings, interrupted occasionally with additions ordered in smaller sections (*Geschichte*, 187). This raises the question of the Chronicler's noncanonical sources. As we have already seen in a few cases, some scholars are of the opinion that sections found uniquely in Chronicles contain material from reliable sources. Welten's research has shown that the amount of this material is greatly overestimated. Though the Chronicler does contain sections that quite probably come from preexilic times, their number is much smaller than is often assumed. The clearest case of material from an outside source is found in the account of the construction of the Siloam Tunnel (2 Chr 32:30). The list of names in 28:7 also probably comes from an outside source, while the language of 28:12–15 and the parallels between 32:2–5 and Isa 22:9–11 might also point to the use of external sources. Moreover, according to Welten, in the "cultic purification" motif, material from older sources might well have been reworked. As for Hezekiah's cultic reforms, however, the Chronicler reworked that account so extensively that no source can be traced. This negative conclusion does not mean that the material unique to Chr is unquestionably false but that, according to the rules of historical criticism, it is not reliable if it cannot be confirmed any other way—for example, through archaeology or extrabiblical sources (see Welten, *Geschichte*, 191–94). As for the construction work, Welten convincingly argues that the Chronicler elaborated a "building" motif that is found (in the chapters about this era) in 2 Chr 27:3–4; 32:5–6a; 33:14. This motif is found only in connection with kings who are given entirely positive assessments, or those kings whose reigns are divided into variously assessed phases, and then only in the positive phases. Building activity is not mentioned in any account of a king who is given a negative assessment. The construction is always of fortresses or fortifications, and, after careful consideration from every angle, these notes have been shown to be mostly the Chronicler's inventions.

Language and the distinctive details (e.g., in relation to Jerusalem) point to postexilic conditions. "If indeed the language and form are so deeply impressed with the Chroniclers' stamp, then a great deal of caution is necessary when using these accounts to reconstruct the preexilic period" (see Welten, *Geschichte*, 42–52). Among other things this means that the Chronicler's entries on Jerusalem cannot be used to resolve questions about the expansion of the city during the era of the monarchy (Welten, *Geschichte*, 197). However, as we will see below, archaeological traces of exactly such an expansion have been found.

In the Bible, all history is theological history. Chronicles, however, is more theological than Kings. While the Deuteronomist draws the lessons of the events he recounts, the Chronicler narrates the events so that the account itself contains the lesson to be drawn from it (van den Born, *Kronieken*, 10). Like his Deuteronomistic predecessor(s), the Chronicler is concerned with legitimate kingship and legitimate cult. This concern also involves the claim that the Jerusalemite kingship and cult were universally valid for all of Israel, as appears most obviously in the account of Hezekiah's cultic reform. According to 2 Chr 31:1, Hezekiah had carried out his cultic purification "in all of Judah, Benjamin, Ephraim and Manasseh" and, according to 30:1, 5 he invited "all of Israel from Beersheba to Dan" to the Passover celebration in Jerusalem. This was very important to the Chronicler:

> From Chr's point of view, the fall of the northern kingdom could not be free of consequences for greater Israel; this consideration led to the considerable role Hezekiah plays in his work, notwithstanding Josiah. Hezekiah is the caesura between the disastrous period of the division of Israel and the growing threat to the rest of Israel by the empires which, though luckily averted in the case of Sennacherib, already greatly threatened the existence of Israel in Manasseh's time.... It is therefore no accident that the reigns of the two kings, Hezekiah and Josiah—both of which mark similar domestic and foreign political turning points in the Chr work—should also stand out cultically: their respective Passover celebrations remain unparalleled for long stretches of history. "There was great joy in Jerusalem," it says in the account of Hezekiah, "for since the time of Solomon son of David King of Israel there had been nothing like this in Jerusalem" (2 Chr 30:26)." (Willi, *Die Chronik*, 211–13)

I. THE BIBLICAL DEPICTION OF THE PERIOD

All of Hezekiah's actions give him the appearance of a new David and a new Solomon. The clearest example of the Chronicler's theological historiography is his ideology of direct retribution: good kings have long, successful reigns, while bad kings have the reverse. This principle is at work in 27:6 (Jotham), 28:5–8, 19 (Ahaz's downfall) and chapter 32 (in which the negative sides of Sennacherib's invasion are trivialized). The most marked example is found in Manasseh's reign: since his fifty-five-year reign is a sign of success, such a king could not have been only a sinner. Therefore, the Chronicler offers us a story of Manasseh's imprisonment as punishment for his sins and of his conversion, for which he is rewarded with liberation and success.

I.2.3. THE PROPHETS

Donner, Herbert. *Israel unter den Völkern: Die Stellung der klassischen Propheten des 8. Jahrhunderts v.Chr. zur Außenpolitik der Könige von Israel und Juda* (VTSup 11; Leiden: Brill, 1964). **Thompson**, Michael E. W. *Situation and Theology: Old Testament Interpretations of the Syro-Ephraimite War* (Prophets and Historians 1; Sheffield: Almond, 1982).

In the third chapter of this volume we will consider the literary aspects of the books passed down as works of the prophets from this period, namely, Hosea, Isaiah, and Micah. Here, however, we will analyze these texts as historical sources, in other words mine them for historical information, evaluate the reliability of this information, and examine the picture they give of this era.

1.2.3.1. Hosea

Alt, Albrecht. "Hosea 5:8–6:6. Ein Krieg und seine Folgen in prophetischer Beleuchtung," in *Kleine Schriften zur Geschichte des Volkes Israel* (3 vols.; Munich: Beck, 1953–59), 2:163–87. **Köcher**, M. "Prophetie und Geschichte im Hoseabuch," *ZTK* 85 (1988): 3–30. **Renaud**, Bernard. "Le livre d'Osée 1–3, un travail complexe d'édition," *RevScRel* 56 (1982): 159–78. **Rudolph**, Wilhelm. *Hosea* (KAT 13/1; Gütersloh: Mohn, 1966). **Ruppert**, Lothar. "Erwägungen zur Kompositions- und Redaktionsgeschichte von Hosea 1–3," *BZ* 26 (1982): 208–23. **Soggin**, J. Alberto. "Hosea und die Außenpolitik Israels," in *Prophecy: Essays Presented to Georg Fohrer on His Sixty-Fifth Birthday, 6 September 1980* (ed. J. A. Emerton; BZAW 150; Berlin: de Gruyter, 1980), 131–36. **Wolff**, Hans Walter. *Hosea: A Commentary on the Book of the Prophet Hosea* (trans. Gary Stansell; Hermeneia; Philadelphia: Fortress, 1974).

As mentioned previously, the superscription to the book of Hosea dates his words to the time of Kings Uzziah, Jotham, Ahaz, and Hezekiah of Judah and

King Jeroboam of Israel (Hos 1:1). If the list of Judean kings is correct, all of the successors of Jeroboam II until the end of the northern kingdom should also have been mentioned for Israel, which would make Hosea contemporary with Isaiah. It is difficult to glean precise historical information from the book, as none of the prophet's words are situated historically. According to 1:4, Hosea was active during Jehu's dynasty, therefore before Zechariah's murder (2 Kgs 15:10). Artur Weiser claims that, according to 7:16; 8:4; 10:3, 15, Hosea lived through the chaos around the throne after Zechariah's murder (Weiser, *The Old Testament: Its Formation and Development* [trans. Dorothea M. Barton; New York: Association Press, 1961], 233). All these texts are about the murder and coronation of kings and are coups lacking any precise historical details. In 5:1–2, place names are mentioned: "you have been a snare at Mizpah, and a net spread upon Tabor, and a pit dug deep in Shittim" (text uncertain). Herbert Donner, concurring with Albrecht Alt, states that these verses presuppose the Syro-Ephraimitic war, as it was exactly these regions that were cut off by Tiglath-pileser III and incorporated as provinces into the Neo-Assyrian Empire (Alt, "Ein Krieg," 187; Donner, *Israel unter den Völkern*, 45). Hans Walter Wolff, on the other hand, believes that this is unsubstantiated, based on the unfounded assumption that 5:1–2 is independent from 5:3–4 and 5:5–7. He believes instead that the passage is alluding to religious offenses (Wolff, *Hosea*, 95–98).

Many authors hold that Hos 5:8–6:11 and perhaps 5:8–7:16 refer to the Syro-Ephraimitic war and its aftermath (Weiser, *Old Testament*; Alt, "Ein Krieg"; Donner, *Israel unter den Völkern*; Soggin, "Hosea," 131–34; Thompson, *Situation*). Wolff sees 5:8–7:16 as a literary unit and not simply a series of sayings preached on different occasions. "These sayings have been combined without any seams. It is therefore … likely that they originated from the same historical occasion and that they were given written form promptly thereafter" (Wolff, *Hosea*, 110–11).

Hosea 5:8–9 refers to a Judean advance on Benjamin in the aftermath of the Israelite siege of Jerusalem, which had been broken by Assyrian attacks from the north. Verse 10 might be an allusion to the annexation by Judah of a strip of Israelite territory judged by the prophet to have been a border violation. In 5:12–14, the vain alliance with Assyria is condemned, though not in concrete historical language. Verse 13b, "then Ephraim went to Assyria and sent to the great king" (correction: אל מלך רב; MT אל מלך ירב) might be an allusion to the tribute Menahem paid the Assyrian king Tiglath-pileser in 738. If, in light of the parallelism with 5:13a, the second part of the verse might still be referring to Judah, there might also be an allusion to Ahaz's call for help from the same king in 735 (see on 2 Kgs 16 above), though this is less probable. In any case, Donner estimates the date of 5:12–14 to be sometime around the end of the Syro-Ephraimitic war (*Israel unter den Völkern*, 50); the wording of the text, however, is too general to decide between these two possibilities.

In Hos 5:15–6:6, the prophet depicts a return of Israel to the Lord (albeit a short-lived one) in the form of a penitential hymn that is then illustrated with a "list of sins" in 6:7–10 (Weiser). It refers to a covenantal violation by Adam, to events in Gilead and on the road to Shechem, as well as to a monstrous crime in Israel (or perhaps in Bethel). All of the events referred to are quite vague, however. According to Michael E. W. Thompson, these verses concern Pekah's coup in northern Israel (*Situation*, 70); however, reference to priests, as well as the vocabulary of these verses (e.g., שעֲרוּרִיָּה, "horrible things") more likely point to cultic offenses rather than political ones. The "day of our king" (7:5) might be the day of an Israelite king's ascension to the throne, perhaps Hoshea's in 732 B.C.E. In fact, the entire diatribe in 7:3–7 may have been prompted by Hoshea's coup against Pekah: the prophet points to malice and deceit and repeatedly uses the image of an oven to describe the turbulent events. The exact events are difficult to discern, though, and in verse 7 the prophet speaks in generalities: "they devour their rulers; all their kings have fallen." As far as history offers any aid, "in the year 733, one could look back upon a series of revolts against the throne: within a period of twelve years, four kings were overthrown" (Wolff, *Hosea*, 125).

In 7:8–12 the prophet moves from internal political chaos back to questions of foreign policy. "Ephraim mixes himself with the peoples" (v. 8); "they call upon Egypt and go to Assyria" (v. 11). According to Wolff, the order of the events—the call to Egypt for help followed by the subjugation by Assyria—does not correspond well to the events during Pekah's succession to Pekahiah's throne, when the order was the opposite. The order does not correspond any better to events during Hoshea's reign (2 Kgs 17:4), even less to those at the succession of Pekah-Hoshea (*Hosea*, 127). The condemnation of see-saw politics between the great powers in general was perhaps implied, in which case these words might have been spoken in the last years of the northern kingdom (so Donner, *Israel unter den Völkern*, 79–80; Soggin, "Hosea," 134–36). Still, it is also conceivable that they do date to Hoshea's time (along with 12:2) but before his break from Assyria, when the decision in favor of Egypt had not yet been made.

In 11:5–6, on the other hand, the reference most likely *is* to Hoshea's break from Assyria, which is depicted as a return to Egypt: "They return to the land of Egypt, but Assyria he is their king." This is the correct translation, in contrast to the more common reading of this verse, which understands it as a judgment: "they shall return to the land of Egypt, and Assyria shall be their king" (NRSV). In Hos 8:7–10, however, Hoshea is accused of submitting to Assyria, either after Tiglath-pileser's expedition in 733, or after the fall of Damascus in 732 (Donner, *Israel unter den Völkern*, 56–57; Wolff, *Hosea*, 142–43). In addition, 9:11–14 can be understood as referring to the end of Samaria, albeit expressed in quite metaphorical language. In these verses the talk is not about cult but about a catastrophe: that is, the final war has begun, and the end is no longer avoidable. These words might therefore have originated after Hoshea's revolt in 724 (Donner, *Israel unter den Völkern*, 83; Wolff, *Hosea*, 166). According to Wolff, 10:1–8 can best be understood as referring to a time when the turmoil of 733, Hoshea's revolt against Pekah, had finally abated for the people (*Hosea*, 173); the references to turmoil and tribute are rather vague, however, and could refer to any number of breaches of alliances.

According to Wolff, Hos 12 and 13 can also be dated quite precisely. In reference to chapter 12, he writes: "Since Gilead has apparently been captured by Tiglath-pileser, and Ephraim again swings between Assyria and Egypt, the time is possibly the beginning of Shalmaneser V's reign" (*Hosea*, 209). He also wants to date chapter 13 to the time of the threat, or to the beginning of the siege of the capital of Samaria, since 13:10–11 presupposes that King Hoshea has already been taken captive by the Assyrians (*Hosea*, 227). However, all of these suspicions are difficult to prove.

According to Wolff, the accounts about Hosea's family are entirely trustworthy. Hosea 1:2–9 was written by an aural witness, and as such a contemporary. In addition, the variations within the frame of the story (the alternation of son and daughter, the weaning of the daughter in v. 8) and the inclusion of the name of his wife suffice to confirm the historicity of the story beyond a doubt (*Hosea*, 11–12). As we will see in the next chapter, however, careful redaction-critical study has demonstrated that the allegory of Hosea's wedding should be ascribed to a later redaction. Only the naming of his children and the deprivation of his wife's freedom are historical actions of the prophet. The terms "wife of whoredom" and "children of whoredom" (1:2) belong to the later redaction; the Hoseanic oracle in 2:4–7, 10–15 originally had nothing to do with Hosea's marriage. Moreover, Hos 3 gives no precise information about the identity of the wife (Gomer?) or her social status (Is she his wife? his slave? How did Hosea purchase her?). Thus, the presentation of Gomer as adulteress is a subsequent fiction with no historical value (cf. Rudolph, *Hosea*, 46–49; Renaud, *Osée*, 175–77; Ruppert, "Erwägungen").

To summarize, it may be said that the book of Hosea does not appear to be a useful historical source, notwithstanding questions of its literary origins. This book offers almost no concrete historical facts, only allusions to political situations that would be enigmatic without previous knowledge of them from 2 Kings—to which it adds no new information.

Hosea's wholly negative perspective on the political situation of the period should be emphasized when trying to understand his view of the era. Hosea strongly condemned the alliance policy of the Israelite kings and the series of coups that accompanied it. In the Syro-Ephraimitic war he came out not only against the alliance between northern Israel and Damascus and their attack on Judah, but also against the Judean conquests of territory to the detriment of the northern kingdom.

I.2.3.2. Isaiah

Ackroyd, Peter R. "Isaiah 36–39: Structure and Function," in *Von Kanaan bis Kerala: Festschrift für Prof. Mag. Dr. Dr. J. P. M. van der Ploeg O.P. zur Vollendung des siebzigsten Lebensjahres am 4. Juli 1979* (ed. W. C. Delsman et al.; AOAT 211; Kevalaer: Butzon & Bercker, 1982), 3–21. **Alt**, Albrecht. "Isaiah 8:23–9:6. Befreiungsnacht und Krönungstag," in *Kleine Schriften zur Geschichte des Volkes Israel* (3 vols.; Munich: Beck, 1953–59), 2:206–25. **Barth**, Hermann. *Die Jesaja-Worte in der Josiazeit: Israel und Assur als Thema e. produktiven Neuinterpretation d. Jesajaüberlieferung* (WMANT 48; Neukirchen-Vluyn: Neukirchener, 1977). **Brunet**, Gilbert. *Essai sur l'Isaïe de l'histoire: étude de quelques textes notamment dans Isa. VII, VIII & XXII* (Paris: A. & J. Picard, 1975). **Budde**, Karl. *Jesaja's Erleben: Eine gemeinverständliche Auslegung der Denkschrift des Propheten (kap. 6,1–9,6)* (Gotha: L. Klotz, 1928). **Dietrich**, Walter. *Jesaja und die Politik* (BEvT 74; Munich: Kaiser, 1976). **Fohrer**, Georg. *Das Buch Jesaja* (3 vols.; ZBK; Zurich: Zwingli, 1966–67). **Hayes**, John H., and Stuart A. **Irvine**. *Isaiah, the Eighth-Century Prophet: His Times and His Preaching* (Nashville: Abingdon, 1987). **Huber**, Friedrich. *Jahwe, Juda und die anderen Völker beim Propheten Jesaja* (BZAW 137; Berlin: de Gruyter, 1976). **Kaiser**, Otto. *Isaiah 1–12: A Commentary* (trans. R. A. Wilson; OTL; London: SCM, 1972). **Kaiser**. *Isaiah 13–39: A Commentary* (trans. R. A. Wilson; OTL; London: SCM, 1974). **Konkel**, A. H. "The Sources of the Story of Hezekiah in the Book of Isaiah," *VT* 43 (1993): 462–82. **Laato**, Antti. *Who Is Immanuel? The Rise and Foundering of Isaiah's Messianic Expectations* (Åbo: Åbo Academy Press, 1988). **Lescow**, T. "Jesajas Denkschrift aus der Zeit des syrisch-ephraimitischen Krieges," *ZAW* 85 (1973): 315–31. **Machinist**, Peter. "Assyria and Its Image in the First Isaiah," *JAOS* 103 (1983): 719–37. **Seitz**, Christopher R. *Zion's Final Destiny: The Development of the Book of Isaiah. A Reassessment of Isaiah 36–39* (Minneapolis: Fortress, 1991). **Smelik**, K. A. D. "Distortion of Old Testament Prophecy: The Purpose of Isaiah XXXVI and XXXVII," *OTS* 24 (1986): 70–93. **Vermeylen**, Jacques. *Du prophète Isaïe à l'apocalyptique: Isaïe, I–XXXV, miroir d'un demi-millénaire d'expérience religieuse en Israël* (EBib; Paris: Gabalda, 1977–78). **Wildberger**, Hans. *Isaiah* (trans. Thomas H. Trapp; 3 vols.; CC; Minneapolis: Fortress, 1991–2002). **Zimmerli**, Walther. "Jesaja und Hiskia," in *Wort und Geschichte: Festschrift für Karl Elliger zum 70. Geburtstag* (ed. Hartmut Gese and Hans Peter Rüger; AOAT 18; Kevelaer: Butzon & Bercker, 1973), 199–208.

I.2.3.2.1. Analysis of Texts from Isaiah with Historical Information

As we will see in the literary analysis of the book of Isaiah, chapters 40–66 were written during and after the exile. As such, information about the Assyrian crisis is only to be found in chapters 1–39. These chapters contain a few statements by the prophet that include dates, though here, too, the majority of the pericopes are undated. In the literary analysis we will see that in chapters 1–39 there are also many strata to discern and much redactional work from different eras. Only statements that can be ascribed to the prophet Isaiah himself or to his contemporaries can be used as a direct source for the history of this era; everything else reflects later ideas and later opinions about this time period.

Not long ago, two American scholars rejected nearly all literary-critical work of the past; they use Isa 1–39 as Isaiah's own writing for historical purposes (John H. Hayes and Stuart A. Irvine). In their view, nearly all of the prophetic quotations—except Isa 34–35—come directly from the prophet himself. The material in Isa 1–27 was ordered chronologically, while Isa 28–33, which pertain to the end of the northern kingdom, and which belong chronologically between Isa 18 and 19, were put in their present place to set the scene for Isa 36–37. The prophetic legends in Isa 38–39 refer to events from the years 713–711 B.C.E. and are from the same historical context as Isa 20–22. They were given their present form and were inserted in their present place as a preparation for the exile and for Deutero-Isaiah's preaching. The prophetic sayings in Isa 1–33 correspond to events in Israelite/Judean history as follows: Isa 1–6 originate from the reigns of Uzziah and Jotham; Isa 7–14 from Ahaz's time; and Isa 15–33 from Hezekiah's. Only a few editorial additions were made, most of which were glosses. According to Hayes and Irvine, the historical settings of the individual pericopes are as follows: Isa 1:1–20 is set during the earthquake in Uzziah's reign (Amos 1:1), which is also referred to in Isa 2:6–22. Many details in Isa 5 point to Manasseh's time (2 Kgs 15:17–22), while Isa 6 describes an experience by the prophet that initiated a new period in his life. Isaiah 7 obviously refers to the Syro-Ephraimitic crisis, as does Isa 8. Isaiah 8:21–9:7 is set during Pekah's coup and Ahaz's subsequent campaign to show his independence from the northern kingdom and avoid involvement in the Syro-Ephraimitic coalition. Isaiah 10:27–12:6 is a single speech given on the eve of Rezin and Pekah's siege of Jerusalem. The oracle in Isa 13 is from the time of Tiglath-pileser's attempts to quell an uprising in Babel. Isaiah 14:1–27 should be read in light of the international situation over the years 729–727, and the king of Babel whose death is announced is Tiglath-pileser! In 14:28–32 his death is already taken for granted, while Isa 15–16 show that Moab participated in an anti-Assyrian coalition in 728/727 that waged a campaign against

I. THE BIBLICAL DEPICTION OF THE PERIOD

Shalmaneser V. According to Isa 17, Damascus and Israel also participated in this coalition. Chapter 18 comes from the same time, and in this chapter the prophet condemns the possibility of alliances with the Ethiopian dynasty in Egypt. The suppression of the Syro-Palestinian coalition by Sargon and his new relationship with the Egyptians in 720 provides the background for Isa 19, while his attack on Merodach-baladan in South Mesopotamia is behind Isa 21. The speech in 22:1–14 is from a celebration in Jerusalem after the withdrawal of the Assyrian army, when Sargon had defeated the anti-Assyrian coalition. The participation in the anti-Assyrian revolt without Hezekiah's cooperation split Judean society, and in 22:15–25 the prophet directs his words against Shebna, the leader of the supporters of the revolt, and his successor, Eliakim, of whom he thought no better. The speech in Isa 23 was occasioned by the decrease of Tyre's power as a result of the Phoenicians' capitulation in Cyprus in the face of Assyria and the alliance of Midas of Phrygia with Sargon in 709. Chapters 24–27, called a "Cantata of Salvation" by Hayes and Irvine, belongs to the period of the Judean revolt against Ashur in 705. Chapters 28–33 reflect the last years of the northern kingdom and therefore belong chronologically after Isa 18. Finally, chapters 36–37 relate to Sennacherib's campaign of 701. Chapters 38 and 39 are later, and were not inserted in the correct chronological spot. Their events occurred much earlier than Sennacherib's invasion, during the period of the anti-Assyrian rebellion of 714–711, and have the same historical background as Isa 20–22. Chapters 34–35 are related to later chapters, 40–66, and were also added subsequently. For the pericopes not mentioned here, less important or more general historical backgrounds are introduced. The authors offer a detailed introduction to the general historical background in support of this exegesis.

This analysis flies in the face of exegetical consensus, which rightly ascribes large parts of Isa 1–39 to later redactions and distinguishes more modest, later additions to other sections. The results of the literary-critical analysis, which will be presented below in chapter 3, are as follows: it is generally accepted that the so-called Apocalypse of Isaiah (Isa 24–27), the "little apocalypse" (Isa 34–35) and Isa 36–39 (cf. 2 Kgs 18:13, 17–20:19) are later, non-Isaian collections. The statements about the foreign nations (Isa 13–23) also seem to have been a later collection incorporated into the text. When one separates out what are most likely Isaiah's actual statements against Ashur (14:24–27), the Philistines (14:28–32), Damascus-Samaria (17:1–6), Egypt (18:1–19:15; 20), and Jerusalem (22:1–9), what remains is a collection of later oracles against foreign nations, all of which have the word מַשָּׂא ("oracle") in their superscription (cf. H.-P. Müller, *TDOT* 9:20–24) (13:1; 15:1; 21:1, 11, 13; 23:1). This collection includes 13:1–22 (against Babel); 15:1–16:14 (Moab); 19:16–25 (Egypt); 21:1–17 (the wilderness of the sea); 23:1–14 (Phoenicians:

Isaian?). Complicating the matter, however, the authentic Isaian sections 17:1–6 and 19:1–15 also have the word משא in their superscription. It is quite possible that these superscriptions changed places or were added when Isaian and non-Isaian collections were combined.

If the *massa*-collection actually existed separately, it also expanded through a few later additions, including 16:13–14; 19:16–25; 21:16–17; 23:15–18. Beyond these collections many other, later additions were inserted between the Isaian units, including 3:10–11; 4:2–6; 10:20–23, 24–27a, 33–34; 11:6–9, 10–16; 12; 22:24–25; 28:5–6; 29:17–24; 30:18–26; 32:6–8; 33. I would like to note in advance that in the most recent edition of his Isaiah commentary, Otto Kaiser views most of the pericopes we are about to consider as non-Isaian.

According to the superscription (Isa 1:1), Isaiah was active during the time of the Judean kings Uzziah, Jotham, Ahaz, and Hezekiah, which is historically sound. Yet even the first chapter is not simply a speech given by prophet. It is formed out of a few smaller units, of which only 1:4–9 can be historically situated with any probability, perhaps to the period during or immediately after the siege of Jerusalem, when Sennacherib left the flats to the Philistine rulers (cf. v. 7; Donner, *Israel unter den Völkern*, 120–21; Dietrich, *Jesaja und die Politik*, 191). The difficult situation is described in poetic language, in general terms, without any historical details. Jacques Vermeylen's analysis—that these pericopes more likely come from Jeremiah's time, from the Deuteronomistic school—is not convincing. Vermeylen is aware of this, too, inasmuch as he admits that the inauthenticity of the section cannot be proven (*Du prophète Isaïe*, 50–57). Hans Wildberger rightly defends its authenticity, although he is perhaps somewhat naïve in his claim that it is undisputed (*Isaiah*, 1:20). According to Vermeylen, though, the whole chapter might have been redacted by the Deuteronomist.

Isaiah 2:6–22 is a later part-exilic/part-postexilic composition that also preserves some Isaian material. It is therefore difficult to conclude whether or not the description in 2:6–8 actually alludes to the religious circumstances in Isaiah's time, either in Samaria or in Judah: "They are full of diviners [from the east?] and of soothsayers like the Philistines, and they clasp their hands with foreigners. Their land is filled with silver and gold, and there is no end to their treasures; their land is filled with horses, and there is no end to their chariots. Their land is filled with idols; they bow down to the work of their hands, to what their own fingers have made." According to Wildberger, the Isaian authenticity of these verses is hardly to be doubted, and I quite agree with him (*Isaiah*, 1:111). In Hermann Barth's opinion, 2:7–17 are Isaiah's words that were later incorporated into the so-called Ashur redaction, which he dates to the close of the seventh century B.C.E., during the reign of King Josiah (*Jesaja-Worte*, 311–12). This would mean that idolatry was imported into the country in Isaiah's time, alongside riches and armaments. Giovanni Pettinato believes that everything in these verses is religious: gold and silver represent the idols, while horses and chariots were the symbols of sun worship in Judah (2 Kgs 23:11; Hos 14:4; Mic 5:9–14; see Pettinato, *OrAnt* 4 [1965]: 1–30). According to Kaiser, however, 2:6–8 is a bridge connecting the core poem, verses 10, 12–17, to the expansion of it, verses 2–5. In his view, all preconditions necessary to identify even the core poem as an original Isaian fragment are lacking (*Isaiah 1–12*, 65–66). Verse 16, "against all the ships of Tarshish," is part of the oracle in 2:12–17, whose Isaian provenance is nearly undisputed. Jehoshaphat had built just these sorts of ships in Elath (1 Kgs 22:48), and since, according to 2 Kgs 14:22 and 2 Chr 26:2 Uzziah reconquered Elath, he probably did the same.

Many scholars date Isa 3:1–12, a herald of anarchy in Jerusalem, to the beginning of Ahaz's reign. However, the descriptions offer no concrete clues that would allow for precise dating. The authenticity of the oracle against the haughty daughters of Jerusalem (3:16–24) is nearly uncontested (with the exception of a later insertion in vv. 18–23), though "[c]oncerning the time when Isaiah spoke this message about the proud daughters of Zion, nothing can be said for sure" (Wildberger, *Isaiah*, 1:148). It is clear, however, that the prophet not only condemned the men in the ruling class but also the women and their luxuries. In 5:13; 6:12; 11:12–16; and 27:8–13 Isaiah seems to know exile, and scholars have therefore labeled these passages non-Isaian. Alviero Niccacci, on the other hand, concluded from these verses that there had been a Judean exile to Assyria after 701 (Sennacherib; Niccacci, *Un profeta tra oppressori e oppressi* [Studium Biblicum Franciscanum, Analecta 27; Jerusalem: Franciscan Printing Press, 1989], 137). The literary critics are correct regarding 11:12–16 and 27:8–13: they belong to a (post)exilic redaction; 6:12 is also clearly exilic. In 5:13, however, under the influence of the Assyrian threat, Isaiah may simply have been envisioning a future exile. In 5:26–28 the prophet paints a picture of Assyria's great military power.

Isaiah's Memoir (*Denkschrift*; 7:1–9:6 or 7:1–8:18) is particularly problematic. Following Karl Budde (*Jesaja's Erleben*), many in scholarly circles hold the *Denkschrift* to be of great historical value, because Isaiah himself allegedly wrote it shortly after the Syro-Ephraimitic war. Literarily, however, the transition from third person (Isa 7) to first (Isa 8) calls into question the unity of the work. Furthermore, the expression often repeated in Isaiah והיה ביום ההוא, "on that day," points to a later redaction, a hypothesis supported by the fact that 7:1 borrows from 2 Kgs 16:5 (cf. Laato, *Immanuel*, 118–19). According to Dietrich, these joints, along with a few additions (e.g., in 7:17, 20; 8:6–7), all point to redaction—which appears to have been done by just one person. "The redactor had a twofold goal for his additions: to organize the disparate material available to him into one overarching context, and to anchor that new whole in a specific historical situation" (*Jesaja und die Politik*, 63–65). According to Dietrich, the redactor took a number of very small pieces and, through transpositions and redactional additions, made them into the literary unit we have today.

Other scholars have also perceived rather complicated redactional processes in this section. Christoph Dohmen, for instance, differentiates three strata in Isa 7:1–17: a base (vv. 3–8a, 9a, 10–13 [ויאמר], 14*, 16–17), a primary reworking (vv. 1–2, 8b), and a secondary reworking (vv. 9b, 13*, 14 [לכן], 15) (Dohmen, *Bib* 68 [1987]: 307–13). Ernst Haag also differentiates three layers of material, but his literary criticism is possibly even more complicated, and he has an entirely different base stratum. He describes the redaction as follows: base: 1a, 2a, 3aα, b, 4a, bβ, 5b, 6, 7b, 8a, 9a, 10, 17aα, b; older reworked stratum: 2b, 3aβ, 4aβ, 9b, 11–13, 14b, 15a, 16a, 17a; newer reworked stratum: 1aβ, b, 5a, 7a, 16b, 17aβ; a few glossed expansions were also added (4b, 8b, 15b). The older reworked stratum is rooted in the interpretation of the Nathan prophecy from 2 Sam 7, especially as it appears in Isa 54, and as such it might have been an exilic/postexilic composition. Obviously, the later reworked stratum would then also be postexilic (Haag, *TTZ* 100 [1991]: 3–22). Barth believes 6:1–8:18* is a collection that Isaiah himself outlined, and he includes 7:2–20; 8:1–8a, 11 as part of this original collection, which was later reworked in the Ashur redaction, while 8:9 and 8:23b–9:6 were added in this redaction (*Jesaja-Worte*, 317–20).

We are interested here in the value of the text of Isaiah as a historical source, however, and we must therefore not go into all the details of the redaction-critical analysis of it. As was mentioned previously, the main part of v. 1 was a late adoption taken from 2 Kgs 16:5. The purpose of this verse is to anchor the Immanuel pericope historically. Even though it was added later, it is nevertheless plausible that it would be based in the Syro-Ephraimitic crisis. Isaiah 7:2–17 has been adapted in 7:4b, 5b, 8b, 15, while 7:4b, 5b, and 8b are explicatory or interpretive glosses. Verse 15 interrupts the naming in 7:14 and the explanation of it in 7:16, which is introduced with the word כי, "because." This verse is an insertion comprising a combination of 7:16a and 22b, as corroborated by the plene spelling of the two infinitives מאוס and בחור, in contrast to 7:16. In 7:17, "the king of Assyria" is a gloss that gives the essentially ambiguous verse the character of a proclamation of doom. In my view, the symbol of Immanuel can only be a promise of salvation, and therefore, without the aforementioned gloss, 7:17 can be understood to mean "the days that YHWH will bring to Judah will be a time of well-being such as Israel has not had since the division of the kingdoms after Solomon." If this verse is to be understood as a proclamation of doom, it cannot be part of the same stratum as 7:14 and 16. Isaiah 7:18–25 undoubtedly originate wholly from a later redaction, even if 7:18–20 might be reworked Isaian material already incorporated into the Ashur redaction (Barth, *Jesaja-Worte*, 318).

Isaiah 8:1–4, whose Isaian authenticity is nearly uncontested, announces the imminent destruction of Damascus and Samaria by the Assyrians in the Syro-Ephraimitic crisis. Thereupon, the prophet heralds disaster for Judah as well (8:5–8): the mighty floodwaters of the (Euphrates) river—the Assyrians, that is—will also flood Judah, "because this people has refused the waters of Shiloah that flow gently," that is, YHWH. The expression "waters of Shiloah" is a reference not to the Siloam Tunnel dug by Hezekiah, but rather to the older canal which flowed through the Kidron Valley, mostly as an open watercourse. Dietrich wants to date this to the crisis during the years 705–701: only the redactional additions in 8:6b, 7ab show clear connections to the Syro-Ephraimitic war. Gilbert Brunet sees here an expression of resistance against the building of the Siloam Tunnel, which was realized only later, under Hezekiah. Dietrich also sees an allusion to this undertaking (*Jesaha und die Politik*, 158–60; Brunet, *Isaïe de l'histoire*, 171–83). According to Donner, however, it is better to see this pericope as referring to "a particular state of events during the course of the Syro-Ephraimitc border war" (cf. *Israel unter den Völkern*, 24). If 8:6b, 7ab and 8b can indeed be considered glosses, Dietrich may be correct. Verses 9–10 do not fit easily into the context, and their historical background is not entirely clear. Because of the literary context, the inclination is to connect them to the anti-Assyrian coalition in 734/733 or even, perhaps, to the period before the Syro-Ephraimitic expedition of 733 (cf. Donner, *Israel unter den Völkern*, 26–27). Because of the broad address to the nations, however, it fits better in the period of Sennacherib's threat (705–701) or, even more plausibly, a redactional addition of later provenance (Ashur redaction; cf. Barth, *Jesaja-Worte*, 319; Huber, *Jahwe, Juda*, 69–82).

According to 8:11–15, Isaiah and his close circle (as shown by the plural) were spurred to distance themselves from those around them. The threat should probably be dated to the Syro-Ephraimitic crisis. In 8:16–18 something of a conclusion is visible: "The prophet draws a very definite line that marks the end of a very specific period of his activity; in fact unless we have been completely misled, that line marks the end of the time when he fought the hardest to be heard, during the time of the Syro-Ephraimitic war" (Wildberger, *Isaiah*, 1:365). The extremely difficult 8:19–23aα come out of the exilic period and are partly Deuteronomistically inspired. K. Jeppesen sees an expression of Isaiah's frustration in 8:21–22 (*VT* 32 [1982]: 145–57).

The authenticity of the section 8:23ab–9:6 is disputed. Barth includes it as part of his Ashur redaction; Vermeylen also favors this dating (Barth, *Jesaja-Worte*, 141–77; Vermeylen, *Du prophète Isaïe*, 245). Others, including

Jochen Vollmer, Fohrer, and Kaiser, are of the opinion that this pericope is postexilic, either because of its vocabulary or because of its content, which betrays postexilic eschatological prophecy (Vollmer, *ZAW* 80 [1968]: 343–50; Fohrer, *Jesaja*, 138; Kaiser, *Isaiah 1–12*, 215–17). According to T. Lescow, the section reflects Sennacherib's withdrawal and grew out of the circle of Jerusalemite court prophecy (Lescow, *ZAW* 79 [1967]: 187–88). It is difficult to decide these questions. Linguistically there are no decisive arguments against Isaian authorship of the poem in 9:1–6. If the section is Isaian, its historical context would have to be that of Assyrian oppression; it is no accident that the prophet used the Akkadian loanword סְאוֹן ("boot") when alluding to the enemy (v. 4). Alt ("Isaiah 8:23–9:6") is of the opinion that 8:23b represents the original introduction to the poem, alluding to Tiglath-pileser's campaign in the Galilee and the annexation of northern and eastern Israel in 732 (cf. 2 Kgs 15:29). If this is so, Isaiah would be announcing a "day of YHWH" in the oracle, one that would bring the liberation of northern Israel by a Davidide. This opinion has become nearly wholly accepted. The meaning of the verse is unclear, however. The traditional translation can hardly be correct: it does not concern an early time in contrast to a later, future time. A literal translation of the words would rather read: "now the first has brought disgrace on the land of Zebulun and the land of Naphtali and the last dealt severely with the way of the sea, the other side of the Jordan, the nations." It seems to me impossible to determine who the *first* and *last* are: Assyrian kings? Israelite kings? For example, the verse could mean that Tiglath-pileser dealt relatively mildly with northern Israel in 732, while Shalmaneser V destroyed it entirely. *Contra* Alt, the redactional character of 8:23b should be emphasized: the verse offers a later historical interpretation. According to Barth, the *terminus a quo* of the Assyrian's withdrawal from the besieged northern West Bank was in the last third of the seventh century, and the king of whom the poem speaks is Josiah (Barth). The poem in Isa 9:1–6 thus offers no reliable historical information.

The beginning of the poem in Isa 9:7–10:4 is directed at the northern kingdom (Ephraim in 9:8). The strophe in 9:8–11 recalls the earthquakes that struck Palestine during Uzziah's reign (cf. Amos 1:1). After this, the prophet mentions hostilities with Aram and the Philistines. The name Rezin in 9:10 cannot possibly be original, as he was Ephraim's allied partner. It is not at all clear to which belligerent events between Israel on the one side and Aram and Philistia on the other side the prophet is referring. As concerns Aram, it could only be referring to hostilities from the period before the alliance between Rezin and Pekah, for example, under Jehoahaz (2 Kgs 13:22). We do not know what difficulties with the Philistines are meant, but Aram and Philistia had indeed on occasion been allied. Amos 1:6–8, too, retains a memory of oppression under the Philistines. It could be said, with Wildberger, that the prophet is looking farther [back] into history. In the second strophe (vv. 12–16), 9:14 is a secondary interpretation, and the authenticity of 9:15–16 is not uncontested either. The prophet has the quick succession of revolutions in mind: Shallum, Menahem, and Pekah (2 Kgs 15:10, 14, 25), and, perhaps most of all, Jehu's revolution (2 Kgs 9–10). Again in 9:17–20 it is difficult to make out the concrete historical circumstances referred to. According to Donner, it is the tribal battle revolving around the usurper Hoshea's ascension to the throne around 732/731 (2 Kgs 15:30; see Donner, *Israel unter den Völkern*, 73). Second Kings 15:30, however, gives no explicit statement of this, and one could just as readily go along with Hayes and Irvine, who see in it the conflict surrounding Pekah's ascension to the throne (*Isaiah*, 188). Isaiah 10:1–4, which was probably originally attached to 5:8–24, turns to the wrongs of Jerusalem. The poem as a whole—which primarily envisions the events before or from the start of Isaiah's prophetic activity—probably originates from a later redaction, like the Ashur redaction. This redaction must also have caused the transposition of Isa 5 and 9:7–10:4.

Isaiah 10:5–15 is a reproach in response to Assyrian arrogance in which the prophet imitates the style of Assyrian glorification speeches. Verse 12 is undoubtedly an addition, and many exegetes also view 10:10–11 as secondary (see Wildberger, *Isaiah 1–12*, 1:413–14). These verses seem to have had the reworked version of the Rabshakeh's speech as a model (cf. 2 Kgs 18:33–35; 19:11–13). If 10:10–11 are original, the section could be dated to the time of Sennacherib's invasion of Judah. If they are a later insertion, however, they lack any concrete reference to Jerusalem, in which case the section 10:5–15* might originate in the period when Sargon II (722–705) consolidated his rule over northern Israel. Dietrich believes that it can be dated more precisely to the period in which Hezekiah had to decide between participating in the planned Ashdodite revolt and acting as a loyal vassal to Assyria, in other words before 713 (cf. Clements, *Isaiah and the Deliverance of Jerusalem*, 36–39; Dietrich, *Jesaja und die Politik*, 118).

Isaiah 10:27b–32 seems to have been taken from a war report. In 701 Sennacherib traveled along the coastal plain, thus from the southwest. If the section is referring to Sennacherib's invasion, then the route described is imaginary, not a *post-eventum* description. The context in Isaiah, however, leads one to suspect an earlier invasion, though we do not learn who the attacker is. Wildberger justifiably claims that the redactor who put this piece where it is—following the Ashur section in Isa 10—believed that the opponent referred to in it was also Ashur. Because Sennacherib is absent, the episode might conceivably be the Ashdodite revolt of 713–711, which Sargon mentions in a number of inscriptions (*AOT*, 351; *TUAT* 1:381; *ANET*, 287; cf. Wildberger, *Isaiah*, 1:450–52). In these inscriptions we learn that Judah also participated in this revolt, and, according to Isa 20, the prophet had warned against participation. The details are completely unknown, however, and there is no clear evidence that 10:27b–32 had anything to do with it. Another possibility is the Syro-Ephraimitic war, in which case the allied Syrian and northern Israelite forces would be the attackers (Donner, *ZDPV* 84 [1968] 46–54; Irvine, *Isaiah, Ahaz*, 278–79). Finally, it might refer to Sargon's western campaign in 720, when he moved through Judah after his victory over the Syrian rebels in Qarqar in order to besiege the Egyptians and the Philistines at Raphia (Marvin A. Sweeney, *Bib* 75 [1994]: 457–70).

In the prophecies about the foreign nations (Isa 13–23), actual Isaian sections are redacted in combination with later oracles. If one considers the original speeches separately, one finds an ordered sequence: east (Assyrians; 14:4–20); west (Philisitines; 14:28–32); north (Damascus and Samaria; 17:1–6); south (Egypt; Isa 18; 20); central (Jerusalem; 22:1–19). The authenticity of Isa 14:4–20 is disputed. There are no references in the song that point unquestionably to Babel; the reference to a king of Babel in the present context is probably secondary. Wildberger has disputed its authenticity using theological and linguistic arguments; H. L. Ginsberg, meanwhile, has offered good arguments in favor of a connection to Sargon II (Wildberger, *Isaiah*, 2:53–54; Ginsberg, *JAOS* 88 [1968]: 47–53). Barth agrees with him, but he sees 14:20b–21 as redactional and is of the opinion that the redacted form of 14:4b–21 can be dated to the final years leading up to the collapse of the Assyrian empire (Barth, *Jesaja-Worte*, 141).

Isaiah 14:24–27 is a threat against Ashur and is often interpreted within the frame of Sennacherib's invasion of Judah. There are no concrete clues supporting any unambiguous historical connection, however. According to R. E. Clements, it is therefore a midrashic elaboration of Isaian themes, and Barth attributes it to the Ashur redaction (Clements, *Isaiah and the Deliverance of Jerusalem*, 45–46; Barth, *Jesaha-Worte*, 103–19). Isaiah 14:28–32 is specifically dated to the year of Ahaz's death, and in the threat the prophet speaks of the joy of the Philistines, "because the rod that struck them is broken." It is not easy to link these two statements. The rod that struck the Philistines should be an Assyrian king. During Isaiah's time three Assyrian kings died, and 14:29–32 have been variously interpreted as connected with each of these dates: Tiglath-pileser III in 727, Shalmaneser V in 722, and Sargon II, whom Sennacherib succeeded, in 705. The "messengers of the nation" in 14:32 are clearly the Philistine envoys in Jerusalem sent to enlist support for a campaign against Ashur. One could then once again envision the Ashdodite revolt, crushed by Sargon in 711. It is possible that the embassy came to Jerusalem at the very beginning of Hezekiah's reign—in other words, in the year of Ahaz's death (around 716)—in which case the date in 14:28 would be correct.

I. THE BIBLICAL DEPICTION OF THE PERIOD

Verse 29 seems to allude to Sargon's demise, however, in which case the oracle should be read in the context of the Philistine embassies during the period of the subsequent rebellion, in which Hezekiah participated, and which led to Sennacherib's invasion. In this case the redacted date given would be false and the text should be ascribed to a redactor who transferred the metaphors in 14:29 to Ahaz in light of the events described in 2 Kgs 18:8. Still, an early point in the year of Ahaz's death opens up another possibility. If Ahaz's death is dated to 728/727 (along with V. Pavlovsky and E. Vogt and others), then the rod in v. 29 refers to Tiglath-pileser, who died in the same year, and who had dealt harshly with the Philistines (cf. *ANET*, 283). According to Dietrich, the whole section is a later imitation, but his linguistic and aesthetic arguments are not convincing (Dietrich, *Jesaja und die Politik*, 208–9). The threat against Damascus and Israel in Isa 17:1–6 undoubtedly dates to the period of the Syro-Ephraimitic war, shortly before Tiglath-pileser attacked in 733 (see Donner, *Israel unter den Völkern*, 41; Wildberger, *Isaiah*, 2:186).

Though the Isaian origin of 17:12–14 is hotly disputed, it is possible that these verses refer to Sennacherib's invasion in 701. However, the content of the oracle is so general that a precise date is impossible, and the expression "the roar of nations"—that is, the idea of the nations against Zion—more likely indicates postexilic eschatological prophecy (Fohrer, *Jesaja*, 218; Huber, *Jahwe, Juda*, 69–82). According to Barth, it belongs to the Ashur redaction.

In Isa 18, verse 7 is a later addition announcing, from an eschatological perspective, the conversion of the Nubians (Kush is the region south of Egypt: Nubia, Sudan, Ethiopia); verse 3 was probably added by the same editor. Since Egypt came under the rule of a Kushite (Greek: Ethiopian) dynasty (the Twenty-Fifth) during Isaiah's time, the prophet means "Egypt ruled by Kush." During Hezekiah's reign, the Egyptians tried to push the smaller Syro-Palestinian states—Judah among them—to revolt against Ashur. The Philistine efforts alluded to in 14:28–32 should be understood similarly. It is unclear, however, whether Isa 18 should be dated to the beginning of these efforts or to a later time, after Sennacherib's succession of Sargon (705), when the relationship between Hezekiah and the Pharaoh was especially close. Dietrich prefers the earlier time, around 713–711, but, according to Donner and Zimmerli, the latter period is the earliest possible, since during that period Hezekiah was trying to form a closer relationship with Egypt and was extremely active in the anti-Assyrian movement (Dietrich, *Jesaja und die Politik*, 128–30; Donner, *Israel unter den Völkern*, 123–26; Zimmerli, "Jesaja und Hiskia," 206–8).

The Isaian authenticity of Isa 19 is generally rejected by scholars. The only sections where Isaian composition is at all possible are verses 1–4 and 11–14. If they are in fact Isaian, the quotation would predate Isa 18: inasmuch as Kush is not mentioned, Egypt was not yet under the rule of the Twenty-Fifth

Dynasty. The section would therefore belong to the troubled period at the end of the Twenty-Second Dynasty. Isaiah 20 recounts a symbolic act by Isaiah. The chapter was therefore not written by Isaiah but could, like Isa 7, have been taken from a cycle of accounts about him. Nevertheless, this chapter offers what is generally taken to be reliable information about an appearance of the prophet in the period during the Ashdod revolt (713–711) (otherwise Kaiser, *Isaiah 13–39*, 99–100: postexilic). As for the oracle in Isa 22:1–14, the Isaian authenticity of verses 1–4, 12–14 is nearly universally accepted, while the authenticity of verses 5–11 is disputed (Kaiser, Fohrer, Vermeylen, and Clements, among others, reject it). The Isaian section is best dated to shortly after Sennacherib's withdrawal from Jerusalem in 701. According to Donner, 22:9b–11a is a very old addition that came from a well-informed source close to the time of the events, though Clements believes that verses 8b–11 are more likely an interpretation added in 587 after the fall of Jerusalem (Donner, *Israel unter den Völkern*, 128; Clements, *Isaiah and the Deliverance of Jerusalem*, 33). The mention of work on the water supply and the defenses is paralleled in 2 Chr 32:2–5 and seems to have come from a reliable source. The oracle against Shebna (22:15–25) is clearly not homogeneous. The base of 22:15–19 is Isaian, though establishing a precise date for it is difficult. It is occasionally dated before Sennacherib's 701 campaign, since in 2 Kgs 18:8 (Isa 36:3) Shebna is called the secretary (סֹפֵר), and had therefore left his position as master of the household (עַל־הַבַּיִת). In the same texts, Eliakim, Hilkiah's son, is already master of the household. Thus, 22:20–23 seems to me to have been added later to bring 22:15–19 in line with 36:3. Isaiah 22:24–36 is an even later prosaic addition.

Chapter 23 includes an oracle against the Phoenicians (vv. 1–14), to which a few verses of prose were added later (vv. 15–18). It is no longer doubted that the addition is postexilic, but there is still ample discussion about the authenticity and dating of 23:1–14, with a host of different opinions. The section is not a prediction but a reflection on the great disaster that struck the Phoenicians. It is probably not Isaian, but may instead have come from the late Assyrian period, and its historical background may be Assarhaddon's punitive expeditions against Phoenicia (681–669; *ANET*, 290–91; cf. Wildberger, *Isaiah*, 2:415–19).

After the so-called Isaiah Apocalypse (Isa 24–27) comes a collection of statements about Israel and Judah (Isa 28–33). In 28:1–13 the redactor took an older statement against the Samarian leaders (vv. 1–4) and transferred it to the Jerusalemite ruling class (vv. 7–13). The Isaian statement can best be dated to the period between the Syro-Ephraimitic war (733/732) and the siege of Samaria by Shalmaneser (725/724). The proclamation of salvation in 28:5–6 is a postexilic insertion. Using 28:7a as a transition, a collector of Isaian state-

I. THE BIBLICAL DEPICTION OF THE PERIOD

ments connected the oracle in vv. 7b–13 to the preceding section. The original form of 28:14–22—an oracle against the alliance with Egypt—may have a basic Isaian component and can be understood as having originated from the period of the revolt against Sennacherib (Wildberger, *Isaiah*, 3:37). In the prophecy about Ariel (29:1–8), only verses 1–4a are Isaian, while 4b is a linking doublet; verses 5–8 stand in contrast to 1–4 both literarily and in their content. The latter verses betray gradual additions which look back on the events of 701 in a legendary version, perhaps as *vaticinia ex eventu* (cf. Isa 36–37; Donner, *Isaiah unter den Völkern*, 154–55; Dietrich, *Jesaja und die Politik*, 188–89). The authentic Ariel saying should probably be dated to shortly before the siege of 701. Dietrich is of the opinion that in 29:13–14 Isaiah is apparently speaking in a service of supplication that may have taken place in 701. Wildberger concurs (Dietrich, *Jesaja und die Politik*, 174; Wildberger, *Isaiah*, 3:89), though in my opinion the evidence for this is extremely vague. Isaiah 29:15–16 probably also pertains to Hezekiah's rebellion in 705–701, particularly in connection with the Judeans' attempts to keep YHWH—the prophet, that is—in the dark about their plans. Isaiah 30:1–5 originated in the same situation and also opposes the attempt to form an alliance with Egypt; 30:6–7 can be counted among the speeches against this policy of alliances as well. Fohrer (*Jesaja*, 2:96) sees 30:8–14 and 15–17 as alluding to Hezekiah's revolt against the Assyrians and his alliance with Egypt. However, outside the fact that most of Isa 28–31 refer to some sort of similar context, there are no direct allusions to this historical setting in 30:8–17. As such, these verses could have originated in some other period of Isaiah's activity.

The authenticity of 30:27–33 is heavily disputed, and the historical referent of this heavily reworked piece is not at all clear. According to Gonçalves, 29:5–7; 30:27–33; 31:5, 8–9 belong to the same redactional layer, while Barth sees 30:27–33 and 31:5, 8b–9 as part of his Ashur redaction (Gonçalves, *L'expédition*, 307; Barth, *Jesaja-Worte*, 334–35). Verses 1–3 of Isa 31 are a self-contained speech against the alliance with Egypt from the same time as 30:1–5. Of the remainder of verses in this chapter, at best 31:4–5 and 31:8a are Isaian in origin. It is still debated whether 31:4 is a threat or a word of salvation. In the case of 31:4–5, verse 5 could only be a secondary interpretation that changes verse 4 into a word of salvation. As mentioned previously, Barth ascribes 31:5, 8b–9 to the Ashur redaction. Fohrer (*Jesaja*, 2:127) calls Isa 32:9–14, a speech against "women who are at ease," the last statement of Isaiah. Its Isaian origin is debatable, though: Kaiser and Wildberger dismiss it, while Barth counts this section among the Isaian texts of his Ashur redaction.

The Proto-Isaian section of the book of Isaiah concludes with Isa 36–39, which are almost entirely parallel to 2 Kgs 18:13, 17–20:19. As mentioned above, the material in these chapters initially circulated separately. The Hezekiah-Isaiah narratives were first worked into 2 Kings, then taken from there and adopted in the book of Isaiah. Some of the details of the text were changed in order to transform Hezekiah into a more ideal figure than he was in 2 Kings. K. A. D. Smelik and Christopher R. Seitz offer a different opinion: the narratives were originally intended to be added as an editorial bridge between the two major sections of Isaiah, and were added to 2 Kings only later, due to Hezekiah's outstanding role in these narratives. This position, however, was convincingly refuted by A. H. Konkel (Smelik, "Distortion," 74; Seitz, *Zion's Final Destiny*, 51–61; Konkel, "Sources").

I.2.3.2.2. Outcome

Isaiah's activity in the greater political scene was primarily connected with the Syro-Ephraimitic crisis, the Ashdod revolt (713–711), and the revolt against Sennacherib (705–701). Most of the references to these events can be found only through an interpretation of the prophet's statements, however, since the facts that directly inspired his words are not usually mentioned explicitly.

We learn from Isa 7:6 that the main goal of the Syro-Ephraimitic campaign against Jerusalem was to replace the king with the son of one Tabe'el (in the MT Tabe'al is a tendentious deformation of the original, Tabe'el; cf. LXX ταβεηλ)—in other words, a threat to the Davidic dynasty. In this situation Isaiah encouraged the king—under the condition that he trust in YHWH alone—and declared the downfall of the coalition (7:5–17*; 8:1–4; 17:1–6). The Isaian texts do not corroborate the account in 2 Kgs 16:7–9 that Ahaz called Tiglath-pileser for help. This makes the account very suspect, as Isaiah would undoubtedly have protested against such a call to the Assyrians for aid. The prophet supported Ahaz's neutrality between Damascus and Assyria and his subsequent resistance against the Syro-Ephraimitic coalition. Irvine is probably correct in stating that Isaiah was not against the king's policies but against the majority of the people (8:12: העם הזה, "this people"), who were well-disposed toward the anti-Assyrian coalition. This does not mean that we can agree with all of the details of his historical interpretation of Isaiah's words, however (Irvine, *Isaiah, Ahaz*). In 8:16–18 the prophet seems to have temporarily retired because of the people's revolt.

It is often quite difficult to differentiate the speeches from the period of the Ashdod revolt and those from the period of the revolt against Sennacherib. In both instances the prophet warned against alliances with Egypt and against Assyria: the symbolic action in Isa 20 is probably datable to the Ashdod revolt, while there is a high probability that Isa 18; 28:14–22; 29:1–4a, 15–16; 30:1–7; and 31:1–3 pertain to the plans to ally with Egypt against Sennacherib. Nowhere does it say that Isaiah condemned disengaging from Ashur.

I. THE BIBLICAL DEPICTION OF THE PERIOD

To the contrary, in 10:15–19* he clearly expressed what he thought about the Assyrians' hunger for expansion; he undoubtedly condemned Sennacherib's campaign against Judah, therefore, and wished for Jerusalem's victory (30:15). He disapproved, however, of Hezekiah's defensive measures, viewing them as an expression of a lack of faith in YHWH (22:8b–11; 30:16). He also fought against alliances, whether with Egypt or with other nations, as with, for example, the Philistines. Dietrich put it aptly: "Isaiah condemns his fellow countrymen for their looking in the wrong direction over the years, 'looking' to Egyptian military power, and to their own defenses, instead of to him who first protected the people and who now wants to punish them, who needs no military support, and who can neither be kept off" (*Jesaja und die Politik*, 158). Isaiah wished for victory for his people and, in the end, was also sure of it. But then Judah suffered a grave defeat (1:4–8; 22:1–14*)—though this did not prevent the people from celebrating Sennacherib's withdrawal from Jerusalem as a victory (22:12–13).

Some texts in the book of Isaiah (17:12–14; 29:5–8; 30:27–33; 31:5, 8–9) allude to the events of 701 and interpret them as a victory against the enemies of Zion, in line with the narratives in Isa 36–37//2 Kgs 18:17–19:34. These verses, however, are not of Isaian origin or were at least reworked at a later time. Gonçalves ascribes them to a redaction in Josiah's time, and Barth also includes these verses in his Ashur redaction (Gonçalves, *L'expédition*, 540; Barth, *Jesaja-Worte*, passim). In this redactional layer, the historical facts of Isaiah's era were reinterpreted by contemporaries of Josiah (around 620–614 B.C.E.): YHWH is justified, while the wisdom of his plans and his works is expounded both in 2:1–14:27* (cf. 14:24–26) and in the didactic poem 28:23–29, a kind of commentary on "YHWH's strange deed" and his "alien work" (28:21). In God's historical plan, the role of the Assyrians as a tool to mete out punishment against his people was limited. The Ashur redaction makes it quite clear "that in YHWH's overall plan the judgment executed by the Assyrians was a necessary intermediate stop; nonetheless YHWH's actions, including the neutralization of all the circumstances which opposed him (not least of which was the wanton oppression by the Assyrians), had a larger goal: the realization of complete salvation for his people" (Barth, *Jesaja-Worte*, 269). Here this people is the greater Israel of the Davidic double monarchy.

It is somewhat surprising that not a single Isaian statement about the fall of Samaria was handed down. Although 9:7–10:4 and 28:1–4 are threats against Ephraim, they are rather vague, and though, according to 8:4, the prophet declared that "the spoil of Samaria will be carried away by the king of Assyria," in this threat Samaria is connected with Damascus. Later the prophet looked back to the fall of Samaria when he confirmed in 10:6 that the destruction of the northern kingdom corresponded to YHWH's intentions: "Against a godless nation I send him [Ashur], and against the people of my wrath I command him, to take spoil and seize plunder, and to tread them down like the mire of the streets" (v. 6). The point of the speech in 10:5–15, however, is that Ashur will not stop: "Is not Calno like Carchemish? Is not Hamath like Arpad? Is not Samaria like Damascus?" (v. 9). "With the names of the cities in verse 9 a north–south line is drawn that ends disturbingly close to Jerusalem. Therefore from the continual expansion of the Assyrian empire, the prophet concludes that Judah's turn would come soon, too" (Dietrich, *Jesaja und die Politik*, 115–16).

As for the social situation in Judah, Isaiah spoke out against injustice, oppression of the poor, bribery, and unfair administration of justice (1:17; 3:13–15; 5:8–24*; 10:1–3), which means that in his time social injustice was a bitter truth. He also reprimanded the women of Jerusalem for their luxuries (3:16–24). Further on we will return to the question of the concrete socioeconomic conditions that gave rise to these condemnations.

I.2.3.3. Micah

Renaud, Bernard. *La formation du livre de Michée: Tradition et actualisation* (EBib; Paris: Gabalda, 1977).**Wolff**, Hans Walter. *Micah: A Commentary* (Minneapolis: Augsburg, 1990).

The first chapter of Micah alludes to historical circumstances: in the trial speech (1:2–7), Samaria's sins are condemned and the destruction of the city heralded, while the lament in 1:8–16 proclaims disaster for twelve cities in southwest Judah. Wolff differentiates three strata in the chapter: 1:6, 7b, 8–13a, and 14–16 form the base layer; 1:3–5, 7a, and 13b belong to the Deuteronomistic redaction; and 1:2 comes from a postexilic, universalist redaction (*Micah*, 45–51). According to Donner and Renaud, all of 1:3–16 (with the exception of 1:5b) can be ascribed to the prophet Micah, who also redactionally assembled 1:2–7, 8–9, 10–16, or 3–7, 8–16. Verse 5b is a later exilic interpretation that expands the trial speech to include Judah (Donner, *Israel unter den Völkern*, 92–105; Renaud, *La formation*, 58–59). According to 1:10–16, Micah expected enemy penetration into his own region, which would also affect Jerusalem; according to 1:15 the conqueror was already there. Here the reference is probably to Tiglath-pileser's campaign to Palestine in 734. Inasmuch as Samaria is in danger but not yet destroyed, the section can be dated to between 724 and 722. This is undoubtedly the case for 1:3–7—assuming that these verses are authentic and should not be assigned to a later redaction (see 178–79)—though 1:8–16 could also have a later date and could be connected to Sennacherib's invasion of 701, although this is difficult to prove. It is less likely that 1:6, 12–13 relate to the Syro-Ephraimitic war, as Henri Cazelles believes (*ErIsr* 14 [1978]: 72).

There are nearly no other historically informative texts in Micah, and, as we will see later, the Mican authenticity of many pericopes is debated. In 2:1–5—the base of which is generally ascribed to Micah—the prophet addresses the greed of the rich, supporting what we read about social injustice in Isaiah. In 6:9–16 he makes the same condemnation, although Wolff doubts the authenticity of these verses (*Micah*, 191). In summary, Micah has a negative opinion of his people's recent history and the state of social justice, and he predicts only disaster for them, denouncing especially the rulers who are responsible (3:1–12).

I.2.4. Further Biblical Sources

Certain psalms are occasionally connected with our era. Ernst Vogt dates Ps 44 to Hezekiah's time (more precisely to Sennacherib's campaign), while J.-M. Carrière believes that Ps 72 comes from the early part of Hezekiah's reign (Vogt, *VD* 45 [1967]: 193–200; Carrière, *Bib* 72 [1991]: 66–69). These dates are anything but secure, however. The question of whether Prov 25–29 originated in Hezekiah's time will be dealt with in the third chapter of this book.

II. The History of the Era

II.1. Sources

II.1.1. Literary Sources

Beer, G. "Das Martyrium Jesajae," in E. Kautzsch, *Die Apokryphen und Pseudepigraphen des Alten Testaments* (1900; repr., Hildesheim: Olms, 1962), 2:119–27. **Josephus**. *Jewish Antiquities* (trans. H. St. J. Thackeray, Ralph Marcus, Allen Wikgren, and Louis H. Feldman; 9 vols.; LCL; Cambridge: Harvard University Press, 1930–65). **Niese**, Benedikt. *Flavii Iosephi opera* (7 vols.; Berlin: Weidmann, 1955). **Norelli**, Enrico. *Ascension du prophète Isaïe* (Turnhout: Brepols, 1993).

In the previous chapter the biblical sources were presented and analyzed in detail. Although not direct historical sources in the strictest sense, the biblical sources do offer historiographically—literarily—reworked information that can be elicited from their present context, which offers an often multifaceted picture of the era that is to be examined critically. There are other historiographical sources, however, outside the Bible, both Israelite-Jewish and foreign.

Among the former, first and foremost is Flavius Josephus's *Antiquitates Iudaicae* ('Ιουδαϊκὴ 'Αρχαιολογία). This work is a history of the Jewish people from creation to 66 C.E., conceived as a counterpart to Dionysius of Halicarnassus's work about Roman history (Ρωμανικὴ 'Αρχαιολογία). As pertains our period, the author mostly relies on the Bible, following its narrative order almost exactly, blending the versions found in Kings and Chronicles. Although Josephus claims that he added nothing to the biblical narrative, he actually took a great deal from extrabiblical traditions. In the sections of interest to us, however, 2 Kgs 15:8–21:26 and 2 Chr 27–33, he added only a few minor details. In *Ant.* 9.235, for instance, he mentions a deportation of Galilean and other northern Israelite groups by Tiglath-pileser, a detail absent in 2 Kgs 15:29, while in 9.253 he claims that not only were the people of Damascus deported (2 Kgs 16:9), but that Assyrians were then settled there. In 9.239 he notably dates the prophet Nahum to Jotham's reign, while critical exegesis dates him sometime in the middle of the seventh century. Occasionally Josephus rationalizes biblical depictions: while 2 Kgs 17:25 claims that YHWH sent lions among the Samaritans, Josephus speaks of a plague (9.289); he also explains the angel, which, according to 2 Kgs 19:35, killed thousands in Sennacherib's camp in front of Jerusalem as having been a plague (10.21). In 10.40 Manasseh was imprisoned not by an Assyrian king but by the king of the Babylonians and Chaldeans (against 2 Chr 33:11). These were the sorts of small details that Josephus added to the biblical narrative, though none offers any historically reliable information.

We have already touched on the apocryphal Prayer of Manasseh. There is also an apocryphal work about Isaiah, the *Ascension of Isaiah*, a Christian composition into which has been incorporated the *Martyrdom of Isaiah* (first century B.C.E.–first century C.E.; *Ascen. Isa.* 2:1–3:12; 5:2–14), a Jewish account of Isaiah's martyrdom. According to the account, Isaiah was sawed to death by Manasseh. Hebrews 11:37 (ἐπρίσθησαν, "they were sawed up") seems to be an allusion to this martyrdom. This legend is found also in the Talmud (y. Sanh. 10; b. Sanh. 103b; b. Yebam. 49b). However, as older sources say nothing of Isaiah's martyrdom, the historicity of this is rather more than suspicious.

II.1.2. Inscriptions

AOT, 345–55. *ANET*, 282–88. *TUAT* 1:370–401. **Aharoni**, Yohanan. *Arad Inscriptions* (Jerusalem: Israel Exploration Society, 1981). **Aharoni**. *Beer-Sheba*, vol. 1, *Excavations at Tel Beer-Sheba, 1969–1971 Seasons* (Publications of the Institute of Archaeology 2; Tel Aviv: Tel Aviv University, Institute of Archaeology, 1973). **Galling**, Kurt. *Textbuch zur Geschichte Israels* (2nd ed.; Tübingen: Mohr Siebeck, 1968), 54–69. **Hallo**, William W. "From Qarqar to Carchemish: Assyria and Israel in the Light of New Discoveries," *BA* 23 (1960): 34–61. **Loretz**, Oswald, and W. **Mayer**, "Pulu-Tiglatpileser III. und Menahem von Israel," *UF* 22 (1990): 221–31. **Luckenbill**, Daniel David. *Ancient Records of Assyria and Babylonia* (2 vols.; Chicago: University of Chicago Press, 1926–27). **Luckenbill**. *The Annals of Sennacherib* (OIP 2; Chicago: University of Chicago Press, 1924). **Luckenbill**. "Azariah of Judah," *AJSL* 41 (1925): 217–32. **Renz**, Johannes, and Wolfgang **Röllig**. *Handbuch der althebräischen Epigraphik* (3 vols.; Darmstadt: Wissenschaftliche Buchgesellschaft, 1995). **Tadmor**, Hayim. "Azriyau of Yaudi," *ScrHier* 8 (1961): 232–71. **Tadmor**. *The Inscriptions of Tiglath-Pileser III, King of Assyria: Critical Edition, with Introduction, Translation, and Commentary* (Publications of the Israel Academy of Sciences and Humanities; Jerusalem: Israel Academy of Sciences and Humanities, 1994). **Timm**, S. "Die Eroberung Samarias aus assyrisch-babylonischer Sicht," *WO* 20–21 (1989–90): 62–82. **Vogt**, Ernst. "Die Texte Tiglath-Pilesers III. über die Eroberung Palästinas," *Bib* 45 (1964): 348–54. **Weippert**, Helga. *Palästina in vorhellenistischer Zeit* (Handbuch der Archäologie, Vorderasien 2.1; Munich: Beck, 1988), 578–87. **Weippert**, Manfred. "Menachem von Israel und seine Zeitgenossen in einer Steleninschrift des assyrischen Königs Tiglatpileser III aus dem Iran," *ZDPV* 89 (1973): 26–53.

Among contemporary sources there are also inscriptions, some from Palestine, more from Mesopotamia. From Hezekiah's time we have the so-called Siloam Inscription, which was discovered in 1880 in the rock face at the outflow of the tunnel dug probably during Hezekiah's reign (*AOT*, 445; *KAI*, 189; *ANET*, 321; Sir 48:17). We gather from this inscription that the tunnel was dug from both sides as "the qyarrymen hewed, each man toward his follow, axe against axe."

The oldest archives found in Israel by archaeologists come from the eighth century. The chronology of the ostraca from Samaria is disputed, but they probably date to the first half of that century—belonging, in other words, to the previous era. From a socioeconomic perspective, however, the information they contain is valid also for the later decades of the century. Excavations at Tel Arad have uncovered a number of ostraca, a few of which come from our era. According to Yohanan Aharoni, one of the archaeologists of Arad, ostraca 60–63, 65–66, and 87 are from layer IX (eighth century until 734), while nos. 40–46, 49–53, and 64 are from layer VIII (from the end of the eighth century). These ostraca are so fragmentary, however, that they offer no meaningful historical information. Only with some difficulty was ostracon 40 understood as having to do with the Edomites in the eastern Negev, but it requires too many hypothetical additions to be used historically. A few ostraca written in Hebrew were also found on Tel Beersheba (Tell es-Seba'). Only one has any significance, because it attests a system of taxes in kind (Aharoni, *Beer-Sheba*, 71, fig 1). An especially important source, though difficult to interpret, is the Bileam inscription from Tell Deir 'Alla, which was originally dated to the end of the eighth century, though recent archaeological study dates it to 800 B.C.E. In her work on Palestinian archaeology, Helga Weippert has exhaustively enumerated all written evidence from Israel and Judah and the neighboring areas (*Palästina*). While these inscriptions cover a considerably longer period, both before and after the Assyrian crisis, they still offer interesting, if fragmentary, information about various aspects of daily life. Both texts and a detailed commentary can be found in Johannes Renz and Wolfgang Röllig, *Handbuch*.

Assyrian inscriptions pertaining to Palestine in our era are readily available. There are the so-called Annals of Tiglath-pileser III, which were engraved

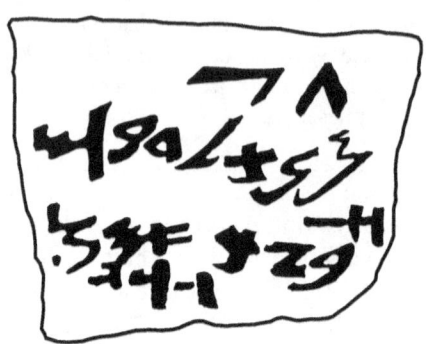

Figure 1. Ostracon from Beersheba (Stratum II) in which deliveries (of wine?) from Tolad and Beth-Amam, villages in the area of Beersheba, were registered.

on stone slabs and found in Kalach. Unfortunately, certain sections were heavily damaged, including damage by the excavators themselves. Although these texts as a whole are important to the historical background of Israel/Judah, spatial constraints prevent us from citing any but those that directly refer to Israelite and neighboring states or monarchies. The annals, lines 103–4 (*AOT*, 345; cf. *TUAT* 1:370) mention an Azriyau of Yaudi, whom many scholars, including Daniel David Luckenbill, William W. Hallo ("From Qarqar," 47), Hayim Tadmor, and Manfred Weippert ("Menachem"), take to be King Azariah of Judah. The poor state of the text makes it nearly impossible to say anything specific about this Azriyau. Since the southernmost territory mentioned is Hamat, however, this ruler could hardly have been the aforementioned Judean king (Loretz and Mayer, "Pulu-Tiglatpileser III," 225; cf. Na'aman, *BASOR* 214 [1974]: 36–39). During this period, Judah was still outside the Assyrian sphere of influence. According to line 150, in an unspecified year Tiglath-pileser collected tribute from Rachianu (= Raṣjān; biblical Rezin; others read Raṣunnu; cf. LXX Ραασον) of the land of Damascus, and Menihimme (biblical Menahem) of Samaria, among many others (*AOT*, 346; *TUAT* 1:371). Menahem is also mentioned in a tribute list on a Stele found in Iran, which refers to Tiglath-pileser's campaign from 738 (*TUAT* 1:378). There is still a debate as to whether this tribute should be dated to 738 or earlier (see M. Weippert, "Menachem," 32; Loretz and Mayer, "Pulu-Tiglatpileser III"). In another fragmentary list, Ahaz of Judah is mentioned alongside Mitinti of Ashkelon and Hanunu of Gaza as having been among those from western lands who owed tribute (*TUAT* 1:374–75). The annals continue (205–40), in a very fragmentary context, to give an account of a westward campaign undertaken by Tiglath-pileser at some point after his ninth year, in which he conquered Damascus, and in which he was active in Israel as well (*AOT*, 346–47; *TUAT* 1:272–73). This must have been his 733–732 campaign, which is noted in the Eponym Chronicle of that year. The same expedition is mentioned in the Nimrud text ND 4301 + 4305, which attests to the annexation of Damascus, the subjugation of Hiram of Tyre, and the enthronement of Hoshea of Samaria (*TGI*, 57–58; *TUAT* 1:377). The Eponym Chronicle from 734 noted

II. THE HISTORY OF THE ERA 71

"to Philistea." This expedition, which reached Gaza and the "Stream of Egypt" (Naḥal Muṣur), is dealt with in Nimrud text ND 400 (*TGI*, 56; *TUAT* 1:375–76). We read in a fragmentary annalistic text (see *AOT*, 348; *ANET*, 283–84; Loretz and Mayer, "Pulu-Tiglatpileser III," 224) that:

> [As for Menahem I ov]erwhelmed him [like a snowstorm] and he … fled like a bird, alone [and bowed to my feet(?)]. I returned him to his place [and imposed tribute upon him, to wit:] gold, silver, linen garments with multicolored trimmings … Israel (lit.: "Omri-Land")] … all its inhabitants (and) their possessions I led to Assyria. They overthrew their king Pekah and I placed Hoshea (A-ú-si) as king over them. I received from them 10 talents of gold, 1,000(?) talents of silver as their [tri]bute and brought them to Assyria. (*ANET*, 283–84)

While one might be tempted to ascribe this text to a campaign against Israel in 738, this overlooks the fact that the name of King Menahem is restored in this text. It therefore should not be used to reconstruct a connection between Tiglath-pileser III and Menahem (Loretz and Mayer, "Pulu-Tiglatpileser III," 225). Incidentally, *TUAT* 1:373–74 offers a different translation. Beyond a doubt, however, Pekah's overthrow by Hoshea in 732 (2 Kgs 15:30) is here confirmed from the Assyrian side.

We have no Assyrian accounts of the reign of Shalmaneser V, and the part of the Eponym Chronicle that pertains to him is only poorly preserved. The conquest of Samaria is ascribed to him in the Babylonian Chronicle: "On the 25th of Tebet Shalmaneser ascended to the throne in Assyria. He destroyed the city of Samaria" (*TGI*, 60). However, Sargon II also boasted many times of the conquest of Samaria. This is found in Sargon's Display Inscription from Khorsabad, lines 23–25 (*AOT*, 349; *TUAT* 1:383; *ANET*, 284–85):

> At the begi[nning of my royal rule, I … the town of the Sama]rians [I besieged, conquered] (2 lines destroyed) [for the god … who le]t me achieve (this) my triumph.… I led away as prisoners [27,290 inhabitants of it (and) [equipped] from among [them (soldiers to man)] 50 chariots for my royal corps.… [The town I] re[built] better than (it was) before and [settled] therein people from countries which [I] myself [had con]quered. I placed an officer of mine as governor over them and imposed upon them tribute as (is customary) for Assyrian citizens. (*ANET*, 284)

He recounts this siege in his annals and mentions it alongside the new settlement of the city. More believable than Sargon's boastful Display Inscription is the Babylonian Chronicle, in which the conquest of Samaria is ascribed to Shalmaneser alone. (Only in the third year of his reign, in 720, did Sargon move westward and thus also against Samaria). In his annals we read "In my second year of reign," but this is impossible, since at that time, according to the Babylonian Chronicle, he was fighting against Humbannikash of Elam. "Since the beginning of my reign" does not make sense in relation to the conquest of Samaria, therefore. He ascended to the throne in 722, but we should not complete Sargon's annals on the basis of his Display Inscriptions, as H. Winckler does (and whom most other scholars follow): "at [the beginning of my reign and in my first year of reign ... I conquered Samar]ina." In 720 he defeated a rebelling Samaria—he does not mention any Israelite king in this context—but Shalmaneser had already taken the city after a three-year siege and had annexed it as a province. The date of this conquest is unknown to us, however, since the commonly assumed date of 722 is based on Sargon's unjustifiably amended annals (see Timm, "Die Eroberung Samarias"). Beyond the conquest of Samaria, Sargon's victories over Hamat and Gaza, alongside the destruction of Raphia in the same campaign, play an important role in his inscriptions. Additionally, in his annals, the Display Inscriptions, and in fragmentary clay prisms he left an account of his campaign against Ashdod (712/711), in which Gat (Akk. *Gimtu*) was besieged and conquered (see *AOT*, 348–52; *TUAT* 1:380, 384, 386). In one of these prisms he mentions Judah, which he claims to have subjugated: "(Property of Sargon, etc.) the subduer of the country Juda (Iaûdu) which is far away" (*ANET*, 287; cf. *AOT*, 330; *TUAT* 1:387). A letter found in Nimrud recounts: "The chiefs of the Egyptians, the inhabitants of Gaza, Judeans, Moabites and Ammonites arrived in Calah on the 12th day." A date during Sargon's time has been proposed for the letter (around 712/711), but the uncertainty of this date greatly diminishes the value of this text as a source.

We have a detailed account from Sennacherib of his expedition against Jerusalem in the so-called Taylor Prism, which, like the Chicago Prism, gives the final version of Sennacherib's Annals. After describing the subjugation of the Phoenician, Israelite, and Philistine cities as well as the kings of Moab and Edom (in varying detail) the Assyrian king dedicates a long section to the conquest of Judah and the siege of Jerusalem (*ANET*, 288; *AOT*, 352–54; *TUAT* 1:389–90; *TGI*, 68–69; fig. 2 below):

> As for Hezekiah the Judahite, who did not submit to my yoke: forty-six of his strong, walled cities, as well as the small towns in their area, which were without number, by levelling with battering-rams and by bringing up seige-engines, and by attacking and storming on foot, by mines, tunnels, and breeches, I besieged and took them. 200,150 people, great and small, male and female, horses, mules, asses, camels, cattle and sheep without number, I brought away from them and counted as spoil. (Hezekiah) himself, like a caged bird I shut up in Jerusalem, his royal city. I threw up earthworks against him—the one coming out of the city-gate, I turned back to

his misery. His cities, which I had despoiled, I cut off from his land, and to Mitinti, king of Ashdod, Padi, king of Ekron, and Silli-bêl, king of Gaza, I gave (them). And thus I diminished his land. I added to the former tribute, and I laid upon him the surrender of their land and imposts—gifts for my majesty. As for Hezekiah, the terrifying splendor of my majesty overcame him, and the Arabs and his mercenary troops which he had brought in to strengthen Jerusalem, his royal city, deserted him. In addition to the thirty talents of gold and eight hundred talents of silver, gems, antimony, jewels, large carnelians, ivory-inlaid couches, ivory-inlaid chairs, elephant hides, elephant tusks, ebony, boxwood, all kinds of valuable treasures, as well as his daughters, his harem, his male and female musicians, which he had brought after me to Nineveh, my royal city. To pay tribute and to accept servitude, he dispatched his messengers. (Luckenbill, *Annals of Sennacherib*)

Sennacherib also left shorter accounts of his Judean campaigns on a stone tablet from Nebi-Junus near Nineveh, on a bull colossus, and on the reliefs in his palace at Nineveh, which will be discussed later (*AOT*, 354; *TUAT* 1:390–91).

We learn something about Sennacherib's mysterious death from Ashurbanipal's annals on the so-called Rassam Cylinder: "The others, I smashed alive with the very same statues of protective deities with which they had smashed my own grandfather Sennacherib" (*ANET*, 288).

In the Babylonian Chronicle we read: "For eight years there was no king in Babylon.... In the month of Tebitu, the 20th day, his son killed Sennacherib, king of Assyrian during a rebellion. [Twenty-thr]ee years was Sennacherib king in Assyria. From the month of Tebitu, the 20th day, there was continuous rebellion in Assyria. In the month of Addaru, the 18th day, Esarhaddon, his son, sat himself on the throne in Assyria" (*ANET*, 302; cf. *TGI*, 69; *TUAT* 1:402). This rebellion, which probably took place in Nineveh on the 20th of Tebet 680, is also described in great detail in the so-called broken Prism B of Esarhaddon, although Sennacherib's murder is not explicitly mentioned in the legible text (*AOT*, 354–57; *ANET*, 289–90; Prism A in *TUAT* 1:393–97). On the same prism we read that Esarhaddon summoned the kings of Hatti and of the seacoast, among them Manasseh of Judah (*ANET*, 291; *AOT*, 357). In commentaries, this account has often been connected with Manasseh's imprisonment, mentioned in 2 Chr 33:11. In a nearly identical list on the Rassam Cylinder, Manasseh is mentioned again among the kings who participated in Ashurbanipal's campaign to Egypt in 667 (*ANET*, 294).

II.2. Archaeological Discoveries

Avigad, Nahman. *Discovering Jerusalem* (Nashville: Thomas Nelson, 1983). **Avigad**.

Fig. 2. Assyrian clay prism, British Museum. On the prism are written in Assyrian cuneiform Sennacherib's annals, with the account of his campaign against Philistia and Judah in 701 B.C.E. © Trustees of the British Museum.

II. THE HISTORY OF THE ERA 75

"The Upper City," in *Biblical Archaeology Today: Proceedings of the International Congress on Biblical Archaeology, Jerusalem, April 1984* (Jerusalem: Israel Exploration Society, 1985), 469-75. **Barnett**, Richard D. *Ancient Ivories in the Middle East and Adjacent Countries* (Qedem 14; Jerusalem: Institute of Archaeology, Hebrew University of Jerusalem, 1982). **Broshi**, Magen. "The Expansion of Jerusalem in the Reigns of Hezekiah and Manasseh," *IEJ* 24 (1974): 21-26. **Dever**, William G. "Ancient Israelite Religion: How to Reconcile the Differing Textual and Artifactual Portraits?" in *Ein Gott allein? JHWH-Verehrung und biblischer Monotheismus im Kontext der israelitischen und altorientalischen Religionsgeschichte* (ed. Walter Dietrich and Martin A. Klopfenstein; OBO 139; Göttingen: Vandenhoeck & Ruprecht, 1994), 105-25. **Fritz**, Volkmar. "Die eisenzeitliche Stadt auf dem Tell es-Seba' im Negev," *Antike Welt* 9/4 (1978): 24-39. **Lemaire**, André. "Les inscriptions de Khirbet el-Qôm et l'Ashéra de YHWH," *RB* 84 (1977): 595-608. **Schoors**, Antoon. *Berseba—De opgraving van een bijbelse stad* (Palaestina Antiqua 5; Kampen: Kok, 1986). **Ussishkin**, David. "The Destruction of Lachish by Sennacherib and the Dating of the Royal Judean Storage Jars," *TAJ* 4 (1977): 28-60. **Ussishkin**. *Excavations at Tel Lachish: Preliminary Report* (Tel Aviv, 1978, 1983). **Ussishkin**. *The Conquest of Lachish by Sennacherib* (Publications of the Institute of Archaeology 6; Tel Aviv: Institute of Archaeology, 1982). **Ussishkin**. "The Date of the Judaean Shrine at Arad," *IEJ* 38 (1988): 142-57. **Weippert**, Helga. *Palästina in vorhellenistischer Zeit* (Handbuch der Archäologie, Vorderasien 2.1; Munich: Beck, 1988), 559-681. **Welten**, Peter. *Die Königs-Stempel: Ein Beitrag zur Militärpolitik Judas unter Hiskia und Josia* (Abhandlungen des Deutschen Palästinavereins; Wiesbaden: Harrassowitz, 1969). **Winter**, I. J. "Is There a South Syrian Style of Ivory Carving in the Early First Millennium B.C.?" *Iraq* 43 (1981): 101-30. **Xella**, P. "Le dieu et 'sa' déese: l'utilisation des suffixes pronominaux avec des théonymes d'Ebla à Ugarit et à Kuntillet 'Ajrud," *UF* 27 (1995): 599-610. **Zwickel**, W. "Wirtschaftliche Grundlagen in Zentraljuda gegen Ende des 8. Jh.s aus archäologischer Sicht," *UF* 26 (1994): 557-592.

The era of the Assyrian crisis falls in the archaeological period designated Iron Age IIC, dated from 850 to 586 B.C.E. and which Helga Weippert characterized as "the period of national cultures, which were ultimately eclipsed by Neo-Assyrian influences" (*Palästina*, 572). It is a remarkably long period that cannot be subdivided because the ceramic typology of Tell Bêt Mirsim is used as the framework for dating in Palestinian archaeology, and its three Iron IIC period layers A1, A2, and A3 are not clearly distinguishable from one another. Excavations by David Ussishkin at Tell ed-Duweir (Lachish) have offered a more precise chronology, however, fixing the date of the end of layers III and II of this tell with a high probability to 701 and 588-586, respectively.

Many locations from the eighth century have been excavated, and the Assyrian conquest of a number of northern Israelite cities is documented in the strata of destruction. In Hazor, for instance, the last walled city was destroyed in the second half of the eighth century. In a modest attempt at reviving the town, only a palace was built, in the Assyrian style. An Assyrian palace was also built after a destruction at Tell el-'Orēme, on the Gennesaret sea. Traces of destruction were also found at Beth-Shean and Tell el-Fār'a. In Samaria, the layer of destruction at the end of stratum VI is attributed to the conquest by the Assyrians in 722–720. In the rubble of the destruction on the northern half of the acropolis a treasure of ivory carvings was found that probably decorated furniture or chests. These carvings are difficult to date: after having been ascribed to Ahab's "ivory house" (Amos 6:4) and as Phoenician imports, it is now accepted that a later date is possible, and that in the collection, southern Syrian and Phoenician styles should be differentiated (see Barnett, *Ancient Ivories*; Winter, "South Syrian Style"; H. Weippert, *Palästina*, 654–57). A few scattered ivory plaques have also been found at other excavation sites. The conversion of Megiddo into the Assyrian provincial capital (stratum III) after its destruction in the eighth century (stratum IVA) is summarized concisely by H. Weippert:

> The new city was equipped with two Assyrian palaces west of the north gate; the streets running through the residential district were laid out like a chessboard, between which houses built tightly up against one another formed right-angled *insulae*. A deep cylinder shaft probably served for stockpiling. With only slight modifications this city plan remained unchanged until the end of the seventh century (Stratum II). Only then does the city wall built in the Iron IIB period seem to have been given up; at this period a palace-like structure was built in the northeast of the city which jutted out beyond the fortification line. (*Palästina*, 588)

After the conquest of northern Israel and its transformation into an Assyrian province, there is visible economic and demographic decline. In Samaria, the palace and the close-fitting houses were not rebuilt, even though it was the capital of the Assyrian province of Samerina—and notwithstanding Sargon's claim that he "made Samaria greater than before." A similar decline can be seen also in places like Megiddo, Hazor, Shechem, and so on. In Judah, on the other hand, there are traces of a great population increase in the second half of the eighth century. This is most visible in the expansion of Jerusalem to possibly more than three times its area until that time (Broshi, "Expansion"), in the increased density in the settlements of central Judah, and in the extension of the area of settlements to the south and to the Shephelah (Zwickel, "Zentraljuda," 565–66). In excavations in the southern section of the present-day old city of Jerusalem, Nahman Avigad discovered many traces of settlement from this period. This section of the city, which lay outside the city walls built in the Davidic/Solomonic period, was itself walled in by a wide wall around 700 (Avigad, "Upper City," 471–75). The area of this expansion is disputed, but the most probable reconstruction estimates it to have been around sixty hectares for the whole city. This maximal reconstruction assumes that the new wall ran from the western wall of the temple district to the present-day citadel, and from there followed the line of the present-day wall southward—but continuing farther south, so that the southern wall would have run past the "City of David"—and finally joining the eastern wall of the "city of David" (fig. 3).

Another sign of this southward expansion is the course of the Siloam Tunnel (fig. 4). This tunnel was dug during Hezekiah's time to run water from the Gihon source into the city, so as to secure the city's water supply in case of siege. The water ran to a pool that lay west of the southern point of the "city of David," where it must have been enclosed by the city walls. It is not absolutely necessary, however, that the walls would have had to extend to the citadel and the present-day city's western walls.

Hezekiah's tunnel is one of the most important archaeological remains of the era that survives to the present day. Given that the distance from the Gihon source and the Siloam Pool is 375 meters (1,230 ft.), one might ask why the tunnel is 512 meters (1,679 ft.) long. Indeed the S-shape of the tunnel has given rise to some speculation. There are hypotheses based on the geological structure of the hill, the presence of fissures, or, most often assumed, the intention to lead the tunnel around the royal necropolis at the southern spur of the hill. The correct interpretation, however, is the geological one. After Sennacherib's campaign in the first half of the seventh century, there was obviously a further influx of refugees to Jerusalem, since excavations on "Mount Zion," in the Armenian garden, and in the citadel show that settlements of that period covered the entire southwestern hill.

Population growth in Judah can be seen in the growth of other cities such as Tell el-Ḥesī, or the new settlements like En-Gedi and Khirbet Qumrān at the Dead Sea, Tel ʿĪrā, Tell Malḥātā and Aroer in the northern Negev. The archaeological survey in Judah (1968) showed that the number of settlements doubled during the period of Assyrian hegemony. Archaeological research has given us a reasonably good picture of the layout and architecture of these cities. The excavation at Tel Beersheba (Tell es-Sebaʿ; Aharoni, *Discovering*, 13–17; Fritz, "Tell es-Sebaʿ") yielded a city plan in stratum II that showed very careful planning (fig. 5). While this plan was already conceived in an earlier era, stratum II, which comes from our era, is the best uncovered and shows clearly what an average city in Judah in the eighth century looked like. The city was surrounded by a casemate wall, which remained from the previous period. Walls built in the eighth century are usually solid with a glacis at the foot of the wall, as in Jerusalem. Lachish and other cities were protected with a doubled circumvallation, a wall around the edges of the hill and a supporting wall underneath. Beersheba was accessible only through a single gate, which led to a circular street that ran parallel to the city walls through the whole city and back to the gate. The buildings on the outside of this ring stood against the walls. There were public buildings on both sides of the gate: to the left administrative rooms and to the right three pillar buildings, which Aharoni believed to be storerooms, although according to others they were probably horse stables. A bit farther from the gate one finds residential houses both outside and inside the ring street. House design was of a consistent type, although it could be varied, particularly to a variant of the so-called four-room house. This type is designated as a three- or four-room house, where both roofed and unroofed sections of the house were considered rooms. It originated in the Iron I period and remained prevalent during our period in its classic form or modified only by additions or incorporations.

Development was not quite so organized in all cities. In Tell en-Naṣbe and Tell Bēt Mirsim, houses of different sizes were built tightly up against one another, and in Megiddo larger and smaller houses alternated. A few city houses in Jerusalem from the eighth century were also dug by Y. Shiloh. In the older northern Israelite capital of Tirzah, excavation uncovered two different sections, one with spacious houses and one with smaller houses built closer to one another, which demonstrates a growing divide between rich and poor. However, it should not be forgotten that this finding is based on the evidence from the remains of only six houses, just three of which survive in their entirety (H. Weippert, *Palästina*, 530). Monumental palace buildings from Iron IIB remained intact until the eighth century, such as the citadel of Hazor, until its destruction, presumably by Tiglath-pileser III; the acropolis of Samaria, until the city's fall in 722/721; and the palace complex in Lachish, until it was conquered by Sennacherib in 701. A palace from the eighth century was found at Ramat Rahel, south of Jerusalem: a rectangular acropolis construction measuring 50 x 75 m (= 64 x 246 ft.) surrounded by a casemate wall, like a miniaturized copy of the acropolis of Samaria. The walls were made of finely dressed ashlars, laid as stretchers and headers. Many decorative architectural pieces were found, such as Proto-Aeolic capitals, pinnacle stones, and stone window or balcony balustrades with palm columns. Rooted in the local building style from Iron IIA and IIB, Ramat Rachel is unique in the eighth century. "Palaces and fortresses in the Assyrian style predominated: this is the case in northern Palestine (Hazor, 'Ayyelet haš-Šahar, Tell-el-'Orēme, Megiddo), the southern coastal region and the Shephelah (Tell el-Baṭāšī, Tell eš-Šerī'a, Tell Ǧemme, Tell Abū Salīma) and Transjordan (Tell el-Mazār, Busēra)" (H. Weippert, *Palästina*, 599–600; fig. 6 below).

The new type of palace arose toward the end of the eighth century B.C.E. The identifying characteristics of this type are: (1) an extensive, rectangular

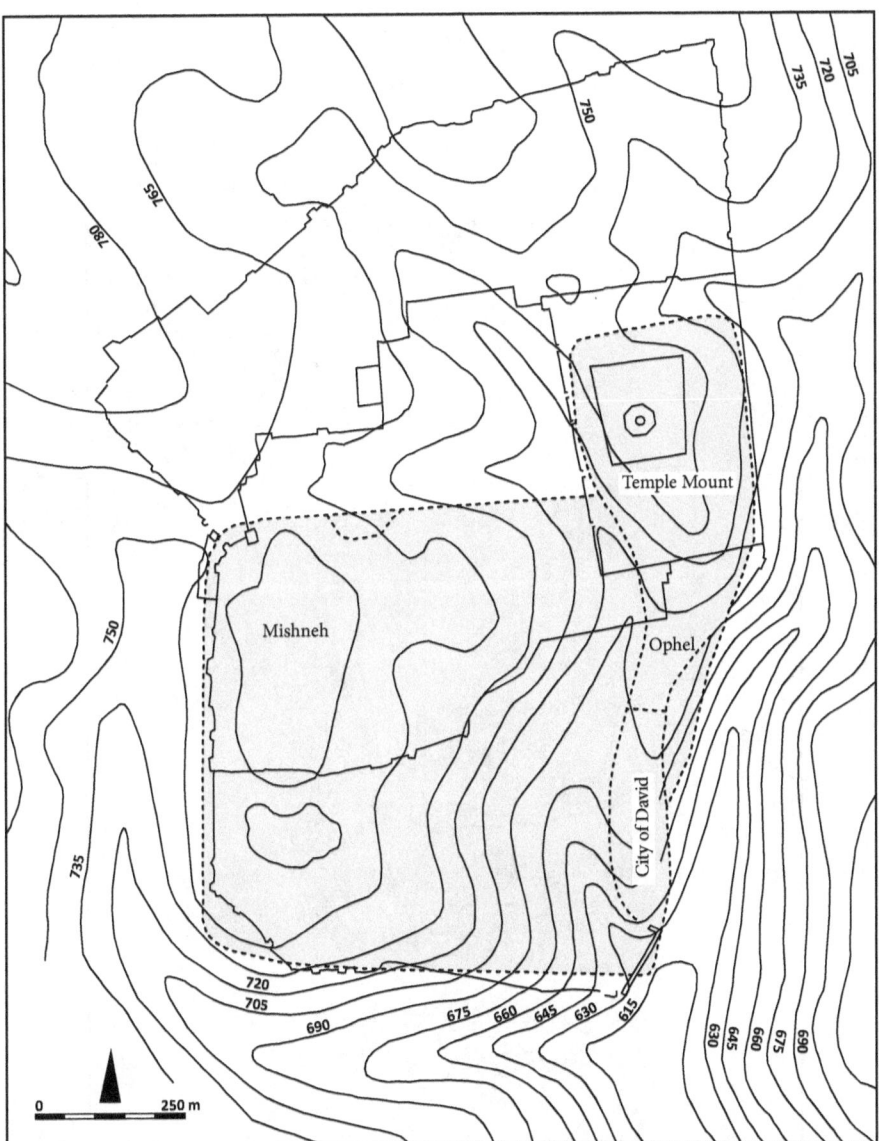

Figure 3. Map of the city of Jerusalem toward the end of the Iron age (eighth to seventh centuries). To the right is the old city of David, which, along with the Ophel and the Temple Mount, made up the city of Solomon of the ninth century. To the left is the expansion of the city (Mishneh) in the eighth century, based on a maximalist reconstruction.

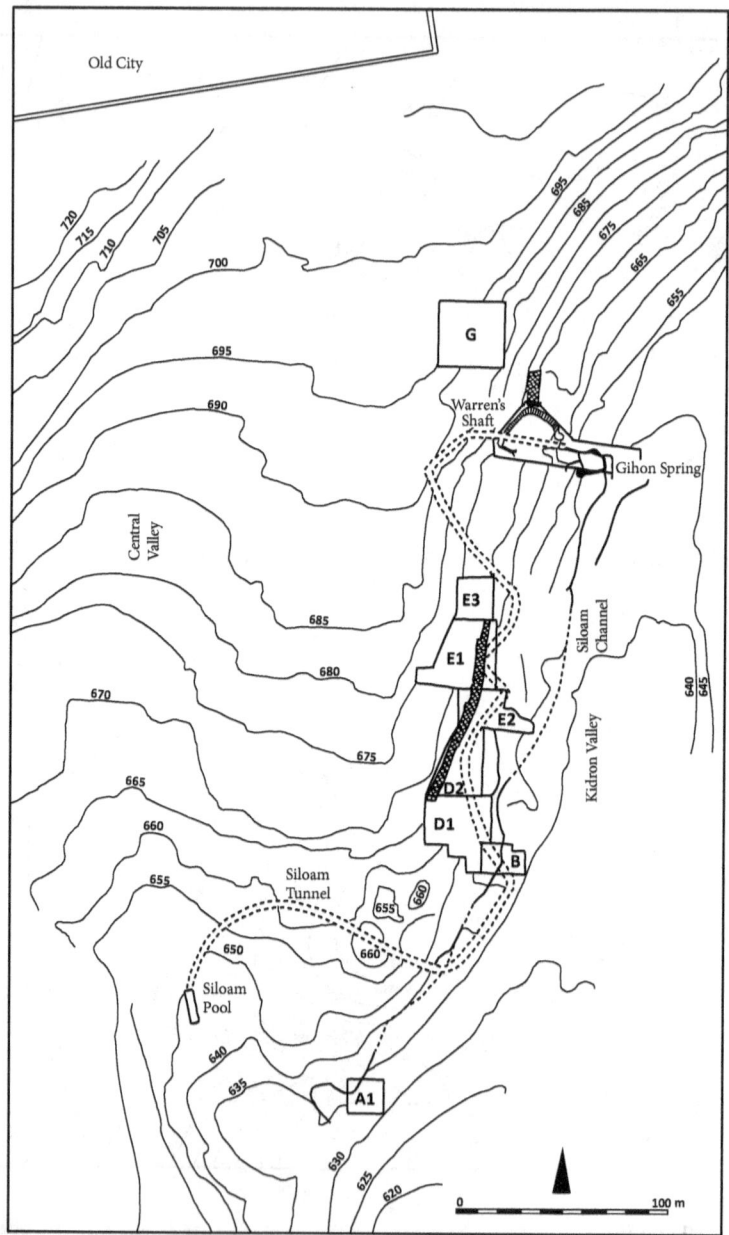

Fig. 4. The Siloam Tunnel, which was made in Hezekiah's time to direct water from the Gihon spring to the so-called Siloam Pool, in what was at that time the south of the city. Points A1, B, D1, D2, E1, E2, E3, G and J are areas excavated in the "City of David Archaeological Project" (Y. Shiloh).

Fig. 5. Map of the city of Beersheba (Tell es-Sebaʿ) in the eighth century (stratum II), showing the careful planning of the city's layout (see further p. 77).

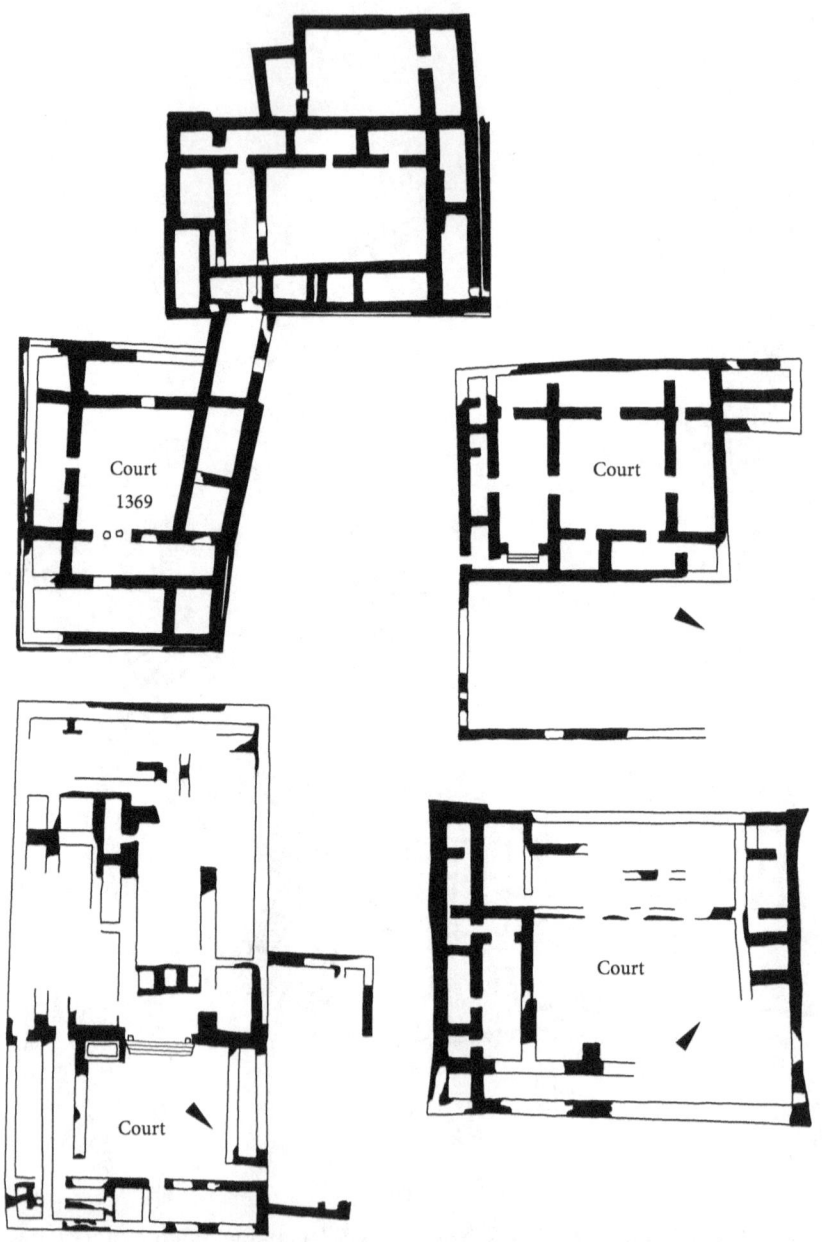

Fig. 6. Assyrian-style palaces. (1) Megiddo; (2) Hazor; (3) and (4) Buṣēra. See further p. 78.

ground plan with closed outer walls; (2) a large central courtyard surrounded by a single or double row of rooms; (3) a main entrance in one of the corners of the house and entrances to rooms in the center; (4) bathrooms and an underground sewer system; (5) finally, the preferred building material was brick (H. Weippert, *Palästina*). Such palaces served as the seat of the Assyrian provincial government, although in the southern coastal region Philistine city kings occasionally may also have built palaces in the Assyrian style. The Assyrian presence is also visible in finds of Assyrian pottery, which differs from the native pottery in its thinner walls and harder firing (H. Weippert, *Palästina*, 647–48).

In the Judean border regions there were also smaller buildings that can be interpreted as fortresses or signal stations. Jerusalem and its surroundings were surrounded by towers (e.g., Tell el-Fūl) and rectangular casemate-type fortresses to the north, west, and south. All of these were visible to one another and offered views of areas of the east Shephelah. These are found especially in the thinly settled areas and were generally built of light materials. It can be assumed, therefore, that they were used to transmit messages. "The defense of the border was a task which was done from the fortified cities, while the fortresses, deep behind the borders only offered support for the defense" (H. Weippert, *Palästina*, 615).

Settlements such as Khirbet Qumrān and Ein-Gedi, founded at the end of the eighth century in the east of Judah, Beersheba in the south, and other Negev forts such as Tel ʿIrā, Tel Malḥātā, and Arad all had similar functions. Deeper in the Negev there were also smaller forts that were used as stopping places.

One of these that became well known only recently is Kuntillet ʿAjrūd, where wall paintings, inscriptions, and votive offerings on the benches point to a pilgrimage shrine. The inscriptions mention El, YHWH of Samaria, YHWH of Teman, Baal, and Asherah, and inscriptions on *pithoi* mention YHWH of Samaria and his Asherah. This way-station was already destroyed around 750 B.C.E., but the one in Kadesh-Barnea was built in the eighth century. The joint worship of YHWH and his Asherah is attested also in a tomb inscription from Khirbet el-Kōm in southern Judah, and this inscription is to be dated in the second half of the eighth century (Lemaire, "Khirbet el-Qôm"). A heated discussion has erupted as to whether Asherah, mentioned alongside YHWH, is a goddess or was rather, a cultic object—usually a holy tree or pole next to the altar and memorial stone (מצבה)— as it is often referred to in the Bible. The grammatical rule that a personal name in Hebrew cannot be attached to a possessive suffix is often used as evidence to show that אשרתה "his [YHWH's] Asherah" cannot refer to a goddess (e.g., Lemaire, "Khirbet el-Qôm," 607). William G. Dever believes it is reasonable to assume that here YHWH's Asherah is the goddess (cf. Ugaritic *aṯrt*), YHWH's *paredros*. In my view he is correct, since texts from Ebla and Ugarit contradict the aforementioned grammatical rule (along with M. Weippert, O. Loretz, H. Niehr, P. Xella, among others).

No temple mentioned in the Bible, such as that of Jerusalem or Samaria, has yet been attested archaeologically.

> Excepting cultic places whose identification is not secure, we know of only one large altar for burnt offerings from Tell es-Sebaʿ and five buildings which are interpreted as shrines from the Iron IIC period. Two of them lie on the southern border of Judah (Arad, Qiṭmīt), two in the middle and southern Negev (Kadesh-Barnea, Kuntillet ʿAjrūd), and one on the eastern side of the middle Jordan valley (Tell Deir ʿAllā). Their geographical distribution shows that these cultic buildings were peripheral institutions, distant from their respective capitals. Add to this that no holy places have been found inside any city. We are dealing, then, with either pilgrim shrines or fortress temples. (H. Weippert, *Palästina*, 623)

There also seems to have been a shrine in Dor, on the Mediterranean coast, since a seal found near Samaria bears the inscription "from Zacharia, priest of Dor" (לזכריו כהן דאר; on this see Nahman Avigad, *IEJ* 25 [1975]: 101–5). The altar in the temple court at the shrine of Arad was abandoned at the end of the eighth century, something the excavators link to Hezekiah's cultic reforms (2 Kgs 18:4). Nevertheless Ussishkin argued persuasively that this shrine was not founded before the eighth century and that consequently changes to it cannot be connected to Hezekiah's reforms (Ussishkin, "Shrine at Arad"). Many cultic objects have been found in residential houses, including small limestone altars and incense plates. In particular, many goddess figurines were found: "The numerous female figurines can be subdivided into rough and naturalistic types. The majority of the hand-formed so-called pillar figurines from the eighth and seventh centuries B.C.E. fall into the first category. The name refers to the pillarlike endings of the bodies of naked, full-bosomed women. Typical of these are arms resting under the breasts. More rare are carefully modeled women's figures with sweeping bell-shaped bodies" (H. Weippert, *Palästina*, 629–30; fig. 7).

We learn from ostraca of Arad and Samaria that grain, oil, and wine were the basic foodstuffs of the period. According to the ostraca, some of these belonged to the state as taxes *in natura* or as products of the royal domains. Winepresses, oil presses, and millstones were found in many settlements, showing the processes used to prepare the agricultural products (cf. *Biblisches Reallexikon2*, 238–40, 362–63). Pillared halls with three naves, like those found in Beersheba and Hazor (see above), were used to store reserves, as were side rooms and cellars in houses and pits in the rock-bed, many of which

II. THE HISTORY OF THE ERA

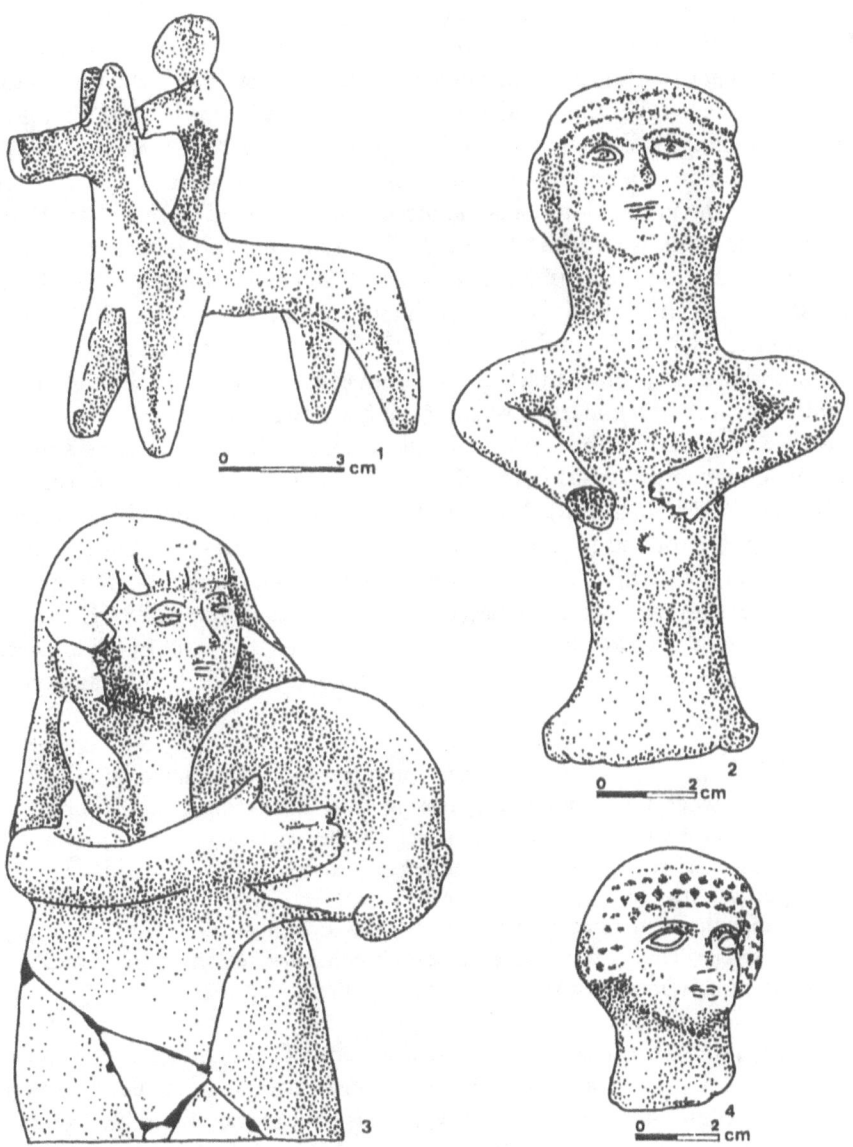

Fig 7. Clay figurines from the eighth and seventh centuries:. (1) figurine of a rider from Lachish; (2) pillar figurine from Beth-Shemesh; (3) female with disc from Tell es-Samak; (4) female head from Lachish (see further pp. 78–79).

were found at Tell en-Naṣbe, Gibeon, and Gibea (Tell el-Fūl), north of Jerusalem. These pits are usually understood to have been cisterns, but, as they had not been plastered, they could not have been put to this use (H. Weippert, *Palästina*, 605). Among the clay vessels, large storage jars from the end of the eighth century in Judah warrant mention: they were marked with typical stamps on the handles (fig. 8), always inscribed with the word למלך, "(belonging) to the king," followed by one of four place names: חברון, Hebron, ז[י]ף, Ziph, שוכה, Sochoh, and ממשת, an otherwise unknown *Mmšt*. Between the two lines of the inscription is a depiction of a four-winged scarab (Class I), or a winged sun (Class II) (see Welten, *Die Königs-Stempel*). More than a thousand of these "king's stamps" have been found. Since the two classes have been found together in stratum III at Lachish and stratum III at Tell el-Baṭāšī, and because the date for the end of stratum III in Lachish has been shown in all likelihood to have been 701 (see above), both can be assigned to the end of the eighth century. This makes these stamps a good tool for dating Judean grave sites, while their distribution also helps mark out Judean territory shortly before Sennacherib's invasion in 701 (Ussishkin, "Destruction of Lachish"; H. Weippert, *Palästina*, 605–6). According to Welten, jars stamped this way contained supply products for the military, which best explains the wide distribution throughout fortified cities and forts. The four places mentioned might be among the cities in which Hezekiah built storehouses (2 Chr 32:28). However, according to W. Zwickel, whose argument is perhaps the most probable, these places were regional centers, set up by the state, from which cultivated land was supervised:

> The wine produced there was taken from these individual cultivated areas to places where it was immediately needed to supply the population or commercial businesses.…Jerusalem and Lachish, the two largest cities of Judah, may have been supraregional commercial centers from which wine was exported. After having been emptied, the jars were returned to the places stamped on them and then distributed to the individual cultivated areas in the regions. Thus it was assured that each cultivated region would always have enough jars at its disposal. (Zwickel, "Zentraljuda," 582)

Many Judean areas were destroyed at the end of the eighth century, something archaeologists usually ascribe Sennacherib's campaign of 701. Although this is difficult to prove in much detail, it is clearest in the case of Tel Lachish. Not only is Sennacherib's siege of this city alluded to in the Bible (2 Kgs 18:17; 19:18), the siege and conquest of the city are depicted in detail on the monumental series of reliefs in Sennacherib's palace at Nineveh (fig. 9). At the tell itself archaeologists, with whom this author had the honor to work, uncovered the siege ramp that the Assyrians had laid, which is also portrayed at

Fig. 8. Above: Storage jar with four handles from Lachish. Below: Stamp imprint on a handle of the same jar: note the scarab and the inscriptions *lmlk* and *ḥbrn* (Hebron).

Fig 9. Scene from the series of reliefs from Sennacherib's palace in Nineveh: Sennacherib on his throne looks at the siege of the city of Lachish and receives the salute from soldiers and prisoners of war (701 B.C.E.); behind the king is his tent.

Nineveh. They also found the counter ramp that the defenders inside the city had set up (Ussishkin, *Conquest of Lachish*).

II.3. Economic and Social History

II.3.1. Economy

Albertz, Rainer. *A History of Israelite Religion in the Old Testament Period* (2 vols.; London: SCM, 1994), 1: 248–55. **Bardtke**, Hans. "Die Latifundien in Juda während der zweiten Hälfte des achten Jahrhunderts v.Chr.," in *Hommages à André Dupont-Sommer* (Paris: Adrien-Maisonneuve, 1971), 235–54. **Chirichigno**, Gregory C. *Debt-Slavery in Israel and the Ancient Near East* (JSOTSup 141; Sheffield: JSOT Press, 1993). **Dearman**, J. Andrew. "Prophecy, Property and Politics," *SBL 1984 Seminar Papers*, 385–97. **Dearman**. *Property Rights in the Eighth-Century Prophets* (SBLDS

106; Atlanta: Scholars Press, 1988). **Donner**, Herbert. "Die soziale Botschaft der Propheten im Lichte der Gesellschaftsordnung in Israel," *OrAnt* 2 (1963): 229–45. **Fendler**, M. "Zur Sozialkritik des Amos: Versuch einer wirtschafts- und sozialgeschichtlichen Interpretation alttestamentlicher Texte," *EvT* 33 (1973): 32–53. **Geus**, C. H. J. de. "Die Gesellschaftskritik der Propheten und die Archäologie," *ZDPV* 98 (1982): 50–57. **Kessler**, Rainer. *Staat und Gesellschaft im vorexilischen Juda: vom 8. Jahrhundert bis zum Exil* (VTSup 47; Leiden: Brill, 1992). **Kraus**, Hans Joachim. "Die prophetische Botschaft gegen das soziale Unrecht Israels," *EvT* 15 (1955): 295–307. **Lang**, Bernhard. "The Social Organization of Peasant Poverty in Biblical Israel," *JSOT* 24 (1982): 47–63. **Loretz**, Oswald. "Die prophetische Kritik des Rentenkapitalismus," *UF* 7 (1975): 271–78. **Premnath**, D. N. "Latifundialization and Isaiah 5,8–10," *JSOT* 40 (1988): 49–60. **Silver**, Morris. *Prophets and Markets: The Political Economy of Ancient Israel* (Boston: Kluwer-Nijhoff, 1983). **Zeeb**, F. "Alalaḫ VII und das Amosbuch," *UF* 27 (1995): 641–56.

It is not easy to get a clear picture of the economic situation of Palestine in the eighth century B.C.E., since written sources offer only incidental and indirect information (e.g., prophetic social criticism) and since archaeology has until recently largely ignored the issue. C. H. J. de Geus put it most clearly ("Die Gesellschaftskritik," 51): "When studying the material culture of a people or an area..., obvious questions to ask would be: 'At what level of wealth did the people in the culture I am studying live?' 'How was this wealth divided?' 'Is there a geographic perspective to this division: city/country; north/south; coast/interior, or was there social variation within a geographically unified area or even within settlements?' 'Did wealth vary in each cultural period? Did it increase? Did it decrease?' ... These questions have been almost entirely disregarded in Palestinian archaeology."

A few things can be gleaned about the economic situation of the land from existing archeological findings. Research into the material culture of Israel shows that there was impoverishment in the Iron IIC period. After a cultural heyday in the ninth century, a turning point came at the beginning of the eighth century. In monumental and residential building, as well as in the production of earthenware, the predominant picture becomes one of stagnation and impoverishment. Most authors justifiably attribute this primarily to the disastrous consequences of the recurring tribute payments to Assyria. Isaiah 1:7 alludes to the situation of the Judean lands after Sennacherib's campaign: "Your country lies desolate, your cities are burned with fire; in your very presence aliens devour your land." The fragmentary inscriptions from the Assyrian kings offer a partial, but striking, picture of this tribute. Tiglath-pileser III speaks of ten talents of gold and an unknown amount of silver that he received from Hoshea of Israel. In 2 Kgs 15:19–20 we read that he received one thousand talents of silver from Menahem, and that "in order to give it to the Kings of Assyria, Menahem exacted the money from Israel, that is, from all the wealthy, fifty shekels of silver from each one." If these numbers are correct, it would mean that there were around sixty thousand wealthy men in the northern kingdom. The Judean king Ahaz also paid a high tribute to the king of Assyria (2 Kgs 16:8). According to the biblical account, Hezekiah had to pay King Sennacherib thirty talents of gold and three hundred talents of silver (2 Kgs 18:14); according to Sennacherib's annals, it was thirty talents of gold and eight hundred talents of silver, as well as a large sum of luxury goods such as ivory and the like. Perhaps this difference can be explained by suggesting that the Bible refers only to treasures from the temple, while Sennacherib refers to the whole amount. Moreover, the Assyrian king notes that he also took countless horses, mules, donkeys, camels, cattle, and small stock from the cities of Judah. These were only the gifts to the ruler and booty: beyond this, yearly tribute had to be given. We have an Assyrian account of grain submissions from the province of Samaria. These tribute payments must have had a disastrous effect on an economy that was wholly agricultural. The farms had to keep up a surplus production of grain that could be sold for the silver and gold needed to make the tribute payments. One archaeological indication of surplus grain production could be the large grain silo in Megiddo from the late eighth century, which had a capacity of at least 450 cubic meters (1,476 cubic feet).

II. THE HISTORY OF THE ERA

In Israel, as in Judah, the people had been used to paying high taxes and engaging in corvée labor since the time of David and Solomon. Although this brought unhappiness and criticism, it did not lead to an economic crisis, since it all flowed back into their own land and brought prosperity to its centers and its new class of craftspeople and merchants. The situation was different in the Assyrian period. De Geus characterizes it in this way ("Die Gesellschaftskritik," 56–57):

> In the Assyrian period the tax burden was even heavier, and all of the money was taken out of the country. This disappearance of capital created an entirely new situation. The stagnation that has been uncovered shows that the Assyrians understood enough to demand the largest possible amount without touching the fundamental production. It goes without saying that it was the inclination from every side to lay the greatest amount of the burden on the weakest shoulders. It seems to me, *contra* Bardtke, that conditions in this period would have been very favorable for the development of latifundia. This development would have emerged directly out of the combination of high production obligation, cheap land and low wages. Unfortunately, archaeologists have yet to uncover such an estate.

Exegetical works often refer to this situation as early capitalism, commenting, for example on Isa 5:8: "Ah, you who join house to house, who add field to field, until there is room for no one but you, and you are left to live alone in the midst of the land" (cf. Mic 2:1–5) or Amos 8:5–6: "You say, When will the new moon be over so that we may sell grain; and the Sabbath, so that we may offer wheat for sale … and selling the sweepings of the wheat." In Hans Bardtke's view, "joining house to house" could not have occurred in the country but assumes an urban setting. The description of the houses as "large and beautiful" (v. 9) might also point to an urban setting. Houses like this have been found at Tell el-Fār'a ("Die Latifundien," 237–38). In Bardtke's opinion, Isaiah's words were directed at refugees from the northern kingdom, mostly from the Canaanite merchant class, who moved to Judah in the years of the Assyrian invasions (733 and 725) and bought houses and land with their money.

Oswald Loretz sees interest capitalism as the cause of the social abuses criticized by the prophets. He takes this name from H. Bobek's term for the economic system characteristic of the Near Eastern, fundamentally city-centered civilization. "Interest capitalism developed out of the commercialization and the reshaping of the interest demands—originally those of the ruling classes—on the rural and commercial lower classes, in an economic spirit based entirely on profit.… it differed from modern-day capitalism in that it was not connected to production but was content to skim off of the yield" (Loretz, "Die prophetische Kritik," 275–76). This explanation is undoubtedly correct, although it does not pertain specifically to the eighth century, and a text such as Isa 5:8 has more to do with the concentration of land ownership than with the indebtedness of small farmers. F. Zeeb has found in the texts of Alalaḫ VII, which are more than eight hundred years older, the expression of interest capitalism, which can be used as a model for interpreting the Amos texts. Here "innocents were sold for money and the poor for a pair of shoes" would reflect a legal transfer of debt slaves to third parties ("Alalaḫ VII").

According to Hans Joachim Kraus early capitalism had begun already in the time of the early kings. This led to an expansion of the wealthy class and heretofore unknown extravagance, which was encouraged and strengthened by the "Baal-izing" of the old YHWH worship. In his opinion, Isa 5:8–10 is directed against the damage caused to the *ius soli* of small Israelite farmers, which had been rooted in the YHWH beliefs and which was no longer in force because of the large-scale landholding inspired by the Canaanites ("Die prophetische Botschaft"). The socioeconomic explanation by de Geus seems more correct to me. As we will see further on, in condemning the oppression of the poor the prophets did not refer to any so-called traditional *ius soli*; nevertheless, the impoverishment did have a socioeconomic, and not a theological, basis.

Herbert Donner also speaks of a form of early capitalism and of a monopolized grain trade in which the Samarian upper class participated ("Die soziale Botschaft," 236). In Mic 2:1–5 Donner finds hints of the expropriation of peasant lands: "They expropriated peasants' land through a rigorous application of debt slavery and, with investment of the funds gained in the Canaanite manner, built latifundia, forcefully interfering in YHWH's traditional *ius soli* rules" ("Die soziale Botschaft," 240). In his opinion, the guilty party is the Jerusalem city-state with its Canaanized upper class. However right this explanation may be, the practice was undoubtedly reinforced by the socioeconomic consequences of the tribute obligations to Assyria.

Explanations such as those of Kraus and Donner use a far too simplified differentiation between Canaanite and Israelite society, which can be summarized in the following schema (see Dearman, "Prophecy," 389):

Canaan	Israel
king, family, city-state	tribe, clan, village
urban, merchants	agrarian, pastoral
centralized bureaucracy	decentralized leadership
land = capital	land = inheritance

There is no proof in the Bible that a difference existed between a so-called Israelite *ius soli* that forbade alienation of family or clan possession and a Canaanite law that permitted it. As we will see below, the formation of latifundia, which Donner adequately described, can be ascribed principally to an inner-Israelite development in royal state administration and feudal land politics. It is also somewhat anachronistic to talk about early capitalism. Rather, Israel and Judah had a redistribution economy in which the initiative for its direction, as well as its objectives, came from the king and his officials. It was precisely the ownership rights, bestowed on royal officials as fiefs in the form of gifts of plots of land or tax relief, that led to the accumulation of land in the hands of a few and the indebtedness of weaker citizens (Dearman, "Prophecy").

The Samarian ostraca, though originating somewhat earlier than the Assyrian era, can nevertheless help shed light on the standard economic and supply practices of this period. These ostraca show that certain citizens, mostly officials in Samaria, had the right to own land and be supported by its yield. Other ostraca are probably receipts for taxes *in natura* and benefited the same official class (Dearman, *Property Rights*, 117–23). Walter Dietrich described in detail how this process led to bondage and impoverishment (*Jesaja und die Politik*, 15; cf. Albertz, *Israelite Religion*, 250–51):

> [C]apital-strong latifundia owners would lend money with high interest to farmers who had fallen into economic trouble. Those who could not pay the debts would be liable with their possessions, or in worse cases, with their and their family's labor. With a veneer of legality, the rich would seize the property of the socially weaker, increasing the size of their productive assets and their workforce, making a high surplus of capital. With their improved liquidity, they could invest in more mortgages which would in turn destroy more family-run farms, etc.

What we are dealing with here is thus legal indentured servitude based on interest-capitalism.

As previously mentioned, urban life in this period witnessed an expansion. Refugees from the north—Bardtke is correct here—evidently enriched trade with new capital and with their experience. To be sure, most cities were destroyed by Sennacherib in 701, but most of these were rebuilt in the seventh century.

II.3.2. Society

Botterweck, G. Johannes. אביון, *TDOT* 1:27–41. **Fabry**, Heinz-Josef. דל, *TDOT* 3:208–30. **Gerstenberger**, Erhard S. ענה II, *TDOT* 11:230–52. **Gunneweg**, A. H. J. *Leviten* *und Priester: Hauptlinen der Traditionsbildung und Geschichte des israelitisch-jüdischen Kultpersonals* (FRLANT 89; Göttingen: Vandenhoeck & Ruprecht, 1965). **Gunneweg.** "עם הארץ: Vollbürger—Laien—Heiden," in *Vom Amt des Laien in Kirche und Theologie: Festschrift für Gerhard Krause zum 70. Geburtstag* (ed. Henning Schröer and Gerhard Müller; Berlin: de Gruyter, 1982), 29–36. **Koch**, Klaus. "Zur Entstehung der sozialen Kritik bei den Propheten," in *Probleme biblischer Theologie: Gerhard von Rad zum 70. Geburtstag* (ed. Hans Walter Wolff; Munich: Kaiser, 1971), 236–57. **Matthews**, Victor H., and Don C. **Benjamin**. *Social World of Ancient Israel 1250–587 BCE* (Peabody, Mass.: Hendrickson, 1993). **Schwantes**, Milton. *Das Recht der Armen* (BEvT 4; Frankfurt am Main: Lang, 1977). **Whybray**, R. N. *The Intellectual Tradition in the Old Testament* (BZAW 135; Berlin: de Gruyter, 1974). **Würthwein**, Ernst. *Der 'amm ha'arez im Alten Testament* (BWANT 66; Stuttgart: Kohlhammer, 1936).

The turbulent period of foreign rule by the Assyrians undoubtedly shook up society in Israel and Judah. After the conquest of Samaria, the upper class was deported and a new upper class was formed by the settlement of foreign peoples from Babylonia and northern Syria (2 Kgs 17:24). We only have sparse information from Samerina and the other provinces of Israel in that period. The Bible is silent about social or political conditions during this period. We learn the title of an official from a cuneiform text found in Samaria, *rab ālāni*, "chief of the cities." Presumably the towns in the province were under his jurisdiction, especially the crown estates, which were allocated to the members of the new upper class (Noth, *History of Israel*, 263).

Biblical and extrabiblical information pertaining to Judah is also meager. It might be possible to form some semblance of a picture of the society using certain prophetic texts in combination with facts from other books and from other eras. The extended family, something presupposed in many biblical texts and described in some biblical commentaries and by some theologians, unquestionably became less connected, most of all in cities. The sense of solidarity decreased, and the individual gradually became freer from the extended family, as, for example, was later established in criminal law (Deut 24:16).

It is also difficult to get beyond the very general picture found in the Bible on the issue of social stratification. In 2 Kgs 15:20 wealthy men (גבורי חיל) are mentioned as the ones who are taxed by Menachem of Israel to pay the tribute to the Assyrian king. This title seems to have originally referred to brave men—in other words, the elite force of the army—but in this context it presupposes the ability to carry a financial load. Thus, wealthy men are meant here, rich landowners who were perhaps obligated to perform military service (*TDOT* 4:351; *HALOT*, 1:311).

According to 2 Kgs 21:24 and 2 Chr 33:25, "the people of the land" (עם הארץ) killed all those who conspired against Amon. In reference to עם הארץ, 2 Chr 26:21 says that Jotham, who was in charge of the palace, governed (שפט)

II. THE HISTORY OF THE ERA

them. Ernst Würthwein (*Der 'amm ha'arez*) has convincingly proven that the term "people of the land" was a technical term for full citizens, probably meaning landowning, and citizens with full rights (Gunneweg, עם הארץ, 30). Whether or not this is a middle class of Judah's landowning farmers (Albertz, *Israelite Religion*, 234-35) is impossible to prove. The impression is given that the two expressions "wealthy men" and "people of the land," respectively, are the Israelite and Judean terms referring to the same social class.

No other classes are specifically mentioned in biblical accounts, though the economic structure described above undoubtedly produced a considerable group of debt servants and other impoverished people. The prophets Amos and Micah use various terms to describe weaker groups in society: אביונים ("the poor"), דלים ("the humble"), עניים/ענוים ("the poor, the wretched"). In certain contexts they almost seem to be technical terms: in the Covenant Code (Exod 23:11) the *'ebyôn* is contrasted with the landowner, meaning that he himself had no land. In Amos's prophecy (2:6; 8:6), sale and purchase of the *'ebyôn* into debt slavery is condemned. This *'ebyôn* is one without possessions who is sold into debt slavery for nothing (a pair of borrowed, but lost, sandals; Botterweck, אביון, *TDOT* 1:31-33). "In the OT the *dal* is not seen fundamentally in relation to the regulations governing the Sabbatical Year, the Year of Jubilee, and letting the land lie fallow. Nor is he reckoned among the four types of dependents in the family (*'ebhedh*, 'male slave,' *'amah*, 'female slave,' *sakhir*, 'hired servant,' and *toshabh*, 'sojourner,' Lev. 25:6). The formula also says that the *dal*, like the *'ashir*, 'rich,' must pay a half-shekel as an inspection fee (Ex. 30:15). It may be concluded, then, that the *dal* was not numbered among the dependents who have no property" (Fabry, דל, *TDOT* 3:219). Instead, he seems to have been a free, full citizen with few possessions and, given the agrarian environment to which the texts mostly point, would probably have been a small farmer. In Amos, however (2:7; 4:1; 5:1; 8:6), he seems to have been a helpless, defenseless person who was subjected to debt slavery, like the *'ebyôn*. This image fits very well with the development of latifundia discussed previously. In Isa 10:2; 11:4 the *dallîm* are mentioned in parallelism with *'aniyyîm/'anāwîm*. Isa 10:2, which can be ascribed to the prophet himself, is an oracle of woe very similar in content to Amos 2:7. The prophet opposes public officers, who probably regulated property law, taxes, and services. Their policies encouraged the existence of latifundia, insofar as they withheld justice from the poor and destroyed their legal rights ("they rob the poor of my people of their right"). The Isaian authenticity of Isa 11:1-5 is debated, but verse 4 expresses the anticipation that the new or ideal king would right the situation he criticizes in 10:2. Although עני and ענו are fundamentally different, in this prophetic context these two words have nearly the same meaning. They describe "someone living in reduced economic circumstances, dependent, in danger of losing the necessities of life" (Gerstenberger, ענה II, *TDOT* 11:243). These became technical terms connoting a social class (11:246–47). Poverty "first appears under complicating social and economic conditions. The development of latifundia, urbanization, monetary economy, centralization of power, and the resultant weakening of both rural family businesses and clan and village structure were the conditions out of which the 'wretched' appeared" (Wildberger, *Isaiah*, 1:284).

Our knowledge of society in that time also includes its offices. What we know about these does not differ significantly from what we know about offices from other eras of the monarchies of Israel and Judah. We know next to nothing about a scribal class; the only relevant mention of the noun סופר refers to the scribe as head of the royal chancellery (2 Kgs 18:18; 19:2; Isa 36:3, 22; 37:2), who was, for example, part of King Hezekiah's embassies to the Rabshakeh and to Isaiah. Still, there must have been professional scribes like those who wrote the Samarian ostraca. The poet of Ps 45:2 speaks of a סופר מהיר, "a skillful scribe." Around a century later the prophet Jeremiah had a scribe/secretary, Baruch; Isa 8:1 takes for granted that the prophet can write. The art was probably not highly unusual in that period, though one can assume that the scribal class had a high reputation, due to their special abilities.

It is generally agreed that during the time of the kings there was a class of professional sages. These would have included the king's advisors, who were also teachers of the king's sons and teachers in the school system outside the court; they were also the authors of wisdom literature. R. N. Whybray challenged the idea of the professional nature of the sage and argued that it was an educated class of wealthy citizens who were active in the study of wisdom. He speaks of an "intellectual tradition," but rejects the idea of a class of professional sages who preserved this tradition (*Intellectual Tradition*). Proverbs 22:17 ("the words of the wise") and 24:23 ("These are also the words of the wise") seem to refer to professional wise persons, though, and an official wisdom position is listed in Jer 18:18 alongside the priests and prophets. According to Jer 8:8, the wise are associated with the scribes. We have no direct information about the wise, and therefore we must consider their words to get a sense of their views.

They cherish the chance to share the fruits of their experience and reflections with their sons (Prov 13:1; 15:5) and with other young people seeking careers at court (25:6–7; 29:26). According to Prov 25:1, proverb collectors were still active until at least Hezekiah's time. Perhaps the court wisdom tradition, which quite naturally viewed wealth as predominantly positive, ideologically abetted the great societal inequality (Prov 18:23; 22:7).

In the immediate religious sphere were the Levites, priests, and prophets. As we saw above, according to 2 Chr 29:3–17 the Levites played a considerable role in Hezekiah's reforms; according to 31:2–19, the same king reorganized the priests and Levites. However, as previously stated, these texts reflect postexilic conditions and interests. Apparently the only reliable evidence for the real Levites—roughly a group of wandering priests—is to be found in the pre-state period; the influence of this Levitical association decreased considerably with the development of a professional priesthood during the period of kings. The Deuteronomic reformers used the term "Levite" to reduce the various local priestly families to a common denominator, both the Jerusalem priests ("Levitical priests") and the priests of the local shrines ("the Levite who is in your gates") (Albertz, *Israelite Religion*, 220). The Levites are noticeably absent in the relevant chapters of 2 Kings.

The Zadokite priests of Jerusalem were rather traditional and not favorably inclined toward innovation; they were royal officials who took orders from the king pertaining to the care of the shrine and its cultic furnishings. Instances of this include the establishment of a new altar upon the orders of King Ahaz (2 Kgs 16:10–16), or the removal of the copper snake by Hezekiah (18:4). Although no such actions are mentioned in relation to the northern Israelite kings, the situation was entirely the same. In Amos 7:13, Amaziah the priest calls the temple in Bethel "the king's sanctuary and a temple of the kingdom." Prophets in both kingdoms reprimand priests for greed and neglect of duty (Hos 4:4–10; Mic 3:11; Isa 28:7–13). The sacrificial feasts in the temple seem to have occasionally degenerated into wild revelry, and decisions by the priests in judicial (Exod 22:8; Deut 17:9) or cultic matters (Hag 2:11–13) were made in a drunken state. Isaiah 28:7–13 and Mic 3:11 are also directed at the prophets. They are referring to official prophets who were on the permanent staff of the temple (cf. also Jer 23:11), who, according to Micah's complaint, told fortunes for money and only prophesied salvation. They were a contemporary Israelite manifestation of common ancient Near Eastern cultic prophecy (see below and Albertz, *Israelite Religion*, 234).

II.3.3. INSTITUTIONS

Begrich, J. "Sofer und Mazkir," *ZAW* 17 (1940–41): 1–29. **Mettinger**, Tryggve N. D. *Solomonic State Officials: A Study of the Civil Government Officials of the Israelite Monarchy* (ConBOT 5; Lund: Gleerup, 1971). **Niehr**, H. ספר, *TDOT* 10:318–26. **Nielsen**, K. קצץ, *TDOT* 13:86–88.

State administration was, on the whole, the same during the entire period of Kings. The king had his employees and advisors, some of whom are mentioned by name in 2 Kings, 2 Chronicles, and in the books of the prophets. They are servants of the king (עבדי המלך) but authorities (שׂרים) for the people. In 2 Chr 29:30 the king and his princes give an order, while "letters from the king and his princes" are mentioned in 30:6. According to 2 Chr 32:3, when Hezekiah saw Sennacherib approaching he held counsel with his officers and heros (גבוריו; probably his military commanders). The most important official was the head of the palace (אשר על הבית). Jotham held this post during his father Uzziah's illness (2 Kgs 15:5), as did Shebna under Hezekiah, who was superseded by Eliakim (Isa 22:15-23; cf. 2 Kgs 18:18). This title is also found in an inscription on a burial cave in the village of Silvan (near Jerusalem) (*KAI*, 192B), which, according to some scholars, might have marked Shebna's grave (N. Avigad, *IEJ* 3 [1953]: 150-51: יהו... filled in as שבניהו, שבנא being its short form). In 2 Chr 28:7 the same office is referred to as נגיד הבית, which was held under Ahaz by one Azrikam. According to Tryggve N. D. Mettinger, the head of the palace in Judah was responsible for the royal estates, royal trade, and the royal mines. He also notes that in the eighth century the head of the palace was the highest official (*State Officials*, 70-110). As such this post entailed even more and was similar to that of the Egyptian grand vizier, who controlled all matters of state. The description of Joseph's position in Gen 41:40-45 describes this official's authority in more concrete terms. In Isa 22:15 Shebna is also called סֹכֵן, a title that is found also both in Assyria (*šᵃkin māti*, land administrator), and in Ugarit (*skn bt mlk*, palace administrator). According to 2 Kgs 18:18, during Sennacherib's siege of Jerusalem the palace administrator Eliakim participated in negotiations with the Rabshakeh, along with the national scribe (הסֹפֵר), Shebna, and the king's spokesperson (המזכיר), Joah. According to 2 Kgs 19:2 the *sōpēr* also took part in the embassy to Isaiah. The parallel between *sōpēr* and *mazkîr* is already found in the early period of kings (2 Sam 8:16-17; 20:15; 1 Kgs 4:3). Shebna the scribe is probably the same person as the palace administrator of the same name who was demoted to scribe, the rank immediately below that of palace administrator. He was the head of the royal court chancellery, a public official who had full power over the royal seal (Niehr, *ThWAT* 10:324). Defining the position of the *mazkîr* is somewhat more difficult. The ספר הזכרנות, "the book of memorable events" (NRSV "book of records") in Esth 6:1 implies a chronicler or archivist. The *mazkîr*'s public appearance during politically important circumstances makes it probable that the office was more important than simply that of an archivist. According to Mettinger, he is a royal herald, like the *whm.w* in Egypt, one who both proclaimed royal edicts and functioned as a *chef du protocole*, reporting to the king all that pertained to the people and the country and expressing the will of the king to the people (*State Officials*, 52-62).

In Isa 1:10; 3:6-7; 22:3; Mic 3:1, 9, קצינים are mentioned. The word means "ruler, head, superior." It could represent a military office, as in Hos 10:24.

However, in Mic 3:1, 9 קצינים and ראשים ("heads") are mentioned as parallel terms to signify rulers who are to know the law and protect the weak. There is no more precise designation of an office of such a description.

The prophets condemn the venality and injustice in the administration of justice (Amos 5:10, 12, 15; Isa 1:23; 5:7, 23). We have no information about whether the judiciary of the eighth century functioned any differently than in the earlier united or divided monarchies. Justice was administered in the common law of the local community. When justice at the gates is mentioned (Amos 5:10; Deut 21:19; etc.), it refers to the local jurisdiction. One gets the impression from the words of the prophets that the judiciary had mostly been rendered inoperative due to social stratification, insofar as it was dominated by the upper stratum and corrupted by bribery. According to 2 Chr 19:4–11, Jehoshaphat (870–848) already engaged in a reform of the judiciary in these local jurisdictions: he appointed judges for every fortified city in Judah, set up a supreme court in Jerusalem, and relieved the king of his post as chief judge. While this account may have been literarily influenced by Deuteronomy and might also partially reflect conditions from the period of the Chronicler, the historicity of Jehoshaphat's reforms is generally accepted. If Rainer Albertz's suggestion that the so-called Covenant Code (Exod 20:23–23:19) was the legal basis for the Hezekian reforms is correct (*Israelite Religion*, 61), then there is much that we could learn from this law about what the new administration of justice at that time was. The procedural law of the book of the Covenant Code seems to have been formulated precisely against the abuses of justice about which the prophets railed:

> You shall not spread a false report. You shall not join hands with the wicked to act as a malicious witness. You shall not follow a majority in wrongdoing; when you bear witness in a lawsuit, you shall not side with the majority so as to pervert justice; nor shall you be partial to the poor in a lawsuit. … You shall not pervert the justice due to your poor in their lawsuits. Keep far from a false charge, and do not kill the innocent and those in the right, for I will not acquit the guilty. You shall take no bribe, for a bribe blinds the officials, and subverts the cause of those who are in the right. (Exod 23:1–3, 6–8)

The Covenant Code also formulates a proper law regarding the phenomenon of debt slavery, regulating this practice and at least reducing its abuse (Exod 21:2–11).

> In addition, the reformers attempted to improve the bad social position of marginal groups through a prohibition with a religoius foundation: the rich upper classes were forbidden to oppress either the landless aliens who were dependent on them or widows and orphans (22.20f.; 23.9), to exact inter-

est from the poor on small loans (22.24), or to take in pledge the cloak of someone overwhelmed with debt (22.25; cf. Amos 2.8). (Albertz, *Israelite Religion*, 185)

A final, religious, institution was the temple, which we will consider below in the section on religious history (§II.5).

II.4. Political History

Herrmann, Siegfried. *Geschichte Israels in alttestamentlicher Zeit* (Munich: Kaiser, 1973), 282–322. **Kitchen**, K. A. *The Third Intermediate Period in Egypt (1100–650 B.C.)* (Warminster: Aris & Phillips, 1973). **Miller**, J. Maxwell, and John H. **Hayes**. *A History of Ancient Israel and Judah* (Philadelphia: Westminster, 1986), 314–76.

Synchronism of Kings

Judah	Israel	Assyria
Jotham (?–742)	Zechariah and Shallum (745)	
	Menahem (745–736)	
		Tiglath-pileser III (744–727)
Ahaz (742–727)		
	Pekahiah (736–735)	
	Pekah (735–732)	
	Hoshea (732–723)	
Hezekiah (727–698)		Shalmaneser V (727–722)
		Sargon II (722–705)
		Sennacherib (705–681)
Manasseh (697–642)		
		Esarhaddon (680–669)
		Ashurbanipal (668–627)
Amon (642–640)		

II. THE HISTORY OF THE ERA

II.4.1. The Assyrian Crisis

Alt, Albrecht. "Das System der assyrischen Provinzen auf dem Boden des Reiches Israel," in *Kleine Schriften zur Geschichte des Volkes Israels* (3 vols.; Munich: Beck, 1953–59), 2:188–205. **Donner**, Herbert. "The Separate States of Israel and Judah," in *Israelite and Judaean History* (ed. John H. Hayes and J. Maxwell Miller; Philadelphia: Westminster, 1977), 381–434. **Forrer**, Emil. *Die Provinzeinteilung des assyrischen Reiches* (Leipzig: Hinrichs, 1920). **Jaroš**, Karl. *Geschichte und Vermächtnis des Königreiches Israel von 926 bis 722 v.Chr.* (EurHS 23.136; Bern: Lang, 1979).

After the death of Jeroboam II, the period of prosperity that had characterized his reign came to an abrupt end. The cause of the fall was primarily the new international situation that began with the reign of Tiglath-pileser III (744–727; fig. 10). Since Adadnirari II (909–889) the Neo-Assyrian empire had been the dominant power, and many conquered areas had been incorporated into it. The attention of the first three Assyrian kings of the eighth century was turned away somewhat from the west to Urartu as well as to internal problems.

Fig. 10. Tiglath-pileser III (744–727). © Trustees of the British Museum.

Tiglath-pileser (Pulu in Babylon and Pul in 2 Kgs 15:19) began a new imperialistic policy that was aimed westward as well, however, to the lands of the Mediterranean coast. He abandoned the system of large provinces, establishing instead smaller administrative regions. He also began to destroy systematically the political independence of Israel's smaller neighbor states, a process that usually occurred in three phases. In the first phase military pressure was used to compel vassalage. If there was an anti-Assyrian conspiracy, military intervention would follow, and a new, "loyal" ruler would be installed. This would be accompanied by a reduction of territory and the deportation of the ruling class. In the final phase, the territory's independence would be abolished and it would become an Assyrian province, with a governor (*šaknu* or *bēl paḫāti*) installed and the upper stratum of the populace deported and replaced by a foreign inhabitants. There were exceptions in which annexation was never complete, however, as in Judah or in Phoenicia. Tiglath-pileser might already have begun conquest of northern Syria in 740. To the best of our knowledge, though, the first extensive campaign there took place in 738: the northern Syrian state of Hamat was annexed, and many Syrian states and Phoenician cities paid tribute, including Damascus, Byblos, and Tyre—and Menahem of Samaria.

II.4.2. THE SYRO-EPHRAIMITIC WAR AND THE END OF THE KINGDOM OF ISRAEL

Alt, Albrecht. "Tiglathpilesers III. erster Feldzug nach Palästina," in *Kleine Schriften zur Geschichte des Volkes Israels* (3 vols.; Munich: Beck, 1953–59), 2:150–62. **Becking**, Bob. *The Fall of Samaria: A Historical and Archaeological Study* (SHANE 2; Leiden: Brill, 1992). **Begrich**, J. "Der syrisch-ephraimitische Krieg und seine weltpolitischen Zusammenhänge," *ZDMG* 83 (1929): 213–37. **Cazelles**, Henri. "Problèmes de la guerre syro-éphraïmite,"*ErIsr* 14 (1978): 70–78. **Cazelles.** "La guerre syro-éphraïmite dans le contexte de la politique internationale," in *Storia e tradizioni di Israele: scritti in onore di J. Alberto Soggin* (ed. Daniele Garronne and Felice Israel; Brescia: Paideia, 1991), 31–48. **Cook**, H. J. "Pekah," *VT* 14 (1964): 121–35. **Day**, John. "The Problem of 'So, King of Egypt' in 2 Kings XVII 4," *VT* 42 (1992): 289–301. **Ehrlich**, C. S. "Coalition Politics in Eighth Century B.C.E. Palestine: The Philistines and the Syro-Ephraimite War," *ZDPV* 107 (1991): 48–58. **Hayes**, John H., and J. K. **Kuan**. "The Final Years of Samaria (730–720 BC)," *Bib* 72 (1991): 153–81. **Irvine**, Stuart A. *Isaiah, Ahaz, and the Syro-Ephraimitic Crisis* (SBLDS 123; Atlanta: Scholars Press, 1990). **Na'aman**, Nahman. "The Historical Background to the Conquest of Samaria (720 BC)," *Bib* 71 (1990): 106–25. **Na'aman.** "Population Changes in Palestine Following Assyrian Deportations," *TA* 20 (1993): 104–24. **Oded**, B. "The Historical Background of the Syro-Ephraimite War Reconsidered," *CBQ* 34 (1972): 253–65. **Otzen**, B. "Israel under the Assyrians," *ASTI* 11 (1978): 96–110. **Thompson**, Michael E. W. *Situation and Theology: Old Testament Interpretations of the Syro-Ephraimite War* (Prophets and Historians 1; Sheffield: Almond, 1982). **Vanel**, A. Tâbe'él en Is. VII 6 et le roi Tubail de Tyr," in *Studies on Prophecy: A Collection of Twelve Papers* (VTSup 26; Leiden: Brill, 1974), 17–24.

Zechariah's murderer and successor, Shallum (745) reigned for only one month and was then himself struck down by Menahem of Tirzah. Menahem voluntarily submitted to Tiglath-pileser III. According to 2 Kgs 15:19, he paid the Assyrian a tribute of a thousand talents of silver, which is confirmed in Tiglath-pileser's annals, as previously mentioned. This must to have occurred during the Assyrian king's first westward campaign, usually dated to the year 738. The biblical text suggests that Menahem submitted not only out of fear of the Assyrian, but also because he needed the support of the Assyrian so that he might help Menahem confirm his hold on royal power. Whatever the case, he held on for ten years (745–736). From that point on, Israel was a vassal of the great Assyrian king. Menahem was the last Israelite king to die a natural death. His son Pekahiah (736–735) was killed by Pekah (735–732) after just two years. As we saw, Tiglath-pileser undertook a campaign in 734 against Philistia, which was aimed primarily at Gaza. In connection with this, Tiglath-pileser took the western part of Pekah's territory, out of which he formed the province of Dū'ru (Dor). According to 2 Kgs 15:29, Pekah also lost control of the Galilee and Gilead.

In 2 Kgs 15:37; 16:5-9; and Isa 7:1-9 we have an account of an attack by Rezin of Damascus and Pekah of Samaria against Judah, the so-called Syro-Ephraimitic war. These two wanted to bring Ahaz of Judah (or probably already Jotham) into an anti-Assyrian coalition of which Rezin of Damascus, Pekah of Samaria, Hiram of Tyre, and the Philistines were all part (*TGI*, 56–59; *TUAT* 1:373–77). Since Ahaz refused, however, they wanted to put a foreigner called Ben Tabe'el on the Judean throne (Isa 7:6). Based on the version of the name given in the Bible, it can be assumed that he was an Aramean, although he could also have been a Phoenician, since a Tubail of Tyre is mentioned on a stele found in Iran (cf. pp. 58–59). The allies could not take Jerusalem. According to 2 Kgs 16:7 Ahaz called for help from the king of Assyria, although in Stuart Irvine's opinion this was a Deuteronomistic invention, and in reality Ahaz remained neutral vis-à-vis the broad anti-Assyrian movement. However, Irvine continues, a large section—perhaps even the majority of the Judean people—favored the coalition, while Isaiah supported the king throughout the conflict (*Isaiah, Ahaz*). Tiglath-pileser's campaign in 734 against Philistia was the beginning of his punitive expedition against the participants of the anti-Assyrian coalition (for another opinion, see Donner, *Israel unter den Völkern*, 60). In 733 he directed his attention inland. In 732 Damascus was taken, Rezin was killed, and his territory was incorporated into the Assyrian provincial system—as were the Israelite regions of Gilead and the Galilee, which became the provinces of Magidu and Gal'aza. Israel became confined to the rump-state of Ephraim (2 Kgs 15:29; Hos 5:1–2; *TGI*, 57–58; *TUAT* 1:377). Pekah was overthrown by his subjects and, with Tiglath-Pileser's permission, was replaced by Hoshea (2 Kgs 15:30; *TGI* 59; *TUAT* 1:373–74). From this point on Judah was also an Assyrian vassal state.

Having come to power in a pro-Assyrian conspiracy, Hoshea (732–723) was also a vassal who paid tribute to Tiglath-pileser (e.g., in 731) and his successor, Shalmaneser V. But it is unlikely that he was forced to do so because of a military campaign, as is stated in 2 Kgs 17:3. In 724 Hoshea rebelled against Assyria for unknown reasons. His rebellion was perhaps part of a larger rebellion in Syro-Palestine (Josephus, *Ant.* 9.283–84; perhaps also Isa 14:28–32) and was supported by Egyptian propaganda and promises of aid (cf. Hos 7:11; 11:5–6). According to 2 Kgs 17:4, Hoshea sent messengers to King So of Egypt.

Inasmuch as this name does not refer to any known pharaoh, and since it is very difficult to believe that So might be a short form of the name Osorkon (IV, ca. 730–715), the best solution is to assume that the word points to the Egyptian city of Sais, where Tefnakht I founded an independent kingdom (Twenty-Fourth Dynasty) around 727. The Einheitsübersetzung correctly translates, "he sent messengers to So to the king of Egypt."[1] The Egyptian help failed to materialize, however, and Hoshea was captured by Shalmaneser and imprisoned. Samaria was besieged for three years before it was conquered (2 Kgs 17:5–6). While both the Bible and the Babylonian Chronicle (*TGI*, 60; *TUAT* 1:401) ascribe the conquest to Shalmaneser, Sargon II also boasted about this victory (*AOT*, 348–49; *TUAT* 1:379, 383). As we saw above, Shalmaneser conquered the city (around 722) and that Sargon put down a rebellion in Samaria in 720 during a western campaign (see §I.2 above; cf. Hayes and Kuan, "Final Years"). Thus, the kingdom of Israel met its end, and the remaining rump-state became the province of Samerina. The city was rebuilt, though archaeology does not support Sargon's claim that it was greater than before. The remaining Israelite troops were drafted into the Assyrian army. A considerable portion of the population was deported, and foreign colonists were brought in to settle Samaria. According to 2 Kgs 17:24, they came from Babylon, Cuthah, Avva, Hamath, and Sepharvaim; in 716 Sargon also settled Arabian tribes in Samaria (*TGI*, 63; *TUAT* 1:386). Many residents of Samaria fled to Judah, which led to a population increase and the expansion of Jerusalem. They brought with them northern Israelite traditions that were recorded in the Bible (e.g., the Elijah and Elisha cycle, Ur-Deuteronomium, and Hosea).

II.4.3. JUDAH UNDER HEZEKIAH

Albright, William Foxwell. "The Date of Sennacherib's Second Campaign against Hezekiah," *BASOR* 130 (1953): 4–11. **Haag**, H. "La campagne de Sennachérib contre Jérusalem en 701," *RB* 58 (1951): 348–59. **Horn**, Siegfried H. "Did Sennacherib Campaign Once or Twice against Hezekiah?" *AUSS* 6 (1966): 1–28. **Laato**, Antti. "Assyrian Propaganda and the Falsification of History in the Royal Inscriptions of Sennacherib," *VT* 45 (1995): 198–226. **Leeuwen**, Cornelis van. "Sanchérib devant Jérusalem," *OTS* 14 (1965): 245–72. **Na'aman**, Nahman. "Hezekiah and the Kings of Assyria," *TA* 21 (1994): 235–54. **Oded**, B. "The Kingdom of Judah during the Reign of Hezekiah," in *Israelite and Judaean History* (ed. John H. Hayes and J. Maxwell Miller; Philadelphia: Westminster, 1977), 441–51. **Yurco**, F. J. "The Shabaka-Shebitku Coregency and the

---

1. Einheitsübersetzung (a German translation of the Bible for use in Roman Catholic worship): "Er hatte nämlich Boten nach So zum König von Ägypten gesandt."

Supposed Second Campaign of Sennacherib against Judah: A Critical Assessment," *JBL* 110 (1991): 35–45.

We have already dealt with Ahaz in the Syro-Ephraimitic conflict, and we will consider his religious projects in §II.5 below, where we will also look at Hezekiah's reforms. Hezekiah's confrontation with Sennacherib of Assyria is most fully attested to in the Bible and in Assyrian sources (2 Kgs 18:13–37; 2 Chr 32:1–23; Isa 36–37; *TGI*, 67–69). "He rebelled against the king of Assyria and would not serve him" (2 Kgs 18:7). The political circumstances seemed good for a revolt: as opposed to 713–711, when Sargon II had put down the Ashdodite rebellion in which Judah, Edom, and Moab had taken part (Isa 20; *TGI*, 63–64; *TUAT* 1:384), at the end of his life he faced trouble in the north with Urartu, while after his death Merodach-baladan led a rebellion in Babylonia. The text 2 Kgs 20:12–19 contains a credible piece of information connecting Hezekiah to these Babylonian rebels. The rebellion was supported in Syro-Palestine by Luli, king of Sidon, and by the Philistine city of Ekron. Perhaps Hezekiah occupied Gath and the region of Gaza, which remained loyal to the Assyrians (cf. 2 Kgs 18:8; 1 Chr 4:34–43 also mentions a Simeonite invasion into this region during Hezekiah's reign). In Egypt the Twenty-Fifth (Nubian) Dynasty seems to have been a powerful ally; we know that Isaiah denounced the Judean attempts to form an alliance with Egypt (Isa 31:1–3). Considerable work on the water supply (the Siloam Tunnel, among others), important construction projects and fortifications, as well as military supply posts are attested to in 2 Kgs 20:20; 2 Chr 32:2–5, 28; and Isa 22:9b–11 and are archaeologically confirmed, as mentioned earlier.

After having put down Merodach-baladan's revolt, Sennacherib turned his attention in his third campaign (701) to the rebellion in Syro-Palestine. He marched along the Phoenician coast to Palestine, meeting little significant resistance along the way. After having taken Ashkelon and Ekron, he then conquered nearly all of Judah—forty-six of the fortified walled cities, according to his own account. Excavation has shown that at the end of the eighth century many Judean towns were destroyed. The capture of Lachish in particular is dramatically confirmed both by its ruins and by the series of reliefs in Sennacherib's palace at Nineveh (see above, pp. 88–89).

Sennacherib also tried to take Jerusalem. We have already analyzed in detail the biblical accounts of the Rabshakeh's embassy, which attempted to cause the city's surrender (2 Kgs 18:17–19:13; Isa 36:2–37:13). According to Sennacherib's annals he had Hezekiah "locked up like a caged bird" (*TGI*, 69). Nevertheless, Jerusalem did not fall. The Bible states that Hezekiah paid a heavy tribute to Sennacherib, but not that Jerusalem was taken. Sennacherib also says nothing about a conquest of Jerusalem, or of Hezekiah's having been deposed. Sennacherib allowed the tribute to be sent to him, pointing to an abrupt departure. The account that YHWH's angel killed 185,000 men in one night in the Assyrian's camp and caused Sennacherib to decamp (2 Kgs 19:35-38) is a later theological interpretation of the sudden departure and presupposes a literary tradition (cf. Exod 12:12; 2 Sam 24:17; 2 Chr 21:15). The historical cause for Sennacherib's action is nearly impossible to ascertain: perhaps he had to lift the siege of Jerusalem early because of an epidemic or because of events in Assyria (cf. 2 Kgs 19:7). Less probable is that his army had been decimated in the battle of Eltheke against the Egyptians (2 Kgs 19:9; *TGI*, 68; *TUAT* 1:389) and that he therefore had no more power to fight against Jerusalem (so Haag, "Le campagne de Sennacherib," 355-58). "Why the city was saved is a particular question that has still not been answered conclusively, since the Old Testament account of it is full of inconsistencies, and comparisons to Assyrian texts do not offer any convincing solution" (Herrmann, *Geschichte Israels*, 319).

The complicated connections between the biblical account (see above I.2.1.2) and the historical problems surrounding Tirhakah, king of Cush, who was not pharaoh before 690, has led some scholars (e.g., Winckler, *Alttestamentliche Untersuchungen*, 26-49; Albright, "Sennacherib's Second Campaign"; van Leeuwen, "Sanchérib"; Horn, "Did Sennacherib Campaign?") to assume that Sennacherib undertook a second campaign against Hezekiah around 688 B.C.E. The first campaign in 701 ended with the payment of tribute, the second with the deliverance of Jerusalem. There are no convincing grounds for this argument, however: there is no mention of any such campaign in Assyrian annals, and the argument that Tirhakah could not have led the Egyptian forces in 701 is based on an incorrect understanding of Egyptian texts. As a twenty-two-year-old in 701, he could well have been the leader of the Egyptian expeditionary corps (Kitchen, *Third Intermediate*, 158). That he is referred to as the king in 2 Kgs 19:9 is an understandable anachronism. A literary analysis of 2 Kgs 18-19 entirely contradicts the theory that Sennacherib had two campaigns. The problems of the biblical account should be solved literarily, not historically.

II.4.4. JUDAH UNDER MANASSEH AND AMON

Dietrich, Walter. "Der eine Gott als Symbol politischen Widerstands," in *Ein Gott allein? JHWH-Verehrung und biblischer Monotheismus im Kontext der israelitischen und altorientalischen Religionsgeschichte* (ed. Walter Dietrich and Martin A. Klopfenstein; OBO 139; Göttingen: Vandenhoeck & Ruprecht, 1994), 463-90. **Ehrlich**, E. L. "Der Aufenthalt des Königs Manasse in Babylon," *TZ* 21 (1965): 281-86. **Rainey**,

Anson F. "Manasseh, King of Judah, in the Whirlpool of the Seventh Century BCE," in *Kinattūtu ša dārâti: Raphael Kutscher Memorial Volume* (Journal of the Institute of Archaeology of Tel Aviv University, Occasional Publications 1; Tel Aviv: Institute of Archaeology, 1993), 147–64. **Tatum**, L. "King Manasseh and the Royal Fortress at Horvat 'Usa," *BA* 54 (1991): 136–45.

Manasseh's evil religious measures are recounted in 2 Kgs 21:1–18 in an entirely Deuteronomistic style. Chronicles offers more political information, in particular about Manasseh's imprisonment in Babylon (2 Chr 33:11–13). We know from Assyrian sources that Manasseh was a vassal of Esarhaddon and Ashurbanipal, and that they commanded him to go to Assyria, either to bring a heavy tribute or to participate in the Assyrian wars (*ANET*, 291, 294; *AOT*, 357). According to the Rassam Cylinder, Manasseh (*Mi-in-si-e*) participated, along with twenty-two other kings from the western part of the Assyrian kingdom, in Ashurbanipal's first campaign against Egypt, which advanced as far as Thebes (667). In the second campaign (663) Thebes (Akk. *Ni-i*; Heb. *No'* [נא]) was conquered again and plundered (Nah 3:8–10; *ANET*, 295). Manasseh's religious measures might in some way be related to his vassalage, though not all scholars believe that the Assyrians attached religious requirements to vassalage. The Assyrian texts make no mention of imprisonment and portray Manasseh only as a loyal vassal; as mentioned above, the "imprisonment–conversion–return" structure was probably invented by the Chronicler. According to Hermann Spieckermann, "the account of his reign of terror" (2 Kgs 21:16) and the accusations that echo throughout 2 Kgs 21 of his suppression of the YHWH religion is all part of the Dtr chamber of horrors" (*Juda unter Assur*, 375). On the other hand, there may be traces of a strong prophetic opposition in the book of Nahum and perhaps also in Habakkuk and Zephaniah (Dietrich, "Der eine Gott"). This would imply that Manasseh did in fact promote religious syncretism and supported the imperial might of Assyria, and that he conducted a bloody form of despotism in Judah.

After the negative Deuteronomistic judgment of Amon, all that is reported is the palace revolution against him, which might have been friendly to Egypt (2 Kgs 21:23–24; 2 Chr 33:24–25). The text ascribes the punishment of the conspirators to the "people of the land." According to Rainer Albertz, this means that the land-owning farmers in Judah teamed up with the royal household against the destructive upper stratum of the capital.

> The free farmers of Judah were evidently concerned right from the start to prevent struggles for power between rival court parties of the kind that had shattered the northern kingdom in its last years. They did not want to forfeit the chance offered by the shift in international power relationships through

a short-term seesaw policy, e.g. reliance on Egypt, but to exploit it for a wide-ranging national renewal. (Albertz, *Israelite Religion*, 201)

The sparse information in the Bible makes it nearly impossible to know what important events were occurring on the international stage. Assyria was at the height of its power and had rendered Egypt entirely powerless. Judah was therefore wholly at the mercy of Assyria and could only engage in a pro-Assyrian policy.

II.5. Religious History

II.5.1. Assyrian Religion

Cogan, Mordechai. *Imperialism and Religion in Assyria, Judah, and Israel in the Eighth and Seventh Centuries B.C.E.* (SBLMS 19; Missoula, Mont.: Society of Biblical Literature, 1974). **Cogan.** "Judah under Assyrian Hegemony: A Re-examination of Imperialism and Religion," *JBL* 112 (1993): 403–14. **McKay**, J. W. *Religion in Judah under the Assyrians, 732–609 B.C.* (SBT 2/26; Naperville, Ill.: Allenson, 1973). **Spieckermann**, Hermann. *Juda unter Assur in der Sargonidenzeit* (FRLANT 129; Göttingen: Vandenhoeck & Ruprecht, 1982), 307–72. **Weinfeld**, Moshe. "The Worship of Molech and of the Queen of Heaven and Its Background," *UF* 4 (1972): 133–54.

It is questionable whether Assyria exercised religious-political pressure on its conquered territories, Judah in particular. Martin Noth was of the opinion that political rulers in the ancient Orient required adoption of the official state cult—not to replace the traditional cults, but to be practiced alongside them (Noth, *History of Israel*, 265–66). J. W. McKay, however, believes that Judah was not under religious compulsion from the Assyrians but did experience a permeation of Syrian-Canaanite syncretism (McKay, *Religion in Judah*). According to Mordechai Cogan, too, vassals were not required to participate in the cult of the Assyrian imperial gods, but the Assyrians required the inhabitants of their provinces to practice the imperial cult. Accordingly, as a vassal, Judah would not have experienced any religio-political pressure from the Assyrian side, while after 722 the then-annexed Israel was faced with just such a requirement (Cogan, *Imperialism*). Using Assyrian sources, however, Hermann Spieckermann convincingly showed that the worship of Assyrian imperial gods was demanded of vassals as well (cf. e.g., *TGI*, 56, 59; *TUAT* 1:373, 376; Spieckermann, *Juda unter Assur*).

It has often been surmised that behind the account of Ahaz's erection of an altar on the Damascene model lies Assyrian religio-political pressure.

Spieckermann is convinced that this is correct, except that it was not the new altar but rather the Solomonic altar that Ahaz had brushed aside that he used to perform his religious vassalic duties (2 Kgs 16:15). All important functions of the YHWH cult would therefore have been moved to the new great burnt offering altar (2 Kgs 16:14). Perhaps the Jerusalem temple, which until that time had not had an altar for burnt offerings, was augmented with one (Zwickel, *Bib* 73 [1992]: 540). Spieckermann concludes "that in 2 Kgs 16:10–16 we have valuable Judean evidence as to how those whose religions did not readily allow for compromise dealt with the religio-political implications of Assyrian supremacy" (*Juda unter Assur,* 369). There is also evidence of the permeation of Assyrian cultic practices in the account of Josiah's reforms, which refers to the worship of heavenly bodies or horses for the sun god (2 Kgs 23:5, 11). It is difficult to know for certain which parts of the heavily Deuteronomistically reworked account about Manasseh (2 Kgs 21:3–18) are historical. Verse 5 ("he built altars for all the host of heaven in the two courts of the house of the Lord"), might have existed before the Deuteronomistic History, "an entirely historically plausible conclusion, since mention of the introduction of the worship of certain astral deities in a particular part of the temple complex would fit very well in Manasseh's time" (Spieckermann, *Juda unter Assur,* 164). The Asherah that was brought into the temple (so 2 Kgs 21:7) was probably the Assyrian goddess Ishtar. Along with these cults, Assyrian forms of divination and exorcism might also have penetrated into Judah, as is suggested by verse 6. These Assyrian customs, however, went syncretistically hand in hand with Canaanite traditions. Child sacrifices, like those that Ahaz and Manasseh offered, according to the Bible (2 Kgs 16:3; 21:6) more likely point to Phoenician-Canaanite tradition. Nevertheless, because of enormous Deuteronomistic revisions, the historical reliability of these accounts is not secure. Scholars are increasingly convinced that the Moloch cult was not concerned with child sacrifice but was a rite in which children were consecrated to the deity (see Weinfeld, "Worship"). The *molek* (מלך) to whom the children were consecrated was the Aramean-Assyrian weather god Adad.

> So in these dedications of children we have an Adad-Yahweh syncretism which came about at the level of family piety. Here in Jewish religious practice, too, the king Adad got a consort, the queen of heaven (*malkat haššāmayim*), worship of whom in the family is often attested in the late monarchy (Jer. 7.18; 44.15–19; cf. Amos 5.26). This refers to an Ishtar figure who is represented in Babylonian and Assyrian religion by the evening star. This means that under Assyrian influence, in the seventh century the new pair of Adad and Ishtar overlaid the male-female divine pair Yahweh and Asherah from earlier personal piety. (Albertz, *Israelite Religion,* 193)

Whatever the case, many syncretistic customs that Jeremiah criticized at the end of the seventh century found their way to Judah in Manasseh's time, especially in private religion—including, for instance, rooftop cultic areas for star worship with incense offerings and libations (2 Kgs 23:12; Jer 19:13; 32:29), and the adoration of the sun god Shamash, a practice also adopted in the Jerusalem cult (2 Kgs 23:11). The numerous horse figurines with discs on their brows, some of which were found in Jerusalem, Lachish, and Hazor, seem to be connected with the sun god (2 Kgs 23:11; cf. H. Weippert, *Palästina*, 629). According to Albertz, in Zeph 1:4 and 2 Kgs 23:5 the idolatrous priests mentioned in connection with the sun cult (כמרים) might be Assyrian or Aramean specialists who had the professional knowledge of the *barû* (priests of hieromancy) or the *asipu* (exorcist priests) (Albertz *Israelite Religion*, 190). The custom of baking cakes for Ishtar (Jer 7:18; 44:19) could hark back to Assyrian influence in Manasseh's time.

II.5.2. Hezekiah's Reform

Aharoni, Yohanan. "The Horned Altar of Beer-sheba," *BA* 37 (1974) 2–6. **Ahlström**, Gösta W. *Royal Administration and National Religion in Ancient Palestine* (SHANE 1: Leiden: Brill, 1982), 65–68. **Borowski**, Oded. "Hezekiah's Reform and the Revolt against Assyria," *BA* 58 (1996): 148–55. **Herzog**, Ze'ev, et al. "The Israelite Fortress at Arad," *BASOR* 254 (1984): 1–34. **Lowery**, R. H. *The Reforming Kings: Cult and Society in First Temple Judah* (JSOTSup 120; Sheffield: JSOT Press, 1991). **Weinfeld**, Moshe. "Cult Centralization in Israel in the Light of a Neo-Babylonian Analogy," *JNES* 23 (1964): 201–12.

Even though the Josian reforms had not yet occurred, the Jerusalem temple was still the center of the Judean cult. As we have seen, the temple also played an important part in the Assyrianization of the religion. There were, however, also shrines outside Jerusalem. The best known is the Arad temple mentioned above, which is probably correctly identified as having been a YHWH temple, given the names of the priests on the ostraca, Meremot and Pashhur (cf. Ezra 8:33; Jer 20:1). Other shrines have been mentioned in the section on archaeological sources, while blocks from a horned altar found on Tel Beersheba show that there may even have been a shrine there that has not yet been excavated (cf. Amos 5:5; 8:14).

Both the Deuteronomistic History and Chronicles mention a cultic reform effected by Hezekiah. In the literary analysis, we saw that what the Chronicler adds to the Deuteronomistic History is historically dubious. However, the Deuteronomistic account of Hezekiah's reform itself experienced heavy literary reworking as well. We have already seen that in light of this Hans Detlef Hoffmann concluded that there was no Hezekian cultic reform. This radical solution has not met with universal acceptance, however. B. Oded has claimed that Hezekiah's reform was authentic, since cultic centralization makes sense in light of his political activities, whose goal was to strengthen the Davidic dynasty and to return to the old borders of the Davidic monarchy (Oded, "Kingdom of Judah," 446; cf. Weinfeld, "Cult Centralization"). Even economic motives might be brought to bear, as cultic centralization would have made it possible to have temple donations flow directly to Jerusalem. Still, Spieckermann has concluded from his analysis that "all of that sounds largely like dtr dogma and little like historical substance" (Spieckermann, *Juda unter Assur*, 171). The only historically secure information is the destruction of the metal snake Nehushtan, but this would hardly be called a reform (see also Herrmann, *Geschichte Israels*, 316–17). Yohanan Aharoni believes that the results of his excavations in Arad and Beersheba show that Hezekiah removed cultic high places (2 Kgs 18:4): in Arad in the late eighth century (stratum VIII) the altar of burnt offerings was taken out of use, as was the shrine itself at the end of the seventh century (stratum VI). The first would be ascribed to the Hezekian reform; the second to the Josian. Later, Ze'ev Herzog and other colleagues of Aharoni date the building of the shrine to stratum VII, connecting the desecration of the altar and the whole shrine to Hezekiah's reform (Herzog et al., "Israelite Fortress," 18–25). As we have already noted, however, David Ussishkin undercut this possibility, since he showed that the shrine could not have been built before the end of the eighth century. According to Aharoni, the profanation of the great horned altar of Beersheba should also be dated some time before 701, making it possible to ascribe this to the Hezekian reform as well (Aharoni, "Horned Altar"). The existence of a temple on Tel Beersheba in the eighth century is entirely hypothetical, however, so its having gone out of use along with its altar is slim proof for an already dubious Hezekian reform.

II.5.3. The Prophets

Ackroyd, Peter R. "Isaiah I–XII: Presentation of a Prophet," in *Congress Volume: Göttingen, 1977* (VTSup 29; Leiden: Brill, 1978), 16–48. **Buss**, Martin J. *The Prophetic Words of Hosea: A Morphological Study* (BZAW 111; Berlin: A. Töpelmann, 1969). **Elliger**, Karl. "Die Heimat des Propheten Micha," *ZDPV* 57 (1934): 81–152. **Fleming**, Daniel E. "The Etymological Origins of the Hebrew *nābî'*: The One Who Invokes God," *CBQ* 55 (1993): 217–24. **Fohrer**, Georg. *Die Propheten des Alten Testaments*, vol. 1, *Die Propheten des 8. Jahrhunderts* (Gütersloh: Mohn, 1974). **Fohrer**. "Wandlungen Jesajas," in *Festschrift für Wilhelm Eilers* (Wiesbaden: Harrassowitz, 1967), 58–71. **Gordis**, Robert. "Hosea's Marriage and Message," *HUCA* 27 (1974): 9–35. **Haag**, Ernst. "Prophet und Politik im Alten Testament," *TTZ* 80 (1971): 222–48. **Høgenhaven**, Jesper. *Gott und Volk bei Jesaja: Eine Untersuchung zur biblischen Theologie* (Acta Theologica Danica 24; Leiden: Brill, 1988). **Johnson**, Aubrey R. *The Cultic Prophet in Ancient Israel* (Cardiff: University of Wales Press, 1944; 2nd ed., 1962). **Junker**, H. *Prophet und Seher im alten Israel* (Trier: Paulinus, 1927). **Koch**, Klaus. *Die Propheten: I, Assyrische Zeit* (Urban Taschenbücher 280; 2nd ed.; Stuttgart: Kohlhammer, 1987). **Levin**, C. "Amos und Jerobeam I," *VT* 45 (1995): 307–17. **Mowinckel**, Sigmund. *Psalmenstudien III: Die Kultprophetie und prophetische Psalmen* (Kristiania: Dybwad, 1922; repr., Amsterdam: P. Schippers, 1961). **Ramlot**, L. "Prophétisme," *DBS* 8 (1972): 811–1222. **Reventlow**, Henning Graf. "Prophetenamt und Mittleramt." *ZTK* 58 (1961): 269–84. **Rosenbaum**, Stanley N. *Amos of Israel: A New Interpretation* (Macon, Ga. Mercer University Press, 1990). **Rowley**, H. H. "Was Amos a Nabi?" in *Festschrift Otto Eissfeldt zum 60. Geburtstage 1 September 1947* (ed. Johann Fück; Halle: Niemeyer, 1947), 191–98. **Scharbert**, Josef. *Die Propheten Israels bis 700 vor Christus* (Cologne: J. P. Bachem, 1965). **Weippert**, Helga. "Amos: Seine Bilder und ihr Milieu," in Helga Weippert, Klaus Seybold, and Manfred Weippert, *Beiträge zur prophetischen Bildsprache in Israel und Assyrien* (OBO 64; Göttingen: Vandenhoeck & Ruprecht, 1985), 1–29. **Wolff**, Hans Walter. "Hoseas geistige Heimat," *TLZ* 81 (1956): 83–94. **Wolff**. "Wie verstand Micha von Moreschet sein prophetisches Amt?" in *Congress Volume: Göttingen, 1977* (VTSup 29; Leiden: Brill, 1978), 403–17. **Woude**, A. S. van der. "The Book of Nahum: A Letter Written in Exile," *OTS* 20 (1977): 108–26.

An important religious phenomenon in this era was the appearance of the prophets, whose words were passed on to us in the books of the prophets. The Bible also offers accounts of prophets in earlier eras, although it is questionable whether all those who are designated with the term נביא ("prophet") throughout history and in all circumstances actually occupy the same place in society. Whatever the case, the etymological meaning of the word נביא itself is heavily disputed. Daniel E. Fleming has come up with a plausible etymology from the Akkadian word *nabû*, in the texts from Mari (eighteenth century B.C.E.) and Emar (fifteenth to fourteenth centuries B.C.E.): "he who calls/invokes God." This emphasizes the prophet's function as intercessor, although this is clearly not an exhaustive definition of the prophet's office.

Prophets are attested in the ancient Near East outside of Israel, in Mari on the Euphrates, for example, as well as in Phoenicia and Syria (cf. the inscriptions of King Zakir of Hamat: *AOT*, 443–44; *TUAT* 1:626–28). They function as royal officials, cultic servants, or ecstatics, and prophets in Israel occasionally are seen serving in all of these roles. According to 1 Kgs 18, in the ninth century Jezebel had 450 prophets of Baal of Tyre in her court. Biblically, prophets are first attested in the time of Samuel (1 Sam 10:10–12) and are found in Judah and Israel (e.g., at the time of Elijah and Elisha), although from the first prophets until Hosea they are more frequently attested in the northern kingdom. They are called בני נביאים ("sons of the prophets"), live in groups, and are often recognizable by their garb, a cloak of haircloth. These prophets seem to have sent themselves into trances with song, repeated calls, and rhythmic movement (1 Sam 10:5; 1 Kgs 22:10; 18:26). This phenomenon of orgiastic fanatics is of Canaanite origin, although over time *nebiism* assumed much of the form and function of the Israelite "seer" (1 Sam 9:9). Samuel was already a singular prophetic figure, standing clearly apart from the ecstatic group. Prophets were also on the staff of the palace court, as individuals or as a group, in order to tell the king God's commands: Nathan and Gad were in David's service (2 Sam 7:1–17; 24:11); Jehoshaphat had his prophets (2 Kgs 3:11–20); and "court prophets" are even attested after the exile (Neh 6:7). There were also prophets employed at the temple, so-called cultic prophets (Jer 35:4). Hananiah, Jeremiah's opponent (Jer 28) seems to have been one; in 2 Chr 20:13–17 a Levite named Jahaziel appeared during the reign of King Jehoshaphat as a cult prophet, and in 1 Chr 15:22, 27 the שׂר המשׂא was probably not the head of transport nor the leader of the singers' performances, but the "leader of the oracle," that is, the cult prophet in the time of David's transportation of the arc of the covenant to Jerusalem. The liturgical style of the book of Joel is a sign that this figure was a cult prophet. One can agree with Ernst Würthwein that, since the work of Sigmund Mowinckel, H. Junker, and Aubrey R. Johnson, the claim that there were cult prophets in Israel can no longer be relegated to the realm of hypothesis (*ZAW* 62 [1950]: 12). There is no doubt that at the time of the Assyrian crisis there were also cult prophets at the Jerusalem temple.

Are all the written prophets cultic prophets, therefore? There has been much disagreement on this question in exegetical literature. A few scholars have argued strongly for the affirmative. In his works on Ezekiel, Amos, and Jeremiah, Henning Graf Reventlow traced the *Sitz im Leben* of the words of the prophets back to a fixed office that was rooted in the traditions of the covenant festival ("Prophetenamt"), though this theory has not found many adherents. In earlier periods already we encounter prophets who seem to be independent of any institution, including Ahijah of Shiloh (1 Kgs 11:29), the unknown "man of God" in 1 Kgs 13, and Elijah. The scriptural prophets—those whose books are still with us—condemn such prophets (cf. Isa 28:7–13; Jer 23:9–24; Ezra 13; Mic 3:5), and Amos does not wish to be called a prophet at all (7:14). Their "office" is more charismatic, and they account for their position based on their calling by YHWH (Isa 6; Jer 1; Amos 7:15). The importance of visions for prophetic identity should not be overestimated, and undoubtedly not all of the scriptural prophets were ecstatic. "The event which led to a man's call to be a *nabi'* is described in a considerable number of different ways, and it is also plain that there was no conventional fashion in which it came about" (Gerhard von Rad, *Old Testament Theology* [2 vols.; New York: Harper, 1962, 1965], 2:56).

Amos and Jeremiah preached their message partly at the sanctuary, but this does not mean they had any fixed connection to the cult. Neither does their relation to tradition in any way exclude an experience of a personal call. When the prophetic texts are read impartially, one gets the impression that several prophets probably experienced temporary abnormal states of consciousness. It is remarkable that Amos is the first prophet from whom we have a collection of sayings in written form, and that in a relatively short span of time several such scriptural prophets appeared (Hosea, Isaiah, Micah). This may be coincidental, but it might also be connected to the social rejection they experienced: "The prophets and their theological circle very soon began to collect, to discuss, to evaluate and to record the message that had found no hearing in the public in order to preserve it as a 'testimony' for later times, should it prove true (Isa. 8.16ff.; 30.8ff.)" (Albertz, *Israelite Religion*, 164). Whatever the case, these prophets had a very critical attitude toward their society. They felt themselves impelled to condemn the social, political, and cultural evils and to expose their devastating consequences. We will deal in greater detail with these messages in chapter IV (see also §II.3 above, "Economic and Social History"). Aside from Isaiah, none of the scriptural prophets of the eighth century is mentioned in the Deuteronomistic History, and it is difficult to understand why: "The suppression of scriptural prophecy is one of the mysteries of the deuteronomistic work" (Koch, *Die Propheten I*, 34).

A number of the great prophetic figures made their appearance in the eighth century, viz., Amos, Hosea, Isaiah, and Micah. **Amos** actually belongs to the former era, since he appeared during the reign of Jeroboam II (785–745), a politically dazzling era in which the northern kingdom was rich and expanding. A Judean from Tekoa, a shepherd (Amos 1:1 and 7:14 have נקד ["shepherd"] and בוקר ["cowherd"], respectively, but צאן in 7:15 points to small stock) and dresser of sycamore trees, he was probably not poor, though he did not belong to the ruling stratum of society. As Helga Weippert says, "Amos was a farmer" ("Amos," 2) and so probably still ran the risk of impoverishment. Stanley N. Rosenbaum (*Amos of Israel*, 41–50), however, holds that he was a regional overseer of the royal herds and a northern Israelite officer who, among other duties, supervised the king's sycamore trees. His horizon was not that of a cultic official. Recently C. Levin has defended an entirely new thesis. In his opinion, the account in Amos 1:1 stating that Amos appeared under Jeroboam II is a date that was imported later based on 7:10ff. In Amos 7, however, Amos's opponent is intended to be Jeroboam I. It would therefore be better not to use that evidence for dating him, but instead to consider the core of his message, found in 8:3: "The end has come upon my people Israel."

The years 734–732, the time of the Syro-Ephraimitic war, can be taken as the time of Amos's appearance. Thus, Amos was a contemporary of Hosea and Isaiah. Levin ends as follows: "The suggestion of this date cannot be founded on more than considerations of plausibility. The traditional date does not even have that, though" ("Amos"). While this may be an interesting hypothesis, in my opinion its plausibility is no greater than that of the *opinio communis*.

According to Amos 7:14, Amos rejected the title of prophet: he was not a prophet nor a prophet's son (meaning a prophet's disciple). He did not deny his prophetic calling, but simply that he was a professional or official prophet. The priest of Bethel, Amaziah, calls him not a נביא but a חֹזֶה "a seer." When Amos gives the motive for his prophetic action, he points to YHWH's irresistible impulse, which tore him from the life he was accustomed to. He prophesied in northern Israel for two years before an earthquake that cannot be precisely dated (sometime around 760). He had been in Samaria, since he apparently knew it very well (3:9; 4:1; 6:1), although the place where he was most active was probably the temple of Bethel (7:10–11). It was there that he foretold that Jeroboam would die by the sword and Israel would be taken into exile. This was something entirely new, as for the first time Israel was threatened with annihilation, which is why Rudolf Smend called Amos "the founder of the new prophecy" (*Lehrbuch der alttestamentlichen Religionsgeschichte* [Freiburg im Breisgau: Mohr, 1899], 183). For this he was expelled from Bethel, after which he returned to Judah. His activity seems to have lasted only a short time, although it is difficult to answer the question of how long he was active as a prophet in Israel. In his prophetic statements he condemns social abuses: the sharp contrast between the luxury of the exploitative large landowners and the plight of the farmers without any rights. He condemns especially injustice in legal proceedings, the hoarding of riches, and the arbitrary impositions and demands of the rich, as well as the religious underpinning of this arrogance by the cult. It is because of these injustices that the end will come to Israel.

Hosea was also active as a prophet in the northern kingdom, but he was a citizen of this kingdom. A few Aramaisms and uncommon linguistic forms point to a northern Israelite idiom. Hosea was an entirely different personality than Amos. The list of kings in Hos 1:1 (Uzziah, Jotham, Ahaz, and Hezekiah of Judah; and Jeroboam II and Joash of Israel) was expanded by the Deuteronomist. A date for Hosea's appearance based on internal criteria is also difficult. Earlier we discussed the historical background of his speeches (§I.2.3.1). He was active beginning in the last years of Jeroboam II, sometime around 752. There is nothing that indicates that he experienced the destruction of Samaria in 722/721, though texts such as 9:11–14 and 11:5–6 presuppose King Hoshea's break from Assyria. The last somewhat datable texts come, therefore, from around 725/724.

> A second major period of Hosea's proclamation is linked with the crucial events of the Syro-Ephraimite War (5:8–11) and the subjugation by Tiglath-pileser III of extensive territory in Israel in the year 733.... The sayings contained in chs. 9–12 are most intelligible if we relate them to the quiet period before and after the accession to the throne of Shalmaneser V in 727. (Wolff, *Hosea: A Commentary on the Book of the Prophet Hosea* [trans. Gary Stansell; Hermeneia; Philadelphia: Fortress, 1974], xxi)

We know almost nothing of Hosea's life beyond his marital problems, although there is no agreement about this either. According to Hos 1:2–8, he married a "wife of whoredom" (אשת זנונים) by the name of Gomer. She is usually assumed to have been a cultic prostitute who participated in fertility rituals. This is not an entirely necessary interpretation, however, as the expression could also refer to a whoring wife. At any rate, Hos 1:2 belongs to a later redaction. The woman's three children are given the symbolic names Jezreel, Lo-Ruhamah (Not Pitied) and Lo-Ammi (Not My People). In Hos 3, Hosea is given the instruction to take back "a woman who has had a lover and is an adulteress." It is generally assumed that the same Gomer is meant. As the prophet has to buy her freedom, she apparently came into another's legal possession after a divorce. In Hosea's prophecies all of this takes on a symbolic meaning, as the covenant between YHWH and Israel, Israel's infidelity, and YHWH's patient love for his people are all represented. The question arises whether these marital problems are historical or only symbolic. We have already seen that, according to Hans Walter Wolff, these texts are historically reliable (cf. 48), and he represents the conviction of the majority of exegetes. The prophet married a woman whom he loved, but she was unfaithful and proved to be an אשת זנונים, and so they divorced. It is possible, however, that in actuality only Jezreel was a son of Hosea, born of Gomer or some other woman. The rest could be taken to be a prophetic naming speech as in Isa 8:1–4 (on this see Buss, *Words of Hosea*, 57). Whatever the case, Hos 1 is redactionally reworked, so the historical picture is hardly discernible.

We have no calling vision for Hosea, but one gets the impression that his recognition of his prophetic calling is intimately tied up with his marital experiences. His unhappy marriage became something like an active prophecy and shaped his whole message. He became convinced that his pain was a symbol for YHWH's behavior toward his people. Because he believed that YHWH was a saving and forgiving God (2:16–25), he also felt himself compelled to take back his unfaithful wife. If this is correct, the symbolic names of his children were added only in the later prophetic interpretation. Hosea seems to have had a close connection to the Levites (on this, see Wolff, "Hoseas geistige Heimat").

The prophet **Isaiah** was born around 765 B.C.E. He is often called "the royal prophet" because he seems to have come from an aristocratic lineage.

II. THE HISTORY OF THE ERA

According to a Jewish tradition from the Talmud he was even of royal blood, but based on his texts (3:1–24; 7:3; 8:1–2; 22:15–16; 36–39), this claim is not convincing. Occasionally it seems as if he was a teacher of wisdom (28:9). He was married (8:3), and from what we can gather from the Bible he had two sons with the symbolic names Shear-jashub (a remnant shall return) and Maher-shalal-hash-baz (the spoil speeds, the booty hastens: 8:2); this could be a fictitious naming story (cf. Hos 1). He lived in Jerusalem, and thus he often took his images from city life. In the year of King Uzziah's death (around 740) he was called to his prophetic position (6:1), meaning that his first oracular sayings should be dated to the first few years after 740. This was already in the middle of the Assyrian crisis. Upon Ahaz of Judah's ascension to the throne (736), Kings Rezin of Damascus and Pekah of Samaria attempted to draw the young king into a coalition against Assyria and, following his refusal, embarked on a military campaign against Jerusalem (2 Kgs 16:5).

We learn from Isa 7:6 that this attack was aimed at replacing the king with a man by the name of Ben Tabe'el, a threat to the Davidic dynasty. It was at that moment that Isaiah became involved in politics, just as the great prophets of the ninth century, Elijah and Elisha, had done. Isaiah had already prophesied against moral corruption and formalistic religiosity, in which external devotion and moral injustice went together hand in hand. Now he went to the king and encouraged him; this was the occasion for the famous Immanuel prophecy (Isa 7). We have already seen that Stuart Irvine is probably correct when he states that Isaiah was not against the politics of the king, who wanted to keep his neutrality, but against the majority of the people who were well disposed to the anti-Assyrian coalition (Irvine, *Isaiah, Ahaz*). According to Jesper Høgenhaven, Isaiah was a supporter of Ahaz's cautious pro-Assyrian foreign policy and later an equally decisive opponent of the actively anti-Assyrian stance taken by King Hezekiah (ibid.). In 8:16–18 the prophet seems to have withdrawn for some time because of the people's opposition. Caution regarding Isaiah's historical role in the Syro-Ephraimitic crisis is advisable, as the bulk of our knowledge is dependent on the depiction of the prophet in Isa 1–12, which is not historical but instead shows a picture that was created over time (Ackroyd, "Isaiah I–XII"). According to 2 Kgs 19:1–7, 20–33; 20:1–19 (parallel to Isa 37:1–7, 21–35; 38–39), Isaiah intervened in politics under Hezekiah, especially during Sennacherib's siege of Jerusalem, Hezekiah's illness, and the embassy of Merodach-Baladan. Because of heavy literary reworking it is difficult to find the historically reliable source material in these texts. Yet Isaiah's involvement in these episodes of Hezekiah's history is possible, even probable. Among the prophet's oracular speeches are some that refer to the Ashdodite revolt (713–711) and the revolt against Sennacherib (705–701), as we saw earlier (cf. p. 63). In the same place we also examined the possible *Sitz in der*

Geschichte of the Isaian pericopes. Georg Fohrer divided Isaiah's prophetic career into four periods: (1) his calling to 736—the oracles refer to Judah's inner religious and moral state; (2) the Syro-Ephraimitic war (735–733); (3) Hezekiah's first years until the failure of the first revolt against Assyria (716–711); (4) the second revolt and Sennacherib's campaign (705–701) (Fohrer, *Jesaja*, 1:5–12). While in principle these divisions are acceptable, Fohrer, along with many others, overestimates the possibility of uncovering historical references in Isaiah's words. In his article about Isaiah's changes he also overestimates the possibility of organizing the development of the prophet's thoughts based on these periods. After 700 Isaiah disappears from sight. As mentioned, according to a Jewish tradition he died a martyr's death.

A younger contemporary of Isaiah was the prophet **Micah**. He came from Moresheth, a small village in the Judean hill country southwest of Jerusalem, not far from Lachish. According to the superscription of the book, Micah was active as a prophet concurrently with the reigns of Kings Jotham, Ahaz, and Hezekiah. It is questionable whether he was really active for such a long period of time, however. According to Mic 1:2–7, he began his activity before the destruction of Samaria, but it is not clear if he lived to see the Assyrian campaign of 701; Mic 1:8–16 might have its origin in connection with this campaign. According to Jer 26:18, he was still active during Hezekiah's reign. According to Wolff, however, Mic 1:8–16 is rhetorically connected to 1:6–7 and should also be dated to before the fall of Samaria. His opinion is therefore that Micah most likely was active between 733 and 723 (Wolff, *Micah*, 3–4). He probably knew Isaiah's words and was influenced by them, too (cf. Mic 1:10–15 with Isa 10:28–32 and Mic 2:1–3 with Isa 5:8–10). He might have begun his activity in his homeland (1:10–15), although he also preached his prophetic statements in Jerusalem (e.g., 3:9–12). He knew from personal experience the social abuses against which he preached, particularly the creation of latifundia, a practice that originated in Jerusalem to the enrichment of large landowners. His main opponents were the "heads" in Jerusalem and their officers in the Shephelah, who were responsible for the course of these events (i.e., 2:1–11*). "The severity of his complaints and the bitterness of his threats, uncommon even by prophetic standards, can be explained by his compassion for the sufferings of small farmers and his contempt for the cultic prophets, who told the rich what they wanted to hear in order to make money" (Fohrer, *Propheten des 8. Jahnhunderts*, 174). In his revolt against injustice he opposed the security of those who believed themselves, as God's people, to be safe from all harm. The deep impression made by his words remained in collective memory for a long time, and a century later the elders of the land of Judah still quoted his words in order to save Jeremiah (Jer 26:17–19). It is impossible to prove if Micah himself was among the elders of the city, as Wolff believes (*Micah*, 6–8).

We know almost nothing about **Nahum**, who can be dated to between 700 and 630, at best estimate. According to the superscription of the book, he was originally from Elkosh. We do not know whether this is to be found in the Galilee (so Jerome) or in Judah (so the Greek *Vita Prophetarum*, PG 43:409). He is usually understood as having been Judean, though according to A. S. van der Woude ("Book of Nahum") he was a northern Israelite who lived in Assyrian exile.

III. THE LITERATURE OF THE ERA

III.1. GENRES

III.1.1. PROPHETIC GENRES

Begrich, J. "Das priesterliche Heilsorakel," *ZAW* 52 (1934): 81–92. **Boecker**, Hans Jochen. *Redeformen des Rechtslebens im Alten Testament* (WMANT 14; Neukirchen-Vluyn: Neukirchener, 1964; 2nd ed., 1970). **Gressmann**, Hugo. "Prophetische Gattungen," in Gressmann, *Der Messias* (FRLANT 43; Göttingen: Vandenhoeck & Ruprecht, 1929). **Gunkel**, Hermann. "Die Propheten als Schriftsteller und Dichter," in Hans **Schmidt**, *Die großen Propheten* (Die Schriften des Alten Testaments 2.2; Göttingen: Vandenhoeck & Ruprecht, 1915), xxvi–lxxii. **Hardmeier**, Christof. *Texttheorie und biblische Exegese: Zur rhetorischen Funktion der Trauermetaphorik in der Prophetie* (BEvT 79; Munich: Kaiser, 1978). **Hempel**, Johannes. "Der Prophetenspruch," in Hempel, *Die althebräische Literatur und ihr hellenistisch-jüdischen Nachleben* (Handbuch der Literaturwissenschaft; Wildpark-Potsdam: Akademische Verlagsgesellschaft Athenaion, 1934), 56–68. **Hölscher**, Gustav. *Die Profeten* (Leipzig: Hinrichs, 1914). **Hunter**, A. Vanlier. *Seek the Lord! A Study of the Meaning and Function of the Exhortations in Amos, Hosea, Isaiah, Micah and Zephaniah* (Baltimore, Md.: St. Mary's Seminary and University, 1982). **Koch**, Klaus. *The Growth of the Biblical Tradition: The Form-Critical Method* (New York: Scribner, 1969). **Köhler**, Ludwig. *Deuterojesaja, stilkritisch untersucht* (BZAW 37; Giessen: A. Töpelmann, 1923), 102–5. **Köhler**. "Der Botenspruch," in Köhler, *Kleine Lichter* (Zurich, 1945), 13–17. **Lindblom**, Johannes. *Die literarische Gattung der prophetischen Literatur* (Uppsala: Lundequistska bokhandeln, 1924). **Lindblom**. *Prophecy in Ancient Israel* (Oxford: Blackwell, 1962). **Rendtorff**, Rolf. "Botenformel und Botenspruch," *ZAW* 74 (1962): 165–77. **Tångberg**, K. Arvid. *Die prophetische Mahnrede: Form- und Traditionsgeschichtliche Studien zum prophetischen Umkehrruf* (FRLANT 143; Göttingen: Vandenhoeck & Ruprecht, 1987). **Warmuth**, Georg. *Das Mahnwort: Seine Bedeutung für die Verkündigung der vorexilischen Propheten Amos, Hosea, Micha, Jesaja und Jeremia* (BET 1; Frankfurt a.M.: Lang, 1976). **Westermann**, Claus. *Basic Forms of Prophetic Speech* (Philadelphia: Westminster, 1967). **Westermann**. "Die Mari-Briefe und die Prophetie in Israel," in

Westermann, *Forschung am Alten Testament* (2 vols.; Munich: Kaiser, 1964), 1:171–88. **Westermann**. *Prophetic Oracles of Salvation in the Old Testament* (Edinburgh: T&T Clark, 1991). **Wolff**, Hans Walter. "Die Begründung der prophetischen Heils- und Unheilssprüche," *ZAW* 52 (1934): 1–21. **Würthwein**, Ernst. "Der Ursprung der prophetischen Gerichtsrede," *ZTK* 49 (1952): 1–16.

The fact that the prophetic books often lack coherence was noted as early as Martin Luther. Wolf Wilhelm Baudissin's view that short, discreet, oral prophetic speeches were the original form of prophecy was thus not entirely novel. According to Carl Steuernagel, two main forms of prophetic speech evolved: accusation directed at the people, and the announcement of divine judgment. When he combines accusation and a call to repentance, however, the evidence "that in the great majority of prophetic speech accusation and announcement of judgment constitute *one* statement" is suppressed (cf. Westermann, *Basic Forms*, 16–21). According to Gustav Hölscher, the original form of prophetic speech was incantation (*Die Propheten*). Although this view is exaggerated, it might elucidate the roots of curses and blessings. Hölscher rightly pointed out that even in its simplest form prophecy had a rhythmic form (92); he recognized the short, rhythmic saying as the basic element of prophetic speech, a view supported also by Hermann Gunkel.

According to Gunkel, these speeches contain visions and words, the latter being by far the more important. From here on these will simply be called oracles. In these oracles the prophet speaks in YHWH's name: the "I" of the oracle is therefore mainly the divine "I," although occasionally the prophet speaks about YHWH's thoughts and plans in the third person. In addition, there is a third form of prophetic speech, wherein the prophet adds his own reflections, speeches, and poetry. There is great variety in these oracles: promises, threats, exhortations, priestly torah, disputations, and all sorts of poetry. Most of these genres are not originally prophetic, but prophecy absorbed a wide range of foreign genres.

As prophets were proclaimers of the future, according to Gunkel, their original genres were promise or threat, depending on whether they were preaching salvation or doom. He includes the future tense of verbs, the prophetic perfect, the use of the second person, and varied uses of the imperative and interrogatives among the characteristics of the genre. New genres were incorporated into prophecy as the prophets became poets and thinkers. As poets they used lyric genres: victory poems, satirical poems, funeral poems, hymns, and laments. In the case of the lament they occasionally added YHWH's response, emulating the liturgical genre. Jeremiah goes so far as to use the individual lament, which focuses on his own situation, not on the word of God.

The prophets also became preachers and teachers and therefore used invective speech, trial speech, admonition, priestly torah, disputations, and so on (see Gunkel, "Schriftsteller und Dichter," xlv–lxxi). The underlying explanation of this argument is this: "*The basic unit of prophetic speech is the short saying, the short single saying which is in itself independent*" (Westermann, *Basic Forms*, 24, emphasis original). Because Gunkel explicitly placed the threat—that is, the oracle of doom—and the rebuke on different levels, he obscured the fact that in reality these two genres do not appear as two separate genres in prophetic texts but as two parts of *one* form of speech: the prophetic trial speech (Gunkel, "Schriftsteller und Dichter").

In his work on Deutero-Isaiah, Ludwig Köhler paid attention to the "messenger formula" (*Botenspruch*) for the first time. This refers to statements introduced with the formula "Thus says x (in prophecy: YHWH)." His study concentrated on Deutero-Isaiah, and he concluded that Deutero-Isaiah used this formula more freely than the earlier prophets. Köhler was therefore forced to limit his study to frame formulae (*Rahmenformeln*), without examining the messenger formula as a genre. Later he dedicated a short article to the genre, in which he found in the message style a characterization of prophecy as such. Thus, he recognized the basic genre of prophetic literature.

Around the same time as Köhler, Johannes Lindblom undertook a study of the messenger formula, which he called the oracle formula (*Orakelformel*) (Lindblom, *Gattung*, 98–113). He determined that the formula "Thus says YHWH" was found exclusively in prophetic literature or prophetic narrative. Therefore, it must express something that is part of the nature of prophecy. Incidentally, these formulae are found more broadly in ancient oriental oracular literature. According to Lindblom, this formula was originally only used to introduce actual oracles, but later it lost this precise meaning and was used to introduce any sort of prophetic speech. In his opinion, the oracle formula goes back, on the one hand, to the proclamation formula in ancient oriental announcements and, on the other, to formulae by which a message would have been introduced. The first origin explains why the formula could also be put in YHWH's mouth; the other emphasizes the messenger's function of the prophet who uses the formula. Oddly enough, however, Lindblom was unable to use this information to characterize the basic prophetic genre. In his entire previous work, he had described the basic form of prophetic literature as revelation and compared it with medieval mystical literature, which also consisted of written revelation. Therefore he thought that he had found an overall genre in which all prophetic texts—admonitions, narratives, monologues, confessions, poems, and so on—could be ordered. Yet there is a nearly complete separation between his definition of the genre of prophetic speech and his analysis of the messenger formula. The latter offers a more solid foundation, because of both its formulaic character and its *Sitz im Leben,* namely, the sending of a messenger. That is much more concrete than obscure revelations of which we know next to nothing. It is not surprising, then, that in his synthesizing work on prophecy Lindblom can do almost nothing with his theory for interpreting the texts (Lindblom, *Prophecy*).

Claus Westermann wonders if, when the prophetic saying as a whole is a messengerial conveyance (*Botenwort*), the character of the message is present only in the framework of the prophetic saying or in its content, too. A few of his predecessors led him to the opinion that the main genre of prophetic speech is the trial speech, which is formed by the prophets in two parts: foundation of judgment and its proclamation (*Basic Forms,* 67–70). In an incisive analysis of the sending of a messenger (*Botensendung*), he shows that the message (*Botenwort*) is characterized not only by the typical messenger formula, but also by a specific form. For the message has a binary structure: it contains a description of the situation (perfect tense) and an instruction, a desire, or something similar (in imperfect tense). Many types of messages can be distinguished from one another, one of which deserves special attention here. Occasionally, in the message of a king to a colleague or vassal, the description of the situation turns into an accusation and the part in imperfect tense becomes a declaration of war. The biblical trial speech is often quite similar to this form.

Westermann paid attention to the prophetic texts from Mari. We cannot cover all of the parallels of these texts with Old Testament prophecy, but Westermann sees "the greatest significance of the Mari texts in the fact that they confirm that the prophetic speech form is the message received and passed on by a messenger sent or commissioned by a god" ("Die Mari-Briefe," 179).

Literary investigation of prophetic literature should also increasingly consider the form and content of the prophetic speeches transmitted in the historical books. In all of the Mari texts, the prophetic message is directed at the king; remarkably, in the biblical historical books all prophetic words are addressed to an individual as well, usually the king. Westermann therefore first examines the trial speech toward individuals. Using three examples (Amos 7:16–17; 1 Kgs 21:17–19; 2 Kgs 1:3–4), he shows the simple structure of the genre: a call to listen, an accusation, a messenger formula, and an announcement. The accusation and the announcement are the main sections. "Only these two together constitute the messenger's speech; both have their existence only as members of the whole. But God's word, in the proper sense, is only the announcement. It is designated as such by the introductory messenger formula (with 'therefore'); the accusation stands *before* the real messenger's speech" (Westermann, *Basic Forms,* 132). One should not attach too much interest to the differentiation between the actual *Botenwort* (i.e., the word of God) and the "simply" prophetic word. The prophet plays a part in the formulation of the whole oracle, and it is the two parts together that make up the *Botenwort*, as Westermann himself remarked. The proclamation of judgment is based on the accusation. This, according to Westermann, is the essential definition of the basic form of prophetic speech. The double structure corresponds to that of a type of law, as in Exod 21:12. Thus, Westermann is inclined to assume a juristic, rather than a cultic origin for the prophetic trial speech (against Würthwein, "Der Ursprung"). Its affinity to the form of the profane message (*Botenwort*) is immediately clear. Westermann correctly noted this, although it might be asked if this structure does not simply impose Deuteronomistic perception on the normal structure of a prophetic word.

The proclamation of judgment against Israel is a development of the individual judgment announcement. Since it is directed to a group or to the whole people, the accusation often has a more complicated form: first it mentions the offense in a generalized, abstract form; the accusation is then developed through concretization, exemplification, or citation ("Israel says…"). The proclamation is often divided into two parts also: the first division marks God's intervention in the first person in the divine speech, while the second part, the judgment—the consequence of the intervention—is in the third person (e.g., Hos 13:8; Isa 8:5–8; 9:7–11). The prophetic trial speech to the people is constructed as follows (Westermann, *Basic Forms*, 130):

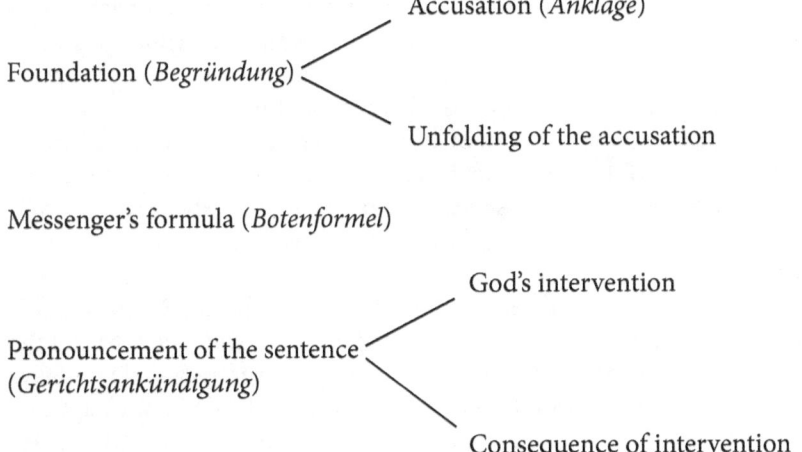

Klaus Koch has rightly pointed out that "prediction of disaster" is a better name than "pronouncement of the sentence," "for it cannot be proved that the prophets saw the disaster which they prophesied as the ruling of a divine court of justice, with judgment following a contest with the accused" (Koch, *Growth of the Biblical Tradition*, 193).

This structure was elucidated by Westermann with the use of Amos 4:1–3; Hos 2:7–9; Isa 8:5–8; 30:12–14; Mic 2:1–4; 3:1–4, 9–12; Jer 5:10–14; 7:16–20. He showed that, although it is justifiable to speak of a basic form of a trial speech or statement of doom against the people, it does not refer to a rigid schema; variations and expansions are entirely possible. The prophets could also dress up their judgments in other borrowed literary forms: the cry of woe, the lawsuit, the disputation,[1] the parable, the lament, or the prophetic torah (*Basic Forms*, 189–94). These forms are borrowed from other situations, but as prophetic messages they should usually be understood in terms of the base form of the trial speech. In this way Westermann unified the diverse world of prophetic genres Gunkel had outlined. In particular in the two-part structure of the trial speech, he brought the threat and scolding speech from Gunkel's arsenal to the unity of the basic form. For this he is especially indebted to Johannes Hempel and Hans Walter Wolff.

When literary genres are reshaped, the rules of the borrowed form must obviously be taken into account. In dealing with a lawsuit between YHWH and his people, attention must be paid to Israelite legal proceedings (see Boecker, *Redeformen*), although perhaps in the prophetic books this so-called lawsuit is more like a debate without appeal to a judge or mediator. Martin J. Buss noticed that Hosea, among other prophets, has hardly any direct connection to secular juridical forms. Instead, the prophetic tradition in which he lived had some connection with legal structures of a more or less cultic type, for example, in the form of curses or condemnations (Buss, *Words of Hosea*, 79). Similarly, a prophetic lamentation should not be separated from psalms of lamentation. According to Christof Hardmeier (*Texttheorie*), the prophetic lament had the function of arousing attention: with it the prophets "expressed the situation of mourning over death and destruction, thus creating an emotionally effective, associational background appropriate to their proclamation" (319). The prophetic lament is an obvious metaphor for a proclamation of doom.

Rolf Rendtorff criticized Westermann's theory (Rendtorff, "Botenformel"). He remarked that the connection between the message (*Botenspruch*) and the messenger formula (*Botenformel*) is loose, so that many messages do not have the typical introductory formula, while the messenger formula often appears in texts with no message. There is no definite genre of profane message. He therefore opposes the two-part structure that Westermann believed to have uncovered. However, Westermann has without a doubt uncovered a characteristic form, even if it is not applicable to the delivery of all messages. More-

---

1. The latter two genres first appear fully in Deutero-Isaiah.

over, according to Rendtorff, there is no direct connection between this structure and the two-part division that Westermann saw in the prophetic word, so the prophetic word does not originate in the message. But Westermann did not claim this. From the I-form and the use of הנה ("see"), which probably come from the messenger's style, Rendtorff himself shows that the prophetic word, although not derived from the message, is still heavily influenced by it. Westermann also implied a formal similarity rather than direct genetic descent. In my opinion, he proved apodictically that the two-part nature is a characteristic feature of the complete prophetic word and, moreover, that it is related to the structure of a specific type of message.

Alongside the main genre of *threat*, Gunkel also identified the category of *promise*, depending on whether the prophecy announced doom or salvation. Westermann, however, paid almost no attention to the *promise* or the *oracle of salvation*. Indeed, he did not hold to the rigid evolutionary schema—which states that the original writing prophets could not prophesy salvation—and demonstrates using the Mari texts that salvation prophecy in Israel has a long ancestry. But in his systematic study of the basic forms he finds no place for salvation prophecy. His work therefore needs to be supplemented. Quite some time ago, J. Begrich dedicated an article to priestly oracles of salvation, although he only dealt with the oracle of salvation in Deutero-Isaiah and read it as an imitation of priestly oracles of salvation, which followed lament and plea in cultic practice. Thus, Begrich does not offer a more general treatment of the prophetic oracle of salvation (Begrich, "Das priesterliche Heilsorakel"). In general there is a dearth of in-depth study of the history of the genre of the prophetic salvation word (*Heilswort*). This is related to the fact that the question of whether the prophets before Jeremiah preached salvation to any noticeable extent is still being argued. In the sayings against the foreign nations (e.g., Isa 13–23), the destruction of the enemies of Israel implies salvation for Israel. From a literary perspective, however, these sayings are not oracles of salvation.

Many years later, Westermann did finally study the prophetic salvation words systematically. Although more extensive than the work on trial speeches, this research is less thorough and unified. It deals more with content and much less with the formal aspects. This is related to the fact that words of salvation have fewer clear genre markings. Westermann is of the opinion that there has never been a period in Israel without words of salvation. He differentiates four main groups among proclamations of salvation: (1) proclamation of salvation and restoration; (2) two-sided announcements—the destruction of the enemy and the salvation of Israel; (3) conditional announcements, connected with parenesis; (4) announcements connected with words of wisdom.

In Isa 1–39 words of salvation of the first group are encountered in narratives (7:1–17; 36–38): the salvation word is formulated out of the situation, and the promised salvation from their distress is quickly fulfilled. In such salvation words the announcement of salvation is often accompanied by a sign (cf. Isa 8:1–4; 36:15 [in the Rabshakeh's speech]; 37:5–7, 30–32; 38:5–8 [actually an individual oracle of salvation]). In spite of their final redaction, these narratives come from the preexilic period about which they tell. The words of salvation outside of the story in Isa 1–39 are generally additions, so that the texts, in liturgical use, would fit into the new situation in which the announced destruction had already occurred. This happened in three steps: single words of salvation were added to some of Isaiah's trial speeches; independent words of salvation were added to the small collections; and Isa 1–39 was joined to collections of words of salvation (chs. 40–55; 56–66). In independent words of salvation God's care for his people and salvation are announced (e.g., 4:2–6; 11:11–16; 29:17–21, 22–24; 30:18–26). There are also additional short salvation speeches with only one motif (e.g., 1:25–26; 10:20–21; 14:1–2; 17:7–8). Occasionally a motif is expanded into a word of salvation, as in promise of a king (9:1–6; 11:1–9:10; 16:4b–5; 32:1–5) or the peoples' pilgrimage, and the peoples' peace (2:1–4; 19:19–25). The relationship between the two short texts (18:7; 16:1, and perhaps 11:10) and the two full ones is understood as the two short texts representing an earlier form, while the fuller show a more developed form (see Westermann, *Prophetic Oracles of Salvation*, 94). Among the motifs are those of God's renewed care and deliverance, and the more descriptive ones of restoration, blessing, or salvation (blessing; restored relation with God; social aspects; security and tranquility and peace; healing of the ill). Westermann also finds similar forms in the twelve prophets. In Amos 9:8b–15 there is a later addendum. In the book of Hosea, following a trial speech there are promises of salvation, as in 2:1–3, 16–25; 3:1–5; 14:2–9, or short additions, mostly so-called Judah glosses, which follow trial speeches (e.g., 1:7; 4:15; 6:11; 12:1b). Micah 4–5 as a whole is a collection of words of salvation from among which independent words (4:1–4 [5], 6–8, 9–12; 5:1–3, 9–13; cf. also 2:12–13; 7:7–20) and short additions (4:13; 5:4–5a, 7, 8, 14) can be distinguished. Westermann makes the same differentiation in the promises of salvation from the twelve prophets as he does in Isaiah: he finds salvation speeches about liberation, gathering, and return (Hos 11:10–11; Mic 2:12–13; etc.), words of God's renewed care, restoration, and blessing (Hos 2:1–3, 16–25; 11:8–9; 14:5–8; Amos 9:11–12; 9:13–15) and the expansions of a motif into a word of salvation (Mic 5:1–3 [5]: royal promise; 4:1–4 [5]: pilgrimage image; Amos 9:8b–10). The motifs are mostly the same as those found in Isaiah: among "announcements of liberation" Westermann includes retrospection on God's earlier acts of salvation, defection from God and God's judgment; lament; God's return of care (forgiveness); liberation; gathering and return; the advance praise of God. Among those of restoration and promise of blessing are the restoration of a sound relationship with God; honor and kingdom; joining of other peoples; the end of the wars; and peace among the peoples. These motifs are not always clearly distinguished.

The second group, two-sided announcements, is a group of statements expressly of political salvation. Their political character is somewhat limited by a lack of certainty about the identity of the people whose destruction is announced. This group of announcements includes a simple form (destruction of the enemy—salvation for Israel, e.g. Isa 8:9–10; 10:24–27; 14:3–4), a more developed form in which the enemies' approach precedes their destruction (e.g., Isa 17:12–14; 29:5b–8; 33:1–16), and large compositions such as Isa 34–35. Chapter 35 is a pure word of salvation of the first group that is similar to Deutero-Isaiah, and chapter 34 was created as an expansion of the simple announcement; Otto Kaiser calls the composition a little apocalypse. The two-sided announcement goes back to the double request that is to be found in many psalms of lament and is rooted in the realm of blessings and curses (Westermann, *Prophetic Oracles of Salvation*, 213–14).

Conditional proclamations of salvation (group 3) are found in Amos 5:4–6, 14, 15; Hos 10:12; and 12:7, 10. However, this is perhaps not prophetic speech; these words might instead belong to the wider context of Deuteronomistic parenesis. Hosea 3 also looks like a Deuteronomistic interpretation of history, an expansion of Hos 1. In Isa 1–39 the conditional proclamation of salvation is rarely relevant, and then only in additions (e.g, 1:19–20; 33:14–16).

The speeches of group 4, which come out of the wisdom tradition, proclaim different fates for the righteous and the sinner. These can consist simply of a wisdom utterance, or they can be connected to a salvation speech (Amos 9:8b–10; Isa 1:27–28; 10:12). "This [type of speech] cannot be included in the prophetic oracles of salvation" (Westermann, *Prophetic Oracles of Salvation*, 251).

Westermann also considers some expressions that are not entirely typical of a genre. The expression ביום ההוא ("on that day") is found forty-four times in Isa 1–39. In the trial speech, this phrase introduces the "consequence of intervention" element (e.g., Mic 2:4 in the judgment word 2:1–4; cf. Isa 2:19–20; 7:17–18). In salvation speeches it can have the same function (e.g., Isa 10:27 in the salvation speech of 10:24–27). Mostly, however, the original function of this expression fades into a stereotyped introduction that links additions to the context (cf. Isa 3:18; 11:10; 12:1; 19:16; 23:15). This leads Westermann to the following conclusion: "[W]hen an oracle of salvation is introduced by the phrase 'In that day,' it is *a priori* likely that this oracle was spoken after the prophecy of judgment had been given" (*Oracles of Salvation*, 257). As an introduction to an announcement of salvation, the expression ימים

בימ ("days are coming") is almost entirely restricted to the book of Jeremiah (cf., however, Amos 9:13). The original use might be found in trial speeches (1 Sam 2:31; 2 Kgs 20:17 = Isa 39:6; Amos 4:2; 8:11). Salvation words outside the narratives in the prophetic books are almost all of later origin, except perhaps Hos 2:16–25, which is closely associated with Hosea's judgment message of Hos 11:8–9. These, then, do not belong to the literature of this era, the subject of this volume.

> From the catastrophe of 587 B.C. on, deliverance of a remnant is announced in terms of rescue from exile. These are new oracles of salvation such as had never before been heard. … Scholarly research shows that the proclamation of salvation after the judgment was more extensive in scope than had previously been assumed. It is heard no only in the individual voices of well-known prophets like Deutero-Isaiah, Trito-Isaiah, Ezekiel, and several of the postexilic minor prophets, but also in the proclamation which extended for decades, or even longer, that God was again attentive to his people. This proclamation is comparable in extent to a major prophetic book. It is a great choir of many voices, proclaiming a message of salvation that to a remarkable degree is consistent and harmonious. Previously the entire scholarly emphasis was on the work of individual prophets of judgment in the preexilic period, but not the emphasis is carried further in the prophecies of salvation after the collapse of the nation, even though these were for the most part transmitted anonymously, and, since they are scattered throughout various prophetic books, their full scope is difficult to recognize. (Westermann, *Prophetic Oracles of Salvation*, 268–69)

Westermann also pointed out the literary couching of oracles in other genres and partially classified the great variety of loan genres. This phenomenon has occasionally been seen as dissolution of the prophetic style connected to a change in content. According to Hempel, the more an oracle was an expression of personal thoughts and independent reflection, that is, the closer it came to preaching while also stating the conditions under which the prophetic word would be fulfilled, the more it would be influenced by nonprophetic genres, especially religious poetry and wisdom sayings ("Der Prophetenspruch," 68). This is genre-critically correct, but genre-historically we should beware of naïve evolutionism. Hempel has pointed out that this situation is already to be found in the oldest writing prophets. Genre-wise, one can find plain oracles just as readily even in the later prophets.

In a genre-critical study of prophetic texts one must therefore ask whether the prophet uses the oracle genre straightforwardly or if he dresses his message in another genre. In the latter case, one must describe the loan genre precisely, because it obviously reveals the intention of the prophet. Beyond that all the data should be interpreted according to their function in the structure of either the oracle genre or the loan genre. Thus, works about psalms or other genres, for example, the introductions to psalms by Gunkel and Begrich or the studies on psalms by Mowinckel, contain important material pertaining to genre-critical analysis of prophetic writings.

There are other sorts of genres in prophetic literature such as exhortations, stories of prophetic call, descriptions of visions, seer's statements, or stories of symbolic actions. Here, too, one must consider the purity of the form, its structure, and its *Sitz im Leben*. The exhortation in particular often appears in the books of the eighth-century prophets as calls to change or to reform (Amos 4:4–5; 5:4–6, 14–15, 24; Hos 2:4ff.; 4:15; 5:15; 6:6; 8:5; 10:12–13a; 12:7; 13:4; 14:2–3; Isa 1:16–17, 18–20; 2:10; 6:9–10; 7:1ff; 28:12, 22; 29:9–10; 30:15). These exhortations, while not having a very rigid structure, are nevertheless recognizable. They consist of two elements: an appeal and a motivation. The appeal is indicated formally by the use of the imperative, jussive, prohibitive, or vetitive. The motivation, which is not always present, consists of a paratactical clause introduced with ו that often contains an indirect jussive or imperative (i.e., with a final sense), or a subordinate clause that is introduced, for instance, with כי ("because") or with פן ("lest").

According to Georg Warmuth, there are no true exhortations in preexilic prophecy. Either they are not used in their exhortative sense by the prophets, or else they come from exilic/postexilic redaction. The true exhortations of the preexilic prophets have the task of describing Israel's failures: they have lost their functions as calls to change. The task of these prophets "is not to improve and save in order to prevent the threatened judgment, but to announce, justify, and make understandable what was to come" (Warmuth, *Das Mahnwort*, 171). Westermann was also of the opinion that the exhortation was not an independent form, but that it can be encountered in connection either with the promise or the accusation, or with statements of threat or judgment—in other words, creating an auxiliary relationship with the two basic forms of trial speeches and salvation words (*Basic Forms*, 47, 55–56). A. Vanlier Hunter followed this opinion: the prophets were preachers of the approaching judgment of God and not simultaneously preachers of conversion. The image of the prophet as preacher of repentance is of Deuteronomistic origin (Hunter, *Seek the Lord*, 28, 45). It may be correct that the prophets did not preach conversion in the sense that one could then avoid destruction. However, this does not mean that they did not speak true exhortations, even if the call for conversion came with an irrevocable announcement of doom. This must be conceded by Warmuth and Hunter, and K. Arvid Tångberg made this the fundamental tenet in his work on prophetic exhortations (*Die Prophetische Mahnrede*). In his opinion Mari prophecy seems to show the exhortation and warning to be age-old functions of prophecy. This is his conclusion:

> The prophetic exhortation to conversion already appears as an independent genre in the oldest written prophets. Certainly in preexilic times it was occasionally inserted as a quote in the prophetic announcement of judgment, and thus has the function of an accusation. The call to repentance presupposes the activity of prophets as exhorters and warners. (*Die prophetische Mahnrede*, 140)

In his opinion, the comparison with wisdom exhortation and Deuteronomistic parenesis confirms that prophetic exhortation was an independent genre, which, like the prophetic trial speech, flexibly used elements of other genres as presentation. One could agree with this, even if perhaps the authenticity of many of his prooftexts is questionable or should be rejected all together (e.g., Amos 5:4–6, 14–15; Hos 10:12; 12:7; Isa 1:18–20).

III.1.2. THE COVENANT CODE

Alt, Albrecht. *Die Ursprünge des israelitischen Rechts* (Leipzig: S. Hirzel, 1934 [= *Kleine Schriften zur Geschichte des Volkes Israel* (3 vols.; Munich: Beck, 1953–59), 1:278–332]). **Beyerlin**, Walter. "Die Paränese im Bundesbuch und ihre Herkunft," in *Gottes Wort und Gottes Land: Hans-Wilhelm Hertzberg zum 70. Geburtstag am 10. Januar 1965* (Göttingen: Vandenhoeck & Ruprecht, 1965), 9–29. **Carmichael**, Calum M. *The Origins of Biblical Law: The Decalogues and the Book of the Covenant* (Ithaca, N.Y.: Cornell University Press, 1992). **Gerstenberger**, Erhard. *Wesen und Herkunft des apodiktischen Rechts* (WMANT 20; Neukirchen-Vluyn: Neukirchener, 1965). **Gilmer**, Harry W. *The If-You Form in Israelite Law* (SBLDS 15; Missoula, Mont.: Society of Biblical Literature, 1975). **Jepsen**, Alfred. *Untersuchungen zum Bundesbuch* (BWANT 41; Stuttgart: Kohlhammer, 1927). **Liedke**, Gerhard. *Gestalt und Bezeichnung alttestamentlicher Rechtssätze: Eine formgeschichtlich-terminologische Studie* (WMANT 39; Neukirchen-Vluyn: Neukirchener, 1971).

Exodus 24:7 states that Moses took the code of the covenant (ספר הברית) and read it out loud before the people. The collection of laws in Exod 20:22–23:33 thus owes its name "Covenant Code" (CC) to this verse. Exodus 23:20–33, with its promises and instructions for the entrance into Canaan, is of Deuteronomistic character and probably did not originally belong in this collection; 23:14–19 also seems to be a later addition. The actual Covenant Code is limited to 20:22–23:13. Earlier exegetes have ascribed it to the E source, which they dated to the eighth century B.C.E. Some scholars who do not recognize an E source nevertheless date the first redaction of the Covenant Code to the eighth century.

Albrecht Alt differentiated between two genres of rules of law: the casuistic rule of law in prose, and an apodictic one that makes rules in short, often rhythmic phrases. The latter do not deal with concrete conditions, and they are often categorical commandments or prohibitions. The legal rules of the first category describe the facts in a conditional sentence and then provide the pertinent legal regulations. They are made of two parts that, following Erhard Gerstenberger (*Wesen und Herkunft*, 25), can be called "definition of facts" and "stipulation of legal consequences." The casuistic legal rule is the prevailing genre in ancient Near Eastern legal corpora. According to Alt, among others, there is a historical-genetic connection between the casuistic legal rules of the Old Testament and those in Israel's environment that were similar in form and content, since they would have made their way into Israelite law through contact with the Canaanites. The apodictic laws are understood to have a specifically Israelite origin. However, this theory of the origins of both legal genres is hypothetical, since no good Canaanite parallels of casuistic law have yet been found. Similarities to Babylonian, Hittite, or Egyptian law codes and decrees should not necessarily be ascribed to direct borrowing. These correspondences only display a shared source, namely, ancient common law, which was adapted in accordance with the various societal attitudes and peoples of different, although similar, character. The concept of a purely Israelite origin for apodictic law is actually problematical, since there are clauses in international Hittite treaties that are quite similar to biblical apodictic commandments and prohibitions: the clause "You should guard the land that I have given you, and you should not covet any part of Hatti-Land" is formulated like the Decalogue commandment "You shall not covet your neighbor's house" (Exod 20:17).

First, the CC contains a number of civil and criminal legal regulations of a casuistic nature (21:1–22:16). According to 21:1, these are generally called *mišpāṭîm* (המשפטים, "the ordinances"). The main case is expressed in a conditional sentence introduced with כי ("because"), and the legal consequences follow in the main sentence. After this, subsets or variations on the main case are dealt with, and are introduced with אם ("if") (in 21:26–27, ואם is parallel to כי). Exodus 21:2–6 is a good example:

Definition of facts Main case: 2 When you buy a male Hebrew slave	Designation of legal consequences He shall serve six years, but in the seventh he shall go out a free person.
Subset 3 if he comes in single,	he should go out single.
If he comes in married	Then his wife shall go out with him.
4 If his master gives him a wife and she bears him sons or daughters,	The wife and her children shall be her master's and he shall go out alone.

5 But if the slave declares, "I love my master, my wife, and my children; I will not go out a free person,"	6 Then his mater shall bring him before God ... and his master shall pierce his ear with an awl; and he shall serve him for life.

Verse 5, which is introduced by ואם, can also be interpreted as a counter case. In verse 7 a new case begins: "When a man sells his daughter as a slave...". If a subcase introduced with אם is followed by a sentence introduced by ואם ("and if"), the latter subcase is a subset of the first subcase. In the aforementioned example, verses 5–6 are therefore a subcase of a subcase. Verses 7–11 are structured in the same manner: (1) Main case (כי; v. 7); (2a) subcase (אם; v. 8); (2b) subcase (אם; v. 10); (3a) subcase of 2a (ואם; v. 9); (3b) subcase of 2b (ואם; v. 11). If, however, a sentence introduced with ואם follows a main case introduced with כי, the former case is coordinated with the main case (e.g., Exod 21:22–23, 26–27). In antecedent sentences with כי or אם, the verb is in the imperfect before the subject, and in the consequent sentences it is in the *perfectum consecutivum* at the front of the sentence—otherwise it is given in the imperfect.

According to Gerhard Liedke, the *Sitz im Leben* of these casuistic laws was the court at the gate, a court of arbitration with no authority to mete out punishment; its judgments, strictly speaking, were only suggestions. The slavery laws in Exod 21:2–11 demonstrate that in the realm of casuistic law there was also arbitration without a gate court of arbitration (*Gestalt*, 52–53). The initial formation point of rules of law was the tradition of accepted judgments. Casuistic laws originated with the junction of judgments and accounts of legal cases divested of their specific circumstances. It must be assumed, contra Alt, that this development might also have taken place in Israel.

A few of the casuistic laws in the CC are formulated in the second person (Exod 21:13–14; 22:24–26; 23:4–5). These "if you" clauses seem to derive their form from covenant regulations, or from regulations of vassal treaties. This formulation is the nucleus of Old Testament parenesis, found above all in Deuteronomy. It bridges casuistic laws (two-part construction and כי) and apodictic ones (second person address) (Liedke, *Gestalt*, 61). In Exod 21:23 there is even a law whose protasis is in the third person while the apodosis is in the second (see Gilmer, *If-You Form*, 70ff.).

Exodus 21:12 contrasts sharply with the previous legal statements, although this is less clear in translation than it is in the original Hebrew text. In a very terse and rhythmically formulated saying, the case is expressed in a nominal clause with a participle, while the stipulation of the legal consequence is a very short and general formula: מכה איש ומת מות יומת, "Who strikes a man and he dies, shall be put to death (cf. vv. 15–17). Such statements are also functionally different from the above-mentioned *mišpāṭîm*: they do not specify a case or consequences but simply establish the undifferentiated principle of capital punishment for murder or cursing parents. Alt and various other authors count these verses among the apodictic laws. In apodictic law they differentiate two different types, prohibitive in the second person (לא תרצח, "you shall not kill") and clauses in the third person singular with participial subjects or relative clauses. As genres go, these two types are entirely different and should not be brough together indiscriminately. The laws in CC that contain מות יומת phrases (Exod 21:12, 15, 16, 17; 22:18) belong to the second type, as well as Exod 22:19, a sentence that varies somewhat from the others (יחרם, "he will be excommunicated"). Liedke counts these among the "apodictic laws" but points out that they are "to be understood as bipartite, that is, with participial protasis and verbal apodosis." These are strikingly similar to a type of saying that is found often in Prov 10–22 (around one hundred times over four hundred verses), for example, זורע עולה יקצור־און ושבט עברתו יכלה, "whosoever sows injustice will reap calamity; and the rod of his fury will fail" (Prov 22:8). Accordingly, these laws seem to originate in ancient tribal wisdom, where the adjudicative power rested in the family or tribe. Whatever the case, these regulations of criminal law are of different origin than the casuistic legal statements of civil law, yet their formal similarity is clear. It is therefore understandable that both types of law are found together in the first section of the CC. Thus in its present context, Exod 21:12 is the main case and precedes a short composition of casuistic rules (vv. 12–15), while the subcases are introduced differently, the first with ואשר, and the second with וכי.

The last section of the CC combines moral and religious/cultic laws (Exod 22:17–23:13). Nearly all of the regulations in this section are formulated in the second person singular. Here we find apodictic commandments and prohibitions very similar to those of the Decalogue (Exod 20:1–17). The prohibitions are in the prohibitive, that is, לא with the nonjussive imperfect, with the commandments usually formulated in the injunctive, a strongly commanding imperfect. Thus, in Exod 22:17 we read מכשפה לא תחיה, "you shall not permit a female sorcerer to live" (prohibitive); and in 22:28 בכור בניך תתן־לי, "the firstborn of your sons you shall give to me."

The CC also includes parenetic verses. These include the addresses with "you" (singular and plural): "you have seen for yourselves," "you [pl.] know" (Exod 20:22; 23:9b); exhortations, as in 23:13: "you shall take heed to all that I have said to you"; and threats including punishment, as in 22:23: "my wrath will burn, and I will kill you with the sword, and your wives shall become widows and your children orphans." Such emphatic and deliberate pronouncements are characteristic of oral performance. Walter Beyerlin disputes the theory that these parenetic verses originate from a Deuteronomistic redaction ("Die Paränese"). In his opinion, the language in Deuteronomy has a noticeably richer vocabulary and is more broadly structured, while in the CC the parallel elements appear to be formulated more tersely and simply. Many are also arranged rhythmically (cf. Exod 23:8b and Deut 16:19b) and are not reflected to the same degree (cf. Exod 22:30 with Deut 14:21). Seventeen percent of the laws in the CC have motivation clauses, whereas in Deuteronomy 60 percent do: this is also a sign that the CC is older. Therefore Beyerlin's conclusion is that "the rules of law of the Covenant Code were already parenetically impressed in the pre-Deuteronomistic period." He also points out that the parenesis is limited to the commandments and the prohibitions and is not found in connection with the *mišpāṭîm*. He infers from this that the series of commandments and prohibitions in Exod 20:22–26 and 22:20–23:19 were worked out parenetically, when the collection of *mišpāṭîm* had not yet been connected with them. The parenesis therefore stems from an early stage.

According to Beyerlin, the cultic ritual commandments and the laws for the protection of the less empowered stem from a cultic legal recitation to the covenant people in the context of the festival cult of the YHWH community. He establishes the origin of these parenetically elaborated laws as having been in the distant past, since they "extend from their [the YHWH community's] beginnings in the desert period all the way to their amphictyonic phase." He is referring to the pilgrimage festivals of the amphictyony, which would have been characterized by YHWH's epiphany and the covenant tradition, and it is in this context that this parenesis is best understood. One objection to this argument is that Beyerlin wrongly includes Exod 20:18–21 as part of the CC; these verses, rather, are an appendix to the Decalogue. In addition, the CC has undoubtedly undergone a Deuteronomistic redaction, as we will see below.

III.1.3. Ur-Deuteronomy

Baltzer, Klaus. *Das Bundesformular* (WMANT 4; Neukirchen Kreis Moers: Neukirchener, 1960). **Craigie**, Peter C. *The Book of Deuteronomy* (NICOT; Grand Rapids: Eerdmans, 1976). **Kline**, Meredith G. *The Treaty of the Great King: The Covenant Structure of Deuteronomy. Studies and Commentary* (Grand Rapids: Eerdmans, 1963). **Klostermann**, August, *Der Pentateuch: Beiträge zu seinem Verständnis und seiner Entstehungsgeschichte* (Leipzig: G. Böhme, 1907). **Mayes**, A. D. H. *Deuteronomy* (NCB; London: Oliphants, 1981). **Merendino**, Rosario P. *Das deuteronomische Gesetz: Eine literarkritische, gattungs- und überlieferungsgeschichtliche Untersuchung zu Dt 12–26*

(BBB 31; Bonn: P. Hanstein, 1969). **Rad**, Gerhard von. *Studies in Deuteronomy* (SBT 9; London: SCM: 1953). **Seitz**, Gottfried. *Redaktionsgeschichtliche Studien zum Deuteronomium* (BWANT 93; Stuttgart: Kohlhammer, 1971).

Ur-Deuteronomy (*Urdeuteronomium*) is the hypothetical version of Deuteronomy, found in 622 by the priest Hilkiah in the temple (2 Kgs 22:8), which inspired King Josiah's reforms (see p. 189). According to August Klostermann, Deut 12–28, the legal portion of the book, is a "collection of material for a public reading of the law (*Der Pentateuch*, 344). Just as with the Covenant Code, this collection includes apodictic rules of law for moral and religious-cultic life formulated in the second person singular (e.g., Deut 14:22; 15:1), as well as casuistic laws (e.g., 13:2–4, 7–12). Here, however, these genres are not used in their pure form; they are integrated into a didactic address in which Moses teaches the people how to organize their religious, political, and social life. The Deuteronomic collection of laws is contained in a speech of a human "I," while all other law corpora are stylized as the word of God. Here laws are interpreted; through the law, and with it, the interpretation itself achieves equal validity (see, e.g., Deut 17:8–13). The original legal statements thus underwent explanatory expansions that not only added much to them but also changed the pure form of the legal statement so that, to give one example, the apodictic laws are formulated in the second person plural or are expanded with casuistic introductions. In other words, the book emerged from a living practice of public law readings. According to Klostermann, this explains its double nature, namely, that it seems to be at one moment the law and at next moment a commentary on it (*Der Pentateuch*, 345–47) "Here Klostermann not only stated something fundamental about the genre of the law corpus, but he also recognized an important moment of the tradition: the juxtaposition of law, interpretation, and illustration as a unique binding word" (Merendino, *Das Gesetz*, 5).

Gerhard von Rad supported a similar view, from a genre-critical and somewhat more detailed perspective: "Deuteronomy is not divine law in codified form, but preaching about the commandments—at least, the commandments appear in a form where they are very much interspersed with parenesis" (*Studies*, 15). He differentiates among a few basic genres. He finds many "apodictic series," the clearest example of which is Deut 16:19:

לא־תטה משפט	You shall not distort justice.
לא תכיר פנים	You shall not show partiality.
לא־תקח שחד	You shall not accept bribes.

There are other series where one can work out the pure apodictic form by removing the parenetic phrasing, such as 16:21–17:1. Also in Deut 22:5–11, verses 5a, 9a, and 10–11 form an apodictic series, as do verses 2–4, 8aα, bα in 23:1–9 (v. 1 is also an apodictic statement, but it belongs to the previous series; *Studies,* 17–21). According to von Rad, there are only a few conditional rules with a looser style of preaching in Deuteronomy, such as 15:12–18, a series pertaining to slaves, which can be compared to the related series in the Covenant Code, Exod 21:2–11, to trace its original genre. At the same time there are more than a few conditional (that is, casuistic) laws, which were adapted simply by having been transformed into the Deuteronomic "you" style, for example, Deut 21:22–23; 22:6–7; 23:22–24, 25–26; 24:10–12, 19 ("When you reap your harvest in your field and forget a sheaf in the field, you shall not go back to get it; it shall be left for the alien, the orphan, and the widow, so that the Lord your God may bless you in all your undertakings"). There are also purely casuistic laws, that is, legal phrasing without a homiletic tone: 21:15–17, 18–22; 22:13–29; 24:1–4; 25:1–3, 5–10, for example, the the levirate law:

> 5 When brothers reside together, and one of them dies and has no son, the wife of the deceased shall not be married outside the family to a stranger. Her husband's brother shall go in to her, taking her in marriage, and performing the duty of a husband's brother to her, 6 and the firstborn whom she bears shall succeed to the name of the deceased brother, so that his name may not be blotted out of Israel. 7 But if the man has no desire to marry his brother's widow, then his brother's widow shall go up to the elders at the gate and say, "My husband's brother refuses to perpetuate his brother's name in Israel; he will not perform the duty of a husband's brother to me." 8 Then the elders of his town shall summon him and speak to him. If he persists, saying, "I have no desire to marry her," 9 then his brother's wife shall go up to him in the presence of the elders, pull his sandal off his foot, spit in his face, and declare, "This is what is done to the man who does not build up his brother's house." 10 Throughout Israel his family shall be known as "the house of him whose sandal was pulled off." (Deut 25:5-10)

In his thorough study, Gottfried Seitz established the most important formal deviation in the casuistic laws as the intrusion of the address form (e.g., 19:16–19; 22:25–27) and the addition of set phrases. Such phrases are "So you shall purge the evil from your midst" (ובערת; 19:19; 21:21; 22:21, 24; etc.); "do what is right in the sight of YHWH" (21:9; cf. the Deuteronomistic assessment of kings in the Deuteronomistic History); "All Israel shall hear and be afraid" (13:12; 19:20; etc.); "Nor shall your eye pity him" (לא תחוס עינך עליו; 13:9; 19:13; etc.). As specific Deuteronomic genres, von Rad mentions parenetic laws, "which treat a subject in an expansive thematic explanation, without the older underlying rule of law being detectable," e.g., in Deut 13:1–6, 7–19;

17:14–20; 18:9–22; 19:1–13. They are to be understood as "sermon-like utterances by the writer of Deuteronomy upon questions which were vital in his own time." Alongside this is another group of laws based on ancient traditions that are not of a legal but of a cultic nature (e.g., 21:1–9; 26:1–11). In Deut 20:1–9, von Rad recognizes ancient norms of holy war (*Studies*, 23).

In his work on Deuteronomic law, Rosario P. Merendino carried out a very detailed genre-critical analysis. I would like to illustrate it with an example:

> A characteristic example of how ancient laws were transmitted is found in section 15:1–3, 7–11: an apodictic commandment (vv. 1–2aα, 3) is explained with a legal interpretation (v. 2aβb), expanded with brief parenesis (vv. 7–8) and impressed with a bit of preaching (vv. 9–11). In the law in 15:12–14a, positive and negative wordings alternate. The law is then expanded with a casuistic interpretation (vv. 16–17). The section 15:19–23 shows the same characteristics. Verses 15, 18 originate from the use of 15:12–17 in preaching. (Merendino, *Das Gesetz*, 400)

As a literary genre, Merendino also discusses the *tô'ēbâ* laws, which borrow their name from the formula תועבת יהוה הוא, "it is abhorrent to the Lord." Almost all the commandments that are based on the *tô'ēbâ* formula are worded negatively, making them apodictic (e.g., 16:21–17:1). The apodictic style also predominates in humanitarian precepts (23:16–24:18). At the same time, Merendino considers the *bi'artā* texts—so called because of the phrase ובערת, "you shall purge"—casuistic legislation (e.g., 17:2–7). A. D. H. Mayes has shown that the *tô'ēbâ* and *bi'artā* texts were for the most part written by the Deuteronomist himself (Mayes, *Deuteronomy*, 51–52). Finally, Merendino tries to characterize the various text collections that combined to form Deuteronomy as follows (see page 195):

> The constant reference to a "you," which almost always characterizes the *Urtexte* and their additions, the effort to justify or explain the laws, and the occurrences of parenesis and sermonizing are all signs that in the transmission of the law, the concern did not simply lie in the preservation of certain ordinances but rather in the actual understanding of the texts, and with the education and edification of people. One thinks of the family, the local community, and later the local levitical education as the standard bearers of this tradition. (*Das Gesetz*, 400–401)

In the 1950s and 1960s Klaus Baltzer (*Das Bundesformular*) and others found the structure of the ancient Near Eastern vassal treaties in the structure of the (Ur-)Deuteronomy. Both contain a historical prologue, covenantal duties (i.e., laws), and a list of blessings and curses. In addition, a few Deuteronomistic terms, expressions, and customs, such as the appearance of the vassal before the king (Deut 16:16–17) or the public reading of the treaty (31:10–13), seem to have such a treaty background. Authors such as Meredith G. Kline and the somewhat more cautious Peter C. Craigie inferred that Deuteronomy originated in the Mosaic period, as the Hittite international treaties can be dated to the fifteenth to thirteenth centuries (Kline, *Treaty*; Craigie, *Deuteronomy*). Against that it should be emphasized that the Ur-Deuteronomy is more similar to the law corpora than it is to the treaties. The correspondence with vassal treaties in Deuteronomy has its origin in the Deuteronomistic redaction that, through the inclusion of the Decalogue, connected the book with the events at Sinai, shaping it into a covenantal book. Thus, the Neo-Assyrian treaties from the ninth to seventh centuries might more likely have been their inspiration (on this, see Mayes, *Deuteronomy*, 53–54).

III.1.4. Wisdom Literature: The Proverbs of Solomon

TUAT 3. **Cox**, Dermot. *Proverbs, with an Introduction to the Sapiential Books* (OTM 17; Wilmington, Del.: Michael Glazier, 1982). **Crenshaw**, James L. *Old Testament Wisdom: An Introduction* (Atlanta: John Knox, 1981). **Duesberg**, Hilaire, and I. **Fransen**, *Les scribes inspirés* (1938–39; repr., Maredsous: Abbaye de Maredsous, 1966). **Eissfeldt**, Otto. *Der Maschal im Alten Testament: Eine wortgeschichtliche Untersuchung nebst einer literargeschichtlichen Untersuchung der genannten Gattungen "Volkssprichwort" und "Spottlied"* (BZAW 24; Giessen: A. Töpelmann, 1913). **Gemser**, Berend. *Sprüche Salomos* (2nd ed.; HAT 16; Tübingen: Mohr Siebeck, 1963). **Golka**, Friedemann W. "Die israelitische Weisheitsschule oder 'des Kaisers neue Kleider,'" *VT* 33 (1983): 257–70. **Golka**. "Die Königs- und Hofsprüche und der Ursprung der israelitischen Weisheit," *VT* 36 (1986): 13–36. **Golka**. *Die Flecken des Leoparden: Biblische und afrikanische Weisheit im Sprichwort* (Arbeiten zur Theologie 78; Stuttgart: Calwer, 1994). **Hermisson**, Hans-Jürgen. *Studien zur israelitischen Spruchweisheit* (WMANT 28: Neukirchen-Vluyn: Neukirchener, 1968). **Maire**, T. "Proverbes XXI 15ss.: Enseignement à Shalishôm?" *VT* 45 (1995): 227–38. **McKane**, William. *Proverbs: A New Approach* (OTL; London: SCM, 1970). **Meinhold**, Arndt. *Die Sprüche* (ZBK 16; Zurich: Theologischer Verlag, 1991). **Murphy**, Roland E. *Wisdom Literature: Job, Proverbs, Ruth, Canticles, Ecclesiastes, and Esther* (FOTL 13; Grand Rapids: Eerdmans, 1981). **Plöger**, Otto. *Sprüche Salomos* (BKAT 17; Neukirchen-Vluyn: Neukirchener, 1984). **Preuss**, Horst Dietrich. *Einführung in die alttestamentliche Weisheitsliteratur* (Kohlhammer Urban-Taschenbücher 383; Stuttgart: Kohlhammer, 1987). **Rad**, Gerhard von. *Wisdom in Israel* (London: SCM, 1972). **Schmidt**, Johannes. *Studien zur Stilistik der alttestamentlichen Spruchliteratur* (Alttestamentliche Abhandlungen 13.1; Münster: Aschendorff, 1936). **Skladny**, Udo. *Die ältesten Spruchsammlungen in Israel* (Göttingen: Vandenhoeck & Ruprecht, 1961). **Westermann**, Claus. "Weisheit im Sprichwort,"in *Schalom: Studien zu Glaube und Geschichte Israels. Alfred Jepsen zum 70. Geburtstag* (ed. Karl-Heinz Bernhardt; Arbeiten zur Theologie 46; Stuttgart:

Calwer, 1971). **Westermann.** *Roots of Wisdom: The Oldest Proverbs of Israel and Other Peoples* (trans. J. Daryl Charles; Louisville: Westminster John Knox, 1995). **Whybray,** R. N. *The Intellectual Tradition in the Old Testament* (BZAW 135; Berlin: de Gruyter, 1974). **Zimmerli,** Walther. "Zur Struktur der alttestamentlichen Weisheit," *ZAW* 51 (1933): 177–204.

There are books in the Old Testament that are generally considered wisdom literature, for example, Proverbs or Qohelet. In this type of literature, the author artfully expresses real experiences and reflections on them. The word חכם ("wise") describes those who, as either professionals or officials, are experts in their field (Exod 28:3; 31:3; 1 Kgs 7:14; Isa 40:20; Ezek 27:8), are experienced advisors/counselors (2 Sam 13:3; 20:16), or are experienced elders (Job 12:12; 15:10) who can read and write and who know how to apply the law (Jer 2:8; 8:8–12). In the Old Testament wisdom means more than being capable of coping with practical life tasks, since wisdom is also permeated by a need to search for and understand the order of the world in both ethical and cosmic spheres (Preuss, *Einführung*, 11, 29). The kings had men in their service who advised them or oversaw their administration. They are often mentioned in the books of Kings, in Isaiah, and in Jeremiah as servants of the king (עבדים), as authority figures or ministers (שרים), as advisors (יועדים). Mostly they appear to have belonged to the scribal class (סופרים). There is a *communis opinio* in exegetical literature that wise men made up a professional group whose members had to complete their education at a suitable school. I quote as an example a statement by Berend Gemser on this matter:

> The concept of "wisdom" has a technical sense from the activity of specific groups that were devoted to the formulation and collection of rules pertaining to life skills and used them to teach youth.... Closely associated with the ruling circles and the official advisors—the "elders," from whose experience many of the life rules were borrowed and placed alongside the popular proverbial wisdom—they were found especially in official circles involved in the development of public policy. The technical term for them was "scribe" (Heb. סֹפֵר). (*Sprüche*, 2)

In Egypt and Mesopotamia as well, the wise men, also called scribes, were important civil servants trained in special schools. The wise man Ahiqar, whose history and words were found on a few sheets of papyrus from the fifth century in Elephantine in Egypt, is introduced in these texts as Assyria's advisor and Sennacherib's seal-bearer. From the eighth century on, wise men are mentioned alongside priests, prophets, and warriors as part of the ruling class (Isa 3:3; 5:21; 19:14; Jer 8:8; 18:18; Ezek 7:26). However, R. N. Whybray has shown that חכם is never given as the title of a person or as a description of a group of people in the historical books, Isaiah, or Jeremiah (Whybray, *Intellectual Tradition*, 17). The common use of the adjective as an attribute of such people is limited to Isaiah, and Whybray believes that in Isaiah's time it showed only that politicians believed themselves to possess superior intelligence. It cannot be proven that schools actually existed in Israel during the monarchy, but in my opinion it is entirely possible, and considering the situation in neighboring lands—not least among them Ugarit—it is quite probable. Jesus Sirach also spoke of a house of study (בית מדרש; Sir 51:23) and of the ישיבה, meaning a place of learning (51:29); however, this evidence is too recent to have probative value. After considering the use of the adjective חכם in wisdom literature, Whybray comes to the conclusion that the adjective is suitable as a name for someone whose great wisdom qualifies him to teach others, but nowhere in the Old Testament does it mean a "teacher," and neither does the plural חכמים represent a class of professional teachers (*Intellectual Tradition*, 48). Nor would there have been a class of scribes who would have been called "the wise men." According to Whybray, Israel's intellectual tradition or an intellectual movement only reflected on the problems of human life; it did not constitute a specific institution with "wise man" as a specific position. Considering that many of the statements are aimed at the young, the educational purpose of the sayings should not be underestimated. Whybray may be correct about this, but the conclusion of his argumentation is solely negative.

The situation in the neighboring countries lends no small amount of credibility to the hypothesis of a professional class of wise men. It is true, however, that education was not only aimed at the training of officials; many of the wisdom sayings pertain to prudent daily conduct of life (see Plöger, *Sprüche*, xxi–xxii). Many of the wisdom sayings come from daily life in Israel and convey the "common sense" of some part of the Israelite people. This hypothesis has rightly been stressed and defended by Friedemann W. Golka, who uses African material for comparison. In his opinion, there is no reason to contest the idea that the proverbs were collected at court, but their origins are in popular speech, since "the genre of the proverb is found among *illiterate* peoples" ("Die Weisheitsschule," 270; see also idem, "Die Königs- und Hofsprüche").

The oldest collections of Proverbs that we know of come from Egypt, especially from the First Intermediate Period (2155–2040 B.C.E.). This was a period of radical social and political change that prepared for the emergence of the literary genre of wisdom teachings (see *TUAT* 3:192). The oldest are the Instruction of Ptahhotep (circa 2000 B.C.E.); Instruction for King Merikare, from the same period; and the Instruction of Amenemhet I (1991–1962). After this came the Instruction of Amenemopet (Twentieth Dynasty, 1186–1070); the Instruction of Ani, from the same period; and the Instruction of Onchsheshonqy; P.Louvre 2414; and P.Insinger. The Instruction of Amenemopet has been of especially great significance in biblical studies, as Prov 22:17–23:11 is indisputably influenced by it (for another opinion, see Maire, "Proverbes XXI"). In Mesopotamia proverbs and collections of proverbs in Sumerian and Akkadian, which were used in classes, had existed since time immemorial (see *TUAT* 3:2). Finally, there is a collection of proverbs in Aramaic under the name of the aforementioned Ahiqar, which is embedded in a narrative. According to Ingo Kottsieper the proverbs of Ahiqar can be used as evidence of the wisdom tradition in the first quarter of the first millennium B.C.E. among the southern Syrian Arameans, a direct neighbor of Israel (3:321). The many parallels in both style and content between the prolific ancient Near Eastern wisdom literature and Hebrew wisdom literature point to a shared *Sitz im Leben*, at least among the collections, which is often very helpful in interpretation. The international character of wisdom also gives Israelite wisdom proverbs a universal tone: they are more secular and intellectual than religious, and there is no mention of the connection between YHWH and his people. This does not mean that God is entirely absent from wisdom thought, though this literature refers to the deity more as the God of creation than as the God of salvation. Plöger rightly pointed out that, in view of the distribution of these writings, the occasional mention of YHWH should not be read as a reinterpretation of older profane wisdom material. "They could indicate that a connection to belief in YHWH was already taken for granted in older wisdom, and did not require that it always be mentioned.... The desire to express this connection more explicitly might have arisen at a later time, as undoubtedly can be assumed of chaps. 1–9" (*Sprüche*, xxxv). (For a thorough analytical overview of ancient Near Eastern wisdom, one might refer to McKane, *Proverbs*, 49–208; for a shorter overview, see Preuss, *Einführung*, 12–30; Meinhold, *Die Sprüche*, 26–37.)

The characteristic genre of biblical wisdom literature is the *māšāl* (משל), which naturally is not analyzed in the Bible. In Hebrew, the Proverbs are called משלי שלמה, "the *māšāl*s of Solomon." Usually this noun is derived from a verbal root that means something like "to be equal." According to K.-M. Beyse, however, there is in the Bible only a denominative verb, derived from the noun *māšāl*, which in the qal and piel means "to make a proverb," in the niphal "to be equated with," in the hithpael "to become equal," and in the hiphil "to compare with" (*TDOT* 9:64–65). While many proverbs are indeed comparative, the term *māšāl* has many other uses in the Bible. The breadth of this genre description can be seen in its synonyms, which are given in Prov 1:6: "To understand a proverb (משל) and a figure (מליצה), the words of the wise (דברי חכמים) and their riddles (חידתם)." Proverbs 1:2–5 explains the content and purpose of these proverbs: "For learning about wisdom and instruction, for understanding words of insight, for gaining instruction in wise dealing, righteousness, justice, and equity; to teach shrewdness to the simple, knowledge and prudence to the young—let the wise also hear and gain in learning, and the discerning acquire skill." The biblical term *māšāl* is not only used for the proverbs typical of Proverbs or Qoheleth. In 1 Kgs 5:12–13 it refers to something more like the "natural scientific" lists similar to those found in Egypt or Mesopotamia. The term has also been used for expansions of individual proverbs into a didactic speech (Ps 49:5) or retrospection on Israel's history in the form of an exhortation or a warning (Ps 78:2). An oracle can also be called a *māšāl* (e.g., the sayings of Balaam in Num 23:7, 18; 24:3, 15, 20–21, 23 or the riddles in Ezek 17:2; 24:3; on this, see Beyse, TDOT 9:65–66).

According to Otto Eissfeldt, the noun *māšāl* originally referred to a folk aphorism; the nuance "wisdom adage" (*Weisheitsspruch*) is an expansion at this original meaning. While the content remained primarily the same, the most prosaic folk aphorism was extended to the art form of *parallelismus membrorum* (Eissfeldt, *Der Maschal*, 45–52). This view of the original meaning of the noun *māšāl* cannot be proven, because in ancient Israel there was no critical reflection on this genre. Indeed, there is no proof that the folk saying was originally prosaic and was only later reworked into *parallelismus membrorum*, and the theory is further contradicted by the African parallels (Golka, "Die Königs- und Hofsprüche"). Whatever the case, some of the sayings that Eissfeldt considered to be folk sayings probably did not have folk origins but came rather out of educated circles, or were at least artfully reworked and honed (see Hermisson, *Studien*, 50). If a saying betrays Egyptian or other foreign influence—though similarity does not necessarily mean influence—it can hardly be of folk composition and should rather be ascribed to scholarly work. In 1968, many years and much research later, Hans-Jürgen Hermisson skillfully summarized a nuanced genre-critical *communis opinio*:

> It is generally acknowledged that at a certain point the proverbs had their *Sitz im Leben*, their place of cultivation, and transmission in a class of the wise, and at the royal court, if one assumes preexilic origin. Here among the "wise" the collections were organized; here at least some of the proverbs were coined or re-coined; and here the proverbial wisdom was used for specific didactic purposes.
>
> The second point of agreement: this *Sitz im Leben* of the proverbs is often not the original one, and its place of transmission is also not its place of origin. One must look further back for the provenance of at least a certain number of the proverbs in the biblical book of Proverbs. It is generally accepted that a great number of *folk aphorisms* were included in the proverbs collected in the book of Proverbs, either unaltered or instead first artistically cast by the wise. (*Studien*, 24; cf. Plöger, *Sprüche*, xvii; Meinhold, *Die Sprüche*, 16)

His own studies led Hermisson to the conclusion that many of the "proverbs from the biblical book are predominantly independent wordings of the wise as representatives of an educated class in Israel" (*Studien,* 81). The number of actual proverbs is relatively small. Probably only a few of them have a folk origin. The exhortations probably stem from Egyptian impulses and belong to didactic wisdom. The wisdom sayings are therefore, for the most part, native to the educated class. As in neighboring countries, this education would have been organized in some sort of school, a place of training not only for officials and scribes but also for the sons of prominent members of society. This does not mean, however, that the collection of proverbs was originally or solely composed for lessons. Surely many of these proverbs originated in lessons and grew into small collections through lesson praxis. The creation of proverbs and the development of the so-called collections was a literary process that presumes an author or collector—all the more so, if Udo Skladny is correct that the contents of the older collections are unified. As Hermisson explains, "The original purpose of the individual collections was not to serve as a textbook—though they would have been used as such—but as reading material for the class educated at the wisdom school, or simply for anyone who could read" (*Studien,* 136). This "education wisdom comes from the circles of the propertied scribe and official classes" (Preuss, *Einführung,* 41).

Hermisson has carefully studied the forms of the wisdom proverbs (*Studien,* 141–92; cf. Meinhold, *Die Sprüche,* 16–21). The basic form of the Proverb is the aphoristic statement, also called the aphorism or *gnomon.* This is "an epigram that organizes matters whose relationships are not obvious" (Meinhold, *Die Sprüche,* 17). Oriental wisdom enjoys expressing itself in statements in which the things, people, or events that at first glance have nothing in common with each other, are connected, contrasted, compared, or set in opposition to one another. The basic form of the proverb's aphoristic sentence is the nominal clause, which expresses an equation by means of a simple coordination, for example, "Whoever loves discipline, loves knowledge" (Prov 12:1a). This form makes it impossible to tell which is the subject and which the predicate. In terms of meaning, however, it is usually clear what a statement is about, for example, "he who destroys his house is one who seeks to make profits" (Prov 15:27a): the meaning is undoubtedly "one who is seeking profits destroys his house." In *parallelismus membrorum,* the poetic feature that is also found in proverbs, these sorts of sentences are placed side by side, for example:

> One who loves transgression loves strife;
> One who builds a high threshold invites broken bones. (Prov 17:19)

Here we must say a little bit about *parallelismus membrorum*. This parallelism between two or three parts of verses or *stichoi*, which usually have three or four accented syllables, appears in the book of Proverbs in three forms. The basic form is the so-called *synonymous parallelism*: both halves of the verse mean the same thing and vary only in wording and association (cf. the previously cited statement, Prov 17:19). This type of parallelism is occasionally chiastically structured, as in Prov 4:24:

> Avoid all falseness of mouth,
> and wrongness of lips keep far from you.

Another form is *antithetical parallelism*, in which each part of the verse is the opposite of the other, for example:

> Those who guard their mouths preserve their lives;
> Those who open wide their lips come to ruin. (Prov 13:3 NRSV)

Antithetical parallelism is the most frequent form in the book of Proverbs.

Finally, in *synthetic parallelism*, the second part of the thought (and third part, if applicable) continues the first: the part of the verse that follows the first part cannot exist without it. The principle of parallelism begins to fall apart here, although this form is quite old and is attested in Ugaritic literature. An example from Proverbs:

> The name of the Lord is a strong tower,
> The righteous run into it and are safe. (Prov 18:10 NRSV)

In the context of the nominal statements, comparative rhetorical devices are to be found, although in their content they are complex constructions: "Cold water to a thirsty soul and good news from a far country." Here the comparative particle (כ-כן) make clear this special form of connection:

> As [כ] in water face answers to face,
> So [כן] the mind of man reflects the man. (Prov 27:19 RSV)

In the nominal sentence an action-result relationship can be expressed through a simple side-by-side placement:

> A wicked man earns deceptive wages,
> but one who sows righteousness gets a sure reward. (Prov 11:18 RSV)

In these comparative statements the "teaching" is implicit and the readers/hearers are challenged to come up with the point based on their own reflection and experience. Often the act–consequence process is made more explicit through particles or nouns (ל, "toward"; אחר, "afterwards"; אחרית, "end"; ראשון, "beginning"; לפני, "before"). The nominal phrase can occasionally be replaced by a verbal phrase with a pendent construction (called a "complex nominal sentence" by Hermisson and others):

> The house of the wicked, it will be destroyed;
> and the tent of the upright, it will flourish. (Prov 14:11)

The statement (*Aussagesatz*) occasionally becomes a judgment, for example, "It is not right to be partial to the guilty" (18:5a). "Here there are no longer two separate phenomena brought into an organized relationship but rather *one* phenomenon is mentioned, set up in a simple value system of good and not good, smart and dumb, wise and foolish, etc." (Hermisson, *Studien*, 154). One special form of the judgment statement is the "better … than" proverb; another is the beatitude (אשרי, "blessed is he"), for example, "Better to be despised and have a servant, than to be honored and lack food" (12:9); and "Happy is the one who is never without fear, but one who is hardhearted will fall into calamity" (28:14).

Judgment statements can be found also in the so-called compound nominal sentence form: the subject in the *casus pendens* is then the expression of the underlying judgment, as in Prov 14:15: "The simple believe everything, but the clever consider their steps"; this means that one who believes every word is an oaf, and so on.

A very commonly used form of the statement is the combined nominal clause in which the finite verb does not describe an action but in which a declaration is made about a subject, for example, "Whoever walks in integrity walks securely, but whoever follows perverse ways will be found out" (10:9). This is applicable also when the *casus pendens* functions in regard to the verb as the direct object or as a prepositional object: "Sinners: misfortune pursues them" (13:21), or: "One who repays good with evil: evil will not depart his house" (17:13). Occasionally proverbs outdo the first statement with the second with אף כי, "how much more so,"

> See, the upright: they are repaid on earth;
> how much more: the wicked and the sinner! (Prov 11:31)

A statement can also take the form of a verbal clause. In that case, it depicts an event that is characteristic of a concrete situation or of a certain person in a concrete situation: "The lazy person buries his hand in the dish, and will not even bring it back to the mouth" (19:24; variant in 26:15). A nominal phrase can precede or follow a verbal phrase: "Bread gained by deceit is sweet, but afterward the mouth will be full of gravel" (20:17). Here wisdom begins to narrate. Examples of wisdom narration are found in Prov 24:30–34; 6:5–11; 7:7–23. These are example narratives, in which the characters are typical ones. A form of statement that is easy to recognize literarily is the numerical proverb (Prov 30:15–33), which is also found in Ugaritic and among the aphorisms of Ahiqar:

> Three things are never satisfied; four never say, "Enough":
> Sheol, the barren womb, the earth ever thirsty for water,
> and the fire that never says "Enough." (Prov 30:15b–16)

The book of Proverbs also contains exhortations, formulated either in the imperative or the jussive, such as Prov 23:31: "Do not look at wine when it is red, when it sparkles in the cup…"; or 6:6: "Go to the ant, you lazybones; consider its ways, and be wise." These are clearer than statements and are explicitly pedagogical; generally they give grounds for the exhortation, which is either joined with כִּי, ("because"), פֶּן, ("lest"), לְמַעַן, ("in order that") or else simply placed alongside in a sentence. "Do not put yourself forward in the king's presence or stand in the place of the great; for (כִּי) it is better to be told, 'Come up here'" (25:6–7).

Hermisson summarizes his findings on the forms of speech in proverbial wisdom, especially indicative statements, as follows:

> The effort expended on organizing phenomena can be seen in the diversity of sentence forms, individual proverbs, as well as the construction of proverbs into collections. Taken as a whole there are three motifs that gave rise to the forms: **theoretical** (regulative-cognitive), **didactic**, and the **aesthetic/artistic moment**. These are found in different degrees in the various forms of wisdom, partly interwoven with one another and partly separate. Thus the proverbs are missing the didactic element, while in the example narratives and exhortations, the motif of the search for order stays somewhat in the background. (*Studien*, 188–89)

Here Hermisson rightly underlines the aesthetic-artistic moment. Many proverbs have a clearly aesthetic function: joy in the beautiful, polished word.

In general, the proverbs are strung together only loosely. Content and connections among key words, associations, and paronomasia all play a role in this. For example, small groups form out of proverbs that begin with the same first letter (11:9–12) or the same first word (10:2–3) or are formulated in the same participial style (26:7–10) or with the same key word (30:18–20: "way"). The same thematic material can also provide the basis of a group (see also Preuss, *Einführung*, 48). Sometimes the connection is no longer recognizable to us or is simply not there. Consequently some proverbs have no context, or at least context does not play the same role as it does in other biblical books (see McKane, *Proverbs*, 10). The case is quite different in the extensive genre of the didactic address (*Lehrrede*), found especially in the later collection Prov 1–9. There is, however, more context in the book of Proverbs than McKane is willing to admit.

III.2. Works

Albert de Pury rightly claims that the period between 750 and 680 appears to have been the first highly productive literary period in Israelite and Judean history.

> The Old Testament contains a great number of literary compositions the first redaction of which may have been written down in this period. These works are of strikingly different literary genres, and although they are of limited proportions, most of these works display thematic coherence, are linguistically succinct, and are of high literary quality—as if the sudden possibility of written literature had released long-bottled-up creative powers. (de Pury, in *Ein Gott allein? JHWH-Verehrung und biblischer Monotheismus im Kontext der israelitischen und altorientalischen Religionsgeschichte* [ed. Walter Dietrich and Martin A. Klopfenstein; OBO 139; Göttingen: Vandenhoeck & Ruprecht, 1994], 417–18)

III.2.1. Prophetic Works

Birkeland, Harris. *Zum hebräischen Traditionswesen: Die Komposition der prophetischen Bücher des Alten Testament* (Oslo: Dybwad, 1938). **Engnell**, Ivan. "Profetia och Tradition," *SEÅ* 12 (1947): 110–39. **Gunkel**, Hermann. *Die Propheten* (Göttingen: Vandenhoeck & Ruprecht, 1917). **Gunneweg**, Antonius H. J. *Mündliche und schriftliche Tradition der vorexilischen Prophetenbücher als Problem der neueren Prophetenforschung* (FRLANT 73; Göttingen: Vandenhoeck & Ruprecht, 1959). **Hardmeier**, Christof. "Verkündigung und Schrift bei Jesaja: Zur Entstehung der Schriftprophetie als Oppositionsliteratur im alten Israel," *Theologie und Glaube* 73 (1983): 119–34. **Millard**, A. R. "An Assessment of the Evidence for Writing in Ancient Israel," in *Biblical Archaeology Today: Proceedings of the International Congress on Biblical Archaeology, Jerusalem, April 1984* (Jerusalem: Israel Exploration Society, 1985). **Mowinckel**, Sigmund. *Prophecy and Tradition: The Prophetic Books in the Light of the Study of the Growth and History of the Tradition* (Oslo: Dybwad, 1946). **Nielsen**, Eduard. *Oral Tradition: A Modern Problem in Old Testament Introduction* (SBT 11; London: SCM, 1954).

Previously it was commonly assumed that the prophets themselves were authors. Indeed, the book of Ezekiel gives the impression of being a unified and closed literary composition, at least in comparison to the other prophetic books. Isaiah 30:8 mentions the writing of the prophet Isaiah, and in Jer 30:2; 36:2 YHWH gives the prophet the task of writing his words on a scroll, which he accomplished by dictating it to Baruch. This cannot be applied to all the prophets, however. The noticeable difference in scope and construction between the Hebrew text of Jeremiah and the LXX version shows that this book, too, had a long formational history. Martin Luther already noticed that individual prophetic books have only minimal internal coherence. He even ventured an explanation for this: the prophetic statements were probably not published by the prophets themselves, but by *scribae*, without any chronological organization.

Hermann Gunkel's view was therefore not entirely novel. He conceived of the origin of the prophetic books as follows: the prophets originally spoke only short oracles; later they or their disciples collected these sayings, which were organized neither by content nor by chronology; still later these collections were brought together in the books in their current form (Gunkel, *Die Propheten*, 114). It follows that in the interpretation of the prophetic books the criterion of coherence should be applied with caution. If one is attempting to describe the structure of a prophetic book, one should first discern whether there is in fact a structure at all.

Along the same lines, Hugo Gressmann called sticking to the idea of the unity of a prophetic book the πρῶτον ψεῦδος of literary criticism (*ZAW* 34 [1914]: 258). This opinion has become commonplace in introductions to the Old Testament or to prophecy. One should be aware of a few important nuances, however. It cannot be presumed a priori that the prophetic books display no order whatsoever: the collections might be based on an organizing principle either of content (e.g., oracles about foreign nations) or form (oracles that are introduced with the same formulae or are connected by key words).

In the beginning were the oral words of the prophet, which should be distinguished from their written record. Some of the prophetic words were transmitted orally for some time. The writing usually followed later, although it might have begun early in certain cases, for example, among disciples of a prophet (see Isa 8:16). The tradition-critical school in particular has zealously explored the oral character of both the origin and transmission of the prophetic texts. Harris Birkeland attempted to prove that oral transmission was the fundamental and formative force of the tradition both in the ancient Near East and in Old Testament, even if certain texts were kept alongside in written form. The only prophetic words that were preserved were those that retained their meaning in transmission, although certain statements could be made suitable for retention through reinterpretation. Moreover, individual sayings were rarely transmitted; rather, tradition complexes were formed. This explains why the question of the origin of the smallest units is often unanswerable. Texts originally belonging together were lost or replaced so that it is not possible to know with any certainty what originated from the prophets and what from the tradition (Birkeland, *Zum hebräischen Traditionswesen*, 18). One must also take into account that the borders between the spheres of tradition (*Traditionskreisen*) were not always entirely clear, and certain material from one cycle might have entered another and produced parallels. The best-known example is the nearly perfect identity between Isa 2:2–4 and Mic 4:1–3. Another close parallel is found in the oracle against Edom in Obad 1–9 and Jer 49:7–22, and another against Moab in Isa 15:1–16:14 and Jer 48:29–39. Although the written concretization of the oral tradition began rather early, the oral tradition continued alongside the written one. It is possible, though unproven, that written documents were corrected on the basis of oral tradition. It might be possible to get some impressions of the great personalities behind the original traditions, but this cannot be accomplished with conventional textual editing (elimination of glosses, filtering out of original speech units). "The question of the *ipsissima verba* of the prophet, if at all solvable, will not be solved literarily, but tradition-critically" (Birkeland, *Zum hebräischen Traditionswesen*, 22). The tradition-critical school was continued in the Scandinavian countries by exegetes like Ivan Engnell, Arvid Kapelrud, and Eduard Nielsen. According to Engnell ("Profetia"), the role of oral tradition was rather limited in books such as Joel, Nahum, and Habakkuk, while it was very important in Amos, Hosea, Isaiah, and Jeremiah. According to Nielsen, the transition from oral to written transmission occurred as a result of a crisis: at the end of the seventh century in Judah and around the middle of the eighth century in northern Israel. In his exegesis, Nielsen believes it is possible to take certain pericopes as authentic prophetic words.

From the extremes of literary criticisim, Birkeland fell into tradition-historical criticism. After this came a healthy reaction intended to lead to a new equality. Sigmund Mowinckel (*Prophecy and Tradition*) dealt with the problem of biblical transmission in general and in prophetic literature specifically. In his view was undoubtedly literary activity, but the long oral tradition can also not be discounted. It was rather free, so long as the transmitted material was not seen as normative. In prophetic circles the independent proverbs were originally handed down literally: signs of this include the metrical form and the manifold "I"-form, for example, in the visions. Certainly much changed during oral transmission, as can be seen in a comparison of Ps 18 and 2 Sam 22. Neither of the two texts is original, but the best text can be uncovered through comparative study of the two. Over the course of the tradition, the text was subject to reshaping, additions, and even mixing and losses. A source-critical study, according to Mowinckel, must take this process of transmission into account, as well as authors who knowingly formed and organized the tradition complexes. Oral and written transmission went hand in hand and influenced one another, although at some point the written form began to predominate.

Mowinckel's general theory can be summarized in four theses: (1) The individual spoken unit is always the starting point of the tradition. (2) Each tradition developed according to psychological, sociological, and artistic laws typical of the *Sitz im Leben* of this tradition. (3) Since this history leaves traces of form and content in traditional material, it is to some extent possible to analyze the course, that is, the origin, growth, and changes in a complex of traditions. (4) For this the role of written sources and recorded traditions must be taken into consideration (Mowinckel, *Prophecy*, 35–36).

Mowinckel dealt separately with tradition criticism in the exegesis of prophetic books. The first task in such a study is to uncover the original units in a tradition complex. For this, the typical genres used by the prophets must be known, meaning one must use the genre-critical method. Between the oral performance of an oracle and its putting into writing lies a whole history of transmission. The tradition creates complexes based on various criteria that must be thoroughly studied. One schema found often is the "threat–promise" succession, which is found in Isaiah, Micah, Hosea, and Amos. The tradition also grew through the addition of later prophetic words and the reworking of earlier ones. The process scholars previously understood as interpolations or additions to a written text is now seen as a later expansion of a prophetic tradition. In practice, however, many literary-critical arguments retain their validity, even when the literary process is increasingly understood as historical growth rather than as mechanistic glossing of the text.

Mowinckel's conclusion is threefold. (1) Tradition criticism should critically sketch out the history of a tradition. Such a study is very complicated: the tradition's strata must be researched as much as possible, determine their tendencies and consider the primary and secondary aspects of their growth. (2) The most common evolution is one in which an oracle of doom is complemented with a promise of salvation. Occasionally the oracle of doom is transformed into an oracle of salvation. In any case, one must look "behind" the tradition, without being overconfident about the possibility of coming to final conclusions. (3) It is not a priori inappropriate to look for the *ipsissima verba* of a prophet (contra Engnell). This is often an impossible task, but when it is possible one should use all available tools to accomplish it.

Antonius H. J. Gunneweg is against a double affirmation: (1) The oral transmission is the most important one, and the written record and prophetic literature are comparatively late. (2) The literary-critical method should therefore no longer be used, as its goal is to divide primary from secondary material; instead one must proceed strictly tradition-critically. An analysis of Isa 8:1, 16 and especially 30:8 shows that, for Isaiah, the most reliable form of transmission was the written one. According to Jer 36 the written word is more lasting and effective than the oral word—nearly magical. These texts, alongside Hab 2:2; Num 5:11–31; Ezek 2:9–10; 43:11–12, show that the prophets, although originally using the spoken word, were also capable of writing it down and did so. Thus, their message became more permanent and acquired a certain universality. Certainly from Isaiah onward "there was a written tradition of prophetic preaching" but "it was not that the newly begun written transmission replaced oral transmission, or even intended to" (Gunneweg, *Tradition*, 48). According to Gunneweg, the traditional-historical method has not yet succeeded in proving with its results that its starting point is compelling. The logically consistent position should be that all literary criticism is impossible, since the final product of the tradition is homogeneous, and it is therefore impossible to differentiate as strata. This does not tally, however, with exegetical practice.

Oral transmission was undoubtedly much more important in Israel than in our milieu, but it was bound by norms, as can be seen from various Old Testament texts (Exod 13:7–8, 14–15; Num 21:27; Deut 4:9–10; 6:6–7, 20–25; 11:19; 32:7; Josh 4:7–22; 22:24–28; Judg 6:13; Pss 44:2; 78:2–6; Isa 38:19). Other texts, however, show the importance of written text. Already pre-Israelite Canaan was familiar with a flourishing written culture (e.g., Ugarit, El Amarna). The ostraca of Samaria, Lachish, and Arad lead to the conclusion that written documents were common. In the Bible as well, there are many examples of written texts such as laws (Exod 24:4; Isa 10:1; Hos 8:12) or books of laws (1 Sam 10:25), poetic collections like the Book of the Wars of the Lord (Num 21:14) and the Book of the Upright (Josh 10:13; 2 Sam 1:18), along with annals, proverbs, letters, and chronicles. Since Isaiah, the prophets also wrote down some of their words (Isa 8:1–2; 30:8; Jer 51:60; Hab 2:2), and we learn of the formation of a prophetic book from Jeremiah (Jer 36).

Thus we must assume the existence of both forms of transmission side by side. Even if certain texts were performed orally, for example, in liturgy, this does not rule out that their written transmission might have been definitive. As pertains to the prophets, an important role must be conceded to the oral tradition in the transmission of independent units and small collections, even in the development of books. Nevertheless, it is indubitable that the prophets wrote down some of their words rather early, and that written collections existed from Jeremiah on, at the latest. It may have happened even earlier, however, since Hardmeier has shown, based on Isa 6:1–8, 18, and

28-30 that the early notation of the prophetic words must be understood as the formation of a dissident literature. "The document served the insider finding and preservation of the identity of a group of followers around the opposition prophet Isaiah" (Hardmeier, "Verkündigung," 131). Accordingly, written prophecy as literature has its roots in the reflection on the experience of refusal of the oral proclamation, as clearly emerges from Isa 30:8-9. I do not partake in the tradition-critical pessimism regarding the possibility of uncovering the original prophetic words; I believe that some prophetic words are well preserved. At the same time, we must always keep a lookout for conscious or unconscious changes both in oral and in written tradition. It is these that often makes the delimitation of original units and the determination of the original text impossible. Yet I believe that many later revisions can still be uncovered with the use of textual criticism, literary criticism, and genre criticism. These methods, however, must always be supplemented by tradition criticism and redaction criticism in order to follow the history of the prophetic words in their various traditional and redacted strata all the way to the final form of the books. What now can we say about the origin of the prophetic works during our period?

III.2.1.1. Amos

Andersen, Francis I., and David Noel **Freedman**. *Amos: A New Translation with Notes and Commentary* (AB 24A; New York: Doubleday, 1989). **Coote**, Robert B. *Amos among the Prophets: Composition and Theology* (Philadelphia: Fortress, 1981). **Fleischer**, Gunther. *Von Menschenverkäufern, Baschankühen und Rechtsverkehrern: Die Sozialkritik des Amosbuches in historisch-kritischer, sozialgeschichtlicher und archäologischer Perspektive* (Athenäums Monografien: Theologie 74; Frankfurt am M.: Athenäum, 1989). **Fritz**, Volkmar. "Amosbuch, Amos-Schule und historischer Amos," in *Gott und Mensch im Dialog: Festschrift für Otto Kaiser zum 80. Geburtstag* (ed. Markus Witte; BZAW 185; Berlin: de Gruyter, 1989), 29-43. **Gordis**, Robert. "The Composition and Structure of Amos," *HTR* 33 (1940): 239-51. **Harper**, William Rainey. *A Critical and Exegetical Commentary on Amos and Hosea* (ICC; Edinburgh: T&T Clark, 1905). **Hayes**, John H. *Amos, the Eighth-Century Prophet: His Times and His Preaching* (Nashville: Abingdon, 1988). **Horst**, Friedrich. "Die Doxologien im Amosbuch," *ZAW* 47 (1929): 45-54. **Jeremias**, Jörg. "Amos 3-6: Beobachtungen zur Entstehungsgeschichte eines Prophetenbuches," *ZAW* 100 Supplement (1988): 123-38. **Koch**, Klaus. *Amos: Untersucht mit den Methoden einer strukturalen Formgeschichte* (AOAT 30; Kevelaer: Butzon & Bercker, 1976)). **Loretz**, Oswald. "Die Entstehung des Amos-Buches im Licht der Prophetien aus Mari, Assur, Ishkali und der Ugarit-Texte," *UF* 24 (1992): 179-215. **Marti**, Karl. *Das Dodekapropheton* (KHC 13; Tübingen: Mohr Siebedk, 1904). **Paul**, Shalom M. *Amos. A Commentary on the Book of Amos* (Hermeneia; Minneapolis: Fortress, 1991). **Reimer**, Haroldo. *Richtet*

III. THE LITERATURE OF THE ERA

auf das Recht! Studien zur Botschaft des Amos (SBS 149; Stuttgart: Katholisches Bibelwerk, 1992). **Schmidt**, Werner H. "Die deuteronomistische Redaktion des Amosbuches," *ZAW* 77 (1965): 168-93. **Sellin**, Ernst. *Das Zwölfprophetenbuch* (2 vols.; KAT 12; Leipzig: Deichert, 1929, 1930). **Vermeylen**, Jacques. *Du prophète Isaïe à l'apocalyptique: Isaïe, I-XXXV, miroir d'un demi-millénaire d'expérience religieuse en Israël, II* (EBib; Paris: Gabalda, 1978) 519-69. **Weimar**, P. "Der Schluß des Amos-Buches: Ein Beitrag zur Redaktionsgeschichte des Amos-Buches,"*BN* 16 (1981): 60-100. **Weiser**, Artur. *Die Prophetie des Amos* (BZAW 53; Giessen: A. Töpelmann, 1929).**Weiser**, and Karl **Elliger**. *Das Buch der zwölf kleinen Propheten* (2 vols.; ATD 24-25; Göttingen: Vandenhoeck & Ruprecht, 1967). **Willi-Plein**, Ina. *Vorformen der Schriftexegese innerhalb des Alten Testaments: Untersuchungen zum literarischen Werden der auf Amos, Hosea und Micha zurückgehenden Bücherim hebräischen Zwölfprophetenbuch* (BZAW 123; Berlin: de Gruyter, 1971). **Wolff**, Hans Walter. *Joel and Amos: A Commentary on the Books of the Prophets Joel and Amos* (Hermeneia; Philadelphia: Fortress, 1977).

The layout of the book of Amos is clear: (1) a great trial speech about the nations and finally about Israel (chs. 1-2); (2) trial speeches (chs. 3-6); (3) trial visions with a declaration of salvation at the end (chs. 7-9). Many scholars in modern biblical scholarship are convinced that the book was written by the prophet himself in this form, excluding 7:10-17, a prose narrative that originated from the circle of Amos's students.

Robert Gordis, for example ("Composition") is of the opinion that the entirety of Amos was edited approximately in historical order: 1:1-7:9 before the incident in Bethel, chapters 8-9 after the incident; 7:10-17 was added to the first collection before the second was joined to it. According to the most recent commentary, the book of Amos stemmed from the prophet himself—his own synthesis and testament—or was written by one of his closest disciples (Andersen and Freedman, *Amos*, 11). John H. Hayes rejected all literary criticism of the last century and, as he did with Isaiah, abstained from engaging with the history of the origin of the book of Amos (Hayes, *Amos*). These views, similar to those also taken by Shalom M. Paul (*Amos*) are consistent with an unfortunate new tendency in certain exegetical circles in the United States.

Literary-critical studies have amply shown that the book did in fact have a literary history. The doxologies (4:13; 5:8-9; 9:5-6) were probably added later, perhaps for reading during worship. Based on their historical references, the oracles against Tyre and Edom (1:9-12) are (post)exilic, and the Deuteronomistic style betrays the (post)exilic origin of the oracle against Judah (2:4-5). The conclusion (9:11-15), too, is (post)exilic and can be ascribed to a Deuteronomistic edition of the book, along with a few other reworkings such as 2:4-5.

Some commentators, for example, William Rainey Harper or Karl Marti, presume more extensive additions. According to Marti the base material is composed of pamphlets: (1) 1:3–5, 13–15; 2:1–3, 6–8, 9–11*, 13–16; (2) chs. 3–6*; (3) 7:1–9; 8:1–3; 9:1–4, 7; 7:10–17. Secondary are (1) the Judah pieces (2:4–5; 3:1b; 6:1), which presume Deuteronomy and the fall of Jerusalem; (2) historical additions of postexilic origin (1:6–12; 2:10; 5:25; 2:12 [at v. 11]; 5:26; 6:2); (3) postexilic theological additions (4:13; 5:8–9; 9:5–6; 3:7; 8:11–14; 5:13; 8:8; 1:2); (4) announcements of salvation (9:8–15). The base material might have been collected during Isaiah's time and after the fall of the northern kingdom (Marti, *Das Dodekapropheton*, 152–53). According to Harper, the base material was probably written during Isaiah's time, and the Judah section (2:4–5) during Jeremiah's, while the remaining additions were written after the exile. (Harper, *Amos and Hosea*, cxxxi–cxxxiv).

It can be said, along with Ernst Sellin, that the basic framework of the three sections, excepting the later revisions, originated with Amos himself, perhaps even in the traditional sequence, even if he did not write it down himself.

Artur Weiser is of the opinion that the recording of the visions did not occur at the same time as the recording of the sayings and was probably not done by the same hand. The visions were written down first, and later another hand wrote down the sayings (chs. 1–6; 7:10–17); these two collections were united into the present book of Amos only later. The heading "The words of Amos of Tekoa, who saw (visions) two years before the earthquake" was originally only the heading for the visions, the collection having been written down by Amos himself shortly after the earthquake. The additions to the visions text (7:9; 8:3, 4–14) originated from the need to add other popular sayings of the prophet to the text, while 9:8, 9–10 arose from the need to defend the words of the prophet from hostile objections. The 7:10–17 insertion was not written by Amos, although the account might have its origins in a story about Amos; it stood originally at the end of the collection of sayings (chs. 1–6) and was shifted during the unification of the two collections, in order to erase the seam that connected them. The collection of sayings was thus originally framed by the introduction in 1:1–2 (first relative clause and time designation in relation to kings; reference to the visions in the prophet's homeland [Zion]) and the ending with 7:10–17. This was done in the circle of the prophet's friends after his death. The collection soon underwent a few expansions (1:9–12; 2:10, 15; 4:7) and a few additions for clarification (e.g., 2:11–12; 5:6, 14–15, 26). According to Weiser, 6:14 and 7:10–17 hint at the catastrophe of 722, meaning that the collection could have been unified only after 722. The conclusion of the whole book, 9:11–15, which presupposes the exile, points to the exile as the time of the final redaction. The hymnic additions 4:13; 5:8; 9:6 are from a yet later period and point to a lively use of the book of Amos in worship at some later time. According to Weiser, there were only two collections in the eighth century, the visions and the collection of sayings, from which the first most likely originated with Amos himself (*Der Prophetie*, 249-90; almost the same in ATD 24).

Hans Walter Wolff is also convinced that the book of Amos underwent a long literary growth. He differentiates between three strata of the eighth century that originated with Amos and his contemporary followers, as well as three further strata of later interpretation. "The words of Amos from Tekoa" was originally the introduction to the collection of sayings in Amos 3–6, whose base material came from Amos himself. The five vision accounts (7:1–8; 8:1–2; 9:1–4) definitely came from Amos, and it can be assumed that the cycle of sayings about the nations (chs. 1–2) was literarily connected to it, as both have five parts, repeat the frame and main sentences, and have final sections that are thematically closely related (2:13–16 and 9:1–4). An early redaction that can be ascribed to an old school of Amos added 7:9, 10–17 to the vision cycle and joined the visions and the "words." "Hence also the recorded cycles are set as brackets around the 'words of Amos from Tekoa'" (Wolff, *Joel and Amos*, 108). The redactive work of the Amos school can also be found in additions to the cycles that were more or less reworked words of Amos: 8:3, 4–14 and 9:7–10 are connected to the fourth and fifth visions, just as 7:9, 10–17 are connected to the third. These redactions present sayings of Amos and are recognizable by their typical language. A few expansions in the "words of Amos from Tekoa" can also be ascribed to them: 6:2 (which interrupts the series of participles in v. 1 and vv. 3ff.); 6:6b; 5:13–15 (which breaks the connection between 5:12 + 16–17, and which can best be understood as a later interpretation of 5:4); 5:5a "do not make a pilgrimage to Beersheba" (there is no corresponding threat in v. 5b; cf. also 8:14). According to Wolff, the Amos school was active in the generation spanning 760–730, and the main period of their work might have been at the beginning of the Assyrian crisis in the northern kingdom in 735. The physical center of their activity was in Judah, which might be signaled by referring to Israel as the "House of Isaac" (7:16) and to shrines as "high places of Isaac" (7:9), and mentioning the shrine in Beersheba (8:14; 5:5a). In this redaction there is a greater interest in cultic matters than Amos himself had. Wolff finds later redactions in a Bethel interpretation from Josiah's time (1:2[?]; 3:14bα; 4:6–13; 5:6, 8–9; 9:5–6), in a Deuteronomistic redaction (1:1b, 9–12; 2:4–5, 10–12; 3:1b, 7; 5:25–26), which W. H. Schmidt had previously recognized ("Die deuteronomistische Redaktion"), and in a postexilic salvation eschatology (9:11–15 and in a few details in 5:22a; 6:5; 9:8b).

According to Jacques Vermeylen (*Du prophète*), the revisions are much more extensive. Klaus Koch prefers to refer to "compositional arches" rather than redactional layers; in his opinion, the book of Amos is neither a simple collection nor an accumulation of strata but a composition that is the work of one person or a school in which existing collections were reworked (3:9–4:3; 4:6–12; 5:9–17; 5:18–27; 6:1–14; 8:4–14a). The collection 3:9–4:3, for example, was aimed at the inhabitants of Samaria, but the redactor inserted two units from the tradition (3:1–2, 3–8) before it, so that the whole would be aimed at all the "Sons of Israel." He then removed 4:1–3 from it and put it in a new complex (4:1–13), whose theme is the cultic places (Koch, *Amos*).

P. Weimar outlines a redactional history of five strata that comes close to Wolff's conception, although differences in many of the details of the stratification cannot be overlooked, and he distinguishes only two strata from the Assyrian period. The original book of Amos consists of three main parts, while the two cycles that frame it correspond closely to one another both formally and thematically. This redactional layer contains only radical prophecy of doom. The Judean redaction gives the book the character of an ultimate exhortation and overlays the social-critical statements with a critical perspective on the cult (1:1*; 2:7a; 3:13a, 14; 4:4–5; 5:4–5, 21–24; 6:8*, 11; 8:4, 7; 9:8–10*). This redaction probably originated in the (late) period of King Manasseh. The later strata are the Deuteronomistic redaction (probably DtrP), with its focus on the proof of guilt; the early postexilic redaction, with its focus on the analysis of social conduct; and the late postexilic, which accentuates the eschatological dimension of YHWH's actions ("Der Schluß," 96–100).

Robert B. Coote (*Amos*) proposed a redactional history in three phases that is influenced by Wolff and probably also by Weimar, although deliberately simplified. The first stratum consists of a few words originally from Amos about social injustice, aimed at the elite of Samaria. They consist entirely of prophecy of doom and were written down in the eighth century (before 722). The second encompasses most of Amos 1:1–9:6; it puts religious politics into the foreground and particularly with Bethel. This section has an exhortative character and is therefore interested in the figure of the prophet, whose task it is to exhort (cf. 2 Kgs 17:7–18 Dtr!). This redaction originated in the seventh century, sometime between Hezekiah and Josiah, or perhaps somewhat later. If the late-seventh-century date is correct, it could be proto-Deuteronomistic. The structure of three large divisions in which five-part sequences are typical also stems from this second redaction. The third stratum (1:9–12; 2:4–5; 9:7–15), dating from the sixth century, is late or postexilic and promises the restoration (for a similar three-phase redactional history, see Jeremias, "Amos 3–6").

Ina Willi-Plein has worked out a hypothesis that assumes a four-stage literary development:

1. Creation of the unit of visions and oracles against the nations, perhaps even during Amos's life, or surely not long after his death—either way still in the eighth century (7:1–8:3*)

2. דברי עמוס collection, which breaks off in chapter 4 (v. 12). This probably also appeared not too long after Amos, since its dating refers to the earthquake (chs. 1–4*)

3. Independent of the Amos 1–4 collection came the collection, redaction, and further composition and updating of Amos's speeches or fragments, which formed a ring around the core of the visions and of the oracles against the nations. This redaction occurred in Judah after the fall of the northern kingdom, probably during Manasseh's reign. (5:1–9:10)

4. Combination of chapters 1–4 and 5–9 by an exilic redactor who, for his part, inserted more updating additions, added the formula נאם יהוה ("utterance of YHWH") nine times, and concluded with the prospect of the erstwhile reestablishment of statehood (1:1–9:12).

Although 9:11 is reminiscent of the end of the Deuteronomistic History, Willi-Plein does not believe in a Deuteronomistic redaction of the book of Amos. Later on came a few expansions, the most important of them being 9:13–15 and the doxologies. According to Willi-Plein, 7:1–8:3 and chapters 1–4 belong to redactional strata from the eighth century (Willi-Plein, *Vorformen*, 58–69).

Haroldo Reimer's study began in the attempt to "work out the cognitive substance of the oldest traceable compositions of the book of Amos"[2] (*Richtet*, 215). In his opinion, 1:3–2:16* formed an originally independent textual unit; the study of the units 3:9–4:3* and 5:2–6:14 showed that they were inextricable from the former. Thus, he comes to the conclusion that chapters 1–6* most probably formed a unified compositional arch, while the visions section 7:1–9:4* formed an independent textual corpus. The book of Amos thus consists of two originally independent textual corpora, chapters 1–6* and 7–9*, which originated in the northern kingdom shortly after Amos's time but still in the pre-Assyrian period, during the reign of Jeroboam II. The compilation into a single "Ur-book of Amos" also involved some reworking, including the addition of textual units such as 4:4–5; 5:4–5; 8:4–7, and the creation of 9:7–10, the conclusion of the "Ur-book." This had occurred already in the northern kingdom. He also sees further reworking: one Judean reworking, not dated precisely; an update in the Josianic period; a Deuteronomistic reworking in the exile; and a postexilic reworking. According to Reimer, the "Ur-book," which underwent only limited further reworking, originated in the eighth century (see Reimer, *Richtet*, 215–25).

---

2. "[D]en kognitiven Gehalt der aufspürbaren ältesten Kompositionen im Amosbuch herauszuarbeiten."

In contrast to Wolff and most others, Volkmar Fritz believes that less of the book originated with Amos. In his opinion, Amos "can only be clearly established in the first two visions 7:1–6, and the sayings announcing a catastrophe affecting the people, 3:12abα* and 5:3" ("Amosbuch," 42). All further sayings from the collection of chapters 3–6, as well as the foundational material of the preceding cycle of speeches about foreign peoples (chs. 1–2*), and further visions (7:7–9:10), including the narrative on Amos (7:10–17), were developed by the Amos school. Its activity is to be estimated from about 750 to 720, while some of the expansions in chapters 3–6 and 7–9 and the shift of the sayings about foreign peoples (chs. 1–2) to the front of the book can be dated to even after 720. Therefore, with the exception of the Deuteronomistic redaction and a few later additions, the entirety of the book of Amos originated in the second half of the eighth century, which corresponds to the findings of most literary-critical scholars. "As a whole the book of Amos mostly styles itself as a great *vaticinium ex eventu*, in order to explain the disaster that had occurred as having been YHWH's just action" ("Amosbuch," 41).

Oswald Loretz proceeds even more radically. On the basis of the form and content of the book of Amos, he is convinced that its origin is to be dated to the postexilic period. Apart from their present context, the visions display no discernible connection to any prophet Amos. Moreover, Loretz claims that the only thing that can be taken from the Amaziah scene (7:1–17) is that in Judah a tradition about Amos was known and that in the present book there is a postexilic version of it with a strong accent on the exile. In the spirit of postexilic Jewish scribal learning, the entirety of the book of Amos can be seen as a midrash-like creation.

Oswald Loretz rightly states: "On the whole, in the future scholars will have to differentiate between the supposed message of Amos, the pre- and postexilic traditions about his activity, and the various (exilic-)postexilic theologies of the book of Amos" ("Die Entstehung," 204). Many redaction critics have tried this, however, and in my opinion their conclusions are no worse than the ones represented here. In my opinion, the structure and literary form of the book of Amos can still be ascribed to an Amos school, while opinion is still divided on the breadth of the prophet's own contribution. Fritz's minimalism, however, and even more that of Loretz, seems to me exaggerated and not provable. The main redaction, which can be dated to the late eighth century or perhaps better in the seventh century, already seems to manifest a three-part structure. After the fall of the northern kingdom, the prophet's words of doom against social injustice were made into an exhortation to the Judeans to turn away from injustice and from the cult at the shrines of Bethel and Gilgal.

This was shown partly through the studies of Gunther Fleischer on social-critical Amos texts. A few are recognizable among these as texts from Amos himself that condemn social offenses toward specific groups of people (דל, עָנִי, נערה, אביון) (e.g., 2:6b*, 7, 13–14; 3:12, 15; 4:1–3; 5:1–2, 7, 10, 16–17, 21–22*, 27; 6:1*, 4, 6a, 11–12). Like Wolff, Fleischer sees Amos's position vis-à-vis the poor as coming from the tribal wisdom tradition (e.g., Prov 14:31; 22:16, 22; 28:3; Fleischer, *Von Menschenverkäufern*, 201–2), just as he sees the use of terminology like משפט and צדקה and other ethical terms as having come from the ethos of tribal wisdom. There are obviously other authentic texts as well. These, according to Fleischer, were first reworked in the period between Amos's expulsion (7:10–17) and the emerging Assyrian threat (4:4–5; 5:4–5*, 12, 23–24). This redaction, principally in the style of the exhortation, is concentrated on criticism of the cult, in that the cult does not exhibit socially just behavior. A further redaction is dated to the period of the Assyrian threat during the years 733–722 (e.g., 2:15–16; 3:9–11; 5:3, 11; 6:2). A Judean redaction, in which the northern kingdom (designated by the name "Joseph") is used as a warning example for Judah, occurred after the end of the northern kingdom (e.g., 5:6, 14–15; 6:1–3, 6b, 7; 8:4–7). Criticism of cults of foreign gods (5:25–26) is to be ascribed to a Deuteronomistic redaction (Fleischer, *Von Menschenverkäufern*, 259–63). Whatever the case may be, Amos is a prophet of doom who severely condemns social injustice and the hypocritical cult connected to it in the northern kingdom, and it is because of these things that he announces divine judgment against the people. From his threats against the foreign nations (chs. 1–2*), it follows that for Amos YHWH is the Lord of all people.

III.2.1.2. Hosea

See also §I.2.3.1. **Andersen**, Francis I., and David Noel **Freedman**. *Hosea: A New Translation with Introduction and Commentary* (AB 24; Garden City, N.Y.: Doubleday, 1980). **Davies**, Graham I. *Hosea: Based on the Revised Standard Version* (NCB; Grand Rapids: Eerdmans, 1992). **Deissler**, Alfons. *Zwölf Propheten; Hosea, Joël, Amos* (NEchtB; Würzburg: Echter Verlag, 1981). **Emmerson**, Grace I. *Hosea: An Israelite Prophet in Judean Perspective* (JSOTSup 28; Sheffield: JSOT Press, 1984). **Good**, Edwin M. "The Composition of Hosea," *SEÅ* 31 (1966): 21–63. **Jeremias**, Jörg. *Der Prophet Hosea* (ATD 24/1; Göttingen: Vandenhoeck & Ruprecht, 1983). **Leeuwen**, Cornelis van. *Hosea* (POT; Nijkerk: G. F. Callenbach, 1978). **Lemche**, Niels Peter. "The God of Hosea," in *Priests, Prophets, and Scribes: Essays on the Formation and Heritage of Second Temple Judaism in Honour of Joseph Blenkinsopp* (ed. Eugene Ulrich et al.; JSOTSup 149; Sheffield: JSOT Press, 1992), 241–57. **Lindblom**, Johannes. *Hosea literarisch untersucht* (Acta Academiae aboensis: Humaniora 5.2; Åbo: Åbo Akademi, 1927). **Mays**, James Luther. *Hosea: A Commentary* (OTL; London: SCM, 1969). **Naumann**, Thomas. *Strukturen der Nachinterpretation im Buch Hosea* (BWANT 131; Stuttgart: Kohlhammer, 1991). **Nissinen**, Martti. *Prophetie, Redaktion und Fortschreibung* *im Hoseabuch: Studien zum Werdegang eines Prophetenbuches im Lichte von Hos 4 und 11* (AOAT 231; Kevelaer: Butzon & Bercker, 1991). **Nowack**, Wilhelm. *Die kleinen Propheten* (HKAT 3.4; 2nd ed.; Göttingen: Vandenhoeck & Ruprecht, 1903). **Robinson**, Theodore H. *Die zwölf kleinen Propheten: Hosea bis Micha* (HAT 14; 2nd ed.; Tübingen: Mohr Siebeck, 1954). **Yee**, Gale A. *Composition and Tradition in the Book of Hosea: A Redaction-Critical Investigation* (SBLDS 102; Atlanta: Scholars Press, 1987).

In reference to the book of Hosea, too, some exegetes are of the opinion that the prophet wrote it in its entirety (e.g., Abraham Kuenen). Similarly, Wilhelm Rudolph is of the opinion that the book of Hosea was for the most part free of later additions; but at the same time he ascribes its redaction to a Judean who, according to 1:7, presupposes Jerusalem's preservation from Sennacherib's attack of 701 (Rudolph, *Hosea* [KAT 13.1; Gütersloh: Mohn, 1966], 25–27). Ernst Sellin develops a similar theory, in which the book of Hosea originated almost entirely from the prophet, and later redactions added only a small number of words in a few places (Sellin, *Das Zwölfprophetenbuch,* vii–viii). Jamse Luther Mays places the entire redaction of the book in Judah, shortly before the fall of Samaria (Mays, *Hosea,* 15–17), and Alfons Deissler holds the opinion that "at its destruction in 722, the Levites of the northern kingdom brought the book (already in its present form?) … to the south. Here the scroll was adapted 'judaically' and the text was expanded accordingly" (Deissler, *Zwölf Propheten,* 10). In critical exegesis, problems in the text of the book of Hosea are often ascribed to large-scale textual corruption (Marti, *Das Dodekapropheton,* 11; Harper, *Amos and Hosea,* clviii, clxxiii; Nowack, *Die kleinen Propheten,* 10; Robinson, *Die zwölf,* 4). Attempts were also made to explain them as northern Hebrew linguistic forms (e.g., Rudolph, *Hosea,* 20–22). There is little evidence to support the assumption of a specific dialect and "whoever assumes this must postulate a priori that the text originates mainly from the northern kingdom" (Nissinen, *Prophetie,* 12). Literary criticism, however, has already made it clear that the evolution of the book is more complicated.

Edwin M. Good assumes that the collections in the book of Hosea have their own evolution, but he believes it is impossible either to synchronize them or to date the phases of their evolution (Good, *Composition,* esp. 62). This view is probably too pessimistic, however. Wilhelm Nowack points out that in Hos 4–14 speech fragments are brought together that did not originally belong together. According to him, Hos 4–14 was not assembled by Hosea himself; the same goes for Hos 1–3. There are later reworkings, for example, 1:7 (which presupposes Sennacherib's campaign); 2:1–3 (uses Jeremiah and Ezekiel); 4:14a (a reader's addition); and so on (Nowack, *Die kleinen Propheten*). According to Marti, Hosea probably wrote down his prophecies himself, but secondary elements were added, such as sections that pertain to Judah (1:7; 2:2; etc.) and the proclamations of salvation (2:1–3, 16–25; 3:1–5; 5:15–6:3, 5b; 11:10–11; 14:2–10). All are (post)exilic, though not simultaneous (Marti, *Das Dodekapropheton*, 5–11). William Rainey Harper approaches the reconstruction of the book's evolution in a more redaction-critical way. It began, in his opinion, with a collection from Hosea himself. This collection was then enlarged through messianic additions, which are to be dated later than Ezekiel and Deutero-Isaiah (2:1–3, 8, 9, 6–18, 20–35; 3:5; 11:8–11*; 14:2–9). After the exile it received a Judean reworking (1:7; 5:10–14 [Israel changed to Judah]; 6:4; 6:11a–8:14; 10:11b; 12:1b, 3) and, finally, it was expanded with a few explicative additions and glosses that are difficult to date (Harper, *Amos and Hosea*, clix–clxii).

According to Hans Walter Wolff, it is as good as certain that part of the written tradition comes from Hosea himself. He believes that Hos 1:2–6, 8–9; 2:1–3:5 can be seen as a first closed tradition complex with its own literary history: the account of Hosea's early period (1:2–4, 6, 8–9) was connected to some of Hosea's writings (2:4–17; 3:1–5) and expanded with a few later words of Hosea (1:5; 2:1–3, 18–25) (*Hosea: A Commentary on the Book of the Prophet Hosea* [Hermeneia; Philadelphia: Fortress, 1974], 12). A second traditional complex was created out of multiple "action sketches" in Hos 4–11 and was framed with the call "hear the word of YHWH" in 4:1, and the formula נאם־יהוה ("utterance of the Lord"). As the sketches probably come from different times, their organization was a specific act, although there is no reason to doubt their chronological arrangement. The remaining, third tradition is Hos 12–14. The three parts "all belong to the same circle of Hosea's contemporary followers, who were also the forerunners of the Deuteronomic movement" (*Hosea*, xxxi). These parts underwent various small redactional expansions. One redactional hand, for instance, glossed certain sayings through the use of other words of Hosea (e.g., 2:10b from 8:4; 13:2; 4:9 from 12:3; 6:10b from 5:3; 7:10 from 5:5). There was also an early Judean redaction that picked up Judean salvation eschatology (1:7; 3:5; 9:4b) and should be differentiated from a later Judean redaction (4:5a, 15; 5:5b; 6:11a). "We are no longer able to determine when the three transmission complexes were combined into the present book of Hosea. This was probably accomplished with the final redaction, when the superscription in 1:1 was added. The superscription is written in the Deuteronomistic language of a circle of redactors who could have edited a series of preexilic prophetic books as early as the 6th century" (*Hosea*, xxxii)

Cornelis van Leeuwen also assumes that the partial collections were the work of the disciples of the prophet, and that the collection of the whole book occurred later, though he rejects Wolff's proposition that it can be ascribed to the Deuteronomistic redactors of the sixth century (van Leeuwen, *Hosea*, 17–19). Jörg Jeremias, too, ascribes the book of Hosea mostly to the prophet, although he sees the final form of the work as a Judean book (*Der Prophet*, 18–20).

Ina Willi-Plein separates the evolution of the book into eight steps:
1. Small compilation(s?) of sayings made while the prophet was active: 5:8–6:6 (between 732 and 722).
2. A biographical memoir on the life and message of Hosea written soon after 722 by his closest disciples: 1:2–3:4.
3. A collection of the prophet's presumably originally oral statements, based predominantly on mnemonic aspects, begun perhaps before 722; probably completed only later, in Judah: 4:1–9:9 (excepting 5:8–6:6; related to the tradents of Amos's words? Cf 4:15).
4. A collection about the history and salvation history of Israel, without reference to the southern kingdom; 9:10–11:9.
5. Updated collection of threats and invective of Hosea, as an exhortation for the southern kingdom after 722, probably during Manasseh's time, and perhaps connected to the origin of Deuteronomy: 12:1–14:9.
6. Collection and arrangement of all traditions into the book of Hosea with the superscription 1:1; after 586.
7. Postexilic expansions and a new organization of the book based on its oral recitation or liturgical use in the postexilic community.
8. Afterword, from a teacher after the end of the prophetic tradition: 14:10.

The five steps belonging to the period of our interest would include only partial collections of the book of Hosea, which were only assembled after the end of the southern kingdom (Willi-Plein, *Vorformen*, 241–53).

In their detailed commentary Francis I. Andersen and David Noel Freedman offer a cautious, yet overly vague and inconsistent picture of the book of Hosea. A first compilation of oracles and narrative pieces originated in the first half of the seventh century, under Manasseh; the book reached its final form during the Babylonian exile. It is difficult, however, to determine what was in the compilations of the eighth or seventh century, and what was added in the sixth century redaction. At the same time, the authors argue that Hosea was spared any later reworkings, though without solid argumentation (Andersen and Freedman, *Hosea*, 52–57).

In Gale A. Yee's study (*Composition*), Willi-Plein's eight steps are reduced to four. The first, the tradition of the prophet Hosea (H), is a *rîb* (ריב, "accusation") that encompasses nearly the entire book (2:4–13:15*) and has its climax in chs. 12–13*. This central tradition is dated to the Syro-Ephraimitic war, alluded to in 5:8–14*, and also mentions Judah (5:10–14; 12:3). After 722, around the time of Hezekiah's reign, a collector (C) recorded the Hosea tradition in writing for the first time and added Hos 1* as a call narrative. Whereas in H the mother "Rachel" and her children, who was accused by the prophet, represented the northern tribes, she now becomes the wife of the prophet, and her children are also the prophet's children. This collector thus created the metaphor of marriage between YHWH and Israel out of the Hosean tradition. The first redactor (R1) is Judean and has clear Deuteronomistic affinities, with a particular interest in Torah, covenant, central shrine, and the fighting of the Baals. His redaction climaxes in ch. 10*, in which the destruction of the northern kingdom is traced back to the sins of Jeroboam. He is dated to the time of Josiah. The final redactor (R2) is a Deuteronomist, whose background includes the exile. With the superscription in 1:1 he situated the prophet and his book in a specific period of the Deuteronomistic History; in 14:10 he gave the book a Deuteronomistic conclusion. He is also responsible for a few important structural changes through the addition of chapters 3; 11; and 14. According to Yee, therefore, the major portion of the book existed both in oral and written form already in the eighth century.

Based on a study of Hos 1–3, Lothar Ruppert comes to a very similar conclusion, although he often takes a very different path when it comes to the details. According to his analysis, the central unit, 2:4–7, 10–15, went through three redactional steps: a redaction from his disciples, which also shifted forward the non-Hoseanic account 1:2–9*, took place at a time when the catastrophe of 725/722 was not yet on the horizon. The second redaction brings us to Josiah's time, while the third is an exilic redaction in Judah that probably has Deuteronomistic traces. In contrast to the Deuteronomistic History, however, salvation for the whole people, Judah and Israel, is awaited. Here, too, the story of Hosea's marriage as an allegory of YHWH's love for his people is ascribed to a later, Josianic redaction, while in the central text only the children have symbolic value and the bride Gomer is not yet called a whore (Ruppert, "Erwägungen zur Kompositions-und Redaktionsgeschichte von Hosea 1–3," *BZ* 26 [1982]: 208–23). Bernard Renaud, on the other hand, differentiates only three strata: original Hosean work (1:2b, 3–4, 6, 8–9; 2:4–7, 10–15; 3:1–4*), a Deuteronomistic reworking, which in Hos 1 and 3 turns Hosea's symbolic actions into allegory, and an eschatologically colored priestly reworking. He therefore concludes that the story of Hosea's marriage has no historical basis in the text ("Le livret d'Osée 13," *RevScRel* 56 [1982]: 159–78).

Based on an analysis of Hos 4 and 11, Nissinen offers a complicated redactional history. The first redaction, which did not yet include Hos 1–3 and which probably had authentic prophetic sayings among its *Vorlagen* (4:1–3*; 11:1–4*), occurred shortly after the dissolution of the northern kingdom (e.g.,

4:1–3*; 5:15–6:3; 7:8–9; 8:7–8; 9:3–6, 10–17; 10:5–8; 11:1–6). In the second redaction, the "lawsuit" (רִיב; 4:1; 12:3) is a compositional umbrella term; this redaction probably connected the first section (chs. 1–3) and its *rîb* theme, to Hos 4–12; it expresses the aspiration of early postexilic Deuteronomistic covenant theology (besides stratum II in ch. 4, at least 6:4–7; 8:1b, 4; 12:1–3; 13:4–8). Nissinen finds a salvation-eschatology redaction in stratum III in chapter 11 as well as in 1:7; 2:1–3, 16–25; 3:1–5; 14:2–9. "Given the variety of forms and themes in these texts it is questionable whether or not one can speak here of *third redaction* or a *final redaction* of the book of Hosea. It is also possible that the aforementioned sections owe their origin to unsystematic updating so that the final 'composition' of the book of Hosea reached its ultimate form by accident" (*Prophetie*, 336–42). Nissinen rightly differentiates between redaction and updating: by *redaction* he means "an activity according to a plan in which larger sections of text are considered and reworked. In redaction, older textual material of a characteristic viewpoint is chosen and adaapted as well as reorganized and reconceptualized. In addition, the redaction can also be literarily productive, i.e. creating new texts.... [I]n contrast, the word *updating* signifies a less systematic, sporadically inspired textual commentary on individual parts" (*Prophetie*, 37). Thomas Naumann also prefers to talk about updating rather than redaction. In his opinion, a group of followers gathered around Hosea, and they qualify as the first collectors and compositors of his words, although it is hardly possible to know how the book first came into being. After 722 B.C.E., residents of the northern kingdom fleeing to Judah might have rapidly brought Hosea's words to the south, where the book achieved its final form as a Judean book. Naumann believes that everything that occurred in connection with this creation of a final form is later interpretation, either preexilic (7:10; 4:15; priestly revision in 14:2–9; Judean updating: 4:5; 5:5; 6:11a; 8:14; 10:11; 12:13) or exilic/postexilic (6:11b; 4:3; 8:1b [Dtr]; 12:6; 11:10; 9:4, 10; 14:4b, 10). He correctly notes that, in reference to the later Judean interpretation, "a 'redactional stratum' should be understood as a reworking of available texts with a similar goal, one that might have occurred over a long period of time and been done by many hands. If this is so, one might speak of a Judean, trial-prophetic redaction in Hos 4–14. If instead this term (i.e., *Redaktionsschicht*) is meant to imply a one-time authorial event, in which a text complex is worked through with a unified theological goal, the term should be avoided. (Naumann, *Strukturen*, 176–77) The differentiation between redaction and updating is obviously valid not only for Hosea but for the evolution of all prophetic books.

The authors are also not in agreement as to the extent of the developing layers of the book of Hosea in the eighth and seventh centuries. The prophet himself announced the destruction of Israel and the symbolic names of his children (1:2–8). In addition, in 2:4–16 as well as in some of the words of 4:1–9:9*, he severely condemns the Baal cult and the break from YHWH and threatens destruction to his people because of them. He also sees Israel's unfaithfulness throughout the whole past history of his people. In relation to politics, he not only condemns the Syro-Ephraimitic war (5:8–12) but also warns of the call of foreign peoples who bring ruin to Israel. He also cries out against social injustice (4:1–3*), although this theme does not match the scope of his condemnation against cultic sins. In particular, he does not defend the poor and the weak or condemn corruption as emphatically as Amos, Isaiah, and Micah (see Buss, *Prophetic Words of Hosea*, 101). A Judean reworking, in which the fate of northern Israel is seen as a warning for Judah, occurred under Hezekiah or Manasseh. The final redaction of the book, however, is partly Deuteronomistic and postexilic. The promises of salvation in Hosea were often ascribed to later postexilic redactions (e.g., Marti, Harper, Nissinen). But this view seems slightly a priori to me, since the prophet himself could not have preached words of salvation himself. Why is it not possible to date the words of salvation like those in 2:1–3, 16–25; 3:1–5; 5:15–6:5 or 14:2–9 to the time of Hosea's life or shortly afterwards, along with Wolff and Willi-Plein? If so, the prophet and his circle of disciples would have hoped for the conversion of Israel or Judah and a consequent restoration. This is also heavily emphasized by Grace I. Emmerson in her doctoral work, in which she highlighted both the Hosean message of salvation and the Judean revision (*Hosea*). Of course each case must be studied literarily to see if a salvation message should to be ascribed to the prophet or redactors at the end of the eighth and the beginning of the seventh century. For Hosea, YHWH is not only a terrifying God, a lion (5:14), or pus[3] for Ephraim (5:12), but also a God who wants to live together with his people.

Niels Peter Lemche's claim that the book of Hosea offers no information whatsoever about the eighth century and originated entirely in the (post-)exilic period is based entirely on the fact that the final redaction of the book is to be dated to the (post-)exilic period. To conclude from this that the book could not include any earlier textual layers is simply unbelievable (cf. Lemche, "God of Hosea").

III.2.1.3. Isaiah

See also §I.2.3.2. **Becker**, Joachim. *Isaias, der Prophet und sein Buch* (SBS 30; Stuttgart: Katholisches Bibelwerk, 1968). **Brekelmans**, C. "Deuteronomistic Influence in

---

3. Cf. NEB, Bible de Jérusalem, *HALOT*, etc.

Isaiah 1–12," in *The Book of Isaiah/Le livre d'Isaïe: Les oracles et leurs relectures unité et complexité de l'ouvrage* (BETL 81; Leuven: Leuven University Press, 1989), 167–76. **Budde**, Karl. *Jesajas Erleben: Eine gemeinverständliche Auslegung der Denkschrift des Propheten* (Gotha: L. Klotz, 1929). **Clements**, Ronald E. *Isaiah 1–39* (NCB; Grand Rapids: Eerdmans, 1980). **Dietrich**, Walter. *Jesaja und die Politik* (BEvT 74; Munich: Kaiser, 1976). **Duhm**, Bernhard. *Das Buch Jesaja* (HKAT; Göttingen: Vandenhoeck & Ruprecht, 1892; 2nd ed., 1902). **Fohrer**, Georg. "Entstehung, Komposition und Überlieferung von Jes 1–39," in Fohrer, *Studien zur alttestamentlichen Prophetie* (BZAW 99; Berlin: A. Töpelmann, 1967), 113–47. **Hardmeier**, Christof. "Jesajaforschung im Umbruch," *VF* 31 (1986): 3–31. **Irvine**, Stuart A. "The Isaianic Denkschrift: Reconsidering an Old Hypothesis," *ZAW* 104 (1992): 216–30. **Jacob**, Edmond. *Esaïe 1–12* (CAT 8a; Geneva: Labor et Fides, 1987). **Jensen**, Joseph. *Isaiah 1–39* (OTM 8; Wilmington, Del.: Michael Glazier, 1984). **Kilian**, Rudolf. *Jesaja 1–39* (EdF 200; Würzburg: Echter Verlag, 1983); **Kilian**. *Jesaja 1–12; 13–39* (NEchtB 17, 32; Würzburg: Echter Verlag, 1986, 1994). **L'Heureux**, Conrad E. "The Redactional History of Isaiah 5:1–10:4," in *In the Shelter of Elyon: Essays on Ancient Palestinian Life and Literture in Honor of G. W. Ahlström* (ed. W. Boyd Barrick and John R. Spencer; JSOTSup 31; Sheffield: JSOT Press, 1984), 99–119. **Mowinckel**, Sigmund. "Die Komposition des Jesajabuches, Kap. 1–39," *AcOr* 11 (1933): 267–92. **Oswalt**, John N. *The Book of Isaiah, Chapters 1–39* (NICOT; Grand Rapids: Eerdmans, 1986). **Perlitt**, Lothar. "Jesaja und die Deuteronomisten," in *Gott und Mensch im Dialog: Festschrift für Otto Kaiser zum 80. Geburtstag* (ed. Markus Witte; BZAW 185; Berlin: de Gruyter, 1989), 133–49. **Rendtorff**, Rolf. "Zur Komposition des Buches Jesaja," *VT* 34 (1984): 295–320. **Scott**, R. B. Y. "Isaiah: Chapters 1–39," *IB* 5:149–381. **Steck**, Odil Hannes. *Bereitete Heimkehr: Jesaja 35 als redaktionelle Brücke zwischen dem Ersten und dem Zweiten Jesaja* (SBS 121; Stuttgart: Katholisches Bibelwerk, 1985). **Werner**, Wolfgang. *Eschatologische Texte in Jesaja 1–39: Messias, Heiliger Rest, Völker* (FzB 46; Würzburg: Echter Verlag, 1982). **Werner**. "Vom Prophetenwort zur Prophetentheologie: Ein redaktionskritischer Versuch zu Jes 6,1–8,18," *BZ* 29 (1985): 1–30.

Contemporary exegetes are generally convinced that Isa 40–55 was written around the end of the exile by an unknown prophet, the so-called Second or Deutero-Isaiah. Since Bernhard Duhm (1892), chapters 56–66 are usually ascribed to one or more prophets whose work in Jerusalem is set after the end of the exile. In any case, chapters 40–66 are clearly differentiated from chapters 1–39, which means we can narrow our focus to the first section of the book of Isaiah; the evolution of the book of Isaiah in its canonical, sixty-six-chapter version is a discussion for a later time. This does not mean that there are no contemporary exegetes who defend the Isaianic authenticity of the book, especially in the United States, for example, John N. Oswalt (*Book of Isaiah*, 17–28).

The actual words of the prophet Isaiah are found in chapters 1–39, although other pieces were added to these chapters during later phases of redaction. John H. Hayes's and Stuart A. Irvine's theory of global authenticity of all the prophetic words in chapters 1–33, discussed earlier (pp. 50–51), should therefore be rejected (see Dietrich, *BO* 48 [1991]: 887–90). The inevitable critical reduction of authentic words of Isaiah should not be misunderstood, however. Here, and regarding the origin of other prophetic books, one should heed Rudolf Kilian's warning: "It would be a misunderstanding of the redacted extension of the ... original so-called real prophetic words to theologically disqualify them and push them off to the side as less important. It is exactly these which show how the old prophetic words were passed on, understood anew and commented on afresh" (*Jesaja 1–12*, 10). It is clear, however, that one must "first ask the question of authenticity before one assesses Isaiah as a prophet and attempts to unfold his message theologically" (Kilian, *Isaiah 1–39*, 138). As pertains the redactional history of the book, Kilian and his student Wolfgang Werner are reasonably skeptical: the final revised form of Isa 1–39 offers no clearly datable redactional strata that extend throughout the whole proto-Isaianic book (Kilian, *Isaiah 1–39*, 14; Werner, *Eschatologische Texte*, 202–3). However, one can still try, and many have, again and again.

It is extremely doubtful that there ever was an original proto-Isaianic book. The original words of Isaiah were compiled in relatively small collections. Joseph Jensen speaks of a "collection of collections" (*Isaiah 1–39*, 14). One can assume that the ancient Isaiah collections were organized chronologically. Klaus Koch differentiates four chronological periods: (1) a social-critical period (Isa 2–5); (2) the Syro-Ephraimitic war (Isa 7–9); (3) the anti-Assyrian uprising under the leadership of Ashdod (Isa 10–23*); (4) the anti-Assyrian uprising after the death of Sargon II (Isa 28–32 (Koch, *Die Propheten: I, Assyrische Zeit* [Urban Taschenbücher 280; 2nd ed.; Stuttgart: Kohlhammer, 1987], 120, 134). Many exilic and postexilic sections were arranged around these collections, characterized primarily by a strong eschatological vision and an almost unconditional message of salvation. These later additions also occasionally assume the form of a collection; in other cases they were added into Isaian collections, such as a series of threats that are brought to a close with an oracle of salvation. Non-Isaian collections are readily recognizable: (1) the so-called Isaiah Apocalypse (Isa 24–27); (2) the small apocalypse (Isa 34–35); (3) the "historical" appendix taken from 2 Kings (Isa 36–39); (4) a possible collection of words about foreign peoples that was worked into chapters 13–23 with a few authentic words as well. Alongside these collections are many small units of more recent date, which were placed between authentic pieces, for example, 3:10–11; 4:2–6; 10:20–23, 24–27a, 33–34; 11:6–9, 10–16; 12; 22:24–25; 28:5–6; 29:17–24; 30:18–26; 32:6–8; 33. The purpose of these additions was to complete the prophet's message of doom with a word of salvation (e.g., 4:2–6), to compensate for the threats against one's own people with a threat against the enemies (e.g., 10:33–34), or to conclude a collection (e.g., Isa 12). Other redactional insertions serve as clarification of a word or as further reflection on an oracle. Most literary and redactional critics agree on this, but in their analyses of the redactional processes of the proto-Isaianic book they often take very different paths.

Bernhard Duhm is an example of earlier literary criticism. He recognized the Isaianic authenticity of many speeches and poems, most of which he could date precisely. The prophet seems to have written two small books himself, 28:1–30:17* (see 30:8) and 6; 7:2–8a, 9–14, 16; 8:1–18. "Both books contain the political-religious legacy of the prophet ... the 'testimony' of what Jahve revealed of his plan for the future, and the commandment to trust in God and believe, which he has qualified as the epitome of religion, had set up" (*Jesaja*, xvi). There may have been several such units, for example, 2:2–4; 11:1–8; 32:1–5, 15ff., but they are now split up. "Because the prophets who lived in this period wrote under their own names, from Isaiah's time until the exile nothing foreign entered the book of Isaiah except a few glosses (7:8b)" (*Jesaja*, XVII). Everything else in the book of Isaiah is (post)exilic: around 540, Isa 40–55 (DtrIsa); around the same time as DtrIsa, another writer who was neither Deutero-Isaiah nor any other known writer: 13:2–22; 14:4b–21, 22–23; 21:1–15; the first half of the fifth century: the servant songs (42:1–4; 49:1–6; 50:4–9; 52:13–53:12), which were later put into Deutero-Isaianic poetry; in Ezra's time: Isa 56–66 (TrIsa) and probably the Isaiah stories in chapters 36–39 as well; in the fourth century: 23:1–14; 19:1–15; 14:29–32, and after Alexander the Great: 23:15–18. The first book of Isaiah seems to have been compiled only after the time of the Chronicler (approximately 6:1–9:6; 20; 36–39 as well as the collection of chs. 40–66, which were united with this book of Isaiah at the end of the third century). Chapter 33 dates from the second century, as do 24–27*; 34–35; and 15:1–9; 16:7–11. All these texts were partly published in collections (e.g., chs. 2–4; 28–33; 24–27). "The scribes who compiled chs. 1–12, chs. 13–23, and chs. 24–35, thus completing the already assembled Isaianic book of 40–66, were probably active in the first decades of the first century B.C.E." (*Jesaja*, xiv–xxi).

According to Duhm, the material of the book of Isaiah has consequently had a long evolution. In today's terminology, the process he describes here could hardly be called a redactional history.

According to Hermann Barth, the redactional history of Proto-Isaiah began "with Isaiah writing down his message, once during the time of the Syro-Ephraimitic war (6:1–8:18*), and then again during the last period of his activity (28:7–30:17*)." Afterwards, the Isaiah tradition crystallized as this collection, so that at the end of the seventh century, alongside a few pieces that had been transmitted, a so-called Ashur redactor came across two collections: chapters 2–11* and 28–32*. Barth admits that the body of evidence used for the assessment of redactive processes in the two collections is extraordinarily difficult. He wonders whether the author of the complex of Isa 2–11* was not Isaiah himself, and in Barth's opinion these revisions would have occurred during the revolts in 713–711 and after 705. It seems possible that chapters 28–32* also were reworked by Isaiah himself, by aligning key words. The aim of the collection was to stress that the announcement of doom was still as valid as before, despite Sennacherib's withdrawal. It was therefore drawn up in 701, after the withdrawal (Barth, *Die Jesaja-Worte*, 277–85). Barth's primary concern is to prove that at the end of the seventh century the so-called Ashur redaction edited the two collections into the Proto-Isaianic book (2:1–32:20*). The message of this redaction is the imminent destruction of Assyria and the liberation of all of Israel by a great king who will bring about complete internal peace. Barth succeeded in making the idea of an Assyrian redaction in the time of Josiah seem plausible, and the theory can be considered demonstrated (Hardmeier, "Jesajaforschung," 10–12). Afterwards the book underwent many exilic and postexilic redactions, for example, the insertion of Isa 34–35 and 24–27 (Barth, *Die Jesaja-Worte*, 285–300; cf. Jacob, *Esaïe 1–12*, 14–19).

With the exception of a few details, Ronald E. Clements follows Barth, though he adds that the narrative of the liberation of Jerusalem from the hand of Sennacherib (chs. 36–37) originated in the same milieu as the Assyrian redaction. In his opinion, Isa 9:1–6 is Isaian, while the promise of the Davidic monarchy in 11:1–5 is exilic (Clements, *Isaiah 1–39*, 2–8). According to Clements, Isa 6:1–8:18*; 2:6–4:1; and 28–31* are the oldest collections that can be ascribed to Isaiah or to those closest to him, although the expanded collection 5:1–14:27* could not have achieved its present form before Josiah's time (end of the seventh century; *Isaiah 1–39*, 4–5).

The thesis that the Isaiah tradition goes back to two written texts from the prophet himself is accepted by many scholars, but the scope of these texts is often estimated quite differently from one critic to another.

R. B. Y. Scott also sees the two written collections as the core of the book. The first of the two, which appeared under Ahaz in 734, was already complex, composed of sayings about Judah and Jerusalem (1:2–26; 3:1–17, 24–26; 4:1, 5; 5:1–24*; 10:1–2) into which other Isaian texts were inserted (2:6–22 with 4:14–16 and 9:7–10:4 with 5:24b–29), as were part of the memoirs (6; 8:1–18). The second collection was written down about 704 by Isaiah when his warnings about intrigues with Egypt were still unsuccessful (28:1–4, 7–13; 28:14–22; 29:15–16; 30:1–17; 31:1–3). The two collections were later expanded, shortly after the death of Isaiah, with the dynastic words 9:1–6; 11:1–9; and 7:1–7, 18–25, among other things (Scott, "Isaiah: Chapters 1–39," 160).

According to Hans Wildberger the first collection (Isa 2:6–11:9*) includes the prophecies of Isaiah from the beginning of his activity through the period of the Syro-Ephraimitic war in a somewhat faulty chronological order. It is organized as follows: (1) sayings from the early period, mostly about domestic affairs (2:6–4:1*); (2) sayings from the early period condemning social abuses (5:1–24* + 10:1–3); (3) a cycle of speeches against Israel (9:7–20* + 5:25–29); (4) the memoir from the period of the Syro-Ephraimitic war (6:1–9:6*); (5) sayings to Judah relating to the growing Assyrian threat (ca. 717–711; 10:5–8, 13–15a + 10:27–11:9). The second main complex (chs. 28–31*) is composed of sayings from the period of Hezekiah's revolt against Sennacherib, around 705–701, and was drawn up by Isaiah himself or under his supervision. According to Wildberger, there was never an Isaian collection of oracles about foreign nations. On the contrary, the late exilic redactor of this collection (chs. 13–23) took only a few authentic Isaian words from the two main collections. Moreover, Wildberger recognizes only exilic and postexilic expansions beyond this and is very critical of the idea of preexilic expansions of the Isaiah tradition. He dates the latest redactions to 400 (11:11–16; 12; 33–35; 19:16–25; 24–27; 36–39). The historical appendix (Isa 36–39) was added "when the process of growth within chaps. 1–35 had substantially reached its conclusion. The expansion that added material now in Deutero- (and Trito-) Isaiah would not yet have been on the horizon," shortly before 400 (Wildberger, *Isaiah*, 3:559).

Isaiah 6:1–8:18/9:6 is recognized by many authors as an original Isaianic collection, the so-called Isaiah Memoir (*Denkschrift Jesajas*). The inventor of this hypothesis was Karl Budde (*Jesajas Erleben*). Hardmeier calls this collection an "autobiographical revelation narrative." In this case אל־ישעיהו ("to Isaiah") in 7:3 is to be emended to אלי ("to me"), and ויאמר ("and he said") in 7:13 is to be emended to ואמר ("and I said"). Joseph Jensen suggests that the collection separated 5:8–24 from 10:1–4a and 5:25–30 from 9:7–20, and thus had been fitted into an already extant collection. This shows that a separate literary unit had existed here. According to Conrad E. L'Heureux, the Memoir—"*Immanuel-Büchlein*," in his words—was surrounded by a double *inclusio*. Responsibility for this lies with a social-justice–minded redaction, which he attributes to the Ashur redaction or at the earliest dates it to the time of Hezekiah, since 9:1–6 was attached to the memoir by someone who equated King Hezekiah with Immanuel (L'Heureux, "Redactional History," 105–16; Hardmeier, "Verkündigung," 123–31; Jensen, *Isaiah 1–39*, 15).

In contrast to the consensus, Jacques Vermeylen differentiates five collections of basic Isaian material in the Proto-Isaianic book, only the first of which was edited by the prophet himself, the others by his disciples: (1) the Memoir (6:1–8:16*); (2) the humiliation of the arrogant (2:12–17; 3:1–9a. 16–17, 24); (3) a *hôy* collection (5:8–23 + 10:1–3); (4) a long poem (9:7–20* + 5:24–29);

(5) another *hôy* collection (10:5–14* + 14:24–25a; 18:1–2, 4; 28:1–4*; 29:1–4*; 30:1–5* + 31:1, 3; 33:1). He then describes a very complicated redactional history, which cannot be explained here in full detail. A first reworking of these collections seems to date to the time of Manasseh and is composed almost exclusively of expansions to the fifth collection that often originate with the prophet himself: 3:12a, 14–15; 7:20 (?); 20:1–6*; 22:1b–3, 7, 12–14, 15–18; 30:6b–8; 31:4; 32:9–14. At the same time, the first, fourth, and fifth collections were reworked in the spirit of the idea of the inviolability of Jerusalem. In the time of Josiah, the book of Isaiah was expanded to include notions of messianic expectations and cultic centralization (2:1–4; 7:15; 8:23–9:6; 11:1–5; 22:19–23*). During the exile there was a double Deuteronomistic redaction, and in the fifth and fourth centuries there are four distinguishable redactional layers (Vermeylen, *Du prophète Isaïe à apocalyptique*, 655–759). According to C. Brekelmans ("Deuteronomistic Influence"), the presence of a Deuteronomistic redaction is unproven, and he warns of pan-Deuteronomism. These warnings of exaggeration are always welcome, but it is hard to deny that in many prophetic books there has been Deuteronomistic redaction or revision. Further, according to a study by Lothar Perlitt, the Deuteronomistic traces in the book of Isaiah are much more limited and less clear, and the role of the Isaianic school is much more important than is often assumed ("Jesaja und die Deuteronomisten").

Otto Kaiser takes an extreme point of view when he regards a smaller collection of prophetic words as the basis of Isa 1–39, a text that presumably appeared at the beginning of the fifth century and was influenced by the theology of the Deuteronomistic historical work (Kaiser, *Das Buch des Propheten Jesaja*, 19). The following conclusion is then unavoidable (p. 24):

> What is laboriously revealed to the researcher and reader piece by piece and step by step in the end mirrors the internal history of postexilic Judaism in Jerusalem, to which the prophetic book owes its present form. Moreover, the figure of the prophet Isaiah, son of Amoz—the man whose name means "Yahweh helped" and whose father's name in its full form means "Yahwe proved himself strong"—receded into the twilight of legend whose brilliance turned him into the symbol of God's help for his people and his city.

This pure redaction criticism and *Tendenz* criticism seems to me a disastrously wrong tack. In my opinion, the late origin of even the core of the book of Isaiah is the starting point for Kaiser's study. Such a working hypothesis is not illegitimate, but it does risk leading to a circular argument. Kaiser too often refers to vague Deuteronomistic influence that cannot be convincingly proven. It is much more straightforward to begin with the assumption that the beginning of the book had something to with the words of the prophet—

which Kaiser has not proven false (see J. Alberto Soggin, *VT* 34 [1984]: 497). In the first edition of his commentary, incidentally, Kaiser already wrote that "at least a foundational layer [*Grundschicht*] from the prophet whose name the book bears should be identified" (*Jesaja* [1973], 4). In this work, for example, he believes the basis of Isa 28–32 to be a collection of words of Isaiah from the period of the Judean, anti-Assyrian revolt of 703–701, consisting of 28:7–12, 14–18; 29:9–10, 13–14, 15–16; 30:1–5, 6–7, 8, 9–17; 31:1–3. The collection achieved its final form between 597 and 587, at the earliest, most likely in the latter year, after the conquest of Jerusalem (*Jesaja*, 287). Kaiser is correct to state that it is too simple to ascribe the Memoir Isa 6:1–8:18 to the prophet himself. It appears as if a redactor composed the so-called Memoir out of a few authentic Isaian texts (e.g., 6:1–11; 7:1–17*; sayings in 8:1–16*; Dietrich, *Jesaja und die Politik*, 62–87). According to Wolfgang Werner ("Vom Prophetenwort zur Prophetentheologie"), the redactor was a Deuteronomist or a theologian influenced by DtrG, although Deuteronomistic influence in the Isaian tradition has not been securely proven to date (see above).

Discussion surrounding the scope of authentic Isaian words or collections also revolves around the theological image of the prophet. If one follows Kaiser, Rudolf Kilian, or Werner in assuming a late date for all of the salvation prophecies in the Proto-Isaian book, then Isaiah is only the prophet of the obduration of Israel. If the basic form of Isa 7:1–17 is Isaian, and if Zion theology was already distinct and Isaiah spoke about it in 14:32 and 28:16, a conditional salvation message can be ascribed to the prophet (Huber, *Jahwe, Juda*, 239; Dietrich, *Jesaja und die Politik*, 211–12). According to Hardmeier, too, it is probable that Isaiah himself proclaimed salvation in the preaching that glimmers behind Isa 7:4–9:11 and 8:1–4 (cf. 17:1–6*; Hardmeier, "Jesajaforschung," 24). One cannot use Isa 6:9–10 to portray Isaiah as only a "prophet of obduration."

We have confined ourselves to the evolution of Isa 1–39* during the hundred years between 750 and 650. Recently, however, redaction critics have examined the redaction of the whole of the book of Isaiah, chapters 1–66. They begin with the assumption that chapters 1–39, 40–55, and 56–66 were not simply mechanically assembled. Thus, Peter R. Ackroyd refers to the *inclusio* of chapters 1 and 66, and, according to Vermeylen, the oldest redaction of chapters 56–66 was closely related to 1:2–2:5 (Ackroyd, "Isaiah I–XII," 42–43; Vermeylen, *Du prophète Isaïe à l'apocalyptique*, 505–11). Rolf Rendtorff shed light on the thematic and theological relationships among the three parts of the book of Isaiah (e.g., Zion, "The Holy One of Israel," justice [צדק, צדקה]) and suspects compositional-historical connections behind them (Rendtorff, "Zur Komposition"). Odil Hannes Steck has definitely shown this great Isaianic redaction through a thorough analysis of Isa 35; chapter 35 never stood on its own; it is a text perfectly suited to go between the complex of oracles in chapters 32–34 and 40:1–11; it is, in other words, a redactional text whose purpose was bridging First and Second Isaiah. In Steck's view, chapter 35 was never a component of a "small Isaiah apocalypse" in the sense of an originally independent variable. Steck finds the same redactional layer in 11:11–16; 27:13; and 62:10–12, which, along with Isa 35 help structure the greater Isaianic redaction. Isaiah 35 joined 40–55* + 60–62* to Proto-Isaiah, thus making the book Isa 1–39*; 40–55*; 60–62* (Steck, *Bereitete Heimkehr*). Meanwhile, Christopher R. Seitz attributes a hinge function to Isa 36–39 in the evolution of the Proto-Isaian book into a (post)exilic book that included chapters 40–55. These Hezekiah narratives, esp chapters 36–38, were already composed before 587, shortly after Isaiah's activity, as a conclusion to the Proto-Isaianic book, and they then might have inspired the author of chapters 40–55 (Seitz, *Zion's Final Destiny*). This assumption, however, is hardly still tenable after the works of Steck and Hardmeier (*Prophetie*). The problem of the redaction of the whole of the book of Isaiah will be covered *in extenso* in the following volumes of the Biblical Encyclopedia.

III.2.1.4. Micah

Allen, Leslie C. *The Books of Joel, Obadiah, Jonah, and Micah* (NICOT; Grand Rapids: Eerdmans, 1976). **Deissler**, Alfons. *Zwölf Propheten II. Obadja–Habakuk* (NEchtB; Würzburg: Echter Verlag, 1984). **Dus**, J. "Weiteres zum nordisraelitischen Psalm Micha 7,7–20," *ZDMG* 115 (1965): 14–22. **Eissfeldt**, Otto. "Ein Psalm aus Nord-Israel, Micha 7,7–20," *ZDMG* 112 (1962): 259–68. **Fritz**, Volkmar. "Das Wort gegen Samaria: Mi 1,2–7," *ZAW* 86 (1974): 316–31. **Jeppesen**, K. "How the Book of Micah Lost Its Integrity: Outline of the History of the Criticism of the Book of Micah with Emphasis on the 19th Century," *ST* 33 (1979): 101–31. **Jeremias**, Jörg. "Die Deutung der Gerichtsworte Michas in der Exilszeit," *ZAW* 83 (1971): 330–54. **Kuenen**, Abraham. *De profetische boeken des Ouden Verbonds* (Leiden: P. Engels en Zoon, 1889). **Lescow**, Theodor. "Redaktionsgeschichtliche Analyse von Micha 1–5; 6–7," *ZAW* 84 (1972): 46–85, 182–212. **Lindblom**, Johannes. *Micha literarisch untersucht* (Acta Academia aboensis: Humaniora 6.2; Åbo: Åbo Akademi, 1929). **Mays**, James Luther. *Micah. A Commentary* (OTL; Philadelphia: Westminster, 1976). **Otto**, Eckart. "Techniken der Rechtssatzredaktion israelitischer Rechtsbücher in der Redaktion des Prophetenbuches Micha," *SJOT* 5 (1991): 119–50. **Renaud**, Bernard. *Michée, Sophonie, Nahum* (Sources bibliques; Paris: J. Gabalda, 1987). **Rudolph**, Wilhelm. *Micha, Nahum, Habakuk, Zephanja* (KAT 13.3; Gütersloh: Gerd Mohn, 1975). **Smith**, J. M. Powis. *A Critical and Exegetical Commentary onMicah, Zephania, Nahum, Habakkuk, Obadiah, and Joel* (ICC; New York: Scribner, 1911). **Stade**, B. "Bemerkungen über das Buch Micha," *ZAW* 1 (1881): 161–72. **Willis**, John T. "The Structure of the Book of Micah," *SEÅ* 34 (1969): 5–42. **Woude**, A. S. van der. "Deutero-Micha: Ein Prophet aus Nord-Israel?" *NedTT* 25 (1971): 365–78. **Woude**. *Micha* (POT; Nijkerk: G. F. Callenbach, 1976).

Literary critics have always recognized that the book of Micah, like the book of Isaiah, had an evolutionary history. In his introduction to the prophetic books, Abraham Kuenen claims that 4:6-8, 11-13 are exilic and 5:9-14 were reworked in the exile; 6:1-7:6, in his opinion, is also not from Micah but perhaps first appeared in Manasseh's time; 7:7-20 is again exilic (*De profetische boeken*, 373-78). In contrast, Ernst Sellin ascribes only a few verses in 4:1-5:8 and three songs at the end (7:8-10, 11-13, 14-20) to revisions from 586 or later (Sellin, *Das Zwölfprophetenbuch*, 260-61). According to J. M. Powis Smith, chapters 4-5 are a collection of pieces with different origins. Chapters 6-7, too, show no logical connection: 6:9-16 and 7:1-6 are possibly from Micah; 6:1-5 is undatable; 6:6-8 and 7:7-10, 14-20 are early postexilic, and 7:11-13 is exilic at the earliest. The redactional history of the book [itself] is no longer possible to reconstruct (Smith, *Critical and Exegetical Commentary*, 12-16). In his commentary, Wilhelm Nowack ascribed a large section of the book to a later hand: 1:2-4; 2:12-13; 4:1-4, 6-8, 12-13; 5:1-8, 14; 6-7 (Nowack, *Die kleinen Propheten*, 204-5). Theodore H. Robinson also dated Mic 4-5 and 6-7 to the exilic or postexilic period; the collection of Mic 1-3, which mainly includes sayings of Micah, appeared shortly after the exile or already during the exile (Robinson, *Die zwölf kleinen Propheten*, 127).

Already in 1881 B. Stade laid out the theory that Mic 4-7 originated in its entirety in the (post)exilic period, and this has been generally accepted up to the present: "The following observations are intended to prove that the *book* of Micah achieved its present form only after the exile, and that only Mic 1-3, with the exclusion of 2:12, 13, can be attributed to the prophet active under Ahaz and Hezekiah" (Stade, "Bemerkungen," 162). According to Karl Marti, the foundational layer of the book—originating from Micah himself, perhaps—encompasses vv 1:5b-6, 8-9, 16; 2:1-4, 5-11; 3:1-2, 3a-12. The oldest additions are 4:1-4; 6:6-8, which are still close to Micah's spirit. Everything else originated later, from circa 500 on into the second century (Marti, *Das Dodekapropheton*, 260-63). Johannes Lindblom, on the other hand, rejects the thesis that Mic 6-7 or 4-7 do not originate from the prophet and should be entirely ascribed to a later hand.

He dates a list of sayings from Micah to specific periods in his life: 1:2-7 and 6:9-16 come from the time before the fall of Samaria (722) and are heavily influenced by Amos and Hosea; later words pertaining to Judah and Jerusalem, for example, the lament in 1:8-16 (around 711) and the invectives and threats 2:1-4, 6-11; 3:1-4, 5-8, 9-12; 4:9-10, 14 from the period between 711 and 701; 7:1-4, 13 from Hezekiah's last years; and 6:1-8 from Manasseh's time. A whole composition was constructed out of these pieces, and looked approximately like this: 1:2-7, 8-16; 2:1-4, 6-11; 3:1-4, 5-8, 9-12; 4:9-10, 14; 6:1-8, 9-16; 7:1-4, 13. Two parts can be differentiated within this composition: Mic 1–4*, which is a well-ordered whole made after 701, and 6:1–7:4, 13, which seems more accidental and was probably added during Manasseh's time. There are additions from a contemporary of Micah (4:11–13 + 5:8), from the exilic period (e.g., 2:12–13; 4:10), and from the period of Trito-Isaiah (7:8–20), as well as later expansions that foretell an ideal future and do not belong to any unified literary stratum (4:1–4, 6–7, 8; 5:1–5, 6–7, 9–14). Lindblom does not offer a real redaction history, and he ends the study with this observation: "I believe that exegetical research trusts itself too much when it claims it can assign the mass of additions to various specific hands or fix them chronologically" (*Micha literarisch untersucht*, 162).

According to Ina Willi-Plein, the literary origin of the book of Micah can essentially be divided into three stages: (1) collection and publication of the preexilic sayings during the period of exile; the content that goes back to Micah himself is confined to Mic 1–3 and 6:9–15, while 5:9–12; 6:2–8 are preexilic and come from Josiah's period. (2) Expansions with a few exilic/postexilic sayings during the fifth century (2:12–13; 4:1–4, 6–7; 4:8 + 5:1, 3; 7:1–4). (3) Eschatological shaping around 350 (4:5, 9–14; 5:2, 4–8; 5:13[–6:1?] and probably also the ending, 7:5ff.) (Willi-Plein, *Vorformen*, 110–14). On the basis of this opinion, authentic Mican sayings are found almost exclusively in Mic 1–3, a thesis that was put forward by Stade and is still found today in many works (e.g., Fohrer, *Die Propheten des 8. Jahrhunderts*, 165–66; Mays, *Micah*, 21).

Theodor Lescow, the author of the first detailed redactional history of the book of Micah, came to similar conclusions: the unit of Mic 1–5 was the result of a long redaction-historical process through which it acquired the structure of a prophetic judgment liturgy directed against the peoples. The foundation material was the prophet's message, which is found only in chs. 1–3. Chapters 6–7, meanwhile, have their own history: in contrast to Mic 1–5, there is no assumption of a slow evolution of Mic 6–7; these chapters are more likely a literary composition that might be described as a large-scale Torah liturgy, probably composed around 330 with the aim of expanding the book of Micah (Lescow, *Redaktionsgeschichtliche Analyse*, 209).

An even more detailed study of the redactional history of the book of Micah is found in the work of Bernard Renaud. He is convinced that there is a core of authentic Mican words that encompasses at least Mic 1–3*. This core includes an oracle against Samaria (1:3–7) and a few words that refer to Judah; these he dates to the time of Hezekiah. It is no longer possible to prove that the prophet himself was responsible for the composition of this collection (contra Volkmar Fritz, "Das Wort gegen Samaria," who wishes to interpret Mic 1:3–7 as a postexilic analogy to 3:12). Renaud ascribes also Mic 6:9–15 to the prophet (so, too, Deissler, *Zwölf Propheten II*, 168). He finds preexilic material, though non-Mican, in Mic 6–7, for example, 6:1–8 and 7:1–6*. The two collections of Mic 1–3 and 6:1–7:7 underwent an extensive exilic redaction, very close in content to the ideas of the Deuteronomistic school. An even later, eschatologically inspired redactor gave the book its final version in the fifth–fourth century through minor retouches and with the addition of Mic 4–5 and 7:8–20, which were edited from older material (Renaud, *Michée*; see also idem, *La formation du livre de Michée*, 161–73). Jacques Vermeylen also assumes Deuteronomistic redaction, although he believes it to be much more extensive than Renaud. He thinks that it occurred in two phases; Jörg Jeremias also discovered a reinterpretation or redactional layer in 1:5b, 7a, 13b; 2:3–4*, 10*; 3:4*; 5:9–13; 6:14b, 16, that might be connected to DtrG and the C-layer from the book of Jeremiah (Vermeylen, *Du prophète Isaïe à l'apocalyptique*, 600–601; Jeremias, *Die Deutung der Gerichtsworte*).

According to Hans Walter Wolff, the beginning of the redactional history of the book of Micah is found in the three sections originating from the prophet himself: 1:6, 7b–13a, 14–16; 2:1–4, 6–11; 3:1–12. These received their first Deuteronomistic commentary through a few additions and changes (e.g., 1:1, 3–4, 5, 7a, 13b). Later additions include the words of salvation for the exiled in 2:12–13 and the call to the foreign nations in 1:2. "From 587 down to the early postexilic period, there accumulated in chaps. 4–5 a collection of sayings from the prophets of salvation" (Wolff, *Micah*, 26). The conclusion of this collection is not conceivable before the dedication of the temple in 515; the editorial insertion of Mic 1–3 through the summons in 1:2 is also connected to this. There must also have been an early postexilic redaction of the text of 6:2–7:7, which connects Micah's accusations to the deplorable contemporary state of affairs. "A final step of redactional activity by this school of tradents prepared the proclamation of Micah (chaps. 1–3), that of the new salvation prophets (chaps. 4–5), and also the later passages from the circles of the social critics (6:2–7:7), for liturgical use as readings within community worship, and added the three psalm texts (7:8–10, 14–17, 18–20) which functioned as the response of the worshiping community" (Wolff, *Micah*, 27).

Not everyone agrees that authentic Mican words are limited to Mic 1–3. Artur Weiser, for example, leans toward seeing 5:1–5, 9–14; 6; 7:1–7 as Mican, and he expressly rejects the oft-stated theory that denies the Mican authenticity of all statements from Mic 4 to Mic 7; he grants, however, that because of a lack of evidence to date these words, no convincing proof of their authenticity can be furnished (Weiser, *Das Buch der zwölf kleinen propheten*, 231–32). Similarly, Leslie C. Allen only denies the prophetic authenticity of 4:1–4 (older than Micah), 6–8; 7:8–20, while Wilhelm Rudolph would only deny Micah 4:1–4; 5:6–8; 7:8–20 (Allen, *Books of Joel*, 241–53; Rudolph, *Micha*).

Against the common tendency to ascribe Mic 6–7 to a postexilic hand, A. S. van der Woude offers the theory that these two chapters—the so-called

Deutero-Micah—were the work of a northern Israelite prophet who was approximately contemporary with the Judean Micah. His most important arguments are the lack of clear agreement between I and II Micah (Micah shows more affinity with Isaiah and Deutero-Micah with Hosea and Ur-Deuteronomy) the geographical and historical hints at northern Israel in Deutero-Micah (6:5, 16; 7:14), the important role of the exodus, desert, and entry in traditions in Deutero-Micah (as in Hosea and Jeremiah); the lack of Zion theology; and vocabulary and way of thinking of Deutero-Micah, which is interested in wisdom and liturgy, and is in the spirit of Hosea, Deuteronomy, and Jeremiah (van der Woude, *Deutero-Micha*; cf. Burkitt, *JBL* 45 [1926]: 159–61; the northern Israelite origin of Mic 7:7–20 was, moreover, already defended by Otto Eissfeldt ["Ein Psalm"] and J. Dus ["Weiteres zum nordisraelitischen Psalm"]). According to van der Woude, chapters 1–5 were redacted by the prophet Micah himself into a book. A Deuteronomist combined chapters 1–5 and 6–7 and only adapted the superscript (1:1) to the new entity. Besides the connection with Deutero-Micah, nothing more was redactionally changed afterwards (van der Woude, *Deutero-Micha*, 11). The thesis of a northern Israelite origin for Deutero-Micah has met with no approval. It is arguable that the similarities to Isaiah, Hosea, and Deuteronomy are clearly distributed between Proto-Micah and Deutero-Micah. It is also too simple to call Jeremiah a northern Israelite.

In summary, it can be said that only Mic 1–3 can be granted to the prophet with any certainty. Other, possibly preexilic pieces were heavily reworked; these are mostly from the end of the monarchy of Judah and, like 7:1–6, are in fact kindred to Jeremiah. The authentic Mican words show a prophet of doom who lived on in the memory of the people in Jer 26:18 (cf. Mic 3:8). He expects only catastrophe, chiefly the destruction of the temple of YHWH. In his opinion, the people have perverted the meaning of the temple by regarding it as a guarantee of divine presence, without respecting the moral consequences of this presence in practice. Micah's complaints therefore pertain more to social injustice than to deficiencies in worship. The Judeans ought to live by divine law (משפט: 3:1, 8, 9), but they have corrupted the law. Perhaps Micah, coming from the countryside, would have felt the injustice committed by officials in Jerusalem more strongly and would thus have accused those in power and in positions of leadership, such as judges, prophets and priests. This is also hard to prove, however. Whatever the case, he saw it as his mission to denounce social injustice and therefore to announce to Judah the destruction of the land and the capital city, Jerusalem. He is "filled with power, with the spirit of the Lord, and with justice and might, to declare to Jacob his transgression and to Israel his sin" (3:8).

III.2.1.5. Nahum

Becking, Bob. "Is het boek Nahum een literaire eenheid?" *NedTT* 32 (1978): 107–24. **Christensen**, Duane L. "The Book of Nahum: The Question of Authorship within the Canonical Process," *JETS* 31 (1988): 51–58. **Deissler**, Alfons, and Mathias **Delcor**, "Les petits prophètes II," in *Le Sainte Bible* (ed. Louis Pirot and Albert Clamer; Paris: Letouzey et Ané, 1964), 8.2. **Dietrich**, Walter. "Nahum/ Nahumbuch," *TRE* 23:737–42. **Haldar**, Alfred O. *Studies in the Book of Nahum* (Uppsala Universitets Årsskrift 7; Uppsala: Lundquistska bokhandeln, 1947). **Humbert**, P. "Le problème du livre de Nahoum," *RHPR* 12 (1932): 1–15. **Jeremias**, Jörg. *Kultprophetie und Gerichtsverkündigung in der späten Königszeit Israels* (WMANT 35; Neukirchen-Vluyn: Neukirchener, 1970). **Junker**, Hubert. *Die Zwölf kleinen Propheten* (Die Heilige Schrift des Alten Testamentes 8.3; Bonn: Hanstein, 1938). **Renaud**, Bernard. "La composition du livre de Nahum: Une proposition," *ZAW* 99 (1987): 198–219. **Schulz**, Hermann. *Das Buch Nahum: Eine redaktionskritische Untersuchung* (BZAW 129; Berlin: de Gruyter, 1973). **Seybold**, Klaus. *Profane Prophetie: Studien zum Buch Nahum* (SBS 135; Stuttgart: Katholisches Bibelwerk, 1989). **Seybold**. *Nahum. Habakuk. Zephanja* (ZBK; Zurich: Theologischer Verlag, 1991). **Sweeney**, Marvin A. "Concerning the Structure and Generic Character of the Book of Nahum," *ZAW* 104 (1992): 364–77. **Vuilleumier**, René, and Carl-A. **Keller**. *Michée, Nahum, Habacuc, Sophonie* (CAT 11b; Neuchâtel: Delachaux et Niestlé, 1971). **Woude**, A. S. van der. *Jona, Nahum* (POT; Nijkerk: G. F. Callenbach, 1978).

It is not self-evident that the prophet Nahum and his book would be discussed here, as there is a widely held opinion that says that his prophecy belongs the period shortly before the conquest of Nineveh, in the year 612 (e.g., George Adam Smith, J. M. Powis Smith, Wilhelm Nowack, Karl Marti, Ernst Sellin, Friedrich Horst, Mathias Delcor, Karl Elliger, Bernard Renaud). According to P. Humbert, the book of Nahum is the text of a liturgy that was celebrated in Jerusalem shortly after the fall of Nineveh ("Le problème"). However, he does not sufficiently deal with the historical growth of the text. According to Hermann Schulz, however, there is no doubt that the composition itself occurred long after 612: he believes that such a profoundly considered engagement with the events of 663 and 612, as in Nah 3:7ff., would not have been at all possible before 612 (*Das Buch Nahum*, 48).

There are good reasons, however, to date the appearance of the prophet—which, in any case, seems to have occurred after Ashurbanipal's conquest of Thebes (No-Amon) in 663 (Nah 3:8–11) and before the conquest of Niniveh in the year 612—to the reign of Manasseh rather than that of Josiah (so Hubert Junker, Carl-A. Keller, Wilhelm Rudolph, A. S. van der Woude, Bob Becking, and Walter Dietrich). According to van der Woude, Nahum was a northern Israelite exile, and the book is a letter he wrote from Assyria aimed at certain people in Judah. He has a few arguments to support this: the relatively high use of Assyrian loanwords (e.g., in 3:17 מנזר ["guards"] from the Assyrian *maṣṣāru* and טפסר ["scribe, official"] from the Assyrian *ṭupšarru*); the announcement of the return of the northern Israelite exiles in 2:1–3, according to his own exegesis; the lack of interest in Jerusalem; the mention of Bashan, Carmel, and Lebanon in 1:4, and the possible location of Elkosh, Nahum's hometown, in the Galilee; his particular knowledge of Nineveh; his calling the whole a ספר ("written document, letter") in the superscription (1:1) (van der Woude, "The Book of Nahum: A Letter Written in Exile"; idem, *Jona, Nahum*, 70–74). This hypothesis is definitely not to be dismissed out of hand, since it has a few things in its favor and it brings certain intractable exegetical problems closer to a solution. It is not compelling, however, and rests on the improbable assumption of the literary unity of the whole book.

The literary and redactional analysis of the book of Nahum is a difficult task. Many scholars, including literary-critical researchers, defend the authenticity of the whole book (e.g., Sellin, Junker, Horst, Delcor, Rudolph, van der Woude, and Becking). Schulz holds the extreme opposite view, that the songs describing the destruction of Nineveh are postexilic poetry, and that is why the prophet Nahum must be considered a postexilic poet. In his opinion, the book of Nahum is the work of a single author; one cannot assume gradual growth. He also rejects the thesis of a prophetic liturgy: "The author wanted to write a prophetic book, not a liturgical form" (Schulz, *Das Buch Nahum*, 105–6, 134). Alfred Haldar also argues that the book of Nahum is a single unity, namely, a piece of political propaganda that was written in a milieu of cultic prophets shortly before 612 (Haldar, *Studies*, 148–49). Duane L. Christensen, however, is of the opinion that the book of Nahum is a unified literary composition that might have given the impulse to Manasseh's rebellion against Assyria (2 Chr 33:14–16) (Christensen, "Book of Nahum"; idem, *ZAW* 27 [1975]: 29). This thesis of the unity of the book is a postulate, however, not the result of research. It seems appropriate to cite Schulz in detail:

> The book of Nahum is the work of an author who, in a varied composition, united a song about the battle in Nineveh and a mocking Qina on Nineveh with a theophanic hymn and a word of salvation directed at Judah into one prophetic book.... [H]e used larger, partly preexisting units, out of which, through new framing and rearrangement, he formed real prophetic words. A succesive growth process is therefore not to be assumed.

Klaus Seybold appropriately remarks: "the last sentence is typical of the self-imposed constraints of the argumentation" (*Profane Prophetie*, 14). Schulz abstains from the diachronic approach on the grounds of methodological stringency, but he does not prove that a diachronic analysis would be false. Jeremias attempted one: in the book he finds trial speeches against Israel, that is, Judah (1:11, 14; 2:2–3; 3:1–5, 8–11), and against Assyria (2:4–14; 3:12–19), both of which go back to Nahum himself. The tradition would have redirected the prophetic words aimed at Judah to Nineveh, respectively Babel. Jeremias finds traces of reworking that betray a (post)exilic origin in 1:2b, 3a, 9–10,12–13; 2:1 (*Kultprophetie,* 12–53). Against this, Seybold correctly argued that in the preserved Nahum texts invectives explicitly against Judah-Jerusalem cannot be proven (*Profane Prophetie,* 12), even if Jeremias's arguments are impressive. In contrast, Seybold makes it clear that the book grew through newer traditions being prefixed to already existing material. This occurred twice so that "the lead sentence of the extant corpus (3:2; 2:2) was taken and turned into the central sentence of a new composition," which resulted in the dovetailing of the textual units. The poems 3:8–19a (around 660), 3:2–3; 2:2, 4–13, and 3:1, 4a (all around 650) stem from the prophet. Everything else is later redaction: 2:14; 3:5–7 (around 615); 1:12–13; 2:1, 3 (around 550); 1:11, 14 and 1:2–10 (around 400; Seybold, *Profane Prophetie,* 32–33). The late character of the alphabetically organized poem Nah 1:2ff. had already often been claimed and is beyond doubt (e.g., J. M. Powis Smith, Nowack, Elliger, Deissler). Bernard Renaud is of the same opinion; he also sees 2:1–3 as a composition of the (post)exilic redactor. In his opinion, everything else was composed by the preexilic Nahum around 630 in the form of individual poems and was transmitted as such, until it was combined into a unit by the final redactor to form the present-day book of Nahum. Renaud also recognizes the dovetailing (2:2; 3:2) that Seybold saw, and which had been in the scholarly discourse even earlier (Renaud, "La composition"; cf. Dietrich, "Nahum/Nahumbuch," 738–39).

Nahum has often been seen as a cultic prophet or a very nationalistic prophet of salvation. The authentic poems give an entirely profane impression, though, and reveal instead a seer and a singer who protested against Assyrian oppression and predicted the bloody end of the Assyrian rule. Conspicuously, there is not a single theological word in his songs and poems; he does not use the name of God YHWH even once. "He saw early on that what happened to No-Amon would happen to Nineveh. He spread this view as a משא, an oracle for his contemporaries.... What did he mean to bring about with this? All that can be said is that he wanted to create some distance in a hectic time, that he wanted to cause people to remember history and its laws, which even Nineveh could not escape" (Seybold, *Profane Prophetie,* 63–64).

III.2.2. THE COVENANT CODE

See also §III.1.2. **Albertz**, Rainer. *A History of Israelite Religion in the Old Testament Period* (2 vols.; London: SCM, 1994), 183–86. **Baentsch**, Bruno. *Das Bundesbuch Ex XX 22–XXIII 33* (Halle: Max Niemeyer, 1892). **Cazelles**, Henri. *Études sur lecode de l'alliance* (Paris: Letouzey et Ané, 1946). **Crüsemann**, Frank. "Das Bundesbuch: Historischer Ort und institutioneller Hintergrund," in *Congress Volume: Jerusalem, 1986* (ed. J. A. Emerton; VTSup 40; Leiden: Brill, 1988), 27–41. **Crüsemann**. *The Torah: Theology and History of Old Testament Law* (Minneapolis: Fortress, 1996), 109–200. **Noth**, Martin. *The Laws in the Pentateuch, and Other Studies* (Philadelphia: Fortress, 1967). **Osumi**, Yuichi. *Die Kompositionsgeschichte des Bundesbuches Exodus 20,22b–23,33* (OBO 105; Göttingen: Vandenhoeck & Ruprecht, 1991). **Otto**, Eckart. *Wandel der Rechtsbegründungen in der Gesellschaftsgeschichte des antiken Israel: Eine Rechtsgeschichte des "Bundesbuches"* (Studia Biblica 3; Leiden: Brill, 1988). **Patrick**, Dale. "The Covenant Code Source," *VT* 27 (1977): 145–57. **Schwienhorst-Schönberger**, Ludger. "'Dies sind die Rechtsvorschriften, die du ihnen vorlegen sollst': Zur Struktur und Entstehung des Bundesbuches," in *Vom Sinai zum Horeb, Stationen alttestamentlicher Glaubensgeschichte* (ed. Frank-Lothar Hossfeld; Würzburg: Echter, 1989), 119–43. **Schwienhorst-Schönberger**. *Das Bundesbuch (Ex 20,22–23,33): Studien zu seiner Entstehung und Theologie* (BZAW 188; Berlin: de Gruyter, 1990).

Concerning the Covenant Code (CC; Exod 20:22–23:13), Martin Noth observed, "It is probable that this collection once formed an independent book of law which has been inserted into the Pentateuchal narrative as an already self-contained entity" (*Exodus: A Commentary* [OTL; Philadelphia: Westminster, 1962], 173). As mentioned previously, many earlier exegetes already dated the CC to the eighth century and even connected it to the prophetic movement (e.g., Rudolf Smend). In more recent commentaries, the CC is often taken to be very old, dating to the pre-state period, as it makes no references to state institutions such as the monarchy (see Cazelles, *Études*). According to Alfred Jepsen, it arose in the period of the judges between Joshua and Samuel, and Noth guessed that its foundational material "was from the start one of the compilations of the 'Amphictyonic law' current in the twelve-tribe confederacy, to which several collections of laws current in the circle of the twelve-tribe confederacy were united to form the existing Book of the Covenant" (Noth, *Laws in the Pentateuch*, 33; cf. Jepsen, *Untersuchungen zum Bundesbuch*, 96–99). Dale Patrick, however, is of the opinion that the CC was part of the E source, which probably originated in the northern kingdom in the ninth century and was brought to Judah after the fall of Samaria ("Covenant Code Source," 156–57). The E-hypothesis has been generally discarded, however. Frank Crüsemann has convincingly proven an eighth-century origin of the CC ("Das Bundesbuch"). He notes that not mentioning certain realities, such as the monarchy, does not signify anything (*argumentum e silentio*). The law of slavery structures the whole first half of the *mišpāṭîm* (21:1–11); before the monarchy, however, there were no slaves as understood in the CC (עֶבֶד עִבְרִי, "a Hebrew slave"; 21:2). The theme of conflict between slave and free-person did not gain importance until the time of the monarchy, especially in prophecy—really, since the time of Amos. In other parts of the CC the theme of גֵרִים ("strangers") is particularly formative: 22:20 and 23:9 enclose the section about the poor with laws about interest, pledges, and conduct before the court. "Historically, based on all that we know from archaeology and from texts, there was not a massive *gērîm* problem in Judah until the arrival of a stream of refugees set off by the fall of the northern kingdom" (Crüsemann, "Das Bundesbuch," 34). It is not impossible that norms and values that ultimately stem from the prestate period were in effect, but the social crisis that had to be solved began in the ninth century and peaked in the eighth. According to Crüsemann, the institutional setting of the CC was the high court, which, according to 2 Chr 19:8ff., was set up by Jehoshaphat in Jerusalem (874–850). At least for the older core of the apodictic part of the CC we should reckon with northern Israelite traditions that came to Judah after 722 (22:17–18, 27–30; 23:10–19). "Then the CC as a whole must be considered an amalgamation of traditions from the northern and southern kingdoms" (Crüsemann, "Das Bundesbuch," 39). According to 2 Chr 19:8, 11, there were also priests and Levites in the aforementioned high court who were responsible for sacral judgments (דְּבַר־יהוה). The CC was probably added into the Sinai tradition in a Deuteronomistic redaction, alongside which came literary revision and theological interpretation. According to Eckart Otto, it was Deuteronomistically reworked in a layer that uses plural verb forms in 20:22–23; 21:1; 22:19b, 20–21, 23, 24b, 30; 23:9, 13 (*Wandel*, 4–6). In Exod 21:2–23:12*, the pre-Deuteronomistic text that formed the basis for the Deuteronomistic reworking, there is evidence of a double chiastic structure (*Wandel*, 9–11):

Exod 21:2–11	Laws for the protection of slaves
Exod 21:12–17	Crimes worthy of the death-penalty
Exod 21:18–32	Laws pertaining to harm of bodily integrity
Exod 21:33–22:14	*yĕšallēm* laws
Exod 22:15–16	Laws pertaining to harm of bodily integrity
Exod 22:17–19a	A list of crimes worthy of death penalty
Exod 22:20–26*	Laws for the protection of strangers and poor
Exod 22:28–29	Rules of selection for YHWH
Exod 23:1–3	Laws for safeguarding judicial institutions

III. THE LITERATURE OF THE ERA 185

Exod 23:4–5   Rules of solidarity with the enemy
Exod 23:6–8   Laws for safeguarding judicial institutions
Exod 23:10–12   Rules of selection for YHWH

According to Otto's analysis, a redactor formed "the first half of the chiastic structure of Exod 21:2–22:26 in 21:2–22:14 by bringing together four originally independent collections (21:2–11/12–17/18–32/33–22:14), while he made the second half, 22:15–16/17–19a/20–26*, out of legal rules that had not yet been put into independent collections" (*Wandel*, 40). This pre-Deuteronomistic collection dates from the era of the monarchy, since the textual history (*Überlieferungsgeschichte*) of deposit law (22:6–14) can be dated to the era of the state (שָׂכִיר, "day-laborer" [22:14] is not documented in the era before the state). A long evolution of Israelite legal history is also reflected in the textual history of the 21:18–32 collection, in which the inclusion of laws about slaves (vv. 20–21, 26–27) reflects the growing social differentiation of the Israelite legal community as farmers became poorer because of the hierachization of the economy. In the social protection provisions (22:20–26*), the direct address adds a parenetic accent. In addition, expressions such as הֶעָנִי עִמָּךְ, "the poor among you" (v. 24), and שִׂמְלַת רֵעֶךָ, "your neighbor's cloak" (v. 25), ground the demand to protect the socially weak in social solidarity. But in framing Exod 22:24–26 with 22:22b, 26b, and especially with the closing formula כִּי חַנּוּן אָנִי, "for I am compassionate," the foundation of the law is theologized:

> Social identity was invoked as grounds in demanding social solidarity to combat the growing social gap between the rich and poor, and to limit the rights of the strong over the weak. The redaction expands social identity as the reason for the law to the theological horizon, grounding it in the will of God.… With this theologization comes the transition from law into ethics. Apodictic and casuistic legal formulae flow into one another and separate themselves from their respective legal institutions in favor of a parenetic function.… Looking at it sociohistorically, the gradual theologization of the legal grounds had its beginning in the growing heterogeneity of Israelite society in the state period.… society, which had become the root of the conflict, could no longer be the basis for alleviating or removing the damage within itself. In this vacuum of legal grounds, the theological legal basis entered: In YHWH, divine king and legal helper of the poor, new legal grounds took effect.… YHWH's requirement of monolatry was realized not only excluding foreign gods from the cult (Exod 22:19a) but also in acting out the norms of the legal collection.… For the redactor it was surely about much more than just collecting various rules into a collection of laws. It was about the unity of Israelite society as '*am YHWH* (see Exod 22:24), which includes the weakest. (Otto, *Wandel*, 39–44)

The pre-Deuteronomistic redaction is marked by YHWH-is-king theology and exhibits a close connection to Jerusalemite cultic theology (cf. Pss 15; 24; 103; 145). The altar law (20:24–26), which contains an older core, was put at the top of this collection by the Jerusalem redactor.

In the collection Exod 22:28–23:12, procedural law (23:1–3, 6–8) is linked to the sacral rules of selection (22:28–29; 23:10–12), and with this theologization, both sacral and profane law lead to YHWH as their shared legal source. The core of the collection is 23:4–5, which is not a justiciable legal rule, but an ethical requirement. The collection stands between the tradition of sacral law, Exod 34:10–26*, and the laws of Deuteronomy: "The tradition-historical analysis of the procedural law collection in Exod 23:1–3, 6–8 shows the eighth century B.C.E. to be the *terminus a quo* for the redaction of Exod 22:28–23:12, which is to be dated as late as preexilic" (Otto, *Wandel*, 49–50). The CC came about through the combination of the two legal collections, 21:2–22:26 and 22:28–23:12. Thus, the rules of selection (22:28–29; 23:10–12) had an ethical buttress in the regulations for the defense of the weak in society (21:2–11; 22:20–26*) (*Wandel*, 52–53). "The Covenant Code shows that sacral law reached out to the everyday world of Israel and that profane law was theologically grounded.... In the theologization of law the innermost nature of this God acted on the law and developed it beyond the possibility of law through the idea of solidarity with even the enemy (Exod 23:4–5)" (*Wandel*, 75). The structure proposed by Ludger Schwienhorst-Schönberger (*Das Bundesbuch*, 23) shows a certain similarity to that proposed by Otto:

21:2–11 Manumission of slaves (six years – seventh year)
       21:12–17   Crimes warranting the death penalty (except v. 13)

       21:18–32   Harm of bodily integrity
       21:33–22:14 Liability in the agricultural and manual work realms
       22:15–16   Kidnapping of an unbethroted girl

       22:17–19   Crimes warranting the death penalty

       22:20–26   Social commandments
       22:27–30   Religious commandments
       23:1–9   Social commandments

23:10–12   Sabbatical year and Sabbath (six years–seventh year)

Schwienhorst-Schönberger does not follow Otto's thesis that the CC is the redacted connection of two originally independent collections. In his opinion, the casuistic part of the CC (Exod 21:12–22:16*) forms its oldest part: "a casuistic law book, which originated and was passed down in the context of administration of justice and juristic learning" (*Das Bundesbuch*, 415). The beginning of this collection was originally 21:12, 18, while 21:12–17 is a secondary composition from the hand of one of the redactors of the CC who transformed it into divine law. This divine law redaction, which Otto also recognized, includes 21:13–17, 20–21, 22aβbβ, 23–24, 26–27, 30; 22:1–2, 9–10*, 15–16, and especially the second half of the CC, Exod 22:17–23:9*, as well as the double frame 20:24–21:11 and 23:10–19. The casuistic part of the CC assumes a sedentary setting of "cattle breeding and agricultural culture of farmers and herdsmen living in open villages and structured in an egalitarian manner based on kinship." Its origin probably dates to the eleventh to tenth centuries, and it must have been passed on and further composed in the ninth to eighth centuries as a law book until it was revised in the eighth to seventh centuries as divine law. "Prompted by the early prophetic criticism, this legal book (i.e., the casuistic section) became connected with divine law and thus became a witness of the connection between social action and YHWH-belief in the proto-Deuteronomic period" (Schwienhorst-Schönberger, "Zur Struktur," 140).

In addition, the altar law (Exod 20:24–26), whose core is possibly very ancient, was probably reworked by the proto-Deuteronomic redaction and incorporated into the CC; it was later again Deuteronomistically reworked. The theologization of law in the CC was advanced by a Deuteronomistic redaction that can be situated in the DtrN circle, and then again by a Priestly redactor (see Schwienhorst-Schönberger, *Das Bundesbuch*, 415–17). Even if they have different opinions on certain details, the studies of Schwienhorst-Schönberger and Otto have elaborated a divine-law redaction that, based on its prophetic inspiration, can justifiably be dated to the end of the eighth century or the beginning of the seventh, a date that corresponds to the findings of Crüsemann.

Like Otto, Yuichi Osumi assumes that two smaller law books stand at the beginning of the compositional history of the CC: the religious law book, Exod 34:11–26, and the casuistic law book, Exod 21:1, 12–22:18*. In his opinion, the greater part of the CC was formed in a composition that joined the two legal books together, which he labels as the "second person singular stratum." The book of *mišpāṭîm* remained almost entirely unchanged, while the law book 34:11–26 was entirely rearranged (22:27–29; 23:10–12, 14–17, 18–19, 20–24*, 32–33*). This composition knits together religious and profane law (cf. the divine-law redaction of Schwienhorst-Schönberger and the theologization of the law according to Otto, which encroach deeper into the casuistic law book.) The second-person singular stratum was reworked in a second-person plural redaction, which mostly agrees with Schwienhorst-Schönberger's Deuteronomistic redaction, although according to Osumi it is pre-Deuteronomistic and comes from the late monarchic period.

According to Rainer Albertz, the CC was actually the legal basis for the Hezekian reform (*Israelite Religion*, 183). He might be correct, provided there was a real reform under Hezekiah. However, one can object to his dating the end form of the CC to the eighth century without assuming any later Deuteronomistic redaction. His arguments are nevertheless applicable for the proto-Deuteronomic redaction (*Israelite Religion*, 184). It cannot be proven that the CC formed the legal basis for the Hezekian reform, since as it is related in 2 Kgs 18:4ff. it has little to do with the demands of the CC, and social reforms are not attested under Hezekiah (Crüsemann, *Torah*, 197). However, with its religious-cultic and social goals, the CC connects well to the prophetic movement of Amos to Micah and therefore would fit perfectly well in the Hezekian period.

III.2.3. Ur-Deuteronomy

See also §III.1.3. **Achenbach**, Reinhard. *Israel zwischen Verheissung und Gebot: Literarkritische Untersuchungen zu Deuteronomium 5–11* (EurHS 23.422; Frankfurt am Main: P. Lang, 1991). **Alt**, Albrecht. "Die Heimat des Deuteronomiums," in idem, *Kleine Schriften zur Geschichte des Volkes Israel* (3 vols.; Munich: Beck, 1953–59), 2:250–75. **Braulik**, Georg. *Die deuteronomischen Gesetze und der Dekalog: Studien zum Aufbau von Deuteronomium 12–26* (SBS 145; Stuttgart: Katholisches Bibelwerk, 1991). **Carmichael**, Calum M. *The Laws of Deuteronomy* (Ithaca, N.Y.: Cornell University Press, 1974). **Crüsemann**, Frank. *The Torah: Theology and History of Old Testament Law* (Minneapolis: Fortress, 1996), 201–75. **Hempel**, Johannes. *Die Schichten des Deuteronomiums: Ein Beitrag zur israelitischen Literatur- und Rechtsgeschichte* (Beiträge zur Kultur- und Universalgeschichte 33; Leipzig: R. Voigtländer, 1914). **Hölscher**, Gustav. "Komposition und Ursprung des Deuteronomiums," ZAW 40 (1923): 161–255. **Horst**, Friedrich. *Das Privilegrecht Jahwes* (FRLANT 45; Göttingen: Vandenhoeck & Ruprecht, 1930) (= TB 12; Munich, 1961, 17–154). **König**, Eduard. *Das Deuteronomium* (KAT; Leipzig: Deichert, 1917). **Labuschagne**, C. J. "Redactie en theologie van het boek Deuteronomium," *Vox Theologica* 43 (1973): 171–84. **Lindblom**, Johannes. *Erwägungen zur Herkunft der josianischen Tempelurkunde* (Lund: Gleerup, 1971). **Loersch**, Sigrid. *Das Deuteronomium und seine Deutungen: Ein forschungsgeschichtlicher Überblick* (SBS 22; Stuttgart: Katholisches Bibelwerk, 1967). **Minette de Tillesse**, G. "Sections 'tu' et sections 'vous' dans le Deutéronome," *VT* 12 (1962): 29–87. **Nicholson**, Ernest W. *Deuteronomy and Tradition* (Oxford: Oxford University Press, 1967). **Oestreicher**, Theodor. *Das deuteronomische Grundgesetz* (Beiträge zur Förderung christlicher Theologie 27; Gütersloh: Bertelsmann, 1923). **Preuss**, Horst

Dietrich. *Deuteronomium* (EdF 164; Darmstadt: Wissenschaftliche Buchgesellschaft, 1982). **Rad**, Gerhard von. *Deuteronomy: A Commentary* (OTL; Philadelphia: Westminster, 1966). **Rose**, Martin. *5. Mose*, vol. 1, *12-25: Einführung und Gesetze* (ZBK 5.1; Zurich: Theologischer Verlag, 1994). **Siebens**, Arthur Robert. *L'origine du code deutéronomique: examen historique et littéraire du sujet à la lumière de la critique contemporaine* (Paris: E. Leroux, 1929). **Staerk**, Willy. *Das Deuteronomium, sein Inhalt und seine literarische Form* (Leipzig: Hinrichs, 1894). **Staerk**. *Das Problem des Deuteronomiums* (Beiträge zur Förderung christlicher Theologie; Gütersloh: Bertelsmann, 1924). **Steuernagel**, Carl. *Die Entstehung des deuteronomischen Gesetzes kritisch und biblisch-theologisch untersucht* (Halle: J. Krause, 1896). **Steuernagel**. *Das Deuteronomium und Josua* (HAT; Göttingen: Vandenhoeck & Ruprecht, 1898). **Veijola**, Timo. *Das Deuteronomium und seine Querbeziehungen* (Schriften der Finnischen Exegetischen Gesellschaft 62; Helsinki: Finnischen Exegetischen Gesellschaft; Göttingen: Vandenhoeck & Ruprecht, 1996). **Weinfeld**, Moshe. "Deuteronomy: The Present State of Inquiry," *JBL* 86 (1967): 249-62. **Weinfeld**. *Deuteronomy and the Deuteronomic School* (Oxford: Clarendon, 1972). **Welch**, Adam C. *The Code of Deuteronomy: A New Theory of Its Origin* (London: J. Clarke, 1924). **Wellhausen**, Julius. *Die Composition des Hexateuchs und der historischen Bücher des Alten Testaments* (3rd ed.; Berlin: Georg Reimer, 1899). **Wette**, W. M. L. de. *Dissertatio critico-exegetica, qua Deut a prioribus Pentateuchi libris diversum, alius cuiusdam recentioris auctoris opus esse monstratur* (Jena, 1805). **Wright**, George Ernest. "Deuteronomy," *IB* 2:309-537.

Critical exegetes no longer follow the Jewish and Christian tradition, which assumes that Moses was the author of the book of Deuteronomy. One of the most important views of critical exegesis is that Deuteronomy is related to Josiah's reform in the last quarter of the seventh century—in other words, that the law book discovered by Hilkiah in the temple in 622 (2 Kgs 22:8) can be found in Deuteronomy. This becomes clear when one considers the parallels between Josiah's actions and the demands in Deuteronomy (7:5; 12-13; 16:1-8, 21; 17:3; 18:10-11). Some of the early church fathers, including Chrysostom and Jerome, were of the opinion that the law book found by Hilkiah was the Mosaic Deuteronomy, and this opinion was stated often across the centuries. W. M. L. de Wette provided the impetus for a new understanding in modern exegesis at the beginning of the nineteenth century. De Wette held that Deuteronomy differed from the early books of the Pentateuch, which stemmed from a more recent author, and that Deuteronomy did not originate too long before its discovery in 622 (*Dissertatio*). Many researchers have even expressed the idea that Deuteronomy was written in Josiah's time for his cultic reform and have suggested a *pia fraus*, a religious deception by the priests, in which they portrayed the discovery of the book of law as accidental. The latter thesis, however, has not met with much approval. Crüsemann claims "that the development of deuteronomic law was connected with circumstances at the beginning of the reign of Josiah." The *'am hā'āreṣ* in particular developed the agenda of Deuteronomy during the reign of the child Josiah (*Torah*, 212–14). It could be said that in the last two centuries of critical exegesis there has been consensus on the following points: (1) Josiah's reform goes back to the discovery of a law book; (2) this law book is to be found in Deuteronomy; (3) the Josian law and our present-day Deuteronomy are not congruent, as Deuteronomy underwent a long and complicated evolution (Loersch, *Das Deuteronomium*, 31–32). According to A. D. H. Mayes, however, the note about the discovery of the law book belongs to the Deuteronomistic redaction; there is thus no historical tradition for this discovery, and so Deuteronomy was not the basis for the Josian reform. According to Mayes, Deuteronomy originated in the period between the reform and the first Deuteronomist and was more likely the reflex of the reform. The connection between Deuteronomy and the reform was the work of the Deuteronomist, who inserted Deuteronomy at the beginning of his historical work, as suited his agenda (Mayes, *Deuteronomy*, 85–103; see also Preuss, *Deuteronomium*, 1–12).

Mayes's thesis, which had a radical predecessor in Gustav Hölscher, must be rejected, as the text found by Hilkiah was only a part of the canonical Deuteronomy, whose core can be deduced from the present-day text. "One needs to separate out an Ur-Deuteronomy" (Wellhausen, *Die Composition*, 191). It is usually assumed that the Deuteronomic law book, Deut 12–26*, is the Ur-Deuteronomy. There is more argument as to whether these chapters are original in their entirety and whether the frame (Deut 1–11; 27ff.) also partly belongs to it. Some scholars include more parenetic parts such as Deut 5–11, and the promises of blessing and threats of curse (Deut 28) as part of Ur-Deuteronomy such that Ur-Deuteronomy would encompass Deut 5–26 (28) (e.g., Abraham Kuenen, August Dillmann, Rudolf Kittel, S. R. Driver, Alfred Bertholet). According to Sigrid Loersch, this is the most common view: "The Dtn law corpus, including the introduction immediately preceding it and ch. 28, were all written by the same hand and thus originated essentially in the same period; the substance of these sections is identical with the book of law found in the temple" (*Das Deuteronomium*, 37).

But even in Deut 12–26 there are irregularities that lead literary critics to look for literary sources or strata. Willy Staerk and Carl Steuernagel have used the switching of number between the "you" singular address and "you" plural as a criterion for differentiating sources. While this criterion is not the only one nor absolutely valid, it is still important for detecting possible sources or redactional layers (on this, see G. Minette de Tillesse, "Sections"). In Deut 12–26, the older texts are undoubtedly found in the singular sections, and in Deut 27ff. the number switch can also be used as a literary-critical criterion (see Preuss, *Deuteronomium*, 35). According to Steuernagel, the law book found by Hilkiah encompassed Deut 12:13–18;

14:22-29; 15:19-23; 16:1-17, 21-22; 17:1; 18:10-12a; 19:3-7, 11-12; 21:1-8, 18-21; 22:5, 13-21; 23:19; 25:5-10, 13-16a; 26:1-11, 12-15. These are all singular texts. This law itself evolved out of various sources, however. Thus, he differentiates laws of centralization, which demand cultic centralization in Jerusalem and the measures that accompany it (12:13-28; 14:22-29; 15:19-23; 16:1-17; 26:1-11, 12-15); laws of the elders, in which the elders play an important role (19:3-7, 11-12; 21:1-8, 18-21; 22:13-21; 25:5-10); and tôʿēbâ sayings (16:21-17:1; 18:10-12a; 22:5; 23:19; 25:13-16a). The law was probably written down at the beginning of Manasseh's reign—shortly after 700, in other words—but the foundational collection of the laws of centralization and the laws of elders must have an older date and might represent part of Hezekiah's edict from his reform (Steuernagel, *Die Entstehung*; idem, *Das Deuteronomium*, xi-xiv). We have seen, however, that Hezekiah's cultic reform is historically questionable.

According to Johannes Hempel, the core of the Ur-Deuteronomy is a source (Q1) that organized the legal life in Israel from the perspective of the cultic centralization. In light of its relation to the CC, Exod 34 (the so-called Yahwistic Covenant Code), and Lev 17-20, it goes back to the period of the judges, or at least to the time of Solomon, and depicts the rules of the old temple in Jerusalem. A redactor found this source already expanded at the beginning of the seventh century and formed the "Josiah book" (Ur-Deuteronomy) out of it, by adapting its legislation to the cultic centralization and writing an Elohist (E)-influenced parenesis. A few more pieces were added in Manasseh's time (Q2) (Hempel, *Die Schichten*, 254-59). Some of this material might go back to the period of the judges, but this is impossible to prove because of the paucity of the sources. Since the biblical history of this period was written by the Deuteronomist, it is unsurprising that Deuteronomistic thoughts and themes are also found there.

Eduard König also takes the view that Ur-Deuteronomy originated around the year 700. He argues from the theme of cultic centralization (Hezekiah!), on the one hand, and the religious-historical background, on the other: The worship of the hosts of heaven (Deut 17:3), which is Assyrian; the prophetic protest against perversion of justice; the mono-Yahwism; and the fight against false prophets all point to a period around 700. After the fall of the northern kingdom (722), the idea of containing idol worship through cultic centralization took hold. König sees the original circle connected to this as having been a priestly circle inclined toward prophetic thought (*Das Deuteronomium*, 48-51). Arthur R. Siebens also points toward a relation to the prophets of the eighth century, which manifests itself in themes such as social justice, fidelity to YHWH, false prophets, and the holiness of YHWH. Condemnation of cultic sites began with the prophets of the eighth century. The *terminus a quo* is Hezekiah, since there is a connection between Ur-Deuteronomy and his reform. The civil laws (chs. 19–25) do not belong to the law book found by Hilkiah but were added after 621 (Siebens, *L'origine*).

Many exegetes have noted the uncontestable dependence of (Ur-)Deuteronomy on prophetic traditions. However, not everyone accepts that cultic centralization was the primary concern of Ur-Deuteronomy. Older authors such as Theodor Oestreicher, Adam C. Welch, and Willy Staerk (*Das Problem*) point out that the expression "the place that YHWH your God will choose" (Deut 12:11, 14, 18, 21, 26; 14:23–25; 15:20; etc.) might have meant multiple places to be chosen by YHWH. Cultic centralization might therefore have been relative: only non-Yahwistic cultic places were precluded. George Ernest Wright is of the same opinion. In his view, the core of the book is an old northern Israelite document that was later reworked—though before 622—in Jerusalem with an eye toward cultic centralization (e.g., in ch. 12). The northern, Levitical origin is supported by the dependence on Hosea and E, as well as by the important place that Shechem holds in Deuteronomy (11:26–32; Wright, "Deuteronomy," 324–26).

The northern Israelite origin of the Ur-Deuteronomy material is assumed by many later researchers and can probably no longer be doubted (see Alt, "Die Heimat"). Important themes such as the dissociation from the Canaanite Baal cult, the militant nationalism, and the revolt against the dynastic monarchy all point to this. "The correspondence between Deuteronomy and the prophet Hosea is especially significant. Hosea's attack on the kingship agrees with Deuteronomy's negative attitude (Deut 17.14ff.; Hos 4.4; 8.4, 10; 13.11). Then, too, the demand to love Yahweh (Deut 6.5 etc.) is probably more or less closely connected with Hosea's message" (von Rad, *Deuteronomy*, 26). "[W]e shall suppose one of the sanctuaries of Northern Israel (Shechem or Bethel?) to be Deuteronomy's place of origin, and the century before 621 must be its date" (26). Von Rad is therefore thinking of the sermons of the Levitical circles in the northern kingdom. Loersch rightly states, "In particular the assumption of a northern kingdom derivation of Dtn forms a fundamental premise of recent works on Dtn" (*Das Deuteronomium*, 86). The Levitical origin also explains the parenetic framework in which the laws were preached. According to Ernest W. Nicholson, it was not the Levites but the prophets who preserved and transmitted the Ur-Deuteronomical material. He finds old traditions in Deuteronomy, such as the observation of the covenantal law, the ideology of YHWH war, the attachment to the principle of charismatic leadership, and a critical attitude to monarchy. The guardians of these traditions can be found in the prophetic group of the northern kingdom. Other Deuteronomic themes such as the theology of election and mono-Yahwism are found in the prophet Hosea. This is connected to the fact that in Deuteronomy Moses is the prophet par excellence who acts as the mediator of the covenant (see 18:15–18; Nicholson, *Deuteronomy*, 65–82). While this might all be true, it remains hypothetical. The role of the Levites, however, is specifically mentioned in Deut 17:18; 27:14–15; 31:9–13 and occupies an important place in the book (12:12, 18–19; etc). Prophets and Levites should probably not be played off against each other. Lindblom convincingly shows that "the authors of the temple document are to be found among the Levites, members of the tribe of Levi, who lived earlier in the land without priestly employment and who sided with the old Zadokite priesthood in Jerusalem" (*Erwägungen*).

After the fall of the northern kingdom, Levites fled to Jerusalem and brought outlines of the law with them to Judah—probably already compiled in a law book—where at some point during Hezekiah's or Manasseh's reign they produced their first edition in the form of Josiah's law book of 622. According to Moshe Weinfeld ("Present State"), the redaction of Ur-Deuteronomy was done not by the Levites but by court scribes. He points out that the promises of blessing and threats of curse in Deut 28 were transposed directly from contemporary Assyrian international treaties (cf. *Bib* 46 [1965]: 417–27; Frankena, *OTS* 14 [1985]: 152–54). The positive attitude toward the monarchy (esp. Deut 17:20) and the dependence on wisdom circles might also point in this direction (see Weinfeld, *Deuteronomic School*, 244–319). The first argument is convincing, but the last is rather weak, since Deuteronomy as a whole is quite negative toward the monarchy. "We can see at once that kingship is conceived, almost reluctantly, as a concession to historical reality. As a matter of fact, this law concerning the king comes very far short of describing correctly the full powers, varied and extensive as they were, of the one who wore the crown. Deuteronomy is concerned only 'to prevent kingship from disturbing the organization of the people's life as set forth in Deuteronomy'" (von Rad, *Deuteronomy*, 119, quoting A. Alt). The dependence on wisdom circles has also been rightly stressed by others (see Labuschagne, *Redactie*; Carmichael, *Laws*). One can agree with Weinfeld, who ascribes the redaction to court scribes, but the Levites are responsible for the preservation and transmission of the older traditions, and their involvement in the Judean redaction cannot be excluded without further evidence. There are such divergent traditions in Deuteronomy (wisdom thought, ancient Near Eastern treaty texts, humanitarian tendencies, laws of war, didactic formulations, cultic centralization, ethics) that we can support Weinfeld's thesis, as Horst Dietrich Preuss does when he says, "All of this seems until now that it can only have been combined by the Jerusalemite court scribes and officials who collected, formed, further reworked and transmitted Dtn" (*Deuteronomium*, 32).

194   ISRAEL AND JUDAH IN THE EIGHTH-SEVENTH CENTURIES

According to Georg Fohrer, the northern Israelite Ur-Deuteronomy encompassed regulations of centralization (e.g., 12; 14:22–29; 15:19–23; 16:1–17) and regulations developed from the CC (15:1–18; 16:18–20; 19:1–13, 16–21). Deuteronomy 14:1–21; 17:14–20; 18:1–8, 15–22 and many doublets in Deut 12 are seen as later additions. The corpus came to Judah in this arrangement, where in further revision it was framed with 4:44–9:6; 10:12–11:32 and 27:1–10; 28:1–68 (Ernst Sellin, *Einleitung in das Alte Testament* [10th ed., ed. Georg Fohrer; Heidelbert: Quelle & Meyer, 1965], 184–91). A second redaction, to which most of the "you" plural pieces belong, must be considered within the framework of the Deuteronomistic History, meaning that the Deuteronomist inserted the Ur-Deuteronomy (the "you" singular pieces) in this history (Deut 1–4 and Joshua–Kings) and at the same time incorporated sections in the plural form into Ur–Deuteronomy in which the exile was in the foreground (on this, see also Minette de Tillesse, "Sections"). Along with Deut 1–4*, 28:69–32:47* is also ascribed to this Deuteronomistic redaction. Later Deuteronomy was removed from the Deuteronomistic History by the P redaction and adopted into the Pentateuch as its conclusion (see Deut 32:48–52; 34:1a, 7–9), but this belongs to a later time.

Rosario P. Merendino (*Das deuteronomische Gesetz*) did a detailed analysis of the phases of growth of the law corpus of Deut 12–26. He localizes the formation of individual complexes and text groups in the pre-Deuteronomic tradition, all of which go back to various independent units, each with its own literary history: (1) cultic texts (14:21b–17:1); (2) *tôʿēbâ* texts (16:21–17:1 [attached to a cultic text]; 18:10–12a; 22:5; 23:18–19; 25:13–16); (3) *biʿartā* texts (a/ 17:2–7; 13:2–12; b/ 19:11–13; 21:18–21; 22:22, 23–25; 24:7); (4) regulations of civil law (19:2–13, 15–21; 21:10–23b); (5) marriage regulations (22:13–29); (6) human rights (23:16–24:18); (7) apodictic series (22:9–11; 23:2–9*); (8) a few liturgical texts (21:1–9; 26:2–15). Mayes is of the opinion that, based on their content, *biʿartā* and *tôʿēbâ* texts could hardly have been original collections. In these groups there are certain laws that were composed by the Deuteronomist himself. He also shaped the *biʿartā* formula to preach Israel's purity, while the *tôʿēbâ* formula was only added in 18:12; 25:16, perhaps pre-Deuteronomically, and in other places by the Deuteronomist himself (Mayes, *Deuteronomy*, 51–52). Merendino describes the composition of these complexes as follows:

> A first collection of the available material was quite probably done during Hezekiah's time within the framework of his reform movement. Of the parts that make up the present law corpus, it included the complex Deut 14:21b–16:19, the *tôʿēbâ* texts and the two groups of *biʿartā* texts, that is, Deut 16:21–17:1; 18:10–12a; 22:5; 23:18–19; 25:13–16 and Deut 17:2–7; 13:2–12, as well

as 13:14–16 and, further on, Deut 19:11–13; 21:18–21; 22:22–25(27–29); 24:7. Deut 18:1–4 and Deut 26:2–11a should be added to this. ...
During the period between Hezekiah and Josiah this collection seems to have undergone a reorganization that was also an expansion. This applies to the second group of *biʿartā* texts, which was expanded with the insertion of civil and matrimonial legal regulations (Deut 21:10–23bα; 22:13–29). Nothing else can be said securely about the pre-Deuteronomic form of the collection. The growth of the pericopes Deut 19:2–13, 15–21; Deut 20 and the Deut 23:16–24:18 complex might go back to an independent tradition." (*Das deuteronomische Gesetz*, 401)

In Merendino's view, this process was followed by yet another redaction, which he calls Deuteronomic, which should not be dated to before Josiah's reform. The collection that was at this redactor's disposal encompassed Deut 12:13–27; 14:4–29*; 15:1–3, 7–23; 16:1–19*, 21–22; 17:1–7; 13:2–12, 14, 16; 17:8–13; 18:1–3, 5–8, 10–12a; 19:2–13, 15–21*; 20:1–14, 19–20; 21–22; 23:2–6*, 6–26*; 24:1–7*, 10–22; 25:1–3, 5–16*; 26:2–15* (*Das deuteronomische Gesetz*, 402). This collection might have formed the legal part of Ur-Deuteronomy found by Hilkiah in the temple, which then later underwent another Deuteronomistic redaction (ibid., 407). Ur-Deuteronomy can thus no longer be considered to have come from the northern kingdom just like that, "as it cannot be proven to have been operative anywhere there, and any more precise explanations remain speculation" (Preuss, *Deuteronomium*, 31). At best one can trace the origin of certain material to the northern kingdom.

Gottfried Seitz undertook an equally detailed study (*Redaktionsgeschichtliche Studien*). He differentiated three redactional stages. In the Deuteronomic collection there were already aggregated laws of war and casuistic regulations of blood and marital law connected with the laws of cultic centralization. The redactor authored further laws with a historicized introduction using available material (12:29–31b*; 13*; 17:14–16, 20*; 18:9–16; 19:1–7, 11–13). This collection came from the prophetic disciples of the Elijah/Elisha circle, but the unit as a whole came about in Isaiah's era. The second phase, the Deuteronomic reworking, which came from the period of Josiah, includes Deut 5–28 (except 27): The parenetic speeches in chs. 5–11* were set up as an introduction to the laws, to which a number of new laws—particularly social ones—were added (15:1–18; 21:22–23; 22:1–12; 23:1–9, 16–24; 24:17–22). The Deuteronomistic reworking followed later. According to research by F. García López, Seitz underestimates the Deuteronomistic redaction of the narrative portions in chs. 5–11, but this no longer belongs to the period under our consideration (García López, *RB* 85 [1978]: 6–33).

In summary, one can say with Preuss that,

in explaining the origin and growth of Deut one must work with a hypothesis of supplementation. Pre-Deuteronomic material of various kinds, possibly present already in small collections, was first collected by circles of the Deuteronomic school and then redacted when it was connected to Deut.... Clearly demarcating an Ur-Deuteronomy, however, became more and more difficult, and we know little more about this book than we did 150 years ago, when we attempt to consider and isolate a coherent "book," a law corpus with an introduction and a final frame. (*Deuteronomium*, 42–43)

Scholars, however, agree on the important parts of the laws in this Ur-Deuteronomy that might have come from the era of the Assyrian crisis. These texts of the (Ur-)Deuteronomy adopt the older regulations from the CC, continue them and update them (cf., e.g., Deut 15:12–18 with Exod 21:1–11; Deut 16:1–17 with Exod 23:14–17). However, Deuteronomy is not tied to the order of the texts in the CC. In contrast to the CC, it shows itself to be more theologically reflective and humanitarian; Deut 15:1–18; 16:18–20; and 19:1–13, 16–21 especially show a close similarity to the CC. It can hardly be claimed that the relationship between Deuteronomy and the CC is one of direct literary dependence (see Preuss, *Deuteronomium*, 104–7).

Immediately after Friedrich Horst recognized "a" Decalogue as having formed the basis of Deut 12–18 (*Das Privilegrecht Jahwes*, 150–54), some scholars assumed the Decalogue's order of the laws to be behind Deuteronomic law. "A significant conclusion of new research awaiting further study and substantiation is that at least some of the parts of Deut 12–25 seem to roughly ... orient themselves according to the order of the laws of the Decalogue (Preuss, *Deuteronomium*, 111–12). Recently, however, Georg Braulik shifted the structuring of Deuteronomy based on the Decalogue to the postexilic period, an analysis that was entirely denied by Reinhard Achenbach.

The Deuteronomic theology is expressed in a formulaic language, which is important for capturing its theological concerns (see Weinfeld, *Deuteronomic School*, 320–65). If one were to characterize the content of Ur-Deuteronomy, one could point to the following important themes (see Seitz, *Redaktionsgeschichtliche Studien*, 305–6; Preuss, *Deuteronomium*, 177–201): The land is the epitome of YHWH's gift of salvation, Israel's נחלה ("inheritance") (perhaps expressed more strongly after the fall of Samaria), but in this land there are many temptations presented by the Canaanite residents, and the law is the remedy. The loss of the land is the fundamental content of the Deuteronomic threats of punishment. In response to Israel's crisis under Assyrian rule, law and obedience become very important, which can be seen in the richness of terminology (חקים/חקות, מצוות, המצוה, משפטים, ברית; covenant, rules of law, the commandment, commandments, decree). The king is viewed critically but not rejected. The prophets had the most direct

III. THE LITERATURE OF THE ERA   197

communication with YHWH, since YHWH aroused them himself. The Levitical priests had great cultic importance and, along with the foreigner, the widow, and the orphan were commended to the charity of the Israelites. Like the CC, Ur-Deuteronomy paid special attention to social justice, such as the just administration of laws or protection of weaker citizens (alongside widows and orphans, now also the "stranger" at your gates; 15:13–15; 16:18; 17:8–13; 24:10–17). In all these areas there is still a need for more research in order to properly differentiate (Ur-)Deuteronomy from Deuteronomistic material.

III.2.4. EARLY ROYAL AND PROPHETIC NARRATIVES

Birch, Bruce C. *The Rise of the Israelite Monarchy: The Growth and Development of 1 Sam 7–15* (SBLDS 27; Missoula, Mont.: Scholars Press, 1976). **Campbell**, Antony F. *Of Prophets and Kings: A Late Ninth-Century Document (1 Samuel 1–2 Kings 10)* (CBQMS 17; Washington, D.C.: Catholic Biblical Association of America, 1986). **Carlson**, R. A. *David, the Chosen King: A Traditio-Historical Approach to the Second Book of Samuel* (Stockholm: Almqvist & Wiksell, 1964). **Dietrich**, Walter. *David, Saul und die Propheten: Das Verhältnis von Religion und Politik nach den prophetischen Überlieferungen vom frühesten Königtum in Israel* (BWANT 122; 2nd ed.; Stuttgart: Kohlhammer, 1992). **Evans**, W. E. "A Historical Reconstruction of the Emergence of Israelite Kingship and the Reign of Saul," in *Scripture in Context II: More Essays on the Comparative Method* (ed. William W. Hallo; Winona Lake, Ind.: Eisenbrauns, 1983), 61–77. **Grønbaek**, Jakob H. *Die Geschichte vom Aufstieg Davids (1. Sam. 15–2. Sam. 5): Tradition und Komposition* (ATDan 10; Copenhagen: Munksgaard, 1971). **Jenni**, Ernst. "Zwei Jahrzehnte Forschung an den Büchern Josua bis Könige," *TRu* 27 (1961): 1–32, 97–146. **Jepsen**, Alfred. *Die Quellen des Königsbuches* (Halle: Max Niemeyer, 1953; 2nd ed., 1957). **Langlamet**, F. "Pour ou contre Salomon? La rédaction prosalomonienne de I Rois I–II," *RB* 83 (1976): 321–79, 481–528. **Langlamet**. "David, fils de Jessé: une edition prédeutéronomiste de l'histoire de la succession," *RB* 89 (1982): 5–47. **McCarter**, P. Kyle. *I Samuel: A New Translation with Introduction, Notes, and Commentary* (AB 8; Garden City, N.Y.: Doubleday, 1980). **McCarter**. *II Samuel: A New Translation with Introduction, Notes and Commentary* (AB 9; Garden City, N.Y.: 1984). **McKenzie**, Steven L. "The Prophetic History and the Redaction of Kings." *HAR* 9 (1985): 203–20. **Mildenberger**, F. "Die vordeuteronomistische Saul-David-Überlieferung" (Ph.D. diss., Tübingen, 1962). **Nübel**, Hans-Ulrich. "Davids Aufstieg in der frühe israelitischer Geschichtsschreibung" (Ph.D. diss., Bonn, 1959). **Rost**, Leonhard. *The Succession to the Throne of David* (1926; Historic Texts and Interpreters in Biblical Scholarship 1; Sheffield: Almond, 1982). **Stolz**, Fritz. *Das erste und zweite Buch Samuel* (ZBK AT 9;Zurich: Theologischer Verlag, 1981). **Veijola**, Timo. *Die ewige Dynastie: David und die Entstehung seiner Dynastie nach der deuteronomistischen Darstellung* (Annales Academiae Scientiarum Fennicae B.193; Helsinki: Suomalainen Tiedeakatemia, 1975). **Vriezen,** T. C. "De compositie van de Samuël-boeken," in *Orientalia Neerlandica* (Leiden: Sijthoff, 1948), 167–86. **Weiser,** Artur. "Die Legitimation des Königs David," *VT* 15 (1966): 325–54. **Würthwein,** Ernst. *Die Erzählung von der Thronfolge Davids: Theologische oder politische Geschichtsschreibung?* (Theologische Studien 115; Zurich: Theologischer Verlag, 1974).

Classical literary criticism often claims that the combination of two or three narrative threads—a continuation of the well-known threads from the Pentateuch—provide the basis of the Deuteronomistic redaction of Joshua–Kings. One of the last to champion this view was Otto Eissfeldt, who, in the last edition of his *Einleitung*, defended the theory that the pentateuchal sources L, J, and E were continued in Samuel–Kings (Eissfeldt, *Einleitung*, 1964, 373; 399–40). R. A. Carlson also argues that J runs from Genesis through to the beginning of 1 Kings (Carlson, *David*, 42–43, 143). However, one should hold strong reservations against the division into two or three continuous literary strands, because arguments linking these narrative strands to continuous source texts are based on evidence that is too weak. "We must start to explain the formation of the books of Samuel by beginning, not as in the case of the Pentateuch, with vertical sections out of the traditional material, but rather with horizontal literary sections, i.e. with greater or smaller groups of narratives which are not so much intermingled with each other as strung after each other, partly on a very loose thread" (Weiser, *The Old Testament: Its Formation and Development* [trans. Dorothea M. Barton; New York: Association, 1961], 162) Leonhard Rost is one of the most important representatives of this view. In his opinion, the following literary units in the books of Samuel were collected and organized chronologically by a Deuteronomistic editor: (a) the narrative of David's succession to the throne (2 Sam 6:16, 20b–23; 9–20; 1 Kgs 1–2), which incorporated an earlier stratum of the Nathan prophecy (2 Sam 7*) and the account of the Ammonite war (2 Sam 10:6–11:1; 12:26–31, as a frame for the Bathsheba story), and which was connected to (b) the ark narrative (1 Sam 4–6*; 2 Sam 6*); (c) the story of Samuel's youth (1 Sam 1–3); (d) a Saul story made out of various components (1 Sam 7–15; 28; 31); (e) the story of David's rise (1 Sam 16–2 Sam 5:25 + 8, with more recent parts in 1 Sam 16:1–13; 17:12ff.; 19:18ff.), and (f) material of various sorts about David's history in 2 Sam 21–24 (on this, see Jenni, "Zwei Jahrzehnte," 111). One might wonder whether some of these *Vorlagen* should not be ascribed to our era.

According to Alfred Jepsen, the basis of the sketch for the historiography of Kings is identified as "synchronistic chronicle S." Short notes about political events and about constructions are enclosed in the chronological details about the rise to power and the death of individual kings. S begins with David and ends with reports about Hezekiah (2 Kgs 18:8). It might have come into

III. THE LITERATURE OF THE ERA

being under Hezekiah, perhaps between 705 and 701. One should differentiate between the notices of the synchronistic Chronicle and the narrative sections which were taken from the Annals of the Kings of Israel and Judah (A) (1 Kgs 5:27-28, 31-32; 6:1-7:51*; 8:2a-8a*; 9:10-11b, 15, 17b-19a; 10:16-20a; 11:27b, 28; 14:25-28; 15:15, 17-22; 2 Kgs 12:5-19; 14:8-14; 16:5, 7-18; 18:14-16). These are not official annals but constitute a historical work stemming from documents from the temple or palace archives. It is possible that the author was a Jerusalemite priest from Manasseh's time (see Jenni, "Zwei Jahrzehnte," 143-44). According to Julius Wellhausen, the composition of the great historical books "probably occurred before the earliest Deuteronomistic reworking, at least in the case of the books of Judges and Samuel" (*Die Composition*, 302). Abraham Kuenen and Rudolf Kittel also reckon with extensive redactions in the first half of the seventh century, that is, under Hezekiah and Manasseh (Kuenen, *Historisch-critisch onderzoek naar het ontstaan en de verzameling van de boeken des ouden verbonds* [2nd ed.; Amsterdam: S. L. van Looy, 1884], 386; Kittel, *Geschichte des Volkes Israel* [2 vols.; Gotha: Perthes, 1916, 1917], 398).

Narratives of the earliest monarchy in Israel (1 Samuel-1 Kings) belong to the final form of the Deuteronomistic History. The Deuteronomistic author, however, here probably DtrP, reworked older traditions that came neither from the earliest monarchical period nor the exilic period, but mainly from the period between them, the era of the monarchy. For instance, two pre-Deuteronomistic textual levels can be differentiated in 1 Sam 15 (Samuel and the Amalekite war): the narrative core in verses 4-8a, 12b-13a, 31b-33 and its design as a paradigmatic narrative in verses 1a, 3, 8b, 9a, 14-16a, 27-28a, 30-31a, 34. Likewise, expanded prophetic narratives were used in 1 Sam 28 (Saul and the necromancer), 2 Sam 12 (Nathan and the Bathsheba scandal) and 2 Sam 24 (Gad and the census of the people), which might have been in a "book of prophetic stories."

> [These traditions] clearly reflect a monarchical-critical and national-critical prophecy which seems to have existed in the northern as well as the southern kingdom or, stated more cautiously, which included both northern and southern Israelite material. This prophecy can be chronologically placed—at first quite roughly—in the era between the early monarchy and the exile, and within this period more likely later than earlier. The so-called classic prophecy, the opposition prophecy of the eighth century, seems to be after this. (Dietrich, *David, Saul*, 38)

This DtrP source seems to constitute a collection of entirely self-contained narratives. These can be followed throughout the books of Kings: 1 Kgs 13 (the Judean man of God in Bethel); 14:1-6, 12-13a, 17-18 (Ahijah of Shiloh); 20; 22 (Micaiah ben Imlah); 2 Kgs 1:2–8, 17a. These narratives of prophetic interventions against northern Israelite kings, which originated in northern Israelite tradition, probably reached Judah after 722. "They then mixed with Judean tradition, meaning that in seventh-century Judah there must have been prophetic circles that were not attached to the court or temple of Jerusalem, and who collected traditions from the north and south, in which they recognized themselves and their standpoints and into which they added their own opinions for clarification" (Dietrich, *David, Saul*, 44). Even the Chronicler seems to have borrowed from these prophetic stories, which are not reworked or are differently reworked in 1–2 Kings, for example, those about Jehu ben Hanani against Jehoshaphat (2 Chr 18–20; cf. 1 Kgs 16:1–4) or about Oded against the victorious northern Israelites in the Syro-Ephraimitic war (2 Chr 28:9–15). The Isaiah narratives (2 Kgs 18:13–20:19) and the Elijah and Elisha cycles (2 Chr 28:9–15) do not seem to have been part of the book of prophetic narratives, but were transmitted separately (see Dietrich, *David, Saul*, 9–48).

The thesis of a pre-Deuteronomistic redaction in Samuel, and partly in Kings—occasionally dated to the eighth century—has met ever-widening acceptance in recent years, as can be seen in works by T. C. Vriezen, Hans-Ulrich Nübel, F. Mildenberger, Weiser (*Old Testament*, 169–70), Bruce C. Birch, W. E. Evans, Antony F. Campbell (ninth century) and the commentaries of P. Kyle McCarter and Fritz Stolz. Thus, the Saul narrative (1 Sam 7–15) underwent a northern Israelite prophetic edition, in which Saul rose as a king anointed by the prophet Samuel and armed with the spirit of God, and was then discarded by God. This edition, which is dated to the second half of the eighth century, most probably after the fall of Samaria, was reworked only slightly by the Deuteronomist (Birch, *Rise*, 140–54). Saul here moves from being a tragic hero to a villain.

McCarter tries to sketch in his Samuel commentary a "prophetic history" that arose in the northern kingdom, and Steven L. McKenzie, following Walter Dietrich, tries to trace it through the books of Kings and dates its ending to the end of the northern kingdom ("Prophetic History"). McCarter systematizes the thesis of a prophetic history and sketches a coherent picture of it. According to him, it shapes the basic form in the beginning of the monarchy in the book of 1 Samuel. It was intended to describe the origin of the kingship as a concession to the unrestrained desire of the people. The king would henceforth be the head of the government, but he would be subject not only to the prophets' teaching and exhortation but also to their choice and dismissal. Anyone who wanted to be king, must, like David, be chosen by YHWH. Such an opinion of kingship, especially as pertains to prophetic choice and dismissal, is entirely northern Israelite (cf. 1 Kgs 11:29–39; 14:1–16; 16:1–4; 2 Kgs 9:1–10) and contradicts the Judean dynastic principle. This "prophetic history" is also geographically northern, centralized around Benjamin and the cities of Ramah and Mizpah. Scholars such as Karl Budde and Adolphe Lods already ascribed an antimonarchical version of the founding of the kingship (1 Sam 7–8; 10:17–25a; 12; 15) to an Elohistic narrator under the influence of the prophets in the eighth century (Lods, *Les prophètes d'Israël et les débuts du judaïsme* [Paris: La Renaissance du livre, 1934], 134). Further, antimonarchical parts of the books of Samuel were sometimes viewed as related to Hosea's so-called antiroyalism.

According to McCarter, this "prophetic history" can be dated to the end of the eighth century, as it betrays a certain Judean orientation, for example, in the recognition of David's legitimacy as successor to Saul. "His background was northern, and he drew the fundamental principles upon which he based his interpretation of history from the teachings of the prophetic circles of the north; but his orientation was to the south, to which he looked for hope and in which he knew the future of Israel to be" (McCarter, *I Samuel*, 22). The author of this history integrated at least three narrative complexes into his work: the ark narrative, the Saul cycle, and the history of David's rise. The prophetic history can be found also in 2 Sam 7:4–9a, 15b, 20–21; 11:2–12:24; 24:10–14, 16a, 17–19. Some of the material that Dietrich and Veijola assigned to DtrP could perhaps also be ascribed to this prophetic redaction (McCarter, *II Samuel*, 7–8), which in a way provided content for the reworking done by DtrP. Stolz dates this stage of the tradition to the wake of the great prophets of the eighth century (Amos, Hosea, Isaiah, Micah) (*Samuel*, 20). This is correct inasmuch as after 722 the northern prophetic tradition in Judah reoriented itself to the Davidic dynasty. Recently, however, Peter Mommer rejected the thesis of a "prophetic portrayal of history" and saw in 1–2 Samuel large narrative blocks (1 Sam 1–7*; 8–14*; 1 Sam 16–2 Sam 5*) that contained individual written traditions and were not reworked further before the Deuteronomistic redaction (*Samuel: Geschichte und Überlieferung* [WMANT 65; Neukirchen-Vluyn: Neukirchener, 1991], 192–202).

According to Dietrich the author of the history of David's rise (1 Sam 16–2 Sam 5 and/or 8) reworked prophetic traditions. The narrative of Saul, who, looking for his father's she-asses would become the king of Israel (1 Sam 9:1–10:16), came from the northern Israelite tradition and served the author only as a prelude to the stories of David's anointing and his protection by Samuel (1 Sam 16:1–13; 19:18–24; see Dietrich, *David, Saul*, 139). He undoubtedly had northern Israelite tradition at his disposal. "It quite probably reached the south along with the stream of refugees after the destruction of the northern kingdom in 722 B.C.E., and it was subject there to a court historiography that wanted to claim that the transfer of power from Saul to David, from the north to the south, was not only legitimate and necessary but willed by God" (ibid.). Some authors and commentators date this history to an earlier period, however, either to the time of David or Solomon or to shortly after the division of the kingdoms in the second half of the tenth century (see Rost, *Die Überlieferung*; Weiser, "Die Legitimation," 349–51; Grønbaek, *Die Geschichte*, 277). The story of David's succession to the throne (2 Sam 9–1 Kgs 2) has been connected to the story of his rise. In the opinion of many authors, the succession narrative originally had a sharp anti-Solomonic tendency that was softened in a pre-Deuteronomistic, pro-Solomonic revision (e.g., Würthwein, *Die Erzählung*; and idem, *Die Bücher der Könige* [2 vols.; ATD 11; Göttingen: Vandenhoeck & Ruprecht, 1977–84], 1:1–2; Veijola, *Die ewige Dynastie*; Langlamet, "Pour ou contre Salomon?"). This revision can be detected in 2 Sam 12; 1 Kgs 1, and already in the text of the Nathan prophecy, which is inserted between the story of the rise and the succession, 2 Sam 7* (in vv. 11bβ, 12aδb, 15b). The story of the succession to the throne seems not to belong to the northern "prophetic history," however, with the exception of a few verses in 1 Kgs 1–2 (Campbell, *Of Prophets*, 81–84).

Two models of a pre-Deuteronomistic "prophetic" source thus stand opposed to each other: on the one hand, Dietrich's model of a mere collection of prophetic narratives that originated in Judah based on northern Israelite traditions after 722 and were used as a source by DtrP; on the other hand, McCarter's model of a "prophetic history," which reworked the ark narrative, the Saul cycle, and the story of David's rise, and which was available as a source for the Deuteronomistic redaction. The question as to which of these is correct cannot be answered with either/or. It could be imagined that there is something correct in both theses: there was a northern-prophecy-inspired pre-Deuteronomistic redaction, which covers large parts of the book of Samuel, and after the fall of Samaria Judah took northern prophetic traditions, revised them under the influence of classical prophecy, and worked them into the pre-Deuteronomistic forms of Samuel and the book of Kings. It was therefore not only the Israelite but also the Judean kingship that was the target of prophetic criticism, and thus the groundwork was laid for the critical attitude of the Deuteronomistic historical work toward the kings and its great interest in the prophets. But despite the sharp criticism, the dynastic principle was clearly never given up in Judah, a position that found ideological support in the expanded form of the Nathan oracle:

> In the expansions of the Nathan oracle we encounter an editor who completes the oracle whose literary horizon reaches from the beginning of the rise narrative to the end of the succession history. Historically he belongs to a period between Solomon and the end of the Judean monarchy. Sociologically he can be found near the king's court in Jerusalem.... Thematically what mattered to our editor was legitimizing the transfer of power from Saul to David and

from David to Solomon—and from there tendentially to the Davidic chain of succession. Literarily, he not only intervened in the rise story at various times but also placed the Nathan prophecy and some other material before it. (Dietrich, *David, Saul*, 127–28)

III.2.5. EARLY FORMS OF THE PATRIARCHAL HISTORY

Berge, Kåre. *Die Zeit des Jahwisten: Ein Beitrag zur Datierung jahwistischer Vätertexte* (BZAW 186; Berlin: de Gruyter, 1990). **Blenkinsopp**, Joseph. *The Pentateuch: An Introduction to the First Five Books of the Bible* (ABRL; New York: Doubleday, 1992). **Blum**, Erhard. *Die Komposition der Vätergeschichte* (WMANT 57; Neukirchen-Vluyn: Neukirchener, 1984). **Gunkel**, Hermann. *Genesis übersetzt und erklärt* (HKAT 1; 5th ed.; Göttingen: Vandenhoeck & Ruprecht, 1922). **Hoftijzer**, Jacob. *Die Verheißungen an die drei Erzväter* (Leiden: Brill, 1956). **Jepsen**, Alfred. "Zur Überlieferungsgeschichte der Vätergestalten," in *Festschrift für A. Alt* (Leipzig, 1953–54), 139–55. **Noth**, Martin. *A History of Pentateuchal Traditions* (Englewood Cliffs, N.J.: Prentice-Hall, 1972). **Otto**, Eckart. *Jakob in Sichem: Überlieferungsgeschichtliche, archäologische und territorialgeschichtliche Studien zur Entstehungsgeschichte Israels* (BWANT 110; Stuttgart: Kohlhammer, 1979). **Pury**, Albert de. *Promesse divine et légende cultuelle dans le cycle de Jacob* (EBib; Paris: Gabalda, 1975). **Pury** (ed.). *Le Pentateuque en question: Les origines et la composition des cinq premiers livres de la Bible à la lumière des recherches récentes* (MdB 19; Geneva: Labor et Fides, 1989). **Pury**. "Le cycle de Jacob comme légende autonome des origines d'Israël," in *Congress Volume: Leuven, 1989* (ed. J. A. Emerton; VTSup 43; Leiden: Brill, 1991), 78–96. **Rendtorff**, Rolf. *The Problem of the Process of Transmission in the Pentateuch* (trans. John J. Scullion; JSOTSup 89; Sheffield: JSOT Press, 1990). **Seebass**, Horst. *Der Erzvater Israel und die Einführung der Jahweverehrung in Kanaan* (BZAW 98; Berlin: A. Töpelmann, 1966). **Westermann**, Claus. *Genesis: A Commentary* (3 vols.; Minneapolis: Augsburg, 1984–1986), vols. 2–3; **Westermann**. *The Promises to the Fathers: Studies on the Patriarchal Narratives* (Philadelphia: Fortress, 1979). **Whitt**, W. D. "The Jacob Traditions in Hosea and Their Relation to Genesis," *ZAW* 103 (1991): 18–42.

The latest development in the history of the exegesis of the patriarchal story manifests two opposite tendencies with regard to the literary stage. The one moves towards an ever-broadening dissolution of the source theory, even to the extent of radically contesting it. M. Noth, H. Seebass, and others understood the traditio-historical method as complementary to the the literary-critical, and the history of the transmission of traditions as closing with the works of J, E, and P. There is now a group of exegetes who want to replace the literary-critical method entirely by the traditio-historical. There remain only traditions and their redaction; writers with an overall plan disappear (e.g., R. Rendtorff). (Westermann, *Genesis*, 2:32)

In older literary criticism, the patriarchal history (Gen 12–50) disappeared somewhat in the traditional J and E sources. More recent exegesis has paid increased attention to the patriarchal narratives, the traditions behind them, and the various redactions. Hermann Gunkel gave the first impulse for this development in his commentary on Genesis with his inquiry into the "smallest units" and the larger collections. He holds the opinion that four groups of legends—the Jacob–Esau complex, the Jacob–Laban narratives, some cultic legends, and narratives about Jacob's children—were woven into a reasonably closed unit (Gunkel, *Genesis*, 291–93). A few individual studies have revealed that the three sections of the patriarchal narrative each had their own histories before they were united into a whole. The Abraham narrative (Gen 12–25) is composed mainly of individual stories; the Jacob narrative (25:19–36:43) comprises larger units; and the Joseph narrative (chs. 37–50) is one long story. "This [difference] cannot be explained by the literary-critical method of division into sources, but only by positing a different origin and growth for each" (Westermann, *Genesis*, 2:33). Concerning the *Gattungen*, these stories also contain itineraries and promises alongside the narratives. Martin Noth, Rendtorff, and Westermann have all pointed out the important role of promises in the patriarchal narrative(s). According to Westermann, the starting point and core of the promise theme in the patriarchal narratives lies in the promise of a son (*Genesis*, 2:126). One can differentiate between promises of land (e.g., Gen 15:7), of offspring (e.g., 16:10) and of guidance (e.g., 26:3) and the blessing that goes along with them (e.g., 12:2). All of these promises come in various forms and combinations that betray the development of each of the patriarchal stories and the compositional connection of the narratives as a whole. It is important to notice if the land is just given to "you," "to you and your seed," or just to "your seed," and whether the presence of these various forms points to certain redactional layers. The Jacob narrative is framed by three promises of guidance (28:15; 31:3; 46:2–4): "The beginning, the turning point, and the end of his 'journey', are each marked out by a divine promise address" (Rendtorff, *Problem of the Process*, 76). Before the Joseph narrative in 35:9–12 come two more divine speeches, the first containing Jacob's renaming, and the other a promise of increase with an additional promise of land. "The framework of the Jacob story, and the theological interpretation that goes with it, obviously did not take place at one stroke; rather it exhibits several stages or layers" (76). The same can also be said of the Abraham narrative and, to a certain extent, the Isaac narrative, which only takes up one chapter and which was worked into the Jacob narrative (see ibid., 43–84).

> [W]e have seen that the promise addresses have on the one hand gone through a varied and many-layered process of development, but on the

other hand have been carefully and consciously made a part of the reworking and theological interpretation of the patriarchal stories. The reworking did not take place at one stroke, but shows signs of different stages and layers. Likewise, the intention and careful planning which have directed the process are in many cases clearly discernible. (Rendtorff, *Problem of the Process*, 82–83)

Rendtorff dates neither these narratives nor the narratives of the patriarchs as a whole, but he seems to be working with a theory of a Priestly editorial stratum—or at least a stratum whose textual concern is generally considered to be P—without presuming a coherent Priestly narrative (*Problem of the Process*, 157). To what period should the patriarchal narrative that later underwent a reworking or an interpretation be dated? Since Rendtorff rejects P as the final redaction of the Pentateuch but still assumes a Deuteronomically reworked stratum, the final form of the narrative of the patriarchs should be pre-Deuteronomic. At the same time, he does not want to exclude the possibility that texts in the Deuteronomic style could already be found from the eighth century B.C.E. onward (*Problem of the Process*, 194–203).

Westermann combines this tradition-historical approach with the literary-critical differentiation between sources. In his opinion, the design of a redactor who wrote a concluding summary lies behind the text of the Abraham narrative. It presupposes the literary works J and P, but retains its own character. Beyond this, it presumes the independent Abraham traditions from which the literary works were put together. The redactor brought together entirely different individual narratives of different origins based on a predetermined sequence of motifs: childlessness of the father/mother–lament of the childless one(s)–promise of a son–(danger to the promise)–birth of a son–danger to the son–continuation of the family through this son. Meanwhile, however, the tradition developed: the redactor added a group of narratives that show the development of the Abraham tradition above and beyond the old stories (Westermann, *Genesis*, 2:123–31). Westermann treats the Jacob narrative in a similar manner. Two works were also combined in Gen 12–36, J and P. The Yahwistic work had a richly developed and varied pre- and post-history (*Genesis*, 2:571), but neither does Westermann give a date to these traditions and redactions. According to Westermann, the Joseph narrative, in the stricter sense (Gen 37; 39–45; 46–50*) is "an artistic narrative, the fruit, not of oral tradition, but of the literary plan of an artist who conceived it in written form" (*Genesis*, 3:26). He also leaves this undated, but seems to situate it at the beginning of the monarchy, since he believes that during the conflict over the emergence of the monarchy in Israel, the narrative intended to portray the positive possibilities of this institution while also clarifying how family values could be protected under the conditions of the monarchy (*Genesis,* 3:248).

In contrast, in his study of the patriarchal history Erhard Blum attempts to elucidate the historical background of the respective traditions as much as possible. Rather than subscribing to a documentary hypothesis (the hypothesis of parallel sources in all of the Pentateuch, e.g., J and E), Blum believe we should have a strongly differentiated textual-historical "reconstruction." He begins his detailed and thorough study with the analysis of the Jacob tradition. In his opinion, at the beginning of the textual history of the "Jacob narrative" (Gen 25:21ff*; 27–33*) there were probably a few individual legends: two individual stories about the purchase of the birthright and Jacob's swindling of the fatherly blessing, which in their present form are attached in a dense compositional context, the cult etiology of Bethel (28:11ff.*) and the tradition of the border agreement in Gilead (31:45–54). They presuppose the importance of the patriarchs as ancestors of the people of Israel, Edom, and Aram. "The existence of these ethnic entities thus forms a sort of *terminus a quo* for these legends" (Blum, *Die Komposition,* 202). Most of the Jacob–Laban episodes, however, were designed from the beginning to be scenes inside a larger narrative. In Blum's opinion,

> a few observations indicate that in our textual tradition the outline of a larger composition can be made out in which the Jacob narrative was already present. This composition might have substantially encompassed the Jacob–Esau narratives (Gen 25B*; 27), Jacob's reception at Laban's, his service for Laban's daughters (the birth of the children), the increase of his flocks, the flight from Laban (theft of the Teraphim) and the accord in Gilead. The composition of the Jacob narrative could link up to this tradition as its foundation. (*Die Komposition,* 174–75)

In other words, according to Blum, the contours of a complete Jacob–Esau–Laban history can still be clearly recognized in the present text.

> This tradition was eventually carried on compositionally and narratively into our "Jacob-narrative" in Gen 25B* and *27–33 with the help of what we call the "composition layer." With it, the Bethel etiology was sewn into the overall arc of the plot (*28:20–22) at the seam between the Jacob–Esau and Jacob–Laban stories with the help of the vow, the tradition of the birth of the sons of Jacob in ch. 29f. was built up, and, last but not least, in a revising continuation of Gen 31 Jacob's stay with Laban is put into a new (and for him positive) light; there God's command in 31:13 creates an important compositional connection with 28:20ff. and at the same time underlines the elements of the divine guidance and the return to the land. Most notably, this

narrative is then artfully rounded off with the uniformly designed finale in ch. 32f. (*Das Komposition*, 203)

The first chronological boundaries for this composition can be designated as the Davidic-Solomonic period as *terminus a quo*, and the end of the seventh century (the destruction of the shrine at Bethel by Josiah) as *terminus ad quem*, since the episode in Gen 28 about Bethel, including the vow, is addressed to those for whom this shrine was part of their daily lives. As for its historical setting, one should first look for both narrator and audience in northern Israel. The Jacob narrative (especially its redactional elements) looks like a script of Jeroboam I's reforms, which he tried to push through in the beginning of Israel's history; it can therefore be dated to the reign of this first northern Israelite king.

How did the Jacob narrative become the Jacob history (Gen 25–50)? A few short itinerary notes (33:18*, 20; 35:6–7*, 8, 16–20) can be considered expansions to the Jacob narrative. The Joseph narrative, however, is a large, originally independent traditional unit (37*; 39–45; 46:5b, 28–33; 47*; 50:1–11, 14–21). An important goal of this narrative is the legitimation of Joseph's preeminence in Israel. A group of texts exist alongside it that are compositionally connected rather than independent and that unambiguously amount to a claim of the primacy of Judah (Gen 34*; 35:21, 22a; 38; 49*). According to Blum, not only is the factual succession of the Jacob and Joseph narratives beyond dispute, but so is the diachronic succession. In the joining of these two into one larger unit, Gen 48* played an important role, as a counterpart to Gen 27. This is how a full history of Jacob evolved, a history encompassing the whole path of his life. This northern Israelite tradition was adapted in Judah with the interweaving of a Judean counterposition, which in the blessing of Jacob (Gen 49*) allowed Judah to take the place of Joseph. This Judean reception should probably be dated after the fall of Samaria, and an appropriate historical occasion for it might have been Judah's claim to power over all of Israel during Josiah's reign. "With regard to this historical situation, the scope of the composition leading up to Gen 49*—the reclamation of the firstborn status among the tribes of Judah—can be understood as a legitimizing explanation of actual historical situations which are taken up opportunistically" (Blum, *Die Komposition*, 261).

An even larger complex is the history of the patriarchs. The Abraham–Lot narrative (Gen 13; 18–19) is undoubtedly a Judean tradition. Blum's thesis is that, when this narrative was attached to the northern Israelite Jacob tradition, the first step was taken in the composition of the history of the patriarchs (*Die Komposition*, 291). In his opinion, the promises in Gen 13:14–17* and 28:13–14 bracket the Abraham–Lot narrative and the Jacob tradition. In this case, too, one would most likely imagine a reception resulting from the transmission of northern Israelite traditions after the fall of Samaria in the eighth century. Jacob Hoftijzer dated those promises to the (post)exilic period, or to a period "in which the existence of the state was seen as threatened, and the possibility of its destruction appeared imminent" (*Die Verheissungen*, 81). But the end of the eighth century was such a time also for Judah. These considerations about the background of the promises and reflection on the formation of the tradition in Judah after the fall of Samaria lead to a "judgment based on indicia" whereby "the connection of the Abraham–Lot narrative and the Jacob history into a compositional unit with the help of the two promise speeches in Gen 13 and 28, can best be dated at the earliest to the period between the political end of the northern kingdom and that of Judah" (Blum, *Die Komposition*, 297). This interpretation must remain somewhat hypothetical, but it is the most obvious if one forgoes the attribution of the texts to parallel pentateuchal sources. With this tradition complex, Blum discovered the first tradition unit that includes the history of multiple patriarchs and thus constitutes the oldest stratum of the patriarchal history (Ph^1). It was reworked and expanded in later stages that are no longer in our era: the historical background of Ph^2 (e.g., 12:6–9, 10ff.; 16*; 21:8–21; 22*; 26*) is the exile, while the Deuteronomi(sti)c and priestly revisions are both dated to the (post)exilic period.

The meaning of the patriarchal history has many dimensions, including its role as paradigm of basic human experience in the world of the family/clan, but its main significance lies elsewhere (see Blum, *Die Komposition*, 478–506). In the oldest "building blocks" of these traditions, as far as textual history can determine, the meaning of the patriarchs as ancestors of Israel is already presupposed. "In the wider sense [the patriarchal history] concerns the etiologies of Israel, etiologies that simultaneously offer orientations of meaning for the present" (ibid., 481). According to Blum, the national-historical importance of the traditions about the patriarchs was there from the outset and does not come from a later stage, as is generally assumed. These traditions presuppose an Israel, such as was reliably documented for the first time in the Davidic-Solomonic period. "Any attempt to get behind this image through textual analysis does not appear very promising" (ibid., 491). One can only speculate about pre-Israelite textual history of the patriarchal traditions. The promises, which, according to Albrecht Alt and many others, determined the religion of the patriarchs actually belong to a later stratum of revision, which likely originated in the context of the late monarchy.

> Whether they [the patriarchal traditions] were aimed at the justification and legitimation of certain foreign and domestic conditions (see the Jacob–Esau narratives, and the Jacob narrative, etc.), or whether they were trying to form

the foundations of a new future for Israel beyond the existentially threatening crisis of the exile (Ph^2), it is almost always essentially about the existence of the nation in their land—often through the differention from and rejection of other peoples. (Blum, *Die Komposition*, 505)

Albert de Pury is of the opinion that the whole design of the patriarchal history encompassing the three patriarchs was later than DtrG—postexilic, therefore, and belonging to the last stage in the evolution of the Pentateuch. In particular, the traditions about Abraham were (post)exilic, supported by the fact that the first mentions of Abraham are all found in exilic texts (Ezek 33:24; Isa 51:1-2). Obviously these texts assume that at that time Abraham was understood as the forefather of the Jewish people and the first proprietor of the land. Jacob, on the other hand, is already mentioned in texts from the eighth century (Amos 7:2; Hos 10:11; 12; Mic 3:1). According to Hos 12, Hosea knew a complete history of Jacob, which he summarized in verses 4-5. De Pury concludes from this, contra Blum, that a Jacob history encompassing at least elements of the narratives about Jacob and Esau, Jacob and Laban, and the theophanies in Bethel and Penuel, was known in northern Israel in the eighth century. In his opinion, the Jacob history (Gen 25–35*) is constructed so logically that it cannot be seen as simply the result of a process of redactional agglutinization. The history was designed as a unity from the beginning—but with later modifications (25:21–34; 27:1–33:20*; 35:1–20*). It fulfills all the conditions of a legend of origin and was also understood as such by Hosea (one might of course ask—along with Joseph Blenkinsopp [*Pentateuch*, 114]—whether Hos 12 really presupposes a coherent narrative known to the prophet). De Pury would even postulate a premonarchical date for its origin (see de Pury, *Le Pentateuque*, 259–70). This does not mean that in his view this cyle would not permit any diachronic views. Doublets show that in the oral tradition the cycle circulated in various versions. Hosea viewed these tribal-oriented and liberal origin legends very negatively and wanted to replace them with the rival Mosaic exodus legends cultivated by the prophetic "YHWH alone" circles. In Judah, the Abraham cycle was set up as a prologue to the Jacob cycle and was thus transposed with it to the south. This first elaboration of the patriarchal history might be situated between 722 and 587, though probably closer to the former date (see de Pury, "Le cycle de Jacob"). De Pury thus comes close to Blum in the dating of the first patriarchal history.

In all likelihood we can postulate a patriarchal history at the end of the eighth century or the beginning of the seventh, whose theological intention has been correctly described by Blum.

III.2.6. Collections of Proverbs in the Book of Proverbs

See also §III.1.4. **Barucq**, André. "Proverbes (Livre des)," *DBS* 8:1395–1476. **Carasik**, Michael. "Who Were the 'Men of Hezekiah' (Proverbs XXV 1)?" *VT* 44 (1994): 289–300. **Kidner**, Derek. *The Proverbs: An Introduction and Commentary* (TOTC; London: Tyndale, 1964). **Krispenz**, Jutta. *Spruchkompositionen im Buch Proverbia* (EurHS 23.349; Frankfurt am Main: P. Lang, 1989). **Ringgren**, Helmer. *Sprüche/Prediger* (ATD; Göttingen: Vandenhoeck & Ruprecht, 1962; 3rd ed., 1980). **Scott**, R. B. Y. *Proverbs, Ecclesiastes: Introduction, Translation, and Notes* (AB 18; Garden City, N.Y.: Doubleday, 1965). **Snell**, Daniel C. *Twice-Told Proverbs and the Composition of the Book of Proverbs* (Winona Lake, Ind.: Eisenbrauns, 1993). **Van Leeuwen**, Raymond C. *Context and Meaning in Proverbs 25–27* (SBLDS 96; Atlanta: Scholars Press, 1988). **Whybray**, R. N. *The Composition of the Book of Proverbs* (JSOTSup 168; Sheffield: JSOT Press, 1994).

According to the superscriptions, the book of Proverbs (משלי שלמה, παροιμίαι, *Liber Proverbiorum*) is a collection of originally independent writings that, from 24:22 onward, differ in order between the LXX and the Hebrew text (cf. 1:1; 10:1; 22:17; 24:23; 25:1; 30:1; 31:1). The fifth collection (chs. 25–29) has the superscription "These are other proverbs of Solomon which the men of King Hezekiah of Judah copied." The author of this superscription betrays that he had at least the first collection, Prov 1–9, and/or the second collection 10:1–22:16 available to him. In the present text only the proverbs in collections 2 and 5 are ascribed to King Solomon. The fifth collection was put together by Hezekiah's men. Many exegetes believe this claim to be true or at least plausible (e.g., Hermann Gunkel, Berend Gemser, J. P. M. van der Ploeg, Helmer Ringgren, Dermot Cox, Arndt Meinhold). Is this historically verifiable? In the biblical view, Solomon is the originator of Israelite wisdom, or at least the first great wise man in Israel (1 Kgs 5:10–14). The queen of Sheba sought him "to test him with hard questions" (1 Kgs 10:1–9). Many highly regarded exegetes assume that the picture of Solomon as the great wise man is historically reliable (e.g., Ernst Sellin, Otto Eissfeldt, W. O. E. Oesterley). This is possible, although there is no direct historical proof, and many scholars agree with James L. Crenshaw that there is not a single sapiential piece of evidence that stems from Solomon's time (Crenshaw, *Old Testament Wisdom*, 99). The small collection Prov 22:17–23:11 is dependent on the Egyptian Wisdom of Amenemope (from approximately between 1180 and 1070 B.C.E.) and therefore could have possibly originated in the preexilic period. It gives special attention to the poor and the weaker groups in society (22:22–23; 23:10–11). Ringgren accurately summarizes the conclusion of critical exegesis regarding the Solomonic origin of Israelite wisdom, the book of Proverbs in particular:

III. THE LITERATURE OF THE ERA 211

> On the one hand, it is quite clear that he [Solomon] could not have written or even collected the book as a whole, since much in it is recognizable as considerably later, and some parts claim to have come from other people. On the other hand, it is not improbable that Israelite wisdom poetry existed in Solomon's time— the extrabiblical evidence is considerably older. Thus, one cannot deny from the outset that part of the book of Proverbs comes from Solomon or from his environment. (Ringgren, *Sprüche*, 3rd ed., 7)

What really does come from Solomon is difficult to decide, and we cannot rule out that the phrase "Proverb of Solomon" is nothing more than a conventional label for a double-line proverb, as this form is characteristic of the "Solomonic" collections (see Scott, *Proverbs*, 83). The same opinion is held by Hans-Jürgen Hermisson, who holds as generally accepted that at least parts of the proverbs are of preexilic origin, even if the book as a whole did not achieve its final form until the postexilic period. In his opinion, at least the collections 10:1–22:16; 22:17–24:22; and chapters 25–29 are essentially preexilic (Hermisson, *Studien*, 15). Proverbs about the king in the first collection mentioned above are an important piece of evidence for this assumption. Gemser brings up further arguments for the preexilic dating of the fifth collection and other parts of the book:

> Wealth in itself is valued, but only when it is acquired according to the way of the fathers, not through speculation. The agricultural ideal is held up (II 12:9–11; 13:23; 14:4; V 27:23–27; 28:19) and farming, established by God, is compared to trade and haste after wealth, especially in the oldest collections (II 10:4–5; 13:11; 19:2; 20:21; 21:5; V 28:8, 20, 22; 29:20). One gets the impression that the wisdom teachers found themselves in the middle of a battle, the same battle the prophets and especially Deuteronomy were waging in the middle of the eighth century. The economic state of agriculture seems hopeless, which can best be explained by the radical social change during late monarchical period. Also related to this are the constant warnings against taking pledges on loans (II 11:15; 17:18; 20:16; V 27:13; III 22:26–27; I 6:1–5). (Gemser, *Sprüche Salomos*, 5)

André Barucq is also of the opinion that the "rich and poor" theme shows that the fifth, and the second collection even more so, are related to Amos and Hosea in certain aspects ("Proverbes," 1434). R. B. Y. Scott also tries to support a date for Prov 25–29 in Hezekiah's time. Hezekiah was the first Judean king after Solomon who reigned without rivals in the north, and he quite possibly may have attempted to collect the historical and religious texts of both states, including the wisdom tradition. According to 2 Chr 29–32, he promoted a national restoration, using Solomon as the model. We have put the historical reliability of this reform into question, however. The prophets of the eighth century show the influence of wisdom, too. For example, Amos and Hosea used the form of the sapiential numerical saying (Amos 1–2; Hos 6:2; cf. Prov 30:15, 18, 29), the question-and-answer form of address (Amos 7:1–6; 8:2), as well as proverbs and rhetorical questions in general. According to Scott, the pedagogical goal of the collection is manifest and, especially in Prov 25–27, the tone is more secular and less moralizing (Scott, *Proverbs*, xxxiv, 21). There is a connection between this humanistic and solitary type of wisdom and the political consequences, which Isaiah decried (Isa 19:11–15; 28:14–29; 29:13–16; 30:1–2; ibid., 17). According to Moshe Weinfeld, Isaiah's prophecies testify to the appearance in this period of the sages as a separate class (Isa 5:21; 29:14); before the Hezekian era the wise do not appear as a proper class or profession. Historically, therefore, Hezekiah can be considered the true patron of wisdom literature (Weinfeld, *Deuteronomic School*, 161–62). Because of the international character of wisdom literature, the possibility of preexilic collections of wisdom proverbs cannot be ruled out with any certainty. The collection Prov 25–29 has too many similarities in both form and content to the collection in 10:1–22:16 (six identical proverbs, e.g., 18:8 = 26:22; seven are almost identical; four cases of identical verse lines; the same virtues praised and the same sins rejected) that it is impossible to prove based on content alone that the fifth collection was more likely Hezekian than the second collection. This is confirmed by Otto Plöger, who states that, based on the material, collections 2 and 5 might be assigned to the middle or late monarchical period (Plöger, *Sprüche Salomos*, xv).

According to Derek Kidner, the fifth collection contains the same concentrated—in his opinion, Solomonic—proverbs as the second collection, but the collectors from Hezekiah's time grouped the proverbs more tightly, for example, the series of statements about kings and courtiers (25:2–7), fools (26:1–12), lazy people (26:13–16), and mischief-makers (26:17–28) (*Proverbs*, 24; cf. Snell, *Twice-Told Proverbs*, 83–85). Dermot Cox, who sees no reason to doubt the ascription of this collection to Hezekiah's men, also believes that it is more unified than the preceding collections (Cox, *Proverbs*, 209). Without delving into the question of the period of origin, Raymond C. Van Leeuwen dedicated a monograph to the literary coherence of Prov 25–27 and established that pericopes 25:2–27; 26:1–12, 13–16, 17–28 could be called proverb poems, in which statements and exhortations were made into larger structures and thematic blocks. Proverbs 27:1–12 can be called a "proverb miscellany," since it lacks an organized and coherent macrostructure and theme extending across its entirety. In Van Leeuwen's opinion, Prov 27:23–27 is a bucolic parable with the goal of exhorting the king and other leaders (Van Leeuwen, *Context*, 146–47). Jutta Krispenz (*Spruchkompositionen*) came to similar conclusions, but none of these scholars could prove the existence of a unified structure or theme for the fifth collection. Arndt Meinhold came closest with his convincing description of the genesis of the fifth collection:

> Going beyond the simple connections between key words or other connections are the numerous *proverb pairs* in which two proverbs are connected into a higher structural unit through various linguistic devices and/or characteristics tied to the situation and/or content. For instance, at one time the two proverbs in 25:16-17 could have stood alone, but because of their similar second half-verses and the orientation of their content toward one another, they hardly would have ever stood alone. The *three-proverbs groups* consist of two related proverbs that have a third added to them, whether at the end (e.g., proverb 25:20, which partly copies 25:19, added to 25:18-19; 26:22 to 26:20-21), preceding (26:23 before 26:24-25), or moved in between them (see 26:1-3). In 30:17-20 one can clearly see that from time to time truly disparate material could be brought together. It is more common, however, that sections related by content are united in *larger groups of proverbs* or *pieces* of a pericope (as in 28:6-11). As a rule, *pericopes* are understood to be larger sections of text consisting of smaller literary units, which have visible marks of their scope and delimitation. This is the case with 25:11-22, which has almost exclusively pairs of comparison proverbs, while 25:23-28 contains individual comparison proverbs, where in the second case the first and last Hebrew word of the section are the same. But in both 25:11-22 and 25:23-28 most of the proverbs deal with sequences of words and related content: moderation and/or self-control. Several sections constitute one or several *chapters* each with a particular central theme (see, e.g., 25; 26; 27). A *partial collection* is formed out of several chapters (25-27 and 28-29). The whole *collection* is made of two *partial collections* (25-29). (Meinhold, *Die Sprüche*, 25-26)

This process of development does not differ from that of the second collection. The division in two partial collections, chapters 25-27 and 28-29, is plausible (5A and 5B; see Ringgren, *Sprüche*, 3rd ed., 100; Plöger, *Sprüche Salomos*, 293): in 5A synonymous parallelism predominates, in 5B antithetical parallelism; in 5A the proverbs are grouped more thematically (see Kidner, Cox, Van Leeuwen); 5B is more explicitly religious; 27:23-27, which interrupts the distichs, seems to have a concluding function. This last pericope praises the secure life of a cattle breeder. This could be a polemic against the luxury of city life, a theme of which there are traces in the words of the prophets Amos, Isaiah, and Micah.

Meinhold assumes, along with many others, that Hezekiah clearly worked hard to cultivate wisdom in Jerusalem, "so the tradition reflected in the superscription (25:1) should not be met with complete mistrust" (*Die Sprüche*, 416). No one, however, has found any proof apart from this superscription.

As mentioned, the collection itself is no more Hezekian than the second collection (10:1–22:6), and inasmuch as the book reached its definitive form in the fourth to third centuries, it is difficult, even impossible, to prove that the superscription in 25:1 is older. André Robert even proposed a date for the second and fifth collections in the time of Ezra-Nehemia (Robert, in *Mémorial Lagrange* [Paris: Gabalda, 1940], 179–81). Michael Carasik asserts with good reason that Prov 25:1 should not necessarily be taken at face value as historical. There are linguistic and topical links that connect Hezekiah with Solomon (e.g., שׂכל hiphil in 2 Kgs 18:7 and 1 Kgs 2:3), and Prov 25 with the historical situation of 2 Kgs 18–19, which might have inspired the author of the superscription. If the superscription *did* present a historical tradition, the Chronicler, who portrayed Hezekiah as a new Solomon, would not have overlooked this mark of Hezekiah's wisdom activity (Carasik, "Who Were the 'Men of Hezekiah'"). Literary-critically, the date of the fifth collection to Hezekiah's time simply remains an unproven possibility.

III.2.7. Conclusion

The section on the works from the Assyrian era can be summarized as follows: the first recordings of the speeches of the prophets Amos, Hosea, Isaiah, and Micah are to be dated to their lifetimes or shortly after. Even though these prophets' books did not reach their final forms until the (post)exilic period, they existed already in complete or partial early versions by the end of the eighth century or the beginning of the seventh. The book of Amos existed in a pre-Deuteronomistic form already in three main parts. The Hoseanic first layer of the book of Hosea, which can be found in 2:4–13:15*, quite probably underwent a Judean revision in the time of Hezekiah or Manasseh and came out of the Assyrian era in this version. Isaiah 40–66 was not part of the preexilic book of Isaiah, and even large parts of the so-called Proto-Isaian book cannot be dated to our era (Isa 24–27; 34–35; 36–39; and a considerable part of Isa 13–23). Hence, the preexilic book of Isaiah could have encompassed only chapters 1–23* and 28–33*. Yet this range also seems improbable. Perhaps in the Assyrian period there were only smaller collections of the words of Isaiah. Two small collections (Isa 2–11* and 28–32*), which were probably constructed of smaller collections in the Assyrian period, were probably available for the so-called Ashur redaction from the end of the seventh century. Micah 1–3* also belongs to this era. Of Nahum, whose appearance can be dated to the reign of Manasseh, we have only a few poems that would later be collected in the book of Nahum.

In its divine-law redaction, the Covenant Code can justifiably be dated to the end of the eighth century or the beginning of the seventh. In addition, Ur-Deuteronomy (Deut 12–26*), which already had a complicated redactional history behind it, was probably redacted in Hezekiah's time out of individual complexes. As for the pre-Deuteronomistic royal and prophetic narratives (1 Samuel–1 Kings*), there was probably a northern prophetically inspired redaction that encompassed already a large section of the books of Samuel; in Judah after 722 the northern prophetic traditions were accepted, further reworked, and incorporated into the aforementioned version of the books of Samuel and Kings. A patriarchal history can most likely be postulated at the end of the eighth century or the beginning of the seventh, in which the Judean Abraham cycle was placed before the northern Israelite Jacob cycle.

Outside of the prophetic books, Prov 25–29 is the only composition ascribed to the Assyrian period in the Bible itself. The genesis of this collection does not differ from that of the collection Prov 10:1–22:16, however, and therefore dating it to Hezekiah's time is, as mentioned, only an unproven possibility.

IV. The Theological Significance of the Era

IV.1. The Prophets

IV.1.1. Theological Significance of the Prophets

Brueggemann, Walter. *Tradition for Crisis: A Study in Hosea* (Richmond, Va.: John Knox, 1968). **Jacob**, Edmond. "The Biblical Prophets: Revolutionaries or Conservatives?" *Int* 19 (1965): 47–55. **Mowinckel**, Sigmund. "The 'Spirit' and the 'Word' in the Pre-exilic Reforming Prophets," *JBL* 53 (1934): 199–227. **Néher**, André. *L'essence du prophétisme* (Paris: Presses universitaires de France, 1955). **Procksch**, Otto. *Geschichtsbetrachtung und geschichtliche Überlieferung bei den vorexilischen Propheten* (Leipzig: Hinrichs, 1902). **Rad**, Gerhard von. *Theologie des Alten Testaments* (4th ed.; Munich: Kaiser, 1965), 2:58–107. **Schmidt**, Werner H. *Zukunftsgewissheit und Gegenwartskritik: Grundzüge prophetischer Verkündigung* (Biblische Studien 64; Neukirchen-Vluyn: Neukirchener, 1973). **Scott**, R. B. Y. *The Relevance of the Prophets* (rev. ed.; New York: Macmillan, 1968).

Prophets have, by their nature, a unique theological position. The prophet knows God speaks to him and that God calls him to serve God's word. He stood in the Lord's council and was sent out as a messenger of YHWH (1 Kgs 22:19–23; Isa 6:8). In biblical culture and in cultures across the ancient Near East, a word was more than simply a demonstrative sign. The word in the Bible was closer to the thing itself; the difference between word and object was not as clear as it is in our rational and technological world. The word had its own dynamic, an idea that has recently gained greater significance in response to extreme rationalism and formalism. As Gerhard von Rad rightly states: "Israel knew of a use of language which did not give highest priority to being heard by an understanding ear at all, but rather 'only' that the words 'only' were spoken—that they were simply set down as a reality full of mysterious power" (*Theologie des Alten Testaments*, 2:94). דָּבָר, almost always translated as "word," describes neither mere communication nor information but an effective power. This is also the meaning of the prophetic concept of "the word of YHWH," as in Isa 9:7–20 + 5:25–30, for example, "the Lord sent a word against Jacob, and it fell on Israel." Such a word remains effective in history (31:2).

The epigraph of the book of Amos (1:2) says, "The Lord roars from Zion, and utters his voice from Jerusalem; the pastures of the shepherds wither, and the top of Carmel dries up," though this probably does not come from the prophet himself and is more likely datable to Josiah's time. Amos 3:8 is probably an authentic statement from Amos: "The lion has roared; who will not fear? The Lord GOD has spoken; who could not prophesy?" Amos intends to make it clear to his enemies that YHWH has spoken to him, has conveyed to him a דָּבָר. This word, compared to the lion's roar, "suggests the authority of the one who must speak out in no uncertain terms against the expectations of the people. He must do this just as surely as Yahweh placed his awesome demand upon him, quite apart from any desire of his own" (Hans Walter Wolff, *Joel and Amos: A Commentary on the Books of the Prophets Joel and Amos* [Hermeneia; Philadelphia: Fortress, 1977], 187).

In the form-critical section of this volume we pointed out the role of the prophet as God's messenger. In the prophetic books, the prophet's call by God (Amos 7:15; Isa 6; Jer 1) and the divine origin of the prophet's words are repeatedly stressed (e.g., Amos 7:1, 4, 7), often with the formula "thus says YHWH." The prophet is occasionally called "a man of the spirit," though this description is seldom used to describe the preexilic prophets (Hos 9:7; Mic 3:8: את־רוח יהוה is a later added commentary here). At no point do early written prophets invoke the spirit (רוח). "The prophets of the eighth and seventh centuries were remarkably strict in their avoidance of speaking about the 'spirit of Yahweh' or the 'power of Yahweh' in reference to their prophetic office" (Hans Walter Wolff, *Micah: A Commentary* [Minneapolis: Augsburg, 1990] 96). The prophet's ecstatic experience, if not entirely a literary fabrication, is nevertheless very rare and unusual, and nowhere are ecstatic techniques alluded to. Thus when Otto Eissfeldt begins his portrayal of prophetic speech with "The ultimate source of the prophetic saying is the state of ecstatic possession" (*Introduction*, 77), it could be called an exaggeration. He himself admits "that all sayings can hardly go back to special inspiration, not even all those which are introduced with the formula: *Thus says Yahweh* (כה אמר יהוה)" (ibid., 78).

According to Werner H. Schmidt, the trial speech heralding Israel's destruction is the first thing in the prophetic message: prophecy begins with a sense of the future.

> Prophetic certainty about the future does not seem to come out of a deep understanding of the reality at hand; the prophet does not intend to divine

where the situation is leading, what must inevitably occur if things continue as they are. Rather the opposite: the intuition of what is coming leads to a penetrating analysis of what already is. Knowledge of the future makes it possible to see the present differently, to have its shortcomings uncovered. (W. H. Schmidt, *Zukunftsgewissheit*, 64)

While this may be true, it cannot be proven. In my opinion, it is likely not correct. When the prophet sees general ethical or religious decay, he cannot but conclude that God must intervene with punishment. And based on what he sees on the international stage, he can assume that the punishment might mean Israel's destruction. Schmidt's opinion ignores the historical human factor. God's message does not come directly from above but is always perceptible in human experience and faithful contemplation of it. The word of the prophet is almost always a faithful interpretation of history, with varying accentuations and different ways of seeing it. In the eighth century in particular, Israel's fate is their perpetual concern. This concern had a national aspect (it pertains to either Israel or Judah) and a religious profundity, the main theme of which was the relation between YHWH and the people. But it also had a noticeable universalistic aspect, since in their eyes YHWH, who guides this history, has power over other peoples, such as Assyria or Egypt.

In this period there were also professional prophets in Jerusalem—we dealt above with cultic prophets, for instance—some of whom Micah attacked for their venality (3:5–8). Micah does not deny that these people are prophets, but he accuses them of misleading the public, as their proclamation corresponds not to YHWH's instruction but to the readiness of their audience to give them extra compensation: "When they have something to eat they cry 'Peace!' but against those who put nothing into their mouths they declare war" (v. 5; cf. v. 11).

IV.1.2. Relationship with God

Boshoff, W. S. "Yahweh as God of Nature: Elements of the Concepts of God in the Book of Hosea," *JNSL* 18 (1992): 13–24. **Crotty**, R. "Hosea and the Knowledge of God," *ABR* 19 (1971): 1–16. **Daniels**, Dwight R. *Hosea and Salvation History: The Early Traditions of Israel in the Prophecy of Hosea* (BZAW 191; Berlin: de Gruyter, 1990). **Fahr**, G. "The Concept of Grace in the Book of Hosea," *ZAW* 70 (1958): 98–107. **Hoffman**, Yair. "A North Israelite Typological Myth and a Judaean Historical Tradition: The Exodus in Hosea and Amos," *VT* 39 (1989): 169–82. **Jeremias**, Jörg. "Der Begriff 'Baal' im Hoseabuch und seine Wirkungsgeschichte," in *Ein Gott allein? YHWH-Verehrung und biblischer Monotheismus im Kontext der israelitischen und altorientalischen Religionsgeschichte* (ed. Walter Dietrich and Martin A. Klopfenstein; OBO 139; Göttingen:

Vandenhoeck & Ruprecht, 1994), 441–62. **Jüngling**, H.-W. "Aspekte des Redens von Gott bei Hosea," *TP* 54 (1979): 335–59. **Köckert**, M. "Verbindliches Reden von Gott in der Verkündigung des Propheten Hosea," *Glaube und Lernen* 3 (1988): 105–19. **Neef**, Heinz-Dieter. *Die Heilstraditionen Israels in der Verkündigung des Propheten Hosea* (BZAW 169; Berlin: de Gruyter, 1987). **Schüngel-Straumann**, Helen. *Gottesbild und Kultkritik vorexilischer Propheten* (SBS 60; Stuttgart: Katholisches Bibelwerk, 1972). **Wolff**, Hans Walter. "'Wissen um Gott' bei Hosea als Urform von Theologie," *EvT* 12 (1952–53): 533–54 (= ThB 22 [1964]: 182–205).

Amos emphasized that the unique relationship between YHWH and Israel was not a natural one: "Are you more than the Cushites to me, O people of Israel? says the LORD. Did I not only bring Israel up from the land of Egypt, but also the Philistines from Caphtor and the Arameans from Kir?" (9:7). No people had a natural advantage over any other. The prophet is opposing the false sense of security that the people derived from the northern Israelite conviction of having been chosen based on the exodus tradition. According to Amos 3:1–2, YHWH led Israel out of Egypt: at that time he knew Israel (ידעתי)—chose them, in other words—from among all the tribes of the earth. This was an election of grace that demanded recognition by the people. Nonrecognition of this election of grace leads to judgment: "therefore I will punish you for all your iniquities" (3:2). Israel's special relation to God is therefore not a law of nature but a moral one. As we will see further on, this justifies the theological connection between belief in God, worship of God, and ethics. The knowledge of God is conveyed through God's word or, more concretely, through the word of the prophet (3:8). According to Mic 6:8, belief in God, worship of God, and ethics go hand in hand: "You have been told, O mortal, what is good; and what does the Lord require of you but to do justice, and to love kindness, and to walk humbly with your God?" This statement makes it clear that the prophets were not preaching a new ethic. The foundation of their ethical message should already have been known to their listeners for a long time, since long ago YHWH had taught them: הגיד לך אדם, "you have been told, O mortal" (read הֻגַּד, with the LXX.)

Just as Amos's message had based his warning of judgment on his condemnation of social injustice (see below), so Hosea's main focus was on the correct understanding of, and proper attitude toward, God (see Jüngling, "Aspekte," 342). YHWH is the God who has made himself known to Israel through his actions in history, ever since their time in the land of Egypt (Hos 12:10; 13:4; cf. 11:1–4). Hosea seems to have been the first to attach typological value to the exodus from Egypt. This was only possible because the exodus tradition already had theological significance in the northern kingdom. Amos confirms that this tradition had a constitutive value there (Amos 2:10–11; 3:1; 9:7), although as a Judean prophet he does not share

IV. THE THEOLOGICAL SIGNIFICANCE OF THE ERA 221

this view (see Hoffman, "North Israelite Typological Myth"). Most exegetes simply assume that Hosea made the loving relationship between a man and a woman a metaphor for the covenantal relationship between YHWH and Israel. We have seen, however, that this metaphor might have been invented by an editor from Hezekiah's time (p. 165). Whatever the case, it belongs to a redactional layer close to the time of the prophets themselves. One can concur with Klaus Koch, who states that, "Because the *bĕrît* between Yahweh and Israel is seen as a marital relationship it has the potential for a wealth of emotional implications" (Koch, *Die Propheten: I, Assyrische Zeit*, 103). It is also therefore understandable why Hosea's God shares so many characteristics with Baal (2:4ff.; 10:12; 13:15): "Baal" also means husband. Divine love could hardly be portrayed more vividly in earthly form than it is here. It is a love that persists even though Israel turned to other gods (3:1). It is God's compassion that that is merciful with Lo-Ruhama (merciless) and says to Lo-Ammi (not my people): you are my people (2:23). It is a love of freedom, as it says in 14:5: אהבם נדבה, "I love them freely." This love shows YHWH's חסד, which can have different nuances depending on the context. God's attitude is not based primarily on respect for the covenant; instead, חסד seems to be at the root of the special relationship between YHWH and his people, and it is therefore probably best understood as God's grace (see Fahr, "Concept of Grace").

The metaphor of God's marriage to Israel implies that the Baal cult can be described as fornication (the word root זנה, "commit fornication," appears nineteen times in the relatively short book of Hosea). The cult of Baal was probably not so much dedicated to other gods as it was a "Baalization" of YHWH, since YHWH was equated with Baal in worship at the high places. Both the unfaithfulness and the fertility rites of the Baal cult are mentioned (see Otto Procksch, *Theologie des Alten Testaments* [Gütersloh: Bertelsmann, 1950], 154–57; von Rad, *Theologie des Alten Testaments*, 148): Israel credits its goods in life and its fertility to the Baals, as her lovers. Hosea's view of the cult, however, is to a great extent setting a new standard polemically. Everything he disqualifies as part of the Baal cult has been part of the YHWH cult for a long time. "Hosea is the first to denounce the 'entirely normal' YHWH cult of his time as a Baal cult—in the context of the religious enemies of the ninth century—and thus as reprehensible syncretism" (Albertz, *Israelite Religion*, 1:73). YHWH is not only the God of history but, like Baal, he is also the God who supports the agrarian cycle, the God who makes the earth produce and generally makes fields, livestock, and people fruitful. Hosea postulates that YHWH is also responsible for the realities of arable land (see Boshoff, "Yahweh"). Hosea's criticism against its being a fertility cult is aimed at its excesses: against worship of Baals, magic, and superstition. One could concur with Jörg Jeremias that, for Hosea, Baal was a cipher for a failed relationship with God, especially for failed worship ("Der Begriff 'Baal,'" 446).

A characteristic term for Hosea is the "knowledge of God" (דעת אלהים: Hos 4:1; 6:6; הדעת: 4:6; ידעת את־יהוה: 2:22; 5:4; 6:3). This is not a theoretical knowledge about God, but rather an intimacy with the revealed law of God (תורת אלהיך//הדעת, "the instruction of your God" in 4:6), the confession to YHWH (Wolff, "Wissen um Gott"). It also has a historical component (11:1; 12:14): because they were freed from Egypt, Israel's existence is an undeserved gift from God. According to Dwight R. Daniels, דעת אלהים is actually an expression for the historical traditions taught by the priests, in contrast to the תורה, an expression for the legal traditions (Daniels, *Hosea*, 112–14). According to Wolff, in Hosea דעת is the essential content of the priestly office: based on 4:6 it would have been the priest's job to transmit דעת to the people (Wolff, "Wissen um Gott," 187). The prophet condemns the lack of knowledge of God, which is rooted in the rejection and contempt for revealed law (4:6; 8:12): "No faithfulness [אמת], no loyalty to the covenant [חסד], no knowledge of God in the land" (4:1; trans. Wolff; cf. Hos 6:6; 10:12). This is why he also rebukes the YHWH cult of his time as Baalistic.

> "Faithful solidarity" (חסד and אמת) is the manner of behaving in accordance with God's acts and God's gifts in "covenant" and "doctrine." … One who would have in the present the faithful connection YHWH showed in earlier times would live in faithful solidarity with him and with the members of the people of the covenant. Thus, as *summa summarum*, "knowledge of God" also involves behavior in accordance with the covenant. (Wolff, "Wissen um Gott," 197)

Here Hosea seems to be very close to the circles in which the (Ur-) Deuteronomium originated, whose texts also state that Israel's experience was the basis of their "knowledge" from the beginning (Deut 4:35, 39; 7:9; 8:2–5; 9:3–8; see Wolff, "Wissen um Gott," 202–5). Although R. Crotty rejects Wolff's interpretation, his own view is not objectively far from it: the lack of knowledge of God means that YHWH's presence was absent as the basis of the covenant relationship, since the channels guaranteeing that presence, kingship, and priesthood had been perverted (see Hos 4:7–8, 11–12; 10:3–4). This is why the cult had become a mechanical device used to exploit God's power. YHWH was no longer present with his Torah in the cult. The Israelites therefore needed to seek (בקש; see Hos 3:5) YHWH, that is, YHWH's epiphany, and Hosea saw himself as the mediator of the covenant in continuity with Moses (Crotty, *Hosea*). In 1969, Lothar Perlitt supported the thesis that the term "covenant," when used to express the relationship between YHWH and Israel, was an invention of the Deuteronomist. However, Hos 6:7; 8:1—texts

IV. THE THEOLOGICAL SIGNIFICANCE OF THE ERA

whose prophetic provenance can hardly be disputed—mention the covenant (ברית), meaning that Hosea already viewed the relationship between YHWH and Israel as a covenant. Thus, the theory of a "covenantal silence" in Hosea (Perlitt; W. Thiel) is highly dubious. Inasmuch as ברית ("covenant") is found as a parallel to תורה ("instruction"), it could be said that God's covenant with Israel becomes concrete in God's laws and that when the Israelites ignore YHWH's covenant and commandments they renounce YHWH himself (see Neef, *Die Heilstraditionen*, 170–74). The covenantal community proceeds from YHWH and is not a contract between equal partners. According to 6:7, the break between the covenantal community and YHWH began with the dispute between Ephraim and Gilead (Judg 12:1–6; cf. also the reference to the Baal-Peor episode in 9:10). The prophet therefore dates Israel's apostasy from YHWH to the crossing from the desert into arable land. It is striking that Hosea saw the time in the desert as an ideal period of harmony between YHWH and his people (Hos 9:10; 13:4–5), something that surely does not reflect either the view of the Yahwist or the canonical historiography on the period in the desert. This does not mean that he supports a nomadic ideal, though, since in 2:16–17; 12:10 he announces Israel's return to the desert out of which it should come to a new conquest.

The prophet Isaiah emphasized a few important points about the relationship with God. He presented faith in God as the fundamental stance of humans in relation to God: "if do you not believe [תַאֲמִינוּ], you will not be established [תֵאָמֵנוּ]" (Isa 7:9; cf. 28:16). The importance of such belief is underscored by the idea of God's having a plan. YHWH's plan makes human plans seem foolish (14:24–27). Part of YHWH's plan is revealed to the prophet, but Isaiah recognizes the strangeness of YHWH's work: "YHWH will do his deed—strange is his deed!—and will work his work—alien is his work!" (28:21; cf. 29:14). Isaiah preaches YHWH's sovereignty and freedom in his historical arrival to his people. Another statement, one that might have originated at the time when Hezekiah was resting its hopes on Egypt, shows that participation in YHWH's promised salvation is dependent on belief: "See, I am laying in Zion a foundation stone, a tested stone, a precious cornerstone, a sure foundation: 'He who believes will not panic'" (28:16). The belief Isaiah preaches frees one from the fear of a dismal fate and opens one up to God's action in history. This is so because YHWH is a king, one who upholds the universal order, which has its center in the Judean national cult and which has cosmic as well as legal and ethical aspects (see Høgenhaven, *Gott und Volk bei Jesaja: Eine Untersuchung zur biblischen Theologie* [ATDan 24; Leiden: Brill, 1988], 217–30). This belief is a fundamental trust in God's enigmatic reality out of which spring calm and peace, which in times of trouble lead to success in life (Koch, *Die Propheten: I, Assyrische Zeit*, 162). We can conclude along with Rainer Albertz that the prophets of the eighth century conveyed three important aspects in the development of the YHWH religion: the universalization and growth of the image of God, the manifold distancing of YHWH (from the economic order, from the kingship, from the policy of alliances, even from his own cult) and the reinforcement of the ethical dimension of the religion (Albertz, *Israelite Religion*, 1:176–77).

IV.1.2.1. Monotheism

Dietrich, Manfried, and Oswald **Loretz**. *"Jahwe und seine Aschera": Anthropomorphes Kultbild in Mesopotamien, Ugarit und Israel. Das biblische Bilderverbot* (Ugaritisch-biblische Literatur 9; Münster: Ugarit-Verlag, 1992).**Dietrich**, Walter, and Martin A. **Klopfenstein** (eds.), *Ein Gott allein? YHWH-Verehrung und biblischer Monotheismus im Kontext der israelitischen und altorientalischen Religionsgeschichte* (OBO 139; Göttingen: Vandenhoeck & Ruprecht, 1994). **Frevel**, Christian. *Aschera und der Ausschließlichkeitsanspruch YHWHs: Beiträge zu literarischen, religionsgeschichtlichen und ikonographischen Aspekten der Ascheradiskussion* (BBB 94; Weinheim: Beltz Athenäum, 1995). **Keel**, Othmar. "Eine Kurzbiographie der Frühzeit des Gottes Israels," *Bulletin der Europäischen Gesellschaft für Katholische Theologie* 5 (1994): 158–75. **Keel**, and Christoph **Uehlinger**. *Göttinnen, Götter und Gottessymbole: Neue Erkenntnisse zur Religionsgeschichte Kanaans und Israels aufgrund bislang unerschlossener ikonographischer Quellen* (QD 134; Freiburg: Herder, 1992). **Kinet**, Dirk. *Ba'al und Jahwe: Ein Beitrag zur Theologie des Hoseabuches* (EurHS 23.87; Frankfurt am Main: P. Lang, 1977). **Kruger**, P. A. "Yahweh and the Gods in Hosea," *JSem* 4 (1992): 81–98. **Lang**, Bernhard. "Die Jahwe-allein-Bewegung," in Lang et al. (eds.), *Der einzige Gott: Die Geburt des biblischen Monotheismus* (Munich: Kösel, 1981), 47–83. **Niehr**, Herbert. *Der höchste Gott: Alttestamentlicher JHWJ-Glaube im Kontext syrisch-kanaanäischer Religion des 1. Jahrtausends v. Chr.* (BZAW 190; Berlin: de Gruyter, 1990).

Scholars dispute the extent to which one can speak of monotheism among the preexilic prophets. Gerhard von Rad writes in *Theologie des Alten Testaments* that "from the beginning the claim of exclusiveness of the Yahweh faith did not tolerate a peaceful side-by-side existence of the religions" (39). Herbert Donner claims the contrary: "Israel first established itself in the cultivated land of Palestine, and with it came its religion. At the cradle of this religion, however, stood *Baal*" (Donner, *Geschichte des Volkes Israel und seiner Nachbarn in Grundzügen*, vol. 1, *Von den Anfängen bis zur Staatenbildungszeit* [GAT 4.1; Göttingen: Vandenhoeck & Ruprecht, 1984], 148). Von Rad's claim is theological, not historical. Contemporary scholars for the most part no longer assume that Israelite religion was entirely monotheistic from the beginning. Other gods were also worshiped, and in the Israelite religion there was no clear and generally accepted picture of YHWH; instead, there was internal religious pluralism.

IV. THE THEOLOGICAL SIGNIFICANCE OF THE ERA 225

> The Deuteronomic authors leave out the title of Jezebel's god as *Tyric* Baal and make it appear as if Elijah was resisting the worship of any deity by the name of Baal. This is the view of a later era, however. It is only a century later that Hosea questions calling YHWH a Baal and tracks down baalizing elements in the Yahweh cult. Elijah did not yet have this mistrust. He did not have any misgivings that the name Baal was used in the Israelite cult at former Canaanite shrines somewhere on the Jezreel plain, and that the image of a bull was used in connection with a fertility rite in the cult of Bethel and Dan. Instead he cared much more about "divinity in Israel" (1 Kgs 18:36; 2 Kgs 1:3, 6, 16), about the oneness of YHWH, and the powers associated with him. (Koch, *Die Propheten: I, Assyrische Zeit*, 45)

As we saw earlier, the likelihood that YHWH and Asherah formed a divine pair seems increasingly probable (83). In most biblical references Asherah is unquestionably a cultic object, but in 1 Kgs 18:19 and 2 Kgs 23:4 the name could scarcely be anything but a reference to a deity. Occasionally one gets the impression that the refusal to see Asherah and YHWH as a pair in the Khirbet el-Kōm and Kuntillet 'Ajrud texts is based more on theological then philological-historical considerations. J. M. Hadley pointed out that Hosea never condemns Asherah by name, even while he does condemn worship of Baal (in *Ein Gott allein?* 240). This could also point to the connection between YHWH and Asherah in the official religion. The prophets categorically reject cultic images, including the image of a bull from Bethel, for example, which not only was worshiped in folk religion as a representation of YHWH (Hos 8:5–6; 10:5–8) but, according to the Deuteronomistic History (1 Kgs 12:28), was also seen by Jeroboam I as YHWH, the God of the exodus. They reject idols (Isa 2:8; 19:1, 3), for which Isaiah uses the term אלילים ("nonentities"). By doing so, he shows that he did not take them seriously, nor the *maṣṣēbôt* (מצבה, "memorial stone"; Hos 10:1–2) and Asherahs (אשרה), which served as symbols of the masculine power of Baal and the fertility of his female counterpart Astarte. This does not mean, however, that the Israelites of this period adhered to strict monotheism. When Hosea attacks the bull image of Bethel, he does so because of the danger of confusing God and image (magic) and the interchangeability of YHWH with other gods who were represented by the image of a bull, or which had a pedestal in the image of a bull, such as El and, above all, Baal.

In the northern kingdom there arose a "YHWH-only movement"—or rather, in the wake of Elijah's activities (among other reasons), a "YHWH-not-Baal movement," according to Othmar Keel. The prophet Hosea is in this tradition and polemicized strongly against the Baal cult. "The book of Hosea is full of the strongest polemic against Baal; indeed the battle against Baal is the main theme of Hosea" (Schüngel-Straumann, *Gottesbild*, 88).

According to Hosea, YHWH is Israel's God, the only one who plays a role in Israel's fate, and the Israelites should worship YHWH to the absolute exclusion of all other gods. With his emphasis on a unique identity and on the differentiation of the YHWH cult from other religions, Hosea set in motion a reform movement, or at least sped one up that already existed. In his religious intolerance he also polemicizes against generally accepted practices such as the consultation of *teraphim*: "[My people] consult a piece of wood, and their divining rod gives them oracles" (4:12). In 13:2 ("people kissing calves"), the plural form "calves" implies that here, too, what is meant is private worship of icons.

One might presume that this movement had an influence on Hezekiah's cultic reforms. As we saw earlier, however, this reform was probably limited to the removal of Nehushtan (see p. 29). Still, this movement unquestionably had a strong influence on the Deuteronomic reform under King Josiah (622 B.C.E.). That the movement flourished precisely in the eighth century might be connected to pressures from the great powers and the problem of national identity. Albert de Pury prefers to see the conflict as an inner-Yahwistic clash between the genealogically structured "Jacob" Israel and the "exodus" Israel based on "call and guidance." The various Jacob and exodus legends would be two individual and mutually exclusive legends of the origin of Israel that were refined in different circles, one among tribal elites and the other within prophetic circles (de Pury, in *Ein Gott allein*, 413–39). One could justifiably ask, however, whether the text of Hos 12 is not being overinterpreted here. Undoubtedly the prophets were not the first to introduce monolatry or the worship of only one God, but neither did any prophet conclude that the gods worshiped by other peoples did not exist at all (cf. Koch, *Die Propheten: I, Assyrische Zeit*, 22–23).

After the fall of Samaria, this movement gained influence in Judah probably due to refugees from the northern kingdom. The prophet Isaiah and seventh-century prophetic opposition literature were all part of this YHWH-only movement (cf. Nah 1:10–11, 14; 2:2–3; see *Ein Gott allein?*). In this context in the eighth century an assimilation of YHWH and the solar deity might be supposed. Perhaps YHWH inherited the care of law and justice from this god, as that was this sun god's realm. "The combination of the militant God in the foreground with the distant sun god (compare, e.g., Isa 28:21 with 18:48) made available to the eighth- and seventh-century prophets a conception of divinity that allowed them to experience and preach YHWH as a God who engages on behalf of his people or intervenes against his people, but who, at the same time, reigns sovereign and imperturbably over events, and who need not be affected by the destruction of his temple" (Keel, "Eine Kurtzbiographie," 169). These prophets, Isaiah above all, see YHWH at work outside of

Israel too; that is, YHWH actively plans the action of foreign peoples against his people.

IV.1.3. Cult

Beyerlin, Walter. *Die Kulttraditionen Israels in der Verkündigung des Propheten Micha* (FRLANT 54; Göttingen: Vandenhoeck & Ruprecht, 1959). **Hentschke**, Richard. *Die Stellung der vorexilischen Schriftpropheten zum Kultus* (BZAW 75; Berlin: A. Töpelmann, 1957). **Hyatt**, J. Philip. *"The Prophetic Criticism of Israelite Worship,"* in *Interpreting the Prophetic Tradition* (Goldenson Lectures 1955–66; Library of Biblical Studies; Cincinnati: Hebrew Union College Press, 1969), 201–24. **Würthwein**, Ernst. "Kultpolemik oder Kultbescheid? Beobachtungen zu dem Thema 'Prophetie und Kult,'" in *Tradition und Situation: Studien zur alttestamentlichen Prophetie. Artur Weiser zum 70. Geburtstag, am 18. 11. 1963* (ed. Ernst Würthwein and Otto Kaiser; Göttingen: Vandenhoeck & Ruprecht, 1963), 115–31.

There is a long-standing conviction, above all among liberal Protestant exegetes, that Hosea entirely rejected burnt offerings and sacrifices. Thus Otto Procksch claims that "Hosea breaks away from every manner and form of cult more absolutely than any other prophet" (*Theologie*, 159). This cannot be inferred from Hos 6:6: "For I desire steadfast love [חסד] and not sacrifice, the knowledge of God rather than burnt offerings." Certainly Hosea stresses the task of the priests to teach the people YHWH's instruction (תורה) and law (משפט) (4:6)—this is more important than offering sacrifices. That, not the absolute rejection of the sacrificial cult, is the message of the verse: "For Hosea, a cultic act of expiation to renew the community with Yahweh is well known. But the prophet denies the value of even this cultic act, precisely because the intention that pleases Yahweh ... is missing from the sacrificers" (G. Sternberg, "Die Buße bei Hosea," *NKZ* 39 [1928]: 454). The priests do not teach justice. They cause the people to sin and then profit from it, since they receive a considerable share of the sin offerings and guilt offerings (Lev 6:19–22; 7:7): "They feed on the sin of my people; they are greedy for their iniquity" (Hos 4:8). Hosea condemns not only the melding of cult and injustice but also that Israel's cult is a form of *do ut des*, as the people offer their goods to Baal or the baalized YHWH in order to receive goods from nature as a reward (e.g., 2:5–12). Further, the connection of the cult with sacred prostitution makes the cult reprehensible in YHWH's eyes. (However, a few scholars doubt there was actual cultic prostitution in Hosea's time. The prophet's allusions to such practices are not exactly direct, and they could also be referring to profane prostitution.)

Although Hosea condemns his contemporaries' cult, he still draws not a little from the theology practiced at northern Israelite shrines. This theology is expressed clearly in Psalms 80–81, which are doubtless of northern Israelite origin and which surely were common in one of the shrines there. The people are called Joseph and sometimes Ephraim, Benjamin, or Manasseh (Pss 80:2–3; 81:6). Ephraim and Manasseh are the two main tribes of the northern kingdom, alongside which Benjamin is occasionally named. Graham I. Davies points out clear parallels between these psalms and Hosea: like the prophet, the psalmists claim that Israel is YHWH's people (80:5; 81:9, 12, 14); they trace this connection back to the exodus (80:9; 81:6–8, 11) and refer to YHWH's constant concern for Israel (80:2, 10–12, 15; 81:8); they expect YHWH's help in battle (80:4–8; 81:15–16); they allude to the absence of loyalty among the people (80:19; 81:12–14); Ps 80:17 points to the special relationship between YHWH and the king; Ps 81:5–6, 9–10 identifies the religious duties that were imposed on Israel in the exodus as the same as those required by Hosea, while this psalm is similar to a prophetic oracle that has many themes in common with Hosea (see Davies, *Hosea*, 32).

Amos's radical judgment of the cult is equally grounded in the recognition that worship of God and morality are the same thing (5:21–24; see Procksch, *Theologie*, 172). "His criticism is aimed above all at the cultic participants, not at the cult itself" (Jochen Vollmer, *Geschichtliche Rückblicke und Motive in der Prophetie des Amos, Hosea und Jesaja* [BZAW 119; Berlin: de Gruyter, 1971], 15).

> For Amos the criticism of societal relations and mode of living necessarily becomes criticism of the cult, as cult and public-religious life and thought are adapted to lifestyle and societal relations, consecrate them religiously, and justify them.… Thus with Amos there is no individual critique of cultic matters, such as discussions about rites or distinctions between types of sacrifices, but simply a fundamental rejection. (Schüngel-Straumann, *Gottesbild*, 78)

According to Amos, his contemporaries' cult is not for YHWH but for the celebrants themselves; the sacrifices and other rites are simply human self-affirmation. In his criticism of the cult he is the defender of YHWH's rule over Israel. Yet, even if Amos might radically reject the cult of his time and all of its components, this does not mean that he rules out all cult in principle (Schüngel-Straumann, *Gottesbild*, 79). His accusation in 5:21–24 contains some terminological parallels with psalms that Amos would probably have come to know only in a cultic setting. His words against pilgrimages show that his criticism of the cult was mainly directed against the connection between the cult and injustice: "Come to Bethel—and transgress; to Gilgal—and multi-

IV. THE THEOLOGICAL SIGNIFICANCE OF THE ERA

ply transgression!" (4:5a). In 5:4–5 he says, "Seek me and live; but do not seek Bethel." This means that looking for (דרש) YHWH, "searching for his will," in other words, is more important than going to a shrine. Further, in the middle of his actual cult polemic (3:13–14; 4:4–5; 5:4–5, 21–24, 26; 8:4)—which probably was the product of the Judean redaction—we again find a juxtaposition of cult and the lack of morality: "Take away from me the noise of your songs; I will not listen to the melody of your harps. But let justice roll down like waters, and righteousness like an ever-flowing stream" (5:23–24). Because justice and righteousness (משפט and צדקה) are operational factors encompassing everything in the life of Israel—both the social realm and the cult—one could not simply repudiate social justice and at the same time uphold cultic justice (see Koch, *Die Propheten: I, Assyrische Zeit,* 68–74).

Like his predecessors, Isaiah attacks the popular cult (1:29; 2:8, 20; 17:10 [the Adonis gardens]). He takes a quite positive position, however, toward the temple in Jerusalem. The temple is YHWH's palace, where the prophet experiences God's presence (ch. 6). He also emphasizes that YHWH dwells on Zion (8:18). Thus when he condemns the sacrificial cult and holidays, it is coming not from an anticultic position but from the conviction that cult without social justice is unthinkable:

> What to me is the multitude of your sacrifices? says the Lord.
> I have had enough of burnt offerings of rams and the fat of fed beasts;
> I do not delight in the blood of bulls, or of lambs, or of goats.
> When you come to appear before me, who asked this from your hand?
> Trample my courts no more; bringing offerings is futile; incense is an abomination to me.
> New moon and sabbath and calling of convocation—I cannot endure solemn assemblies with iniquity.
> Your new moons and your appointed festivals my soul hates; they have become a burden to me, I am weary of bearing them.
> When you stretch out your hands, I will hide my eyes from you; even though you make many prayers, I will not listen; your hands are full of blood.
> Wash yourselves; make yourselves clean; remove the evil of your doings from before my eyes;
> cease to do evil, learn to do good; seek justice, rescue the oppressed, defend the orphan, plead for the widow. (Isa 1:11–17)

In 22:13, Isaiah also attacks the participants, not the cult itself. Nor can Mic 6:6–7, a text that is unquestionably preexilic (though not necessarily to be ascribed to Micah himself), be read simply as a rejection of offerings. In combination with 6:8, it points rather to a proper ethical life as being more important than any sacrifice (in contrast, see Beyerlin, *Die Kulttraditionen,* 95).

Prophetic sayings about the cult are noticeably coherent: YHWH does not accept offerings with pleasure (רצה, a technical term in cultic language); he does not hear prayer and does not see, or he hates, the ritual acts; his attitude is often motivated by the attitude of the cultic partners, or else something is demanded of them (Amos 5:21-27; Hos 6:6; 8:13; Isa 1:10-17; Würthwein, "Kultpolemik"). If YHWH does not receive a sacrifice with pleasure, it is because the relationship with God is deeply disturbed, because YHWH's sovereignty over the all of life goes unrecognized. Injustice or the spirit of whoredom "must be eliminated for the offering to reach YHWH and the blessing of the community of God to be received.... Accordingly, in some cases, and given certain conditions, the prophets preach that YHWH does not accept sacrifice and prayer. It is entirely misleading to read in these a fundamental and general rejection of sacrifice and prayer" (Würthwein, "Kultpolemik," 125-26).

IV.1.4. Law and Justice: The Ethics of the Prophets

Bach, Robert. "Gottesrecht und weltliches Recht in der Verkündigung des Propheten Amos," in *Festschrift für Günther Dehn zum 75. Geburtstag am 18. April 1957* (Neukirchen: Kreis Moers, 1957), 23–34. **Bohlen**, R. "Zur Sozialkritik des Propheten Amos," *TTZ* 95 (1986): 282–301. **Borchert**, R. "Zur sozialen Botschaft der Propheten des 8. Jahrhunderts," in *Festschrift für Siegfried Wibbing* (Landau, 1986), 2–21. **Davies**, Eryl W. *Prophecy and Ethics: Isaiah and the Ethical Traditions of Israel* (JSOTSup 16; Sheffield: JSOT Press, 1981). **Hardmeier**, Christof. "Die judäische Unheilsprophetie: Antwort auf einen Gesellschafts- und Normenwandel im Israel des 8. Jahrhunderts vor Christus," *Der altsprachliche Unterricht* 26/2 (1983a): 20–44. **Kaiser**, Otto. "Gerechtigkeit und Heil bei den israelitischen Propheten und griechischen Denkern des 8.–6. Jahrhunderts," *Neue Zeitschrift für Systematische Theologie* 11 (1969): 312–28. **Kapelrud**, A. S. "New Ideas in Amos," in *Volume du congrès: Genève, 1965* (VTSup 15; Leiden: Brill, 1966), 193–206. **Niehr**, Herbert. "Bedeutung und Funktion kanaanäischer Traditionselemente in der Sozialkritik Jesajas," *BZ* 28 (1984): 69–81. **Schottroff**, Willy. "Der Prophet Amos: Versuch einer Würdigung seines Auftretens unter sozialgeschichtlichem Aspekt," in Schottroff and Wolfgang Stegemann, *Der Gott der kleinen Leute* (2 vols.; Munich: Kaiser, 1979), 1:39–66. **Wolff**, Hans Walter, *Mit Micha reden: Prophetie einst und jetzt* (Munich: Kaiser, 1978). **Würthwein**, Ernst. "Amos-Studien," *ZAW* 62 (1950): 10–52.

The prophets of the eighth century indisputably have a social-ethical message, which is expressed in their indictment of social injustice. They know that without justice there would be neither peace nor salvation. We will show how each of the prophets expressed this and give our attention, when possible, to the various theological presentations and nuances of these indictments.

IV. THE THEOLOGICAL SIGNIFICANCE OF THE ERA 231

As we saw, Amos is a prophet of doom who strongly condemns social injustice in the northern kingdom and the hypocritical cult connected with it and announces to the people the divine judgment for it. The offenses he recounts pertain to matters of justice (see משפט ["law"] and צדקה ["justice"] in 5:7, 24; 6:12), above all in legal proceedings (5:10–12: בשער ["at the city gate," the place of the administration of justice]), in the accumulation of riches (האוצרים חמס ושד בארמנותיהם, "who store up violence and robbery in their strongholds"; 3:10), in the oppression of the poor (4:1), and in misplaced trust in the cult (5:21–24). "Thus the criticism of the cultus goes hand in hand with legal and social criticism" (Wolff, *Joel and Amos,* 104) though in the Judean redaction, from the beginning of the seventh century, criticism of the cult seems to have been more strongly distinguished (3:14; 4:4–5; 5:4–5, 21–24). Amos attacks the ruling classes (6:4–7), and his condemnation is in some sense pioneering. In Israel it was not a sin to be rich—indeed, just the opposite—and in the wisdom tradition in particular wealth was the privilege of the צדיק, "the upright." Amos did not condemn wealth or luxury in itself, nor was he proposing a sort of asceticism, like that of the Rechabites. For him, however, the wealthy, ruling classes in society are the oppressors, and the צדיקים are now to be found among the oppressed poor, as seen in a parallelism in 2:6: "because they sell the righteous [צדיק] for silver, and the needy [אביון] for a pair of sandals" (cf. 5:11–12; see Kapelrud, "New Ideas," 202–3). Amos's attacks are directed at those whose property grew at the cost of the poor (see Schottroff, "Der Prophet Amos"). Here Amos intends צדיק to refer to those who continued to hold fast to the old order of the apodictic law, as was written in his time in the Covenant Code and perhaps Ur-Deuteronomy. Amos's accusations generally seem to be based on apodictic law (see Bach, "Gottesrecht," 28–34). According to 2:6, the just poor are threatened with debt slavery. Amos seems especially to attack so-called interest-capitalism and its associated debt slavery: rich city-dwellers lead a life of shameless luxury (6:1, 8); small farmers work the land and are exploited by the landowners (5:11); if for any reason the former have too much debt, they are forced into debt slavery (2:6; 8:5; cf. Prov 22:7). Alongside the profits made in this manner, another important source of income for the upper class is the manipulation of the grain trade, which strengthened their position of economic power (see Lang, "The Social Organization of Peasant Poverty in Biblical Israel," *JSOT* 24 [1982]: 47–63). Amos does not pillory the institution of debt slavery itself, as it is supposed by the law (Exod 21:3–6; Deut 15:12–18). Rather, he condemns the unjust abuse of this institution. The same could be said about his stand on liens (2:8), which in practice disregard the established legal protections of the poor. In 4:1–3 Amos points to the connection between the poverty of the exploited and the wealth of the rich. He expresses this even more directly in 3:10: "They store up violence and robbery in their strongholds"—just as Isaiah does, "the spoil of the poor is in your houses" (Isa 3:14). Both divisions of estates and population growth might also have been factors of increasing pauperization (so G. Fleischer, *Von Menschenverkäufern*), though Amos's condemnations show the aforementioned socioeconomic outrages to have been the main causes. With their unfeeling exploitation of credit laws, the upper class destroyed social solidarity, while the administration of justice was not sufficiently independent from the upper class to obtain justice for the oppressed.

Oppression of the weak is generally a main theme of prophetic accusation in the eighth century. This accusation was aimed especially at the oppression of the weak by the powerful, of the poor by wealthy officials and landowners, who, in the words of Isaiah, "join house to house, who add field to field" (Isa 5:8; Amos 2:6–7; 4:1; 5:11; Mic 2:2). It is not impossible, however, that large landowners who took ownership of small farmers indebted to them alongside their land were acting within their legal rights. The prophets also reprimand judges who accepted gifts and bribes in exchange for judgments (Mic 3:11), "who acquit the guilty for a bribe, and deprive the innocent of their rights" (Isa 5:23; cf. Amos 2:7; 5:10, 12). Apparently the powerful made the laws that legalized their moral injustice (Isa 10:1–4). Or perhaps the phrase "disastrous laws and unbearable regulations" refers to legal recommendations from the Jerusalemite judicial officials, who encouraged the perverted judicial decisions at the gates of the country towns (so Hardmeier, "Die judäische Unheilsprophetie," 29). Those who did so were probably royal officials to whom the administration of justice was given, but who sought with their laws to give preference to those residing in their own districts. A particular threat to the poor came with the administration of justice. "In the newly formed justice system created by the king and his officials the poor were even more systematically threatened than they have been in the legal system of lay judges" (Schwantes, *Das Recht der Armen* [BEvT 4; Frankfurt am Main: Lang, 1977], 106). In 3:14–15 Isaiah attacks the ruling classes as a whole: "The Lord enters into judgment with the elders [זקנים] and officials [שרים] of his people: It is you who have devoured the vineyard; the spoil of the poor is in your houses. What do you mean by crushing my people?" "Internally (within the tribe) the elders have ruling and judicial functions and, externally, representative functions; the officials exercise military, administrative, and judicial functions in the king's stead" (Wildberger, *Isaiah: A Continental Commentary* [3 vols.; Minneapolis: Fortress, 1972], 1:142). Just as in the Covenant Code (Exod 22:24), the poor are in parallelism to the people of YHWH. The accusation of the behavior of the upper classes toward the poor, then, has a principled and radical character. Isaiah vividly summed up his judgment

IV. THE THEOLOGICAL SIGNIFICANCE OF THE ERA 233

of the people's social behavior in his vineyard song: "he expected justice [מִשְׁפָּט], but saw bloodshed [מִשְׂפָּח]; righteousness [צְדָקָה], but heard a cry [צְעָקָה]!" (5:7). The belief that Isaiah's social criticism was aimed "exclusively at the Canaanite or Canaanized upper class and civil servants, at their interference in the old regulations of legal life and in problems with respect to landownership" (so Donner, "Die soziale Botschaft," 243–44; Niehr, "Bedeutung") can no longer be historically sustained, since this view betrays both a naïve understanding of the legal organization and an uncritical conception of the relationship between Canaanites and Israelites, based on the Deuteronomistic History. When the prophets make an accusation of the exploitation of weaker groups, they appeal not to a positive Israelite *jus soli* against a Canaanite civil service but to a just social order—not a positive legal category but an ethical one.

According to Micah, the sin of Judah is concentrated in Jerusalem (Mic 1:5). He identifies those who are oppressed with "the free men (2:2) in YHWH's community (2:5) who suffered under the Jerusalemite officials. His use of language makes perfect sense as that of an elder from the countryside who is closely connected to his fellow citizens" (Wolff, *Mit Micha reden*, 36). This rural prophet does not fail to notice the defects of life in the capital. He protests that under Hezekiah the expansion of the capital was carried out with blood (דָּמִים) and injustice (עַוְלָה; 3:10); one need only think of the example of the Siloam tunnel. According to his message, the root of the evil was the disregard and perversion of justice on the part of Jerusalem's leading class: "Listen, you heads of Jacob [רָאשֵׁי יַעֲקֹב] and rulers of the house of Israel [קְצִינֵי בֵּית יִשְׂרָאֵל]! Is it not your duty to know the law?" (Mic 3:1). They should have known it, since the prophet, or perhaps an unknown seventh-century author, reminds his audience of God's revelation of his will as expressed in the laws: "He has told you, O mortal, what is good; and what does the Lord require of you but to do justice" (6:8; see Beyerlin, *Die Kulttraditionen*, 50–52). Here, according to Beyerlin, the heads (רָאשֵׁי יַעֲקֹב) are the tribal and family leaders who were responsible for the administration of justice at the gates (see Exod 18:25–26); the leaders (קְצִינֵי בֵּית יִשְׂרָאֵל) could be the Jerusalemite royal officials who in the later monarchy practiced an independent royal administration of justice (ibid., 52–53), although admittedly this is impossible to prove with any certainty through the texts. These judges violated the law, which was intended to protect the weak in society, and turned it against those who were in need of protection. More concretely, we might say that they contravened the laws of the Covenant Code (Exod 23:1–3, 6-9) and Ur-Deuteronomy (Deut 16:19). At the same time, they felt themselves to be protected by their cultic institutions, like those in Hosea's and Isaiah's audience:

> Hear this, you rulers of the house of Jacob and chiefs of the house of Israel,
> who abhor justice and pervert all equity,
> who build Zion with blood and Jerusalem with wrong!
> Its rulers give judgment for a bribe [שחד], its priests teach for a price,
> its prophets give oracles for money; yet they lean upon the Lord and say,
> "Is not the Lord in the midst of us? No harm shall come upon us." (Mic 3:9–11)

The prophets do not attempt to incite the oppressed classes of people to revolt; they are not revolutionaries with a socioeconomic program of their own. Instead they direct their speeches directly at the oppressors and charge that their behavior conflicts with the law sanctioned by YHWH. Isaiah, whose message is directed at the royal court and the Jerusalemite aristocracy, also denounces social injustice:

> Like Amos, Isaiah was an unrelenting guardian of, and spokesperson for, divine law. He continues the indictment against every form of perversion of justice and discrimination against the legally weak with such breadth and intensity to warrant the assumption that the prophets of the eighth century already had a certain tradition, a practice with respect to the themes of prophetic address. (von Rad, *Theologie des Alten Testaments*, 2:156)

The terms "justice" and "law" play a central role in Isaiah's preaching (צדק[ה]: 1:21, 26; 5:7, 23; 9:6; 28:17; משפט: 1:17, 21; 4:4; 5:7; 9:6; 10:2; 28:17). By these terms he means a community organized in solidarity, one that guarantees the basic rights of all its citizens. For Isaiah, the administration of justice was crucial for society's proper connection with God; it demonstrates how serious one is about God. That is why time and again he condemns oppression of the poor, bribery, unjust administration of laws, and the latifundia economy of the ruling class, which leads to the exploitation of the weak (1:17, 21–28; 3:13–15; 5:7, 8–10; etc.). Even if this economic system were legal, it would result in the bitter poverty of subsistence farmers and probably their loss of representation in the community's assembly of full citizens (Davies, *Prophecy and Ethics,* 102). He also thunders against the luxuries of women of higher status (3:16–24) and against banquets and drinking parties (5:11–12). These views are similar to those of Amos, and Isaiah was probably influenced by him, too, while in his fight against landlordism he resembles Micah (Mic 2:1–5). Isaiah's ethical claims are related to the importance of YHWH's holiness in his prophetic experience and theology. YHWH is Israel's Holy One, an epithet used almost exclusively in Isaiah (twenty-four times, compared with five times in other books). YHWH's holiness is not simply of heavenly significance; YHWH is holy in and with Israel. "As 'Israel's Holy One' YHWH reigns

IV. THE THEOLOGICAL SIGNIFICANCE OF THE ERA 235

less *over* the people than he reigns through them" (Koch, *Die Propheten: I, Assyrische Zeit,* 169). As the Holy One, YHWH has a special connection with Israel that includes his demands that his people be correspondingly holy. In his holiness YHWH must be feared (8:13), since it is he who mercilessly punishes sins. As a moral characteristic YHWH's holiness consists in his justice, and therefore he expects justice from his people. Thus injustice is ingratitude to YHWH, he who in his holiness lavished on his people so much love and care (Isa 5:1–4) According to Isaiah, haughtiness or overestimation of one's own abilities are the root of all human injustice in Judah (Isa 2:6–19*; see the theme of arrogance in 3:16–26; 9:7–20 + 5:25–29).

Milton Schwantes comes to the following conclusion about Amos, though it can equally be said of Isaiah and Micah:

> Reference to the poor is found not in the prohibition itself, as in Zech 7:10a, but in the accusation that serves as the grounds for the declaration of damnation in the prophetic judgment. The poor get their rights not through the prohibition, but through the announcement and justification of the outcome. The rights of the poor are not expressed as a right to be advanced but as one that is disregarded at the gates, in economics. and in human relations. (Schwantes, *Das Recht der Armen*, 99)

According to Christof Hardmeier, Amos goes beyond traditional ethics insofar as he sees the typical social behavior of the upper strata as a social dimension and no longer one of individual, personal behavior. His younger contemporaries Micah and Isaiah even go a step further in their social criticism, in that they envision changes in the economic structure, that is, the stealing of land and the formation of latifundia, which were destroying the agricultural economy of small farmers. The prophets consistently judged the social developments in the communal fields of economy and the new morality of exploitation on the damage and the victims they made. This is traditional solidarity ethics, something also found in proverbial wisdom (e.g., compare Prov 31:6–7 and Isa 1:16–17), whose "final goal is to secure each and every disadvantaged person their rights, to bring them back into society and not consign them to further impoverishment and isolation" (Hardmeier, "Die judäische Unheilsprophetie," 30–33).

> Thus the social accusation of the prophets is not an objective analysis of society but is deliberately one-sided and partisan. In the name of God the prophets show up the apparently autonomous critical social development of their time as the guilty behaviour of the upper classes, and in so doing clearly put themselves on the side of the lower classes, who are getting poorer. For them, those with economic strength who are profiting from the develop-

ments are clearly the guilty ones, whereas the economically weak, the victims of this development, are really innocent (*ṣaddīq*, Amos 2.6; 5.12). ... [T]hey pointed out that an economic and legal order which is no longer orientated on the basic norms of *mišpāṭ* and *ṣedāqā* and no longer gives special protection to the rights of marginal groups in society is unjust, however legal the proceedings may be. (Albertz, *Israelite Religion*, 1:165–66)

IV.1.5. POLITICS

Dietrich, Walter. *Jesaja und die Politik* (BEvT 74; Munich: Kaiser, 1976). **Gelston**, A. "Kingship in the Book of Hosea," *OTS* 19 (1974): 71–85. **Gonçalves**, Francolino J. "Isaïe, Jérémie et la politique internationale de Juda," *Bib* 76 (1995): 282–98. **Hoffmann**, Hans Werner. *Die Intention der Verkündigung Jesajas* (BZAW 136; Berlin: de Gruyter, 1974). **Høgenhaven**, Jesper. "Prophecy and Propaganda: Aspects of Political and Religious Reasoning in Israel and the Ancient Near East," *SJOT* 1 (1989): 125–41. **Huber**, Friedrich. *Jahwe, Juda und die anderen Völker beim Propheten Jesaja* (BZAW 137; Berlin: de Gruyter, 1976). **Keller**, Carl-A. "Das quietistische Element in der Botschaft des Jesaja," *TZ* 11 (1955): 81–97.

The prophets received their inspiration not only from visionary revelations and Israelite traditions; they also lived through changes in the national and political sphere and reflected on them. It could even be said that their faithful and engaged reflection on contemporary political and social events was the main source of their prophetic words. It was therefore very clear to Amos that the northern kingdom would succumb to a military catastrophe and be led into exile (2:13–16; 3:11; 5:3). He interprets these political developments as the judgment of YHWH. In this way, for instance, the conquest of the land and the looting of the palaces (3:11) are seen as divine punishment for violence and oppression (3:9–10). The prophet also uncovered the cause of the disaster through careful consideration of social circumstances. Hosea recognizes the execution of divine judgment in the palace revolutions (8:4): "I gave you a king in my anger, and I took him away in my wrath" (13:11). He does not seem to speak against kingship in general or reproach the monarchy of northern Israel in particular with apostasy from the house of David; rather he reprimands the contemporary northern Israelite monarchy for apostasy against YHWH and general moral decay (Hos 7:3–7; 8:4; 13:10). Or is the "evil in Gilgal" (9:15) perhaps an insinuation about Saul's elevation to the throne (1 Sam 11:15)?

In Hos 10:4; 12:2 the prophet turns against Israel's policy of alliances. Since the making of treaties is listed among Israel's sins in both verses, it is clear that "in Israel's alliances with foreign powers Hosea saw a break in the relationship/fellowship with YHWH" (Neef, *Die Heilstraditionen*, 164–72): in the policy of alliances Israel loses its identity and breaks away from YHWH, its only helper. The work of Herbert Donner on the position of the classical prophets of the eighth century on the foreign policies of the kings of Israel and Judah (*Israel unter den Völkern*)—which we looked at in detail in our consideration of the prophetic books as historical sources—is also important, especially as pertains to the prophets' political positions. In his opinion, Isaiah was decidedly against military and political alliances either with or against Assyria. He supported neutrality, which Donner calls a realistic and intelligent view (see also Dietrich, *Jesaja und die Politik*, esp. 255–56). Hans Werner Hoffmann reacts to this in the negative: "Each of his political demands was in the first place a demand for belief" (*Die Intentionen*, 76). This is probably correct, but the sharp contrast between the rational and the faithful Isaiah is an undemonstrated and unfortunate allegation made by a theologian. Nor is Isaiah a quietist, as Carl-A. Keller would have it, who believes, for instance, that Isaiah condemned all defensive measures (with reference to Isa 7:4, see Keller, "Das quietistische Element"). The quietism of such words should not be exaggerated, however, as the prophet's security—a motive in the war speeches in the so-called YHWH-war—includes the participation of warriors. According to Donner, it is not a negative neutrality but a positive conception, a sense of security based on trust in YHWH's word. All resistance against Assyria is pointless, and, according to Isaiah, the politics of resistance without YHWH is even a sin. In other words, Judah's alliance should be only with YHWH (see Donner, *Israel unter den Völkern*, 169–72). Through Isa 7:1–9; 14:29–32*; 18:1–6*; 20:1–6, Hoffman also shows that Isaiah tried to convert his people from military-political alliances to faith in YHWH, and he sees the work of the prophet as moving the government and the nation as a whole to a right existence desired by God (*Die Intentionen*, 49–77). However, as we have seen (p. 117), according to Jesper Høgenhaven (*Gott und Volk bei Jesaja*) Isaiah supported the cautious and pro-Assyrian foreign policies of King Ahaz and decidedly opposed the actively anti-Assyrian line of King Hezekiah (cf. Isa 30:1–7). In his opinion, the Isaian prophecies were tightly bound up with the interests of the Jerusalemite court during the Syro-Ephraimitic war and should be understood as a legitimation of Ahaz's pro-Assyrian policies. The condemnation of these policies can only be ascribed to a later redactional layer. In the crisis at the end of the ninth century, the prophet always condemned coalitions with Egypt and other nations against Assyria. At the same time, the friendly relationship between Isaiah and Hezekiah in Isa 36–37 is not relevant to the discussion, as these chapters should be read within the framework of the Deuteronomistic History and are not an authentic Isaiah tradition (*Gott und Volk bei Jesaja*, 164–65). According to Isa 39:1–8, Hezekiah received ambassadors from the Babylonian king Merodach-Baladan (Marduk-apla-iddin) and showed them his storehouses. If this is historical, the Judean king sought to bring not only Egypt but also the Babylonian usurper Merodach-Baladan into his coalition (cf. 2 Chr 32:25ff.). "Isaiah was not satisfied with attacking these people because of their support of revolutionary policies (against Assyria) but ascribed their wrongheaded position on foreign policies to a fundamental attitude that is characterized by arrogance, carefree self-assertion, and disastrous self-deception and that had an effect on the entire behavior of those concerned" (Høgenhaven, *Gott und Volk bei Jesaja*, 187; see also idem, "Prophecy and Propaganda"). Stuart A. Irvine (*Isaiah, Ahaz*) rejects the traditional picture of an Isaiah who condemned Ahaz for his appeal to Tiglath-pileser III against the Syro-Ephraimitic coalition. This picture is supported in the text of Isaiah, but only in the combination of prophetic material with the negative Deuteronomistic portrayal of Ahaz's reign in 2 Kgs 16:7ff. This is pure Deuteronomistic invention, and in reality Ahaz would have remained neutral in the wider anti-Assyrian movement in the Syro-Palestinian area in the years after 740. He would have been one of the few Palestinian rulers who did not participate. On the other hand, a large sector of the population—the majority of the Judean inhabitants, even—would have supported the coalition, while the prophet supported the king during the entire conflict (cf. pp. 102–4).

Whatever the case, Isaiah was, first of all, YHWH's messenger, and only under this condition did he intervene in politics. "Isaiah did not fundamentally expect earthly powers to abandon their own political efforts and objectives, nor did he raise belief to a political program. At the same time, the particular intentions of YHWH, Lord of the earth, were his standard for evaluating all political programs" (Dietrich, *Jesaja und die Politik*, 235). In any case, he was distrustful of political alliances with neighboring states, for in such alliances he sees a lack of trust in YHWH and a reinforcement of the more powerful social class: Isaiah "believed in a God who fundamentally wanted to secure the right of the weak against the more powerful.... This holds for the sociopolitical as well as the foreign political realm" (Dietrich, *Jesaja und die Politik*, 268; cf. Gonçalves, "Isaïe," 289–91).

IV.1.6. JUDGMENT AND CONVERSION

Dietrich, Walter. "JHWH, Israel und die Völker beim Propheten Amos," *TZ* 48 (1992): 315–28. **Hardmeier**, Christof. "Jesajas Verkündigungsabsicht und Jahwes Verstockungsauftrag in Jes 6," in *Die Botschaft und die Boten: Festschrift für Hans Walter Wolff zum 70. Geburtstag* (ed. Jörg Jeremias and Lothar Perlitt; Neukirchen-Vluyn: Neukirchener, 1981), 235–52. **Haspecker**, Josef. "Natur und Heilsdenken bei den Propheten," *BibLeb* 9 (1968): 237–49. **Herrmann**, Siegfried. *Die prophetischen Heilser-*

wartungen im Alten Testament: Ursprung und Gestaltwandel (BWANT 85; Stuttgart: Kohlhammer, 1965). **Hesse**, Franz. *Das Verstockungsproblem im Alten Testament: Eine frömmigkeitsgeschichtliche Untersuchung* (BZAW 74; Berlin: A. Töpelmann, 1955). **Kilian**, Rudolf. *Jesaja 1–39* (EdF 200; Darmstadt: Wissenschaftlight Buchgesellschaft, 1983), 112–30. **Keel**, Othmar. "Rechttun oder Annahme des Gerichts? Erwägungen zu Amos, dem früheren Jesaja und Micha," *BZ* 21 (1977): 200–218. **Reimer**, Haroldo. *Richtet auf das Recht! Studien zur Botschaft des Amos* (SBS 149; Stuttgart: Katholisches Bibelwerk, 1992). **Schenker**, Adrian. "Gerichtsankündigung und Verblendung bei den vorexilischen Propheten," *RB* 93 (1986): 563–80. **Schmidt**, J. M. "Gedanken zum Verstockungsauftrag Jesajas," *VT* 21 (1971): 68–90. **Schmidt**. "Ausgangspunkt und Ziel prophetischer Verkündigung im 8. Jahrhundert," *VF* 22 (1977): 65–82. **Sternberg**, G. "Die Buße bei Hosea," *NKZ* 39 (1928): 450–62. **Vollmer**, Jochen. *Geschichtliche Rückblicke und Motive in der Prophetie des Amos, Hosea und Jesaja* (BZAW 119; Berlin: de Gruyter, 1971). **Wolff**, Hans Walter. *Die Stunde des Amos: Prophetie und Protest* (Munich: Kaiser, 1969). **Zenger**, Erich. "Die eigentliche Botschaft des Amos: Von der Relevanz der Politischen Theologie in einer exegetischen Kontroverse," in *Festschrift J. B. Metz* (Mainz, 1988), 394–406.

In their trial speeches the prophets repeatedly announced the annihilation of the country. In these statements they are not particularly interested in the political consequences of such annihilation, such as the loss of political independence. Their words are directed more to the loss of the goods of the land, such as the devastation of farmland or the destruction of cities (see Haspecker, "Natur," 240–41). In their image of the future they project catastrophes that occur fairly often. For the prophets of the eighth century it is above all social transgressions that bring about disaster, and a connection can often be seen between the content of the sin and that of the punishment. For example, in Isa 5:8–13, to those who tack house upon house it is said that all their houses will be deserted; in Mic 2:1–5, those who want fields and seize them are told: "Therefore you will have no one to divide a field with a measuring line in the assembly of the Lord"; in Mic 6:9–15, those who enriched themselves in the city have the loss of their riches foretold (ibid., 247). On the other hand, the statement "the end has come upon my people Israel" (Amos 8:2) is something new and unprecedented: it expresses nothing less than a prediction of calamity for the whole people (see W. H. Schmidt, *Zukunftsgewissheit*, 15). Even if one translates קץ as "harvest" and not "end," it remains a vision of radical destruction. In Amos's trial speeches as well as in his visions he expresses his certainty that Israel is doomed to destruction (7:1–3, 4–6, 7–8; 8:1–2; 9:1–14). Israel would be torn apart as by a lion (3:12), and the day of YHWH, a special festival of the deity the people hoped would be a day of triumph, will have not light but darkness (5:18–20). In a very careful study, however, Haroldo Reimer has expounded the thesis that the heralding of destruction would not affect the people of Israel as a whole but was rather directed at particular segments of community and class.

> If we list all the people, important figures, or institutions in the northern kingdom that were to meet their "end" in some manner in the coming doom according to the earliest compositions, the following are represented: the military (2:13–16; 5:2–3 + 6:13–14), the representative buildings and defensive installations of the kingdom (3:11, 15; 6:8, 11), the rulers in the capital (3:12; 4:1–3; 6:7; 7:9b; 8:1–3), the capital itself (6:11), the prophets of salvation and the priests officiating at the state shrines (5:18ff., 21ff., 27; 9:1ff.; cf. also 5:5), as well as the rich Israelites in all fortified cities and villages (5:10ff., 16–17). (Reimer, *Richtet*, 229)

Walter Dietrich ("JHWH") has a similar perspective on the trial speech concerning the neighboring peoples and Israel (1:3–2:16*). While the trial speech comes close to announcing a complete destruction of the nation, one should nevertheless take seriously this idea of a restricted judgment and give it greater than usual attention. As Reimer rightly says, "The 'judgment' is great, but it does not mean a total end for the whole nation." The oppressed poor are not to be included in the judgment, for instance, as this would be an unbearable injustice (see Koch, *Die Propheten: I, Assyrische Zeit*, 56). Less convincing, however, is Reimer's claim that Amos is hinting at a leaderless society after the calamity. In Amos 4:4–12*, the prophet replaces the one-sided tradition of YHWH's acts of salvation with a statement of his uninterrupted acts of destruction. It is true that even this divine act has a salvific purpose, "but because of the persistent refusal of conversion YHWH's acts of calamity has become a history of calamity whose goal is the obliteration of Israel" (Vollmer, *Geschichtliche Rückblicke*, 20).

Hosea's words express the same conviction. The symbolic names of his children in 1:2–9—even if they do stem from an eighth-century redaction of a disciple (see 164)—clearly express that, in his view, the tradition of election no longer had any validity: לא רחמה ("not pitied") and לא עמי ("not my people"). In 2:16–22* he writes of the possibility of Israel's going through a judgment of purification. According to Vollmer, it was only later that the prophet's view of judgment moved in this direction (*Geschichtliche Rückblicke*, 122). In my opinion this cannot be proven, and the message of the judgment of purification could just as well be changed to one of destruction. Again according to Vollmer, Isaiah "initially held the view that a judgment of purification would suffice to return Israel to complete communion with YHWH. After the second meeting with Ahaz, however, when the latter refused the offer of a sign, Isaiah announced a judgment of total destruction" (ibid., 199–200; cf. Fohrer, *Die Propheten des Alten Testaments*, 1:158). Hoffmann even holds the opinion that until a turnabout in 701 (seen in Isa 22:1–14; 29:9–10), at the end of his prophetic activity, Isaiah had been a prophet demanding only conversion (Hoffmann, *Die Intentionen*, 49–59, 125). Hoffmann thinks that, in a second period of his career Isaiah no longer called the people of Judah-Jerusalem YHWH's people but "this people" and that this reassessment of the people is also expressed in 6:9–10 (ibid., 22–23). He attaches too much importance, however, without sufficient grounds to his correct thesis that the intent of a great part of Isaiah's words of calamity was to cause the people to change (see Isa 1:16–17; 28:22). He does so because he did not take into account important parts of the text adduced by Vollmer (6:11, among others), or because he did not interpret them in a satisfactory manner (e.g., the song of the vineyard, 5:1–7; 29:1–4), while at the same time because of his thesis he overinterprets other texts (e.g., 1:2–3). For his part, Vollmer did not give enough weight to texts such as 1:10–17, 18–20 or 2:7–17*. In addition, in 1:21–28* Isaiah sees the possibility of a judgment of purification. He "speaks of judgment and destruction of the defective and at the same time of the possibility of a restitution initiated in the middle of the judgment, whose roots are in the present, " (Herrmann, *Die prophetischen Heilserwartungen*, 128). Hoffmann and Vollmer both see something valid, but one should not absolutize either of their theses. "The chronological succession of the various phases cannot be proven" (Rudolph, *Hosea*, 259). Werner H. Schmidt is also of the opinion that, according to Isaiah, reform is impossible and there is no way open to salvation in the present. He also sweeps the prophet's words of exhortation and warning under the carpet too easily, reading them as offering only apparent possibilities or as being the expression of a missed opportunity (see W. H. Schmidt, *Zukunftsgewissheit*, 39–54). In relation to Amos, too, Hans Walter Wolff claims that the prophet is assured of the coming destruction and rejects any interpretation that "would falsify" his concern into a call for repentance (Wolff, *Joel and Amos*, 103). Similarly, nothing resembling a call for change could be found in the texts of Micah. There is therefore a whole line of exegetes who defend the absolute radicalism of prophecy of calamity (Wolff, Jörg Jeremias, F. Hecht, Helen Schüngel-Straumann, Werner H. Schmidt, G. Warmuth, Klaus Koch, H. V. Hunter; cf. J. M. Schmidt, "Ausgangspunkt"). One could argue, however, along with Christof Hardmeier, that the logic of the prophecy of calamity is based on the act–consequence process—the guilt rebounds to the actor as a punishment—and that the intention of their proclamations was to keep open the guilt–calamity process by clarifying the guilt in hopes of moving the guilty to change and avert the coming calamity: "Amos's intercession for his people in his visions, as well as Isaiah's thirty-year activity as a preacher, notwithstanding the command given to him to be obdurate, demonstrate that the proclamation of guilt and calamity had in fact the aim of averting the doom that threatened them as a consequence of their guilt by enlightening the people" (Hardmeier, "Die judäische Unheilsprophetie," 38–40).

Erich Zenger also made it clear that Amos "was neither the herald of the absolute end nor the exhorter to change, but the preacher of God's judgment and God's justice" ("Die eigentliche Botschaft," 405). Such a message was meant not only to shake up those who exploit the weak with an easy conscience, but it could also bring hope, especially to the exploited.

In Isa 6:9–10 we read the most theologically difficult text in the Bible, the so-called command of stubbornness (*Verstockungsauftrag*):

> Go and say to this people:
> Hear and hear, but do not understand; see and see, but do not perceive.
> Make the heart of this people fat, and their ears heavy, and shut their eyes.

In later statements Isaiah pronounced these thoughts of obduration again (29:9–10). In light of theological reservations about this verse—a God who hardens people or, rather, gives the order for it—many clarifications have been attempted: the obduration was a punishment for sin; the imperative in verse 9 was only a strong expression of the future; the Semitic mind did not differentiate between types of causality, so what God permits he causes; the *hiphil* forms in verse 10 are not causative but should be interpreted as permissive; the prophet afterwards interpreted his mission as one of obduration, as he saw that it led, de facto, to obduration. Each of these explanations includes some measure of truth. Behind these verses is the well-known prophetic view on the dynamic power of God's word. The *dābār* is a tool God uses to guide history. The prophet receives the order at once to announce YHWH's judgment on his people through the word and, at the same time, to carry it out. In v. 9 the prophet is sent with a word of command (*Machtwort*); the imperatives mean that the prophet puts his listeners in a state of "hearing but not understanding."

This condemnation presumes sin, however. The people have already done something from which they can return (שׁוב; v. 10). Isaiah says that the time of conversion is passed and that now, with his message, the time of punishment has come. The obduracy of the people is punished with more obduracy. "Obduracy does not come about by accident; it is a lamentable result of a long prophetic/divine experience with these people" (Koch, *Die Propheten: I, Assyrische Zeit*, 126). According to Gerhard von Rad, in the message–rejection dialectic the rejection itself has a place in God's plan: "this means, however, that we must relearn to view the statement of obduracy as part of salvation history" (von Rad, *Theologie des Alten Testaments*, 162). This view of the statement of obduracy as part of salvation history is based on the assumption that YHWH's plan is unchanging. As we will see further on, according to

IV. THE THEOLOGICAL SIGNIFICANCE OF THE ERA

the prophetic view, God's actions are based not only on his plan but also on human behavior. Hardmeier is right in claiming that one cannot depict Isaiah as a pure "prophet of obduracy" (see 174). The prophet's efforts at clarifying guilt cannot be denied. Throughout the stages of his preaching he tries again and again to bring about the realization of sin as a prerequisite for forgiveness and conversion. He tries to clarify the "theologically perceived sociopolitical correlation of guilt with its threats of judgment in order to remove and prevent it. Instead of understanding and recognition, however, which could have resulted in conversion, he experiences nonunderstanding and rejection, which he understands *in retrospect* as YHWH's having caused an obduracy that runs counter to the intent of his preaching" (Hardmeier, "Jesajaforschung im Umbruch," 30–31; see also Dietrich, *Jesaja und die Politik*, 175–80). Hardmeier convincingly showed that, in contrast to its literary context in the so-called memoir (*Denkschrift*), the statement of obduracy in Isa 6:9–10 is from a later period:

> This order [7:2–9] stands in glaring contradiction with the obduracy command in the vision narrative. The narrated proclamation is only meaningful if the prophet and his God assume at the beginning of the war that the politics of the hard-pressed king would be determined by this promise of well-being. Historically, in this phase there could not have been any awareness of a command of obduracy. Thus the order in Isa 6 is shown to be a retrospective interpretation of the experience. (Hardmeier, "Verkündigung und Schrift bei Jesaja," 127)

This would be true if Isa 6:9 was in fact an order of obduracy. However, Adrian Schenker demonstrated quite convincingly that obduracy is not the point of this section—blinding is. Obduracy is fixation of the will in a wrong choice; blinding is fixation of the mind in an error, which is what we have here. Isaiah not only has the order to blind, but also the order to reveal YHWH's true intent with it, and that has its reason: "Since blinding makes the *right decision* impossible, it leads assuredly to disaster. At the same time YHWH cannot go so far as to be *untrue* for the sake of bringing about this punishment. Thus, he never blinds entirely, and *therefore no doom, no matter how firmly he is resolved to it, is inescapable*" (Schenker, "Berichtsankündigung," 577). This opinion is confirmed by the fact that in the so-called Isaiah Memoir, 6:9–10 forms an *inclusio* with a statement of hope in 8:17.

Unlike his Judean contemporary Isaiah, Micah announces the destruction of Jerusalem, including the temple (Mic 3:12), a threat that remained in memory in Jeremiah's time (Jer 26:18). His criticism of Jerusalem is also radical, and he sees no salvation for the capital. The capital, however, is not the whole nation.

IV.1.7. History, Eschatology, and Messianism

IV.1.7.1. Conception of History

Wolff, Hans Walter. "Das Geschichtsverständnis der alttestamentlichen Prophetie," *EvT* 20 (1960): 218–35.

Hans Walter Wolff pointed out, correctly, that the prophetic understanding of history must first be understood as the understanding of history from the perspective of its future. The future appears here as YHWH's future (e.g., Hos 5:14), which takes shape at the outset in the prophetic word. The prophetic word, however, is aimed at the conversion of the listener and consequently the nonfulfillment of what was threatened, thus demonstrating the dialogical character of history: "Prophetic history is the purposeful dialogue of the lord of the future with Israel" (Wolff, "Das Geschichtsverständnis," 324). It is discernible as a continuous unity, since at all times and in all places it is infused with the sameness of the God of Israel. Already in Amos the history of Israel is viewed in relation to the history of the nations (9:7), and in the eighth century Assyria is recognized as YHWH's instrument in his actions throughout history (Isa 10*). Thus an interest in universal history awakens in prophecy that increasingly recognizes the God of Israel as the sole God of all reality. This view is still a guide for us today: "Contingent events are rooted in the freedom of God's discussion with humanity; at the same time the continuity of the totality of history is rooted in God's superior, all-encompassing faithfulness" (ibid., 335). According to Dwight R. Daniels, Hosea in particular was aware of a continuity in Israel's history intended by YHWH; it is therefore justifiable to speak of a salvation history in Hosea (Daniels, *Hosea and Salvation History*, 124–25). In Nahum, too, one can see a straight course running through world history: "The fate predicted for the capitals of the world (more concretely Nineveh) is fulfilled with eerie, even frightening precision" (Seybold, *Nahum, Habakuk,* 14)

In a thorough study, however, Vollmer has shown that for the great prophets of the eighth century, Amos, Hosea, and Isaiah, the continuity of history is very relative: "Indeed, Yahweh brought about the history of Israel, but that this history went this way and not some other way is not based on some plan of Yahweh's that he brought to life step by step since primeval times but should rather be attributed to individual human decisions for or against Yahweh" (Vollmer, *Geschichtliche Rückblicke,* 202 and passim). YHWH guides history, not because he predetermines events but because he offers humans a path that they can follow or reject. As mentioned, the content of the message of these prophets is YHWH's coming in judgment. When they look back in history it is not to confirm the validity of the salvation-historical traditions, to explain them, and thus confirm the way the hearers see themselves, but in order to show the lapses into guilt and to justify their predictions of judgment. We learn from Amos 2:9, read in its context, that the prophet did not entirely hold to the validity of the gift of the land. He denies the traditional idea, whereby YHWH stands on Israel's side forever. In 9:7 he maintains the equal status of the other nations alongside Israel before YHWH.

According to Isa 6:11, Isaiah should announce the complete destruction of Israel (cf. 5:1–7). He outlines a history of calamity in which, compared to the previous reformation judgments, the imminent judgment of destruction appears to be something entirely new (9:7–20 + 5:25–29*). In 28:14–22 and 29:1–4, he turns the tradition of David's victories and his conquest of Jerusalem around to mean the opposite. All of this collides with a widespread opinion, one expressed, for example, by von Rad as follows: "We see how deep they [the prophets of the eighth century] are rooted in the religious traditions of their people, probably much deeper than any of their contemporaries; one could even describe almost all of their preaching as a single, up-to-date dialogue with the tradition" (*Theologie des Alten Testaments*, 183). Vollmer's conclusion does more justice to the original texts of the prophets:

> One must argue, in contrast to the current widespread reading, that the prophets did not change or update the tradition, but instead demanded, with unheard-of abruptness, absolute and sole trust in Yahweh as the only path to life itself—in contrast to faith in the tradition, which was only an expression of the self-assertion of rebellious humanity against Yahweh. (*Geschichtliche Rückblicke*, 211)

IV.1.7.2. Eschatology and Messianism

Bright, John. *Covenant and Promise: The Prophetic Understanding of the Future in Preexilic Israel* (Philadelphia: Westminster, 1976). **Kilian**, Rudolf. *Jesaja 1–39* (EdF 200; Darmstadt: Wissenschaftliche Buchgesellschaft, 1983), 5–39. **Kinet**, Dirk. "Eschatologische Perspektiven im Hoseabuch," in *Eschatologie: Bibeltheologische und philosophische Studien zum Verhältnis von Erösungswelt und Wirklichkeitsbewältungen. Festschrift für Engelbert Neuhäusler* (St. Ottilien: EOS, 1982), 41–57. **Leeuwen**, Cornelis van. "De heilsverwachting bij Amos," in *Festschrift H. A. Brongers* (Utrecht, 1974), 71–87.

In traditional Christian interpretation, the prophets are presented too one-sidedly as predicting the eschatological future and messianism. True eschatology in eighth-century prophecy is difficult, if not impossible, to find. The prophets see the future as a historical event—not the end of history (Wolff,

"Das Geschichtsverständnis," 323). Many exegetes call these expectations of a new history, or a repeat of the great events in salvation history like the exodus or the election of David or Zion, eschatology. This blurs the univocal meaning of the terms, however: if this is eschatology, we have to invent a new term for what is traditionally referred to as eschatology, namely, the doctrine of "last things," "notions of faith concerned with the final fate of individual men as well as the end-time history of the world as a whole" (Lanczkowski, *LTK* 3 (1959): 1083; seeNéher, *L'essence du prophétisme*, 131–32). It is an attractive idea to identify Israelite eschatology with the expectation of the coming of YHWH, but YHWH's coming is only eschatological when it occurs in the end-time, that is, when it heralds the end of history. Nor should one view the prophecy of the future reestablishment of the fallen booth of David in Amos 9:11–15 as eschatological. The authenticity of this prophecy is doubted by many. Gerhard von Rad, however, is of the opinion that, as a Judean, Amos has given expression to a Judean tradition concerning the house of David (*Theologie des Alten Testaments*, 144–45). According to Klaus Koch this prophecy reveals the general Israelite attitude of Amos's expectation of salvation, awaiting a restoration of the Davidic empire (*Die Propheten: I, Assyrische Zeit*, 81–83). The pericope belongs to postexilic salvation eschatology, however, and its authenticity has with good reason been rejected by most literary-critical exegetes (e.g., Wolff, Ina Willi-Plein, Jacques Vermeylen et al.). Instead it should be ascribed to a later, final redaction of the book of Amos. Similarly, Hos 3:5 ("Afterward the Israelites shall return and seek YHWH their God, and David their king; they shall come in awe to YHWH and to his goodness in the latter days") could only have come from a later redaction (e.g., Willi-Plein, Gale A. Yee, Bernard Renaud, Martti Nissinen). In Amos 5:15, a text that might be ascribed to the Amos school of the eighth century, we find the first mention of the idea of the remnant: שארית יוסף ("the remnant of Joseph"). This expression refers to the diminished northern kingdom. It speaks only hesitantly about the possible salvation of the remnant: "it may be that the YHWH, the God of hosts, will be gracious to the remnant of Joseph." This is in no way the same as the later eschatological hopes for the remnant. Amos 9:8–9, which considers the possibility of a remnant of the house of Israel, also comes from the Amos school or perhaps an even later redaction.

In any case, the preexilic prophets preached more than just doom. Isaiah breaks out of the traditional pattern of the trial speech in 1:21–26 by making a purification process out of the punishment and by allowing the condemnation to flow into a promise of salvation: "And I will restore your judges as at the first [כבראשנה], and your counselors as at the beginning. By "first time" (ראשנה) he probably means the time of David and Solomon. He does set up "the *original-time/end-time equation* for the first time," however, "which later becomes an apocalyptic motif" (Koch, *Die Propheten: I, Assyrische Zeit*, 152–53); non-Isaian according to Kilian, *Jesaja 1–39*, 35–38). In Isa 8:1–4 the prophet might again be announcing not an eschatological salvation but a historical one. According to this prophet, though, the salvation will occur only after judgment, and it will be something new, a new beginning after the catastrophe. The continuity between destruction and salvation is ultimately based only in God himself. In Amos 5:4–5 we find a statement of admonition, which includes a conditional promise of salvation, "Seek me and you will live," but the authenticity of this word is not entirely unquestioned. In the book of Hosea there are also promises of salvation whose context was reworked literarily, which go back, at least partly, to the prophet (Hos 2:17–25*). YHWH attempted to win his people back with a salvation-pedagogic sanction, thus leading them back to salvation (2:4–17*). "And so it is hinted at that in reality no judicial action can turn Israel to conversion. The only way that remains open for YHWH is a further and even more intense event in which YHWH changes Israel from the inside out and equips them with the corresponding disposition" (Kinet, "Eschatologische Perspektiven," 50). Hosea is convinced that YHWH is God and no man, that there are impulses in him that maintain themselves against all human reason, and that therefore, despite his anger he can love his people (11:8–9). For Israel there is still an unearned future, given as a gift from YHWH.

IV.1.7.2.1. Zion according to Isaiah

Kilian, Rudolf. *Jesaja 1–39* (EdF 200; Darmstadt: Wissenschaftliche Buchgesellschaft, 1983), 40–97. **Wanke**, Gunther. *Die Zionstheologie der Korachiten in ihrem traditionsgeschichtlichen Zusammenhang* (BZAW 97; Berlin: Töpelmann, 1966).

In Isa 1–39 the expectation and the promise of a long-awaited time of salvation are mentioned often, though only in rather late texts, particularly in chapters 24–27 and 34–35. Chapter 35 holds out the prospect of the definitive glorification of Zion with the return of the Diaspora (cf. Isa 4:3–6). Isaiah 2:1–4—a promise found also in Mic 4:1–3—declares Zion to be the center of the worship of YHWH for the nations as well. This is seen by some scholars as a development of Isaian theology wherein Zion is the center. According to Isaiah, Zion is sacrosanct because it was established by YHWH (14:32; 17:12–14): YHWH defends it against all attacking enemies (31:4–5, 8–9). Here the prophet would be dependent on older traditions, found in the so-called songs of Zion (Pss 46; 48; 76). Gunther Wanke, however, concluded from his analysis of the Zion psalms that there was no such thing as a pre-Isaian Zion tradition (*Die Zionstheologie*, 106–13). The question is whether this thesis goes too far. There are good reasons to accept a preexilic Zion tradition in which YHWH chose Zion as his residence and protected it from enemies (Laato, *Who Is Immanuel?* 81–88). This does not mean, however, that Isaiah believed Zion to be inviolable. Isaiah 17:12–14 comes from the postexilic period (see above, 59), but it is hard to deny that 14:32 is Isaianic. Isaiah 14:32 is not an assurance of inviolability but a rejection of the policy of alliances: the poor are YHWH's protégés, and the king should stand up for them, relying on YHWH's support. In Isa 31:4–9, only verse 4 might be considered originally Isaian (the rest is later expansion), but that verse can only be interpreted as meaning a war against (עַל) Zion (Vermeylen, *Du prophète Isaïe à l'apocalyptique*, 421–24; see above 60). The theme of "the nations" makes it impossible to date Isa 2:1–4 to the eighth century. In Isa 28:16–17a, it appears that YHWH's presence among his people on Zion is bound to faith: the edifice of God's people will be tested on the cornerstone of Yahwistic belief; law and justice will be the plumb line and the level, which alone can guarantee its stability. Because this belief is constantly lacking, it is not surprising that Isaiah also levels threats at Zion (29:1–4; 28:17b–22). "Isaiah promises neither unconditional protection or rescue for Jerusalem, nor a future salvation through judgment" (Fohrer, *Jesaja*, 2:61) In other words, Isaiah most probably knew the tradition of YHWH's founding of Zion, but he used it against Israel.

According to Rudolf Kilian, none of the texts in Isaiah pertaining to the Zion tradition (1:21–26; 2:2–4; 8:9–10; 10:27b–34; 14:24–27, 28–32; 17:12–14; 28:16–17; 29:1–8; 30:27–33; 31:1–9) has been proven authentic/original to Isaiah. Everything rather suggests that "this evidence is of exilic or even postexilic origin" (*Jesaja 1–39*, 95–96). This may be correct for some of the texts, but the overall picture is more complex.

IV.1.7.2.2. The Messianism of Isaiah and Micah

Hermisson, Hans-Jürgen. "Zukunftserwartung und Gegenwartskritik in der Verkündigung Jesajas," *EvT* 33 (1973): 54–77. **Schoors**, Antoon. "The Immanuel of Isaiah 7,14," *OLP* 18 (1987): 67–77. **Seybold**, Klaus. *Das davidische Königtum im Zeugnis der Propheten* (FRLANT 107; Göttingen: Vandenhoeck & Ruprecht, 1972). **Stegemann**, U. "Der Restgedanke bei Isaias," *BZ* 13 (1969): 161–86. **Wegner**, Paul D. *An Examination of Kingship and Messianic Expectation in Isaiah 1–35* (Lewiston, N.Y.: Mellen Biblical Press, 1992). **Werner**, Wolfgang. *Eschatologische Texte in Jesaja 1–39: Messias, Heiliger Rest, Völker* (FzB 46; Würzburg: Echter Verlag, 1982).

In connection with the view that Isaiah was a prophet of messianism, the idea, allegedly propagated by him, of the remnant is often brought to the fore. At the same time, the ambiguity of this idea is often highlighted: through

IV. THE THEOLOGICAL SIGNIFICANCE OF THE ERA 249

YHWH's judgment only a small remnant of God's people would be be saved, and in this sense the idea of the remnant belongs with prophecies of calamity. At the same time, out of the divine judgment a remnant *would* be saved; thus the idea of the remnant also includes a message of salvation. Yet nowhere is it expressly stated—except in commentaries—that the remnant that would be saved would form the nucleus of the renewed kingdom. Moreover, the idea of the remnant from a salvation perspective is found only in later strata of the book of Isaiah (4:3; 6:13; 10:20–21; 28:5). Isaiah's authentic words relate only to the meaning of the "remnant," in line with the original sense of the idea, that only a small group would escape extermination. The smallness of the remnant shows the magnitude of the catastrophe. In my opinion, even the symbolic name of the prophet's son שאר ישוב (7:3) has a threatening meaning. The common translation "a remainder will return" does not take into consideration the order of the two words, which should instead be translated "only a remainder will return." In the context of Isa 7, one might think first of the armies of the Israelites and Arameans. But the name also contains a warning for Ahaz, the threat of great calamity and an incentive for belief as the only way left to avoid the calamity (see Werner, *Eschatologische Texte*, 89–147). In addition, the statement in Amos 5:15 skeptical of the possibility of salvation for a remainder from Joseph, which breaks up the coherence of the text, is probably an interpretation of 5:4–5 and should be ascribed to a later glossator. The same holds for Amos 9:8, "I will not entirely destroy the house of Jacob." "The whole quote in 9:8–10 includes an interpretation to update the text and an independent continuation of Amos's message from a later time (seventh century) for the southern kingdom" (Willi-Plein, *Vorformen*, 56).

Beyond the idea of the remnant, many commentators find a number of other prophecies about the messiah and his kingdom in Isaiah. The prophet is called the evangelist of the Old Testament—in the words of Jerome, "non tam propheta dicendus est, quam evangelista." The important messianic prophecies are found in the triad 7:14; 9:1–6; 11:1–9. These statements are not messianic, however, for the simple reason that in Isaiah's time there was no messianic expectation, and it has not been shown that Isaiah initiated it (11:1–9 probably does not come from Isaiah; but cf. Hermisson, "Zukunftserwartung," 58–66). Immanuel in Isa 7:14 is not a messiah, not a savior, and not a redeemer but a "sign" of the successful outcome of the Syro-Ephraimitic war. The sign is the whole situation that is announced: the enemy will soon perish and Ahaz therefore has reason to call the son that he is perhaps expecting soon *God-with-us*. All of this is a sign that YHWH is capable of saving David's dynasty, which is precisely the core of the promise. In 9:1–6, a text whose Isaianic authenticity is not uncontested, the child is the expected (or already born) son of the king. Expectations of good fortune are connected with his birth. This could be called messianism if one is content with vague terms, but in that case every king of Israel is a messiah, as every king is anointed and represents God, and with each new king comes the hope that all will be better. If one does not intend "messiah" to mean the ideal Davidic king of the end-time, or at least an eschatological savior, one ought not use this word in reference to Isaiah. Yet most defenders of the messianic interpretation use the word with precisely this meaning. This messiah, however, is not to be found in Isaiah. The success of the messianic interpretation of the texts in question is found in the New Testament, which is at least partly related to the Jewish milieu of its time. If this interpretation had never occurred in the New Testament, no one today would think to label these texts messianic.

It is correct, though, that Isaiah sets great store in the Davidic dynasty. It represents a historical and still valid political system that, for Isaiah, has a salvation-historical character. In this sense, in 7:4–9 he is close to Nathan's prophecy (2 Sam 7) when he asserts that those who threaten Ahaz would have no success. Isaiah makes the promise more nuanced, however, by imposing a condition: belief in YHWH. He also calls the Davidic king "prince" or "minister" (שׂר) and his office "rulership" (מִשְׂרָה; 9:5–6), perhaps to suggest that he remains a vassal, subordinate to the divine king (מלך), YHWH.

Micah 5:1–5 also contains a statement that is believed to be messianic. It involves an expectation of the future, that a special ruler would come from Bethlehem. The original statement might include only verses 1, 3a, 4a, 5b, and according to Wolff (Wolff, *Micah*, 136–39) even these verses are probably correctly dated to the period of the siege of Jerusalem by Nebuchadnezzar:

> But you, O Bethlehem of Ephrathah, who are one of the little clans of Judah,
> from you shall come forth for me one who is to rule in Israel,
> whose origin is from of old, from ancient days.
> And he shall stand and feed his flock in the strength of the Lord,
> in the majesty of the name of the Lord his God.
> and he shall be the one of peace.
> he shall rescue us from the Assyrians
> if they come into our land or tread within our border.

If these verses are authentic, Micah would be expecting David's rebirth or rather a ruler from another family or dynasty of the descendants of Jesse (1 Sam 17:12) whose origins hark back to the time before David, "from of old." He would therefore be awaiting something new, even while his expectation is directed entirely to the near future of his own time: the new ruler is to save Judah from Assyria. These words would have been spoken during the crisis that ended in 701 with the siege of Jerusalem by Sennacherib and his retreat (Herrmann, *Die prophetischen Heilserwartungen*, 146–52).

IV.2 THE LAWS

IV.2.1. LAW AND PROPHETS

Dion, Paul-Eugène. "Le message moral du prophète Amos s'inspirait-il du 'droit de l'alliance'?" *ScEs* 27 (1975): 5–34. **Jensen**, Joseph. "Eighth-Century Prophets and Apodictic Law," in *To Touch the Text: Biblical and Related Studies in Honor of Joseph A. Fitzmyer, S.J.* (ed. Maurya P. Horgan and Paul J. Kobelski; New York: Crossroad, 1989), 103–17. **Klopfenstein**, Martin A. "Das Gesetz bei den Propheten," in idem, *Leben aus dem Wort: Beiträge zum Alten Testament* (BEATAJ 40; Bern: P. Lang, 1996), 41–57. **Tucker**, Gene M. "The Law in the Eighth-Century Prophets," in *Canon, Theology, and Old Testament Interpretation: Essays in Honor of Brevard S. Childs* (ed. Gene M. Tucker et al.; Philadelphia: Fortress, 1988), 201–16. **Zimmerli**, Walther. *The Law and the Prophets: A Study of the Meaning of the Old Testament* (James Sprunt Lectures 1963; Oxford: Blackwell, 1965). **Zobel**, Konstantin. *Prophetie und Deuteronomium: Die Rezeption prophetischer Theologie durch das Deuteronomium* (BZAW 199; Berlin: de Gruyter, 1992).

According to Julius Wellhausen, the law is more recent than the prophets, and the prophets are therefore no longer to be seen as interpreters of a legal tradition that began with Moses but rather as trailblazers of ethical monotheism (Wellhausen, *Prolegomena to the History of Israel* [Edinburgh: A. & C. Black, 1995], 399ff.). Haroldo Reimer follows along the same lines in claiming that Amos's radical prophecy had a strong reception in the Covenant Code (Reimer, *Richtet*, 233). According to what we have seen of the ethical message of the prophets and their role in the development of monolatry, the term "ethical monotheism" is well chosen. Several later scholars have put forward the thesis that the charges leveled by the first writing prophet, Amos, were based on legal tradition (Würthwein, "Amos-Studien," 40ff.; Bach, "Gottesrecht"). Gene M. Tucker ("Law") extended this to include all the prophets of the eighth century. In his view, however, the prophets do not depend on the legal corpora so much as on traditional rules according to which the courts judged. Eryl W. Davies believes that Israelite law was such a limited and imperfect instrument that one could harbor grave doubts about the prophets' dependence on legal tradition (Davies, *Prophecy and Ethics*, 26). It has been pointed out that clear references to the Decalogue can be found in Hosea: the self-introduction formula in 12:10 and 13:4; the second commandment in 8:4–5 and 13:2; the laws of the second tablet: perjury, lie, murder, theft, adultery in 4:1–3 (see, e.g., Brueggemann, *Tradition for Crisis*, 38–43; Neef, *Die Heilstraditionen*, 175–209). This does not necessarily mean that Hosea knew of the Decalogue. It is more probable that he harks back to older traditional material, a sort of early version of the Decalogue. Such an early version must therefore have been known by the inhabitants of the northern kingdom.

It was not only the prophets who claimed injustice; they were not alone in speaking up for a just social order, and the laws in the Covenant Code and in Ur-Deuteronomy betray the same concerns. There are clear parallels between Deuteronomy and Hosea: compare, for instance, Deut 12:2–3 (on places of cultic worship) with Hos 4:13; 8:11; 10:1; or Deut 14:1–2 with Hos 7:14 (on self-laceration in fertility cults); Deut 17:14–20 with Hos 8:4; 13:10–11 (on kings); Deut 19:14; 25:13–15 with Hos 5:10; 12:8 (on the movement of border markers and business fraud); Deut 27:15 with Hos 4:12; 8:4b; 11:2; 13:2 (on idol worship; see Brueggemann, *Tradition for Crisis*, 43–50). The question has been raised as to whether the moral message of prophets like Amos or Isaiah had been inspired by the laws. Recent study has heavily qualified the thesis of the dependence of the prophets on law. Paul-Eugène Dion has shown that, on the one hand, Amos knew the legal rules quite well and took them into account: reference to the law is clearly discernible in 2:8a (the moderation of pawnbroking; Exod 22:25–26; Deut 24:12–13, 17) and 2:7b (respect for female slaves in the house; Exod 21:7–11); in 5:10–12 (integrity of community justice; Exod 23:1–3; Deut 16:19) and in 8:5b (against fraud in business; Deut 25:13–15); allusions to debt slavery in 2:6b and 8:6a might be read in connection with Exod 21:2–11. On the other hand, Amos condemns offenses beyond those found in ancient Israelite law, for example, his condemnation against luxury, against greed (8:5a), and against ritualism (4:4–5; 5:4–5, 21–24), none of which was forbidden by the law. His demands do not always go along with those of the law; in 2:6b and 8:6a, for instance, he opposes legal practice. He never argues on the basis of the law, nor does he invoke it. The correspondence of his accusations to some rules of law does not necessarily make them the main source of his preaching. In 5:14–15 he expresses the central principle of his moral judgments: "Seek good and not evil.... Hate evil and love good." Amos goes further than the law, and in 1:3–2:3 he shows that he was aware of it and that some of his moral values were known outside the people of Israel (Dion, "Le message"). The justice preached by the prophets was not simply legal correctness; it was a justice that involved compassion and ethical feeling.

Nevertheless, it is not easy to prove whether the prophets were dependent on the law or the law (e.g., Ur-Deuteronomy) on the prophets. According to Konstantin Zobel, substantial portions of the prophecy of the eighth century flowed into Deuteronomy: he mentions the Hosean theology of love, and the phrase "seek YHWH" as a paraphrase of a conversion to YHWH, embedding prophetic demands in Deuteronomistic legal exhortation. Zobel is working only with the final form of Deuteronomy, however, not the Ur-Deuteronomy of the eighth century. Many parallels between the law in Ur-Deuteronomy and in Hosea (and to a lesser degree among the other eighth-century prophets)

IV. THE THEOLOGICAL SIGNIFICANCE OF THE ERA

point to a common contemporary background—in particular a northern Israelite one—and a shared set of concerns among the prophets and lawgivers.

IV.2.2. The Religious and Ethical Message of the Laws

Blenkinsopp, Joseph. "Deuteronomy and the Politics of Post-mortem Existence," *VT* 45 (1995): 1–16. **Hamilton**, Jeffries M. *Social Justice and Deuteronomy: The Case of Deuteronomy 15* (SBLDS 136; Atlanta: Scholars Press, 1992). **Kaufman**, Stephen A. "A Reconstruction of the Social Welfare Systems of Ancient Israel," in *In the Shelter of Elyon: Essays on Ancient Palestiniah Life and Literature in Honor of G. W. Ahlström* (ed. W. Boyd Barrick and John R. Spencer; JSOTSup 31; Sheffield: JSOT Press, 1984), 277–86. **Marshall**, Jay W. *Israel and the Book of the Covenant: An Anthropological Approach to Biblical Law* (SBLDS 140; Atlanta: Scholars Press, 1993). **Otto**, Eckart. *Theologische Ethik des Alten Testaments* (Theologische Wissenschaft 3.2; Stuttgart: Kohlhammer, 1994). **Schenker**, Adrian. *Versöhnung und Widerstand: Bibeltheologische Untersuchung zum Strafen Gottes und der Menschen, besonders im Lichte von Exodus 21–22* (SBS 139; Stuttgart: Katholisches Bibelwerk, 1990). **Schwantes**, Milton. *Das Recht der Armen* (BBET 4; Frankfurt am Main: Lang, 1977).

The oldest sections that refer to the poor are found in the Covenant Code (Exod 22:24; 23:3, 6, 11). Exodus 23:3 and 6 combat a dispensation of justice judged according to property: verse 3 against preference for the poor and verse 6 against discrimination against them. In Exod 22:24 a casuistic rule of law, whose regulation of legal consequences is in the form of a prohibition, stands up for the rights of the poor in matters of lending. "Verse 24a, singular in the OT, intends to protect person and property from the reach of the creditor in cases of nonfulfillment of a loan contract; it intends to protect the poor (עָנִי) from debt slavery" (Schwantes, *Das Recht*, 63). Deuteronomy 24:10–13 is similar to this prohibition, taking up extreme cases of poverty (עָנִי) in 24:12–13, where one has only a coat as a pledge. This text probably does not belong to Ur-Deuteronomy, but to later Deuteronomistic preaching (Merendino, *Das deuteronomische Gesetz*, 302). As we saw, the penultimate redactional layer of the Covenant Code comes from the eighth century. According to Rainer Albertz, it forms the legal basis of the Hezekian reform. In support of this thesis, Albertz points to the poor, who are to be protected and looked after (22:20–21, 24–26; 23:3, 7, 11), to debt slavery as one of the main problems (21:2–11), and to the protection of the stranger, which responds to the refugee problem after the fall of Samaria. The Covenant Code attempts to get under control the worst social circumstances of its time: it combats partiality and corruptibility in the judicial process (23:1–8), creates laws for debt slavery and, through religiously grounded prohibitions, protects the socially weak groups: widows and orphans, strangers, and heavily indebted small farmers (22:20ff.). It also attempts "to clearly connect Israel as a cultic community to Yahweh and to mark it out from the surrounding world" through cultic commandments and laws of differentiation (e.g., against magic, sodomy: 22:17–18). Accordingly, the Hezekian reform would have been not only cultic but also social (Albertz, *Israelite Religion*, 1:184–86). We must not forget, however, that the Covenant Code does not protect only the weaker strata of society but also the rights of free proprietors with respect to their lives, bodily harm, and economic loss (see Marshall, *Israel and the Book*, 113–30). It is certainly not sufficient to abolish social stratification in Israel, but its great care for weaker groups cannot be denied. On the whole, however, the significance of the Hezekian reform seems to me to be overestimated here.

In Deut 15:1–11 the indebted poor are again protected. The law of remission (שמטה) is found in verses 1–2, while verses 3–11 are later Deuteronomistic preaching in which the rights of the poor are promoted through exhortation, promises, and threats (see Schwantes, *Das Recht*, 69–75). The remission year originated out of the fallow period of the Sabbath year, which, according to the Covenant Code (Exod 23:11), was instituted to care for the poor, though this would not have been its original purpose. In the laws, mention of the poor is almost always connected with the possessive suffix of the second person, for example, אביונך, "your poor person" (Exod 23:6), אביוני עמך, "the poor of your people" (Exod 23:11), העני עמך, "the poor among you" (Exod 22:24), אחיך האביון, "your poor brother" (Deut 15:7, 9), לאחיך לעניך ולאבינך, "your poor and needy brother" (Deut 15:11). "The poor person is viewed in relation to the one who is addressed" (ibid., 83); he is a fellow citizen, his brother. As Schwantes summarizes:

> Notable in the legal texts the predominant texts are not those that require care for them but those that secure the claims of the poor as part of the people. The point of departure is what is due to the poor: just legal decisions, loans without liability or interest . . . humane pledges. But the care, too, has a special feature: it is not the kind donation of the rich; the care of the sacred fallow year and the harvest customs is YHWH's care; he feeds the poor from his property. (*Das Recht,* 81)

Ur-Deuteronomy also reformed regulations concerning the manumission of debt slaves by including female slaves and providing them with material assistance upon their manumission (Deut 15:12–18). Further, it adopts the instructions of the Covenant Code (Exod 21:2–11). This means, however, that the freed slave does not regain possession of his land, since otherwise the presentation of these gifts on the part of the master would have been unnecessary. The social justice supported by these laws comes out of an ideology that can be paraphrased as follows: Social justice is not an abstraction but something concrete: justice for the poor is a central part of social justice and is symptomatic of the health of a society as an inclusive, not exclusive, one; as a guarantor of the inclusive character of the society, God is the defender of the powerless (see Hamilton, *Social Justice*, 135–38).

In Deuteronomy there are also regulations pertaining to the cult of the dead and contact with the deceased, including, for example, "You must not lacerate yourselves or shave your forelocks for the dead" (Deut 14:1). In 18:10–12 there is a list of people who should not be found among Israel: "No one shall be found among you who makes a son or daughter pass through fire, or who practices divination [קוסם קסמים], or is a soothsayer [מעונן], or an augur [מנחש], or a sorcerer [מכשף], or one who casts spells [חֹבֵר חָבֶר], or who consults ghosts [שׁאל אוב], or a clairvoyant [ידעני] or who seeks oracles from the dead (דרש אל־המתים). For whoever does these things is abhorrent to the Lord." According to Joseph Blenkinsopp, nearly all of these people are in some way connected with communication with the dead or who at least could occasionally do so. The legal opposition to these practices is, in his opinion, part of a broader strategy to loosen the system of family bonds and to replace it with a bond with the broader community ("Deuteronomy and the Politics"). This is an interesting hypothesis, though it is obviously difficult to prove; furthermore Blenkinsopp did not demonstrate that these prohibitions were already found in Ur-Deuteronomy.

IV.3. Narrative Literature

V.3.1. The Early Kingship Narratives

Earlier we made an observation about the theological interests of the pre-Deuteronomistic strata in Samuel–Kings (see 202). The major theme in the collection of prophetic tales (which Walter Dietrich calls the "book of prophetic narratives" [*Prophetengeschichten*] and which, in his opinion, was used as a source by DtrP) is the prophetic criticism of the monarchy. These texts air the fears of prophetic circles "that state power likes to be absolute and tolerates nothing and no one above it. This is impossible for a people who are not only people of the state but should also be people of God." Such an opposition to monarchy continues throughout prophecy. Israel seems to have been especially capable of resisting the temptations of power, and this was thanks to the opposition religion that was carried on by the prophets. This does not mean that the prophets rejected the monarchy entirely but that they remained critical of it. As was shown above, northern Israelite traditions were incorporated into the David–Saul history in Judah after the fall of the northern kingdom in 722 B.C.E., to legitimate the transition of power from the north to the south and show it to be divinely intended (see Dietrich, "JHWH, Israel," 138–39).

IV.3.2. The History of the Patriarchs

Alt, Albrecht. *Der Gott der Väter*, in Alt, *Kleine Schriften zur Geschichte des Volkes Israel* (3 vols.; Munich: Beck, 1953–59), 1:1–78. **Fritz**, Volkmar. "Die Bedeutung der vorpriesterschriftlichen Vätererzählungen für die Religionsgeschichte der Königszeit," in *Ein Gott allein? JHWH-Verehrung und biblischer Monotheismus im Kontext der israelitischen und altorientalischen Religionsgeschichte* (ed. Walter Dietrich and Martin A. Klopfenstein; OBO 139; Göttingen: Vandenhoeck & Ruprecht, 1994), 403–11. **Schreiner**, J. "Zur Theologie der Patriarchenerzählungen in Gen 12–36," in *Alttestamentlicher Glaube und biblische Theologie: Festschrift für Horst Dietrich Preuss* (ed. Jutta Hausmann and Hans-Jürgen Zobel; Stuttgart: Kohlhammer, 1992), 20–34.

As we saw earlier, the oldest stratum of the history of the patriarchs (*Vätergeschichte*: Vg¹) was from the eighth century and was intended to offer etiologies for Israel and that at the same time oriented meaning in the present. According to J. Schreiner, in its final form the message of the history of the patriarchs is that everything that happened to David had been planned and prepared long before by the God of Israel. To make this planning visible, the Israelites looked to the distant past in which the patriarchs lived. "Thus both David's empire and the kingdom of Judah, weaker after the separation, could be shown to have been planned and supported by YHWH, initiated by his promise, and established by his working" (Schreiner, "Zur Theologie," 28). In any case, already in the older version these narratives intended to communicate history, that is to say, historical aspects of the origin of Israel in their theological sense. As the promises in Gen 13:14–16a, 17 and 28:13*, 14 connect the Abraham narrative and the Jacob tradition, they belong to the core of the message of the oldest version (though they also play an important role in later redactions): YHWH will give the land to the numerous descendents of the patriarchs. Along with Erhard Blum, we should stress in connection with this the discoveries of tradition history: "In the older content of the narrative there are no promise texts; without exception these belong to 'later' compositional and reworked strata. As we saw, their historical context is found at the earliest in the late monarchy, the exile, and after" (Blum, *Die Komposition der Vätergeschichte*, 497). These narratives are almost always about the life of the nation in its land.

IV. THE THEOLOGICAL SIGNIFICANCE OF THE ERA

The image of God in this pre-Priestly patriarchal narrative is within the monolatric horizon, notwithstanding the multiple names for gods (El-Roï: Gen 16:13; El Olam [God, the eternal]: Gen 21:33; El of Bethel: Gen 31:13; God, the God of Israel: Gen 33:20; God, the God of your father: Gen 46:3; see Fritz, "Die Bedeutung," 403–11). Whatever the case, it is no longer possible to accept Albrecht Alt's hypothesis of the "nomadic" gods of the patriarchs: there are too many attestations of the formula "God of my father" from urban cultures for this. This formula seems to have belonged to the context of personal or familial piety (see Albertz, *Israelite Religion*, 29–34).

IV.4. Proverbs

IV.4.1. Prophecy and Wisdom

Fichtner, J. "Jahwes Plan in der Botschaft des Jesaja," *ZAW* 63 (1951): 16–33. **Vermeylen**, Jacques. "Le Proto-Isaïe et la sagesse d'Israël," in *La sagesse de l'Ancien Testament* (BETL 51; Leuven: Leuven University Press, 1990), 39–58. **Whedbee**, J. William. *Isaiah and Wisdom* (Nashville: Abingdon, 1971). **Wolff**, Hans Walter. *Amos' geistige Heimat* (WMANT 18; Neukirchen-Vluyn: Neukirchener, 1964).

In recent decades exegesis has taken into account the effect of wisdom on the prophets, especially Isaiah. Although this prophet rebuked the wise for self-satisfaction and short-sighted politics, he nevertheless adopted some terminology and thought from them. This influence of wisdom is especially evident in the context of the Syro-Ephraimitic war, above all in the title פלא יועץ (Isa 9:5), "Wonderful Councilor," or better, "Wonderful Administrator" (as יעץ does not mean "advise, give advice" but "make decisions, rule"). The binomial עצה and גבורה, which is found in the titles "administrator" and "hero," belong to the terminology of government and officers, as can be seen clearly in Isa 36:5: "Do you think that mere words are strategy [עצה] and power [גבורה] for war?" But these terms are at home in wisdom, as in Prov 20:18: "Plans are established by counsel." Further, the title אבי־עד, "Everlasting Father," in Isa 9:6 can be connected with a proverb from the collection of "Hezekiah's men": "If a king judges the poor with equity, his throne will be established forever" (כסאו לעד יכון; Prov 29:14; cf. also Prov 16:12; 25:5; see Ramlot, "Prophétisme," 1175–76). One must consider, however, that the Isaian authenticity of Isa 9:1–6 has recently been disputed. Meanwhile, J. William Whedbee is of the opinion that the terminology of so-called technical wisdom is not strong proof, though he believes that the dispute between Isaiah and the "wise councilors" is a strong argument that the prophet borrowed his wisdom forms from professional wise men and not folk wisdom (*Isaiah and Wisdom*). It is also reasonable that in his dispute with self-satisfied sages and officials the prophet should use their terminology. There are some notable points of contact between Isaiah and Prov 25–29: compare Isa 5:21 with Prov 26:5, 12, 16; Isa 1:25 with Prov 25:4. From this discussion, Eryl W. Davies rightly concludes that on this question no clear line can be drawn between folk wisdom and "technical" wisdom and its *Sitz im Leben* in the instruction of the wise (*Prophecy and Ethics*, 36). He is convinced that there is no wisdom background in Isaiah's prophecy against injustice (ibid., 107; see also Vermeylen, "Le Proto-Isaïe," 40–44). Yet it can hardly be disputed that in their more ethical approach to the legal institutions the prophets were oriented to wisdom norms (see Jensen, "Eighth-Century Prophets," 113–17).

With Amos, Hans Walter Wolff found clear traces of tribal wisdom, such as in the graded numerical dictum (Amos 1:3–2:8), in the didactic questions, in the formation of sets (*Reihenbildung*) in the method of argument by analogy within the disputation (3:3–8), and in the cries of woe (5:18; 6:1; Wolff, *Amos' geistige Heimat;* idem, *Joel and Amos,* passim). The most important influence, however, was the orientation toward tribal wisdom mentioned previously. Thus, Amos 2:6–7 was inspired by an ethics expressed in Prov 22:22, while Amos 8:4–6 can be compared with Prov 11:1 and 20:23; and Mic 3:9, 11 and Isa 1:23; 5:23 with Prov 17:15.

According to Gunther Fleischer, however, Amos did not base his words on law, nor does he have any discernible roots in wisdom. He argues independently, out of the background of the norms of the ethos of tribal solidarity. Traces of the influence of juridical and wisdom formulations are not perceptible until the redactional texts (*Von Menschenverkäufern*, 344–45). Still, the ethos of tribal solidarity is a sort of wisdom. Such parallels with the wisdom ethos can also be found in Micah and Isaiah.

IV.4.2. The Theology of Proverbs

Dearman, J. Andrew. *Religion and Culture in Ancient Israel* (Peabody, Mass.: Hendrickson, 1992). **Gese**, Hartmut. *Lehre und Wirklichkeit in der alten Weisheit: Studien zu den Sprüchen Salomos und zu dem Buche Hiob* (Tübingen: Mohr, 1958). **Schmid**, Hans Heinrich. *Wesen und Geschichte der Weisheit: Eine Untersuchung zur altorientalischen und israelitischen Weisheitsliteratur* (BZAW 101; Berlin: A. Töpelmann, 1966). **Washington**, Harold C. *Wealth and Poverty in the Instruction of Amenemope and the Hebrew Proverbs* (SBLDS 142; Atlanta: Scholars Press, 1994).**Whybray**, R. N. *Wealth and Poverty in the Book of Proverbs* (JSOTSup 99; Sheffield: JSOT Press, 1990).

IV. THE THEOLOGICAL SIGNIFICANCE OF THE ERA

It is often assumed that wisdom in Israel was originally a secular concept. William McKane, for example, differentiates between proverbs that pertain to the secular education of the individual, those that pertain to the behavior of the individual in reference to the community, and those that refer to religious education. The nonreligious proverbs would be the oldest. In other words, Old Testament wisdom would originally have been purely worldly, or secular, and would have only gradually been theologized (McKane, *Proverbs*, 11). This assumption, however, has lost its validity. Neither in the ancient Near East nor in Israel was wisdom ever entirely secular. Hartmut Gese and Hans Heinrich Schmid showed that the moral organization sought by ancient Near Eastern and Israelite sages in the cosmos and in human relations was a creation of the gods. Even the proverbs that seem secular and do not mention divinity presume that human actions are subject to the order of the world created by the gods (see Dearman, *Religion and Culture*, 200–204). According to 1 Kgs 3:3–28, Solomon beseeched YHWH for wisdom in order to rule the people. Wisdom in Israel, therefore, had a theological significance. This theology is unquestionably different from that of the prophets and of the greater biblical history works, however. As mentioned, wisdom is interested in the cosmic order and lived human experience, not history. Wisdom seeks guidelines for private and community life. The cosmic order expresses itself in a specific connection between the persons' deeds and what happens to them. The prevailing attitude in the book of Proverbs is anthropocentric; the human being is the center of interest. "Despite all appeal to God's satisfaction or repulsion, one always asks about the consequences for people that result from the behavior in question" (Ringgren, *Sprüche/Prediger*, 3rd ed., 10) The moral optimism of the proverbs is in keeping with this: the wise person is acting correctly, and people also unquestionably have the power to do so. This optimism betrays a strong belief in a just world order that results in the welfare of the just and disaster for the godless (ibid., 46). Although the consequences for the person in question are a motivation for correct action, this optimism still displays a deep conception of human solidarity (Prov 17:5). Some proverbs speak of YHWH: these contain primarily a declaration of belief about God's work, about the mysteries of God's activity in the world, and about God's part in maintaining the act–consequence process. So, for instance, Prov 16:1–4:

> The plans of the mind belong to humankind,
> but the answer of the tongue is from the Lord.
> All one's ways are pure in one's own eyes, but the Lord weighs the spirit.
> Commit your work to the Lord, and your plans will be established.
> The Lord has made everything for its purpose, even the wicked for the day of trouble.

Moral behavior is not unimportant to YHWH: like the prophets, the wise teacher is convinced that sacrifices by sinners are an abomination to YHWH. Religion and morality go together: "To do righteousness and justice is more acceptable to the Lord than sacrifice" (Prov 21:3; cf. 15:8–9). According to 16:6–7 guilt is pardoned through love and truth (בחסד ואמת), not simply through ritual.

We read in the proverbs from the Hezekian collection that "if a king judges the poor with equity, his throne will be established forever" (כסאו לעד יכון; Prov 29:14; cf. 16:12). Here is the concern for the upright administration of justice that we also found in the prophets (cf. Prov 17:8, 15, 23, 26; 18:5, 16). As mentioned above, this formulation is quite similar to Isaiah's oracle for the king: the awaited king establishes (להכין) and upholds his throne (כסא) with justice and righteousness, and receives the name "Everlasting Father" (אבי־עד; Isa 9:5–6). It has been pointed out that concern for the poor is also a theme of the wisdom traditions (e.g., Prov 22:22–23, which is dependent on the Wisdom of Amenemope; see Whedbee, *Isaiah and Wisdom*, 44). As Harold C. Washington and others have shown, the influence of Amenemope and other Egyptian wisdom texts on Prov 22:17–24:22 is considerable, also regarding its concern for the poor (cf. Prov 22:22–23, 28; 23:4–5, 10 with Amenemope 4:4ff.; 7:12–19; 8:9–10; 9:10–10:5; 20:21–21:8). R. N. Whybray pointed out that an unusually large number of the proverbs in Prov 10–22 and 25–29 refer to property, poverty, and social status. Care for the poor is lauded (14:31; 19:17; 28:8); contempt for and oppression of the poor are threatened with punishment (14:21; 28:8). We find this also in the Hezekian collection of proverbs: "A ruler who oppresses the poor is a beating rain that brings no bread" (28:3; cf. vv. 6, 8, 16, 27; 29:4, 7). The final guarantor of protection for the poor is YHWH himself: "Those who mock the poor insult their Maker; those who are glad at calamity will not go unpunished" (17:5; cf. 22:23). This is not a reference to the God of history, but to the God of creation. Therefore, care for or violation of the poor is "involvement with God himself. One encounters God in the poor" (Schwantes, *Das Recht*, 264). At the same time, there are also proverbs in the biblical book that betray a different attitude toward the poor and oppressed. The contrast between poverty and wealth is often set up as an unavoidable part of human existence that must be accepted and not viewed as an injustice (22:12 and, in the Hezekian collection, 29:13). Poverty is further described as a consequence of laziness, and diligence is recommended as a means against poverty (10:4; 20:13). It is therefore foolish to be lazy; in the end poverty can be attributed to stupidity—the poor are therefore the dumb. "Leading to poverty: idle laziness (Prov 10:4; 20:13; 24:30ff.), aimless haste (21:5; 28:19, 22 [Hezekian collection]), delight in merrymaking (21:17; 23:19ff.), thrift (11:24), stupidity (13:18), wickedness (13:25). In this context there is no talk of rights for the poor. Here the poor lose their claim" (Schwantes, *Das Recht,* 221). This evaluation could be connected with the *Sitz im Leben* of proverbial wisdom. Such statements were formulated on an empirical basis and were widely held in the international wisdom of that time (and all times). Exegesis often regards them as inspired by an ethic of self-interest, but their origin can just as readily be situated in traditional folk wisdom, independent of urban culture. This sort of evaluation of the poor is not found among the prophets. It is, however, probably not accidental that in the Hezekian collection of Proverbs the legal rights of the poor are underlined: "A righteous man knows the rights of the poor" (29:7). "Rich and poor" is an important theme in chapters 28–29, and here, too, there is no positive judgment of wealth, as is often found in other collections of proverbs. The greedy are reprimanded, and the subjugation of the poor is strongly condemned (28:3, 8). This doubtless has to do with the excruciating poverty of the small tenant farmers as a result of latifundia economics and the debt slavery attached to it. This is more likely prophetic influence on wisdom than the reverse. In particular, the proverbs in which God (YHWH or the creator) is connected with property and poverty (10:3; 15:25; 19:17; 25:21–22) and is called the creator of the poor (14:31; 17:5; 22:2; 29:13) are probably relatively recent, originating in the eighth century.

IV.5. THE IMPORTANCE OF PROPHETIC THEOLOGY FOR OUR TIME

Kraus, Hans-Joachim. *Prophetie heute! Die Aktualität biblischer Prophetie in der Verkündigung der Kirche* (Neukirchen-Vluyn: Neukirchener, 1986).

> "What will become of Christian preaching if it always passes over the texts of the Old Testament prophets? Or worse: what will happen to the church and the world if this voice is withheld?" (Hans Walter Wolff, *Die Hochzeit der Hure: Hosea heute* [Munich: Kaiser, 1979], 9)

The prophets of the eighth century still have a message for us that can guide and nourish our belief and our theological reflection. Obviously we must avoid timeless interpretations that take biblical statements and bring them into the contemporary world and contemporary situations without any further comment. That would be fundamentalism. It is equally false to think that these ancient texts have nothing to offer us in our times. If we confront our life with the prophetic message of the eighth century B.C.E., it can offer us models and inspiration for true life.

The first thing that prophetic literature teaches us is the importance of prophecy itself. The prophets were critical observers of civil and religious society, and their literature was opposition literature. Prophecy retains an important function in the contemporary polis and church. Politicians and church leaders who keep an eye on order and peace often have stark reservations toward prophecy. As in ancient Israel, prophets today speak out against the distance between reality and the demands of God, in the area of social relations as well as that of belief. Church preaching should not only be educational but also prophetic. "In the crisis of the church, of communities, of schools, our preaching should not become babbling platitudes four-fifths of which might be ignored with impunity" (Wolff, *Mit Micha reden*, 55). Modern prophets should perhaps shun party politics. The ancient prophets did not attempt to exert influence through the power of a party or an institution.

One thing we cannot take from the biblical prophets without further thought is the ability to speak in the name of God. We moderns are more cognizant of the fact that the word of God is almost never available "pure": it is speech spoken through people in human circumstances that comes into being through faithful interpretation of historical reality. Prophets can hear the word of God only from the Bible, from the church, and through encounters with people and events in daily life; then prophets speak according to their own conviction with the hope that they are remaining faithful to their God in their critical speech.

The biblical prophets paid special attention to the correct relationship with God. They offer us the image of a living God, a personal God who enters our lives with ethical demands. Religion is not a special human activity but a way of living according to God's will. According to Hosea, recognition of God is intimacy with his will. Religion is not indifferent to ethics, and it cannot simply be restricted to formulaic ritual actions. As is emphasized in the New Testament as well, religion and ethics must form a vital unity. It is not the form of worship that matters but its objectives. Our worship should be a sign of a faithful, just, merciful, and simple life. In contrast to the image of a more static God in older philosophy—Blaise Pascal's "le Dieu des philosophes"—in the modern age the image of a living God has become current and prevalent. At the same time, recent insights into the history of monotheism compel us to conceive of the image of the God involved in history as more incarnational. YHWH did not so much get involved in events "from above"; instead he became the God of Israel and finally the God of the whole monotheistic world through Israel's long struggle with its history and with the words of its prophets. The recognition that the one God had, so to speak, a polytheistic prehistory should make us aware of the richness of a God who, among other things, unified the qualities of Baal and Asherah. The Christian doctrine of the Trinity is one version of the attempt to attain a view of the inner richness of God. The belief that was so important to Isaiah is essential for this: if one does not counter the events of our world with the belief that God keeps his promises, one will be forced to worship the contemporary Baals or idols of property, power, and prestige and obey their will.

Closely linked with this is an reasonable view of salvation history. As we saw, among the prophets the continuity of history was relative. History is not predetermined by God but is rooted in the freedom of God's dialogue with human beings. This also contrasts with an all-too-static view of God. In my opinion, a well-thought-out image of God in the manner of "process theology" does the most justice to this conception of history and the ethical life of humans. Hosea or his school elucidated the relationship between YHWH and his people with the metaphor of the loving relationship between a man and his wife. This metaphor, along with New Testament texts about marriage (e.g., Eph 5:22–33) was misused as an ideological support for the subordination of women, particularly in marriage, but also in society in general. This bears witness not only to biblical fundamentalism, as found in some traditional church statements, and not only about women. It is also a methodological mistake to twist this metaphor. The metaphor starts from the social reality of married relationships in that time, to clarify how the covenantal relationship between God and his people might be imagined. One cannot infer from this theologoumenon of the covenantal relationship, in which Israel takes an inferior position vis-à-vis God, the correct hierarchy of marital relations. The fact that in the covenantal relationship Israel is the unfaithful and therefore sinning party should in no way lead to the opinion, in connection with Gen 3, that woman is the origin of the world's sinfulness.

We have already touched on the relationship between belief and cult. The prophetic preaching about this is taken up again by Jesus, quoting Hos 6:6 in Matt 9:13, and it is still relevant today. As Hans-Joachim Kraus writes, "Prophetic preaching does not affect only the *homo naturalis*, but also the *homo religiosus*, who lives in the *Pseudos* of his devoutness seeking protection in worship as a fortress while living a daily life of social injustice, irreconcilability, and unkindness" (Kraus, *Prophetie heute!* 39–40). Cultic formalism, even the feeling of superiority—in which one feels oneself at peace with God because one has performed rites or recited prayers, while being unconcerned about the requirements of social justice—is still widespread in our churches. Related to this is the problem of the correct understanding of the prophetic message, which, incidentally, was supported by the law corpus of its time. In the Christian church it has been customary for too long to see the prophets primarily, if not exclusively, as those who predicted Jesus Christ and his church. Jesus' disciples and the church saw Jesus as the fulfillment of prophetic expectations, and they read him into specific texts with this assumption in mind. This may be a legitimate hermeneutic of faith, under the condition that one does not overlook the differentiation between the king awaited by Israel and Christ. But because of this, the social-ethical message of the prophets has often been obscured. The church always preached justice and love, but the prophets can give this preaching and the practice that stems from it some special nuance. The prophets mostly indict the whole people and thus teach us to pay attention to collective responsibility. They also teach the importance not only of helping unfortunate individuals but also of tackling poverty that has structural socioeconomic causes with all suitable political and other means. Against the feeling of impotence that comes from often impersonal and seemingly immutable structural factors that play a large role in the current problems of poverty, unemployment, and exploitation, one could say along with Christof Hardmeier: "However much it is necessary today for a social ethic or an ethic of political action to expose autonomous structural laws and anonymous, nonindividual mechanisms that lead to the disadvantage and oppression of minorities and even of whole nations, it should never be forgotten that it is never a fated process that we are at the mercy of" (Hardmeier, "Die judäische Unheilsprophetie," 25). These processes are always kept going by human actions and can therefore also be changed by humans. The prophets almost never pointed out political or other strategies for the improvement of the social-ethical situation, but rather they were oriented to an ethic of solidarity. From this the following basic criterion of social ethics can be formulated, along with Hardmeier: "The criteria for judging new fields of technological-economic progress in existing and new forms of organization in government and economy should be determined by the sacrifices and the harm they cause and never by their usefulness and benefit, no matter how great the group to which the usefulness and benefit is a blessing" (ibid., 35). This should be preached during the worship service as well, lest we be reproached for cultic formalism. Church and social ethics are not separable. The prophets do not separate the spirit and the world, the kingdom of God and the kingdom of humans. Therefore we, too, can integrate much from the worldly wisdom of proverbs in the prophetic message. "With all that can rightly be said against a reduction of the biblical message to social politics, one thing must remain clear: the biblical witnesses of the kind of Micah unavoidably impress upon us that the true preacher is also a champion of the distressed and the powerless abused" (Wolff, *Mit Micha reden*, 80).

The social and the political are closely intertwined. In politics, too, the faithful citizen or politician needs to take the words of the prophets to heart. Certain prophetic statements against alliance policies of their contemporary kings are not concrete or directly applicable rules for present-day politics. But believers cannot practice just any sort of politics. They can never accept policies that favor only the interests of the powerful. True, politics is always the

IV. THE THEOLOGICAL SIGNIFICANCE OF THE ERA

art of the possible, and it cannot manage without compromises. At the same time, one often gets the feeling that many Christian politicians' readiness to compromise is much greater than their prophetic passion.

Should the Christian people of God no longer take seriously the judgment speeches of the prophets? Christological preaching and the formation of the church established the conviction that redemption was a definitive accomplishment. If one reads the prophetic message of doom with these presuppositions, it has become harmless in advance. But even today the great injustices in the world cry out for a catastrophic requital. The redemption achieved salvation, not as a guaranteed right but as an offering of grace that calls us to a just life and allows us to hope for salvation. This is also a critique of too self-confident messianic belief. The kingdom of God has still not been realized, as is clear from the contemporary situation of the world. The people of God still have to hear the prophets' accusations and their messages of calamity, and they still must convert. But, like the prophets, they must also preserve their hope, be it hesitantly, as in Amos 5:15, or with greater confidence, as in Isa 1:26–27; 7:14; or 9:1–6.

Index of Names

Abraham 204–5, 207–9, 215
Adadnirari 101
Ahaz 2–5, 7–9, 14–17, 29–30, 32–36, 45–46, 50, 52–53, 58–59, 62, 70, 90, 97–98, 100, 102–3, 105, 108–9, 115, 117–18, 171, 176, 237–38, 240, 249–50
Ahijah 28, 113, 199
Ahiqar 141, 143, 148
Alalah 92
Amaziah 97, 115, 160
Amenemhet 142
Ammon, Ammonite(s) 3, 33, 72, 198
Amon 8, 15, 27, 29–32, 43, 94, 100, 106–7, 180, 182
Amos 9–10, 50, 56, 76, 89, 91–92, 95, 97, 99–100, 109–10, 112–15, 121, 124, 126, 128–32, 151–52, 154–64, 167, 176, 184, 188, 201, 209, 211–14, 218–20, 228, 230–32, 234–36, 238–42, 244–47, 249, 251–52, 257–58, 265
Ani 142
Arad 68–69, 75, 83, 84, 110–11, 153
Aram, Aramean(s) 3–4, 16, 34–35, 56, 103, 109–10, 206
Ashdod 9, 60, 62, 72–73, 169
Ashkelon 70, 105
Ashurbanipal 3, 41, 73, 100, 107, 180
Assur 2, 25, 41–42, 51–52, 54–55, 57–59, 63–64, 170–72, 214
Assyria, Assyrian(s) 1–7, 9, 13–14, 16, 19–25, 28, 30, 34, 35, 39, 41, 42, 46–51, 53–60, 62–64, 68–78, 82–83, 90–94, 98, 100–110, 113, 115, 117–19, 140–41, 157–59, 161, 169, 171–72, 174, 180–82, 191, 193, 196, 214–15, 219, 237–38, 244, 250
Avva 2, 3, 104
Azariah 3, 70
Babel 25–26, 50–51, 58, 182
Babylon, Babylonian(s) 2–3, 8, 22, 25, 31, 35, 40–42, 71–73, 101, 104–7, 109–10, 133, 164, 237–38
Baruch 96, 150
Bathsheba 198–99
Beersheba 5, 36, 44, 69–70, 77–78, 81, 83–84, 110–11, 157
Benjamin 38, 44, 46, 94, 201, 228
Ben Tabe'el 103, 117
Bethel 3, 14, 28, 47, 97, 115, 155, 157–58, 160, 192, 199, 206–7, 209, 225, 228–29, 257
Beth-Shean 76
Byblos 102
Cuthah 2, 104
Damascus 2–5, 35, 48–49, 51, 55, 58–59, 62–64, 68, 70, 102–3, 117
Dan 5, 28, 36, 44, 225
David 5–8, 13, 17–18, 23, 28–30, 35, 38, 40, 45–56, 62–63, 76–77, 91, 111, 113, 117, 171, 198, 200–203, 207–8, 236, 245–46, 249–50, 256
Dor 84, 103
Edom, Edomite(s) 10, 16, 72, 105, 151, 155, 206

Egypt, Egyptian(s)   2, 6, 9, 21, 41, 47, 48, 51, 58–59, 61–63, 71, 73, 98, 100, 102–8, 133, 141–42, 144–45, 171, 210, 219–20, 222–23, 237–38, 260
Ekron   73, 105
Elath   4, 16, 53
Eliakim   21–22, 51, 60, 98
Elijah   104, 112–13, 117, 195, 200, 225
Elisha   104, 112, 117, 195, 200
Elkosh   119, 181
Emar   112
Ephraim   36, 38, 44, 46–48, 56, 63, 103, 167, 223, 228
Esarhaddon   41, 73, 100, 107
Ezekiel   24, 25, 113, 130, 150, 162–63
Gad   113, 199
Galilee   2, 36, 56, 103, 119, 181
Gath   105
Gaza   6, 35, 70–73, 103, 105
Gihon   8, 77, 80
Gilead   2, 47–48, 103, 206, 223
Gilgal   160, 228, 236
Gomer   48, 116, 165
Habakkuk   107, 151, 175
Hamath   2–3, 21, 64, 104
Hanunu   70
Hazor   2, 75–76, 78, 82, 84, 110
Hebron   86–87
Hezekiah   5–10, 13, 15–26, 29–32, 35–45, 49–52, 55, 57–59, 61–63, 65, 69, 72–73, 75, 77, 80, 84, 86, 90, 96–98, 100, 104–6, 110–11, 115, 117–18, 158, 165, 167, 172, 175–77, 188, 191–95, 198–99, 210–15, 221, 223, 226, 233, 237, 257
Hilkiah   21, 60, 137, 189–90, 192, 195
Hinnom   3, 33
Hiram   70, 103
Hosea   8–10, 45–48, 104, 111–16, 121, 126, 128–30, 151–52, 154–56, 161–67, 176, 179, 192, 201, 203, 209, 211–12, 214, 217, 219–28, 233, 236, 239–41, 244, 247, 251–52, 261–63
Hoshea   2, 5, 12–13, 18, 28, 47–48, 57, 70–71, 90, 100, 103–4, 115

Hozai   8, 42
Immanuel   4, 9, 31, 49, 53–54, 172, 248–49
Isaiah   4, 6–10, 14, 16, 19–20, 22–23, 25–27, 29–30, 39–40, 45–46, 49–65, 68, 89–91, 96–98, 102–3, 105, 111, 114–18, 121, 123, 126–30, 141–42, 150–56, 163, 167–77, 179, 195, 200–201, 212–14, 223, 225–26, 229–30, 232–35, 237–38, 240–50, 252, 257–58, 260, 262
Ishtar   109–10
Jacob   179, 204–9, 215, 218, 226, 233–34, 249, 256
Jehoshaphat   53, 99, 113, 184, 200
Jehu   1, 12, 46, 57, 200
Jeremiah   24–25, 41, 52, 96, 110, 113–14, 118, 122, 127, 130, 141–42, 150–51, 153, 156, 162, 178–79, 243
Jericho   4, 34
Jeroboam I   1, 12, 14, 28–29, 165, 207, 225
Jeroboam II   1, 8, 46, 101, 114–15, 159
Jerusalem   4–10, 13–16, 18–21, 24–25, 27–28, 30, 36–42, 44, 46, 50–53, 57–58, 60, 62–64, 68, 72–73, 75–79, 83–84, 86, 92, 97–99, 103–6, 109–11, 113, 117–18, 149, 156, 162, 168, 171, 173–74, 176, 179–84, 186, 191–93, 200, 202, 213, 218–19, 229, 233–34, 241, 243, 245, 248, 250
Jesse   250
Jesus Sirach   142
Jezreel   116, 225
Joseph   98, 161, 204–5, 207, 228, 246, 249
Josiah   8, 11, 16, 18, 23, 26–27, 30–31, 35–37, 44, 52, 56, 63, 109, 137, 157–58, 165, 171, 173, 177, 180, 189–91, 193, 195, 207, 218, 226
Jotham   3, 8–9, 12, 15–16, 29, 32–33, 45, 50, 52, 68, 94, 98, 100, 103, 115, 118
Kadesh-Barnea   83, 84
Kalach   70
Khirbet el-Kōm   75, 83, 225

INDEX OF NAMES

Khirbet Qumrān 77, 83
Kuntillet 'Ajrud 75, 225
Kush 59
Lachish 6, 20, 22, 75, 77–78, 85–88, 105, 110, 118, 153
Lo-Ammi 116, 221
Lo-Ruhamah 116
Luli 105
Maher-shalal-hash-baz 117
Manasseh 5, 8, 13, 15–16, 26–32, 36, 38, 41–45, 50, 68, 73, 75, 100, 106–7, 109–10, 158–59, 164, 167, 173, 176–77, 180–81, 191, 193, 199, 214
Manasseh (tribe) 228
Mari 112, 121, 124, 127, 131, 154
Megiddo 76, 78, 82, 90
Menahem 1, 11–13, 46, 57, 68, 70–71, 90, 100, 102–3
Merikare 142
Merodach-Baladan 19, 30, 40, 117, 237–38
Micah 9–10, 45, 64–65, 95, 97, 114, 118–19, 121, 128, 152, 167, 175–79, 188, 201, 213–14, 218–19, 229, 233–35, 241, 243, 248, 250, 258, 264
Micaiah ben Imlah 200
Mitinti 70, 73
Mizpah 46, 201
Mmšt 86
Moab 50–51, 72, 105, 151
Moabites 72
Moloch 109
Moresheth 118
Moses 5, 132, 137, 189, 193, 222, 251
Nahum 68, 107, 112, 119, 151, 175, 180–82, 214, 244
Nathan 54, 113, 198–99, 202–3, 250
Negev 4, 35, 69, 75, 77, 83–84
Nineveh 22, 73, 86, 88, 105, 180–82, 244
Oded 4, 34, 200
Onchsheshonqy 142
Pekah 2–4, 11–12, 16, 33, 47–48, 50, 56–57, 71, 100, 102–3, 117
Pekahiah 1–2, 11–12, 47, 100, 103

Philistia 34, 56, 74, 103
Philistine 52, 58–59, 72, 83, 105
Philistines 4, 6, 9, 17–18, 34, 51–52, 56, 58–59, 63, 102–3, 220
Phoenicia 60, 101, 112
Phoenician 72, 76, 102–3, 105, 109
Phoenicians 51, 60
Ptahhotep 142
Qarqar 58, 68, 70
Qiṭmīt 84
Ramah 201
Ramat Rahel 78
Raphia 58, 72
Rezin 3–4, 16, 33, 50, 56, 70, 103, 117
Sais 104
Samaria 1–4, 6, 9, 13–14, 18, 21, 28, 36–37, 48, 51–52, 55, 58, 60, 63–64, 69–72, 76, 78, 83–84, 90, 93–94, 102–4, 115, 117–18, 153, 158, 162, 175–77, 183, 196, 200, 202, 207–8, 226, 253
Samuel 113, 199
Sargon II 9, 51, 57–59, 71–72, 76, 100, 104–5, 169
Saul 198–203, 236, 256
Sennacherib 6–7, 9, 14, 19, 22–24, 27, 29–30, 35, 38–39, 44–45, 51–53, 55–63, 65, 68, 72–75, 77–78, 86, 88, 90, 93, 98, 100, 104–6, 117–18, 141, 162, 171–72, 250
Sepharvaim 2–3, 21, 104
Shallum 1, 11, 28, 57, 100, 102
Shalmaneser V 2, 13, 48, 51, 56, 58, 60, 71–72, 100, 103–4, 116
Shear-jashub 117
Shebna 22, 51, 60, 98
Shechem 47, 76, 192
Shephelah 4, 35, 76, 78, 83, 118
Shittim 46
Sidon 105
Silvan 98
So 103
Sochoh 86
Solomon 6, 10, 27, 36–38, 44–45, 54, 79, 91, 140, 143, 191, 202–3, 210–11, 214, 246, 259

Syria	4, 94, 101, 112	Tifsah	13
Syrian	58, 75–76, 102, 108, 143	Tiglath-pileser	1–2, 4, 16, 34–35, 46–48, 50, 56, 58–59, 62, 64, 67, 69–71, 78, 90, 100–103, 116, 238
Tabeal	4		
Tabe'el	62		
Tabor	46	Tirhakah	6, 22, 106
Tel Arad	69	Tirzah	1, 78, 102
Tel Beersheba	69, 77, 110, 111	Tyre	51, 70, 102–3, 112, 155
Tel 'Īrā	77, 83	Ugarit	75, 84, 98, 142, 153–54, 224
Tell Bēt Mirsim	75, 78	Uriah	5, 16
Tell Deir 'Allā	84	Uzziah	3, 8–9, 15, 32, 35, 45, 50, 52–53, 56, 98, 115, 117
Tell el-Baṭāšī	78, 86		
Tell el-Fār'a	91	Zechariah	1, 11, 46, 100, 102
Tell el-Fūl	83, 86	Zedekiah	12, 24
Tell el-Ḥesī	77	Zephaniah	110
Tell el-'Orēme	76	Zion	9, 24, 30, 53, 59, 62–63, 77, 156, 174–75, 179, 218, 223, 229, 234, 246–48
Tell en-Naṣbe	78, 86		
Tel Malḥātā	83		
Thebes	107, 180	Ziph	86

Index of Authors

Achenbach, Reinhard 188, 196
Ackroyd, Peter R. 31, 36, 41, 49, 111, 117, 174
Aharoni, Yohanan 68, 69, 77, 78, 110, 111
Ahlström, Gösta W. 31, 42, 110, 168, 253
Albertz, Rainer 88, 93, 95, 97, 99, 100, 107, 108, 109, 110, 114, 183, 188, 221, 223, 224, 236, 253, 254, 257
Albright, William Foxwell 104, 106
Allen, Leslie C. 175, 178
Alt, Albrecht 45, 46, 49, 56, 101, 102, 132, 133, 134, 135, 188, 192, 193, 203, 208, 256, 257
Andersen, Francis I. 154, 155, 161, 164
Avigad, Nahman 73, 76, 84, 98
Bach, Robert 230, 231, 251
Baentsch, Bruno 183
Baltzer, Klaus 136, 139
Bardtke, Hans 88, 91, 93
Barnett, Richard D. 75, 76
Barth, Hermann 49, 52, 54, 55, 56, 58, 59, 61, 63, 170, 171
Barucq, André 210, 211
Baudissin, Wolf Wilhelm 122
Becking, Bob 102, 180, 181
Beer, G. 5, 36, 67, 68, 69, 110, 157
Begrich, J. 97, 102, 121, 127, 131
Benjamin, Don C. 94
Benzinger, Immanuel 31, 36, 38, 39, 41, 42
Berge, Kåre 203
Bertholet, Alfred 190
Beyerlin, Walter 132, 136, 227, 229, 233
Beyse, K.-M. 143, 144
Birch, Bruce C. 197, 200
Birkeland, Harris 149, 150, 151
Blenkinsopp, Joseph 161, 203, 209, 253, 255
Blum, Erhard 203, 206, 207, 208, 209, 256
Bobek, H. 91
Boecker, Hans Jochen 121, 126
Bohlen, R. 230
Borchert, R. 230
Born, A. van den 31, 39, 44
Borowski, Oded 110
Boshoff, W. S. 219, 221
Botterweck, G. Johannes 93, 95
Brettler, Marc Zvi 10
Bright, John 245
Broshi, Magen 75, 76
Brueggemann, Walter 217, 251, 252
Brunet, Gilbert 49, 55
Budde, Karl 49, 53, 168, 172, 201
Buss, Martin J. 111, 116, 126, 167
Campbell, Antony F. 197, 200, 202
Camp, Ludger 14, 19, 20, 22, 23, 24, 25, 30
Carasik, Michael 210, 214
Carlson, R. A. 197, 198
Carmichael, Calum M. 132, 188, 193
Carrière, J.-M. 65
Cazelles, Henri 31, 65, 102, 183
Childs, Brevard S. 14, 20, 39, 251

Chirichigno, Gregory C. 88
Christensen, Duane L. 180, 181
Chrysostom, John 189
Clements, R. E. 14, 23, 57, 58, 60, 168, 171
Cogan, Mordechai 14, 16, 108
Cook, H. J. 102
Coote, Robert B. 154, 158
Cox, Dermot 140, 210, 212, 213
Craigie, Peter C. 136, 140
Crenshaw, James L. 140, 210
Crotty, R. 219, 222
Crüsemann, Frank 183, 184, 187, 188, 189
Daniels, Dwight R. 219, 222, 244
Davies, Eryl W. 230, 234, 251, 258
Davies, Graham I. 161, 228
Day, John 102
Dearman, J. Andrew 88, 92, 93, 258, 259
Deissler, Alfons 161, 162, 175, 177, 180, 182
Delcor, Mathias 31, 180, 181
Dever, William G. 75, 83
Dietrich, Manfried 224
Dietrich, Walter 10, 13, 15, 26, 49, 52, 53, 54, 55, 57, 59, 61, 63, 64, 75, 93, 106, 107, 149, 168, 169, 174, 180, 182, 197, 199, 200, 201, 202, 203, 219, 224, 236, 237, 238, 240, 243, 255, 256
Dillard, Raymond B. 31, 37, 38, 40, 42
Dillmann, August 190
Dion, Paul-Eugène 251, 252
Dohmen, Christoph 54
Donner, Herbert 45, 46, 47, 48, 52, 55, 57, 58, 59, 60, 61, 64, 89, 92, 93, 101, 103, 224, 233, 237
Driver, S. R. 190
Duesberg, Hilaire 140
Duhm, Bernhard 168, 170
Dus, J. 175, 179
Ehrlich, E. L. 31, 42, 102, 106
Eissfeldt, Otto 42, 112, 140, 144, 175, 179, 198, 210, 218
Elliger, Karl 13, 31, 49, 111, 155, 180, 182

Emmerson, Grace I. 161, 167
Engnell, Ivan 149, 151, 152
Evans, W. E. 197, 200
Fabry, Heinz-Josef 93, 95
Fahr, G. 219, 221
Fendler, M. 89
Fichtner, J. 257
Fleischer, Gunther 154, 160, 161, 232, 258
Fleming, Daniel E. 111, 112
Fohrer, Georg 45, 49, 56, 59, 60, 61, 111, 118, 168, 177, 194, 240, 248
Forrer, Emil 101
Fransen, I. 140
Freedman, David Noel 154, 155, 161, 164
Frevel, Christian 224
Fritz, Volkmar 75, 77, 154, 160, 175, 177, 256, 257
Galling, Kurt 68
García López, F. 195
Gelston, A. 236
Gemser, Berend 140, 141, 210, 211
Gerstenberger, Erhard 93, 96, 132, 133
Gese, Hartmut 31, 49, 258, 259
Geus, C. H. J. de 89, 91, 92
Gilmer, Harry W. 132, 134
Ginsberg, H. L. 58
Golka, Friedemann W. 140, 142, 144
Gonçalves, Francolino J. 14, 23, 35, 61, 63, 236, 238
Good, Edwin M. 161, 162
Gordis, Robert 112, 154, 155
Gressmann, Hugo 121, 150
Grønbaek, Jakob H. 197, 202
Gunkel, Hermann 121, 122, 123, 126, 127, 131, 149, 150, 203, 204, 210
Gunneweg, A. H. J. 93, 94, 95, 149, 152, 153
H. 31
Haag, Ernst 54, 112
Haag, H. 14, 31, 37, 39, 104, 106
Hadley, J. M. 225
Haldar, Alfred O. 180, 181
Hallo, William W. 68, 70, 197

INDEX OF AUTHORS

Hamilton, Jeffries M. 253, 255
Hardmeier, Christof 10, 12, 14, 18, 19, 24, 25, 26, 30, 121, 126, 149, 153, 154, 168, 171, 172, 174, 175, 230, 232, 235, 238, 241, 242, 243, 264
Harper, William Rainey 154, 156, 162, 163, 167
Haspecker, Josef 238, 239
Hayes, John H. 49, 50, 51, 57, 100, 101, 102, 104, 154, 155, 169
Hempel, Johannes 121, 126, 130, 188, 191
Hentschke, Richard 227
Hermisson, Hans-Jürgen 140, 144, 145, 147, 148, 211, 248, 249
Herrmann, Siegfried 100, 106, 111, 238, 241, 250
Herzog, Ze'ev 110, 111
Hesse, Franz 239
Hoffmann, Hans Detlef 10, 13, 15, 17, 28, 29, 30, 31, 111
Hoffmann, Hans Werner 236, 237, 240, 241
Hoffman, Yair 219, 221, 237
Hoftijzer, Jacob 203, 208
Høgenhaven, Jesper 112, 117, 223, 236, 237, 238
Hölscher, Gustav 121, 122, 188, 190
Horn, Siegfried H. 104, 106
Horst, Friedrich 154, 180, 181, 188, 196
Huber, Friedrich 49, 55, 59, 174, 236
Humbert, P. 180
Hunter, A. Vanlier 121, 131, 241
Hyatt, J. Philip 227
Irvine, Stuart A. 14, 16, 49, 50, 51, 57, 58, 62, 102, 103, 117, 168, 169, 238
Jacob, Edmond 168, 171, 217
Japhet, Sara 31
Jaroš, Karl 101
Jenni, Ernst 197, 198, 199
Jensen, Joseph 168, 169, 172, 251, 258
Jeppesen, K. 55, 175
Jepsen, Alfred 132, 140, 183, 197, 198, 203

Jeremias, Jörg 154, 158, 161, 164, 175, 178, 180, 182, 219, 222, 238, 241
Jerome 119, 189, 249
Johnson, Aubrey R. 112, 113
Josephus, Flavius 67, 68, 103
Jüngling, H.-W. 220
Junker, H. 112, 113, 180, 181
Kaiser, Otto 23, 49, 52, 53, 56, 60, 61, 94, 100, 121, 122, 129, 154, 168, 173, 174, 217, 227, 230, 236, 239, 261
Kapelrud, A. S. 151, 230, 231
Kaufman, Stephen A. 253
Keel, Othmar 224, 225, 226, 239
Keller, Carl-A. 180, 236, 237
Kessler, Rainer 89
Kidner, Derek 210, 212, 213
Kilian, Rudolf 168, 169, 174, 239, 245, 247, 248
Kinet, Dirk 224, 245, 247
Kitchen, K. A. 100, 106
Kittel, Rudolf 190, 199
Kline, Meredith G. 136, 140
Klopfenstein, Martin A. 75, 106, 149, 219, 224, 251, 256
Klostermann, August 136, 137
Köcher, M. 45
Koch, Klaus 94, 112, 114, 121, 125, 154, 157, 158, 169, 221, 223, 225, 226, 229, 235, 240, 241, 242, 246, 247
Köckert, M. 220
Köhler, Ludwig 121, 123
Konkel, A. H. 49, 62
Kooij, Arie van der 14, 22, 23
Kottsieper, Ingo 143
Kraus, Hans Joachim 89, 92, 261, 263
Krispenz, Jutta 210, 212
Kruger, P. A. 224
Kuan, J. K. 102, 104
Kuenen, Abraham 162, 175, 176, 190, 199
Laato, Antti 49, 53, 104, 248
Lang, Bernhard 89, 224, 231
Langlamet, F. 197, 202
Leeuwen, Cornelis van 14, 104, 106, 161, 163, 164, 245

Lemaire, André	75, 83	Néher, André	217
Lemche, Niels Peter	161, 167	Nelson, Richard D.	10, 14, 73
Lescow, T.	49, 56, 175, 177	Niccacci, Alviero	53
Levin, C.	112, 114, 115	Niehr, H.	84, 97, 98, 224, 230, 233
L'Heureux, Conrad E.	168, 172	Nielsen, Eduard	149, 151
Liedke, Gerhard	132, 134, 135	Nielsen, K.	97
Lindblom, Johannes	121, 123, 124, 161, 175, 176, 177, 188, 193	Niese, Benedikt	67
Lods, Adolphe	201	Nissinen, Martti	161, 162, 165, 166, 167, 246
Loretz, Oswald	68, 70, 71, 84, 89, 91, 154, 160, 224	Norelli, Enrico	67
Lowery, R. H.	110	Noth, Martin	10, 11, 13, 16, 18, 27, 31, 33, 34, 35, 36, 38, 40, 42, 94, 108, 183, 203, 204
Luckenbill, Daniel David	68, 70, 73		
Luther, Martin	122, 150	Nowack, Wilhelm	162, 176, 180, 182
Machinist, Peter	49	Nübel, Hans-Ulrich	197, 200
Maire, T.	140, 143	Oded, B.	102, 104, 111
Marshall, Jay W.	253, 254	Osumi, Yuichi	183, 187, 188
Marti, Karl	154, 156, 162, 163, 167, 176, 180	Oswalt, John N.	168
		Otto, Eckart	175, 183, 184, 185, 186, 187, 203, 253
Matthews, Victor H.	94		
Mayer, W.	68, 70, 71	Otzen, B.	102
Mayes, A. D. H.	136, 139, 140, 190, 194	Pascal, Blaise	262
Mays, James Luther	161, 162, 175, 177	Patrick, Dale	183
McCarter, P. Kyle	197, 200, 201, 202	Paul, Shalom M.	154, 155
McKane, William	140, 143, 149, 259	Perlitt, Lothar	168, 173, 222, 223, 238
McKay, J. W.	108	Pettinato, Giovanni	53
McKenzie, Steven L.	10, 197, 200	Plöger, Otto	140, 142, 143, 144, 212, 213
Meinhold, Arndt	140, 143, 144, 145, 210, 213	Premnath, D. N.	89
Merendino, Rosario P.	136, 137, 139, 194, 195, 253	Preuss, Horst Dietrich	140, 141, 143, 145, 148, 188, 190, 193, 195, 196
Mettinger, Tryggve N. D.	97, 98	Procksch, Otto	217, 221, 227, 228
Meyers, Jacob M.	31, 42	Provan, Iain W.	10, 15, 17, 18, 20
Michaéli	31, 41, 42	Pury, Albert de	149, 203, 209, 226
Mildenberger, F.	197, 200	Rad, Gerhard von	94, 114, 137, 138, 139, 140, 189, 192, 193, 217, 221, 224, 234, 242, 245, 246
Millard, A. R.	149		
Miller, J. Maxwell	100, 101, 104		
Mommer, Peter	201	Rainey, Anson F.	106
Moriarty, F. L.	31, 37	Ramlot, L.	112, 257
Mowinckel, Sigmund	112, 113, 131, 149, 151, 152, 168, 217	Reimer, Haroldo	155, 159, 189, 239, 240, 251
Murphy, Roland E.	140	Renaud, Bernard	45, 48, 64, 165, 175, 177, 178, 180, 182, 246
Na'aman, Nahman	70, 102, 104		
Naumann, Thomas	161, 166	Rendtorff, Rolf	17, 121, 126, 127, 168, 174, 203, 204, 205
Neef, Heinz-Dieter	220, 223, 236, 251		

Renz, Johannes 68, 69
Reventlow, Henning Graf 112, 113
Ringgren, Helmer 210, 211, 213, 259
Robert, André 214
Robinson, Theodore H. 162, 176
Röllig, Wolfgang 68, 69
Rose, Martin 189
Rosenbaum, Stanley N. 112, 114
Rost, Leonhard 197, 198, 202
Rowley, H. H. 112
Rudolph 31, 34, 36, 41, 45, 48, 162, 175, 178, 180, 181, 241
Ruppert, Lothar 45, 48, 165
Scharbert, Josef 112
Schenker, Adrian 31, 239, 243, 253
Schmid, Hans Heinrich 258, 259
Schmidt, Hans 121
Schmidt, J. M. 239, 241
Schmidt, Johannes 140
Schmidt, Werner H. 155, 157, 217, 218, 219, 241
Schniedewind, William M. 42, 43
Schoors, Antoon 75, 248
Schottroff, Willy 230, 231
Schreiner, J. 256
Schulz, Hermann 180, 181
Schüngel-Straumann, Helen 220, 225, 228, 241
Schwantes, Milton 94, 232, 235, 253, 254, 260, 261
Schwienhorst-Schönberger, Ludger 183, 186, 187, 188
Scott, R. B. Y. 168, 171, 210, 211, 212, 217
Seebass, Horst 203
Seitz, Christopher R. 49, 62, 175
Seitz, Gottfried 137, 138, 195, 196
Sellin, Ernst 155, 156, 162, 176, 180, 181, 194, 210
Seybold, Klaus 112, 180, 181, 182, 244, 248
Shiloh, Y. 78
Shiloh. Y. 80
Siebens, Arthur Robert 189, 191, 192
Silver, Morris 89

Skladny, Udo 140, 145
Smelik, K. A. D. 49, 62
Smend, Rudolf 115, 183
Smith, George Adam 180
Smith, J. M. Powis 175, 176, 180, 182
Snell, Daniel C. 210, 212
Soggin, J. Alberto 45, 46, 47, 102, 174
Spieckermann, Hermann 14, 17, 26, 31, 107, 108, 109, 111
Stade, B. 20, 32, 175, 176, 177
Staerk, Willy 189, 190, 192
Steck, Odil Hannes 168, 174, 175
Stegemann, U. 230, 248
Sternberg, G. 227, 239
Steuernagel, Carl 122, 189, 190, 191
Stolz, Fritz 197, 200, 201
Sweeney, Marvin A. 58, 180
Tadmor, Hayim 14, 16, 68, 70
Tångberg, K. Arvid 121, 131
Tatum, L. 107
Thompson, Michael E. W. 45, 46, 47, 102
Timm, S. 68, 72
Tucker, Gene M. 251
Uehlinger, Christoph 224
Ussishkin, David 75, 84, 86, 88, 111
Vanel, A. 102
Van Leeuwen, Raymond C. 210, 212, 213
Veijola, Timo 189, 197, 201, 202
Vermeylen, Jacques 49, 52, 55, 60, 155, 157, 172, 173, 174, 178, 246, 248, 257, 258
Vogt, Ernst 14, 22, 23, 59, 65, 69
Vollmer, Jochen 56, 228, 239, 240, 241, 244, 245
Vriezen, T. C. 198, 200
Vuilleumier, René 180
Wanke, Gunther 247
Warmuth, Georg 121, 131, 241
Washington, Harold C. 258, 260
Wegner, Paul D. 248
Weimar, P. 155, 158
Weinfeld, Moshe 108, 109, 110, 111, 189, 193, 196, 212

Weippert, Helga   10, 15, 17, 26, 69, 70, 75, 76, 78, 83, 84, 86, 110, 112, 114
Weippert, Manfred   69, 70, 84
Weiser, Artur   46, 47, 155, 156, 157, 178, 198, 200, 202, 227
Welch, Adam C.   31, 35, 189, 192
Wellhausen, Julius   189, 190, 199, 251
Welten, Peter   32, 33, 34, 35, 38, 40, 42, 43, 44, 75, 86
Werner, Wolfgang   168, 169, 174, 248, 249
Westermann, Claus   121, 122, 123, 124, 125, 126, 127, 128, 129, 130, 131, 140, 141, 203, 204, 205
Wette, W. M. L. de   189
Whedbee, J. William   257, 260
Whitt, W. D.   203
Whybray, R. N.   94, 96, 141, 142, 210, 258, 260
Wildberger, Hans   14, 23, 25, 26, 49, 52, 53, 55, 56, 57, 58, 59, 60, 61, 96, 172, 232
Williamson, H. G. M.   31, 32, 33, 34, 36, 37, 38, 42
Willi-Plein, Ina   155, 158, 159, 164, 167, 177, 246, 249
Willis, John T.   175
Willi, Thomas   32, 35, 36, 43, 44
Winckler, Hugo   10, 72, 106
Winter, I. J.   75, 76
Wolff, Hans Walter   45, 46, 47, 48, 64, 65, 94, 112, 116, 118, 119, 122, 126, 155, 157, 158, 160, 161, 163, 167, 178, 218, 220, 222, 230, 231, 233, 238, 239, 241, 244, 245, 246, 250, 257, 258, 261, 262, 264
Woude, A. S. van der   112, 119, 175, 178, 179, 180, 181
Wright, George Ernest   189, 192
Würthwein, Ernst   22, 23, 94, 95, 113, 122, 125, 198, 202, 227, 230, 251
Xella, P.   75, 84
Yee, Gale A.   162, 164, 165, 246
Yurco, F. J.   104
Zeeb, F.   89, 92
Zenger, Erich   239, 242
Zimmerli, Walther   49, 59, 141, 251
Zobel, Konstantin   251, 252, 256
Zwickel, W.   75, 76, 86, 109

Index of Subjects

ABBJ narrative 24, 26, 30
Abraham–Lot narrative 207
accusation 125
act–consequence process 147, 241, 259
Adad-Yahweh syncretism 109
alliances, policy of 16, 49, 61, 63, 224
Ammonite war 198
Amos, school of 157, 158, 160
annals 10, 12, 14, 15, 16, 17, 18, 27, 39, 43
Annals of the Kings 11, 12, 13, 19, 27, 40, 42, 199
Annals of the Kings of Judah 19
aphorism, folk 144
apodictic law 133
Arad, ostraca 69
Arad, temple 84, 110, 111
Ascension of Isaiah 68
Ashdodite revolt 57, 58, 60, 62, 117
Asherah 41, 83, 109, 225, 262
Ashur redaction 52, 54, 55, 57, 58, 59, 61, 63, 171, 172, 214
Ashur redactor 170
Baal 2, 9, 13, 28, 41, 83, 92, 112, 167, 192, 219, 221, 222, 223, 224, 225, 227, 262
Baal, and Asherah 83
Baal cult 221
Babylonian Chronicle 71, 72, 73, 104
belief 223
bi'artā texts 139, 194, 195
Bileam inscription 69
capitalism, early 91, 92

capitalism, interest 91, 92
casemate wall 77, 78
casuistic 138
casuistic law 132, 133, 134, 135, 137, 139, 187
Chicago Prism 72
child sacrifice 8, 16, 33, 109
Chronicler 1, 4, 5, 6, 7, 8, 31, 32, 33, 34, 35, 36, 37, 38, 39, 40, 41, 42, 43, 44, 45, 99, 107, 110, 170, 200, 214
city of David 5, 8, 35, 77, 79
construction motif, Chronicler's 33, 35, 38, 39, 42, 43, 44
court at the gate 134
covenant 222
Covenant Code 95, 99, 132, 136, 137, 138, 183, 186, 191, 215, 231, 232, 233, 251, 252, 253, 254
cult 263
cultic centralization 28, 30, 111, 173, 191, 192, 193, 195
cultic prophecy 97
cultic reform 27, 29, 30, 42, 44, 110, 111, 189, 191
cult of the dead 255
cult prophet 113
cult prostitute 116, 227
cult purification 5, 36, 38, 43, 44
Davidic dynasty 13, 28, 62, 111, 117, 201, 250
David, rise of 201
debt slavery 92, 95, 99, 231, 252, 253, 261

-277-

debt slavery, law of	99	Isaiah, redaction of	174
deportation	67, 68	Israel, end of kingdom	2
Deutero-Micah	179	Israel, obduration	174, 242
Deuteronomistic History	10, 11, 12, 13, 16, 18, 27, 109, 110, 114, 138, 159, 165, 194, 199, 225, 233, 237	ius soli--italics	92, 93
		ivory	73, 76, 90
		Jacob–Esau–Laban narratives	204
Deuteronomy	23	Jacob narrative	204
dissident literature	154	Jeroboam, sins of	27, 28
divine law redaction	187	Judean redaction	158, 161, 163, 193, 229, 231
Dtr	11		
DtrG	11, 13, 15, 18, 19, 25, 174, 178, 209	judgment formula	30
		jurisdiction, local	99
DtrH	11, 13, 15, 16, 19, 26, 28, 30, 31	justice, administration of	64, 99, 187, 231, 232, 233, 234, 260
DtrN	11, 13, 19, 20, 25, 26, 28, 30, 31, 187		
		kingship	193
DtrP	11, 26, 27, 29, 30, 158, 199, 201, 202, 255	king's stamps	86
		latifundia, development of	91, 92, 93, 95, 96, 118, 234, 235, 261
Edomites, war with	35		
Egypt, alliance with	6, 9, 61, 105	law	38
Elijah-Elisha cycle	104	legal grounds, theologization of	185
Eponym Chronicle	70	Levites	5, 6, 35, 36, 38, 96, 97, 116, 162, 184, 192, 193
Ethiopian dynasty	51, 59		
exhortation	131, 148	Manasseh, conversion of	41
foreign nations, prophecies about	58	Manasseh, imprisonment of	41
fortifications	39, 42, 44, 105	Manasseh, prayer of	42
genres, loan	130	māšāl	143, 144
God, knowledge of	220, 222, 227	mazkîr	98
God, relationship with	223	mazza, feast of	35
Hezekiah, cult reform	5, 6, 20, 21, 29, 30, 31, 35, 37	messenger formula	123, 124, 126
		midrashic revision	39
Hezekiah, illness	7, 25, 26, 30, 35, 39	mišpāṭîm	133, 135, 136
Hezekiah narratives	175	monotheism, ethical	251
high places	2, 3, 5, 6, 8, 14, 15, 18, 21, 28, 29, 30, 32, 38, 111, 157, 221	Nehushtan	5, 18, 29, 30, 38, 111, 226
		Nimrud text	70
Hosea, marriage	9, 48, 116, 165	Nineveh, fall of	180
host of heaven	2, 8, 13, 26, 28, 109	number, switching of	190
house, four-room	78	offices	96
Immanuel prophecy	4, 117, 172	oracle of salvation	127
Immanuel symbol	54	oral transmission	153
injunctive	135	ostraca	69, 84, 93, 96, 110, 153
inscriptions, Assyrian	69	palace buildings	78
Iron Age IIC	75	palace, head of the	98
Isaiah Apocalypse	9, 60, 169	*parallelismus membrorum*	144, 145, 146
Isaiah Memoir	53, 172, 243	parenesis	127, 129, 132, 134, 136, 137, 139, 191
Isaiah, Proto-	169, 214		

Passover	5, 35, 36	scribe, national	98
patriarchal history	215	scribes	96
peasant lands	92	scribes, court	193
Pentateuch, sources	198	Siloam Inscription	69

Passover 5, 35, 36
patriarchal history 215
peasant lands 92
Pentateuch, sources 198
people of the land 8, 27, 94, 95, 107
Philistines, war 18, 34
pillar figurines 84
P law 37
politics 264
poor 95
poverty 260
prediction of disaster 125
priests 35, 36, 38, 47, 96
prohibition 133, 135, 136, 253
pronouncement of the sentence 125
prophecy 261
prophet, call of 218
prophetic history 200, 201, 202
prophetic redaction 166, 201
prophetic stories, book of 199
prophets 8–10, 26, 27, 28, 29, 96
prophets, court 113
purification, judgment of 240, 241
Rabshakeh 6, 20, 21, 22, 23, 30, 57, 96, 98, 105, 128
Rassam Cylinder 73, 107
redaction, pre-Deuteronomistic 15, 186, 200, 202
redaction, versus updating 166
reform, Josiah's 189
remission year 254
remnant, idea of 249
retribution, direct 33, 34, 35, 38, 42, 45
sages, professional 96
salvation history 263
Samaria, capture of 13, 18, 72
Samaria, ostraca 69, 93, 96

scribe, national 98
scribes 96
scribes, court 193
Siloam Inscription 69
Siloam Tunnel 17, 38, 40, 43, 55, 77, 80, 105, 233
social injustice 64, 65
sōpēr 98
strata, destruction of 75
sun cult 110
sun god 109, 110, 226
supplementation hypothesis 196
symbolic act 9
Syro-Ephraimitic war 3, 4, 9, 16, 46, 47, 49, 53, 55, 58, 59, 60, 65, 103, 115, 118, 164, 167, 169, 170, 172, 200, 237, 249, 257
Taylor Prism 72
tôʻēbâ formula 139, 194
tradition-critical school 150
tradition criticism 152
trial speech 64, 123, 124, 125, 126, 128, 129, 132, 155, 218, 239, 240, 246
tribute, payment of 70, 71, 73, 90, 92, 94, 102, 103, 105, 106, 107
updating, versus redaction 166
Ur-Deuteronomy 136, 137, 140, 179, 188, 190, 191, 192, 193, 194, 195, 196, 197, 215, 231, 233, 252, 253, 254, 255
vassal treaty 134, 139, 140
violence 231
women, status of 48, 234, 263
word 217
YHWH alone 62, 209
YHWH war 192
Zion theology 24, 30, 174, 179
Zion tradition 247, 248

Index of Biblical References

Genesis

3	263
12–25	204
12–50	204
12:2	204
12:6–9	208
12:10	208
13	207, 208
13:14–16	256
13:14–17	207
13:17	256
15:7	204
16	208
16:10	204
16:13	257
18–19	207
21:8–21	208
21:33	257
22	208
25:19–36:43	204
25:21	206
25:21–34	209
25–35	209
25–50	207
26	208
26:3	204
27	206, 207
27–33	206
27:1–33:20	209
28	207, 208
28:11	206
28:13	256
28:13–14	207
28:14	256
28:15	204
28:20	206
28:20–22	206
29–30	206
31	206
31:3	204
31:13	206, 257
31:45–54	206
32–33	207
33:18	207
33:20	207, 257
34	207
35:1–20	209
35:6–7	207
35:8	207
35:9–12	204
35:16–20	207
35:21	207
35:22	207
37	207
37–50	204
38	207
39–45	207
41:40–45	98
46:2–4	204
46:3	257
46:5	207
46:28–33	207
47	207
48	207
49	207
50:1–11	207

INDEX OF BIBLICAL REFERENCES

50:14–21	207	23:4–5	134
		23:6	253, 254
Exodus		23:6–8	99
12:12	106	23:6-9	233
13:7–8	153	23:8	136
13:14–15	153	23:9	99, 135
18:25–26	233	23:11	95, 253, 254
20:1–17	135	23:13	135
20:17	133	23:14–17	196
20:18–21	136	23:14–19	132
20:22	135	23:20–33	132
20:22–26	136	24:4	153
20:22–23:13	132	24:7	132
20:22–23:33	132	28:3	141
20:23–23:19	99	30:15	95
21:1	133	31:3	141
21:1–11	196	34	191
21:1–22:16	133–34		
21:2–6	133	Leviticus	
21:2–11	99, 134, 138, 252, 254	6:19–22	227
21:3–6	231	7:7	227
21:7–11	134, 252	15:31	37
21:12	125, 134, 135	17–20	191
21:12–15	135	25:6	95
21:13–14	134		
21:15–17	135	Numbers	
21:22–23	134	5:11–31	153
21:23	134	9:9–11	37
21:26–27	133, 134	18:8–24	38
22:8	97	21:14	153
22:17	135	21:27	153
22:17–23:13	135	23:7	144
22:18	135	23:18	144
22:19	135	24:3	144
22:20–21	99	24:15	144
22:20–23:19	136	24:20–21	144
22:23	135	24:23	144
22:24	100, 232, 253, 254	28–29	38
22:24–26	134		
22:25	100	Deuteronomy	
22:25–26	252	1–4	194
22:28	135	1–11	190
22:30	136	4:9–10	153
23:1–3	99, 233, 252	4:35	23, 222
23:3	253	4:39	23, 222

Deuteronomy (cont.)

4:44–9:6	194	17:9	97
5–11	190, 195	17:14–20	139
5–28	195	18:9–22	139
6:5	192	18:10–12	255
6:6–7	153	19:1–13	139
6:20–25	153	19:13	138
7:9	222	19:14	252
8:2–5	222	19:16–19	138
9:3–8	222	19:19	138
10:12–11:32	194	19:20	138
11:19	153	20:1–9	139
12:2–3	252	21:1–9	139
12–26	**188–97**, 215	21:2–11	253
12–28	137	21:9	138
13:1–6	138	21:15–17	138
13:2–4	137	21:18–22	138
13:7–12	137	21:19	99
13:7–19	138	21:21	138
13:9	138	21:22–23	138
13:12	138	21:24–26	253
14:1	255	22:5–11	138
14:1–2	252	22:6–7	138
14:21	136	22:13–29	138
14:22	137	22:17–18	254
15:1	137	22:20	254
15:1–3	139	22:20–21	253
15:1–11	254	22:21	138
15:7	254	22:24	138
15:7–11	139	22:25–27	138
15:9	254	23:1–8	253
15:11	254	23:1–9	138
15:12–14	139	23:3	253
15:12–17	139	23:7	253
15:12–18	138, 231, 254	23:11	253
15:15	139	23:16–24:18	139
15:16–17	139	23:22–24	138
15:18	139	23:25–26	138
15:19–23	139	24:1–4	138
16:5	37	24:10–12	138
16:16–17	140	24:10–13	253
16:19	136, 137, 233, 252	24:12–13	252
16:21–17:1	138, 139	24:16	94
17:2–7	139	24:17	252
17:8–13	137	24:19	138
		25:1–3	138

INDEX OF BIBLICAL REFERENCES

25:5–10	138	19:18	198
25:13–15	252	19:18–24	201
26:1–11	139	28	198, 199
27:1–10	194	31	198
27:15	252		
28	190, 193	2 Samuel	
28:1–68	194	1:18	153
28:69–32:47	194	6	198
31:6	39	6:16	198
31:10–13	140	6:20–23	198
32:7	153	7	54, 198, 202, 250
		7:1–17	113
Joshua		7:4–9	201
4:7–22	153	7:15	201
10:13	153	7:20–21	201
22:24–28	153	8:16–17	98
		9–20	198
Judges		9–1 Kgs 2	202
6:13	153	10:6–11:1	198
9:10	223	11:2–12:24	201
12:1–6	223	12	199, 202
		12:26–31	198
1 Samuel		13:3	141
1–3	198	20:15	98
1–7	201	20:16	141
2:31	130	21–24	198
4–6	198	22	151
7–8	201	24	199
7–15	198, 200	24:10–14	201
8–14	201	24:11	113
9:1–10:16	201	24:16	201
9:9	113	24:17	106
10:5	113	24:17–19	201
10:10–12	112		
10:17–25	201	1 Kings	
10:25	153	1	202
11:15	236	1–2	198, 202
12	201	2:3	214
15	199, 201	3:3	18
16–2 Sam 5	201	3:3–28	259
16–2 Sam 5:25	198	3:16	12
16:1–13	198, 201	4:3	98
17:12	198, 250	5:10–14	210
18:5	17	5:12–13	144
18:27	17	5:27–28	199

1 Kings (cont.)		22:48	53
5:31–32	199		
6:1–7:51	199	2 Kings	
7:14	141	1:2–8	200
8:2–8	199	1:3	225
9:10–11	199	1:3–4	124
9:15	199	1:6	225
9:17–19	199	1:16	225
10:1–9	210	1:17	200
10:16–20	199	3:11–20	113
11:27–28	199	6:16	39
11:29	113	8:18	16
11:29–39	200	8:27	16
12:26–32	13	9–10	57
12:26–33	2	9:1–10	200
12:28	2, 225	9:7	29
12:31–13:34	14	10:28–33	12
13	113, 199	10:30	1, 12
13:33–34	28	12:3–4	15
14:1–6	199	12:4	18, 32
14:1–16	200	12:5–19	199
14:7–11	29	13:22	56
14:8	28	14:3–4	15
14:12–13	199	14:4	18, 32
14:16	28	14:8–14	199
14:17–18	199	14:22	53
14:22–24	18	15–16	15
14:25–28	199	15:2	15
15:14	18	15:3–4	15
15:15	199	15:4	18, 33
15:17–22	199	15:5	3, 98
16:1–4	200	15:6	17
16:2	29	15:8	11
18:4	29	15:8–10	1
18:19	225	15:8–31	11
18:26	113	15:8–21:26	**10–31**, 67
18:36	225	15:9	11
20	200	15:10	11, 12, 46, 57
21:17–19	124	15:11	17
21:22	29	15:11–12	11
22	200	15:12	12
22:10	113	15:13	11
22:19–23	217	15:13–16	1
22:43–44	15	15:14	11, 12, 57
22:44	18	15:15	11, 17

INDEX OF BIBLICAL REFERENCES

15:16	11, 12	16:14	109
15:17	12	16:15	109
15:17–22	50	16:17–18	5
15:18	12	16:20	5
15:19	1, 101, 102	17:1–5	2
15:19–20	12, 90	17:1–6	13
15:20	1, 94	17:2	28
15:21–22	12	17:3	103
15:22	12	17:4	47, 103
15:23	12	17:5	18
15:23–25	2	17:5–6	18, 104
15:24	12	17:6	14
15:25	12, 57	17:7–17	18
15:26	12	17:7–18	158
15:27	12	17:7–23	2, 13, 14, 28
15:27–29	2	17:14–15	2
15:28	12	17:16	2
15:29	56, 68, 103	17:23	2
15:29–30	12	17:24	14, 94, 104
15:30	2, 12, 57, 71, 103	17:24–41	3, 14
15:31	12	17:25	68
15:32–38	15	17:25–28	3
15:33	12, 15	17:29–31	14
15:34	32	18–19	106, 214
15:35	3, 18, 27, 33	18–20	17
15:36	33	18–21	15
15:37	3, 33, 103	18:1–2	17
15:38	33	18:1–12	18
16	16	18:1–16	19
16:2–4	3, 33	18:2	15
16:3	109	18:3	5, 30
16:3–4	29	18:3–8	17, 18
16:4	30	18:4	5, 6, 27, 30, 35, 36, 38, 84, 97, 111, 188
16:5	3, 33, 53, 54, 117, 199		
16:5–9	103	18:5–7	20, 38
16:5–18	16	18:7	105, 214
16:6	4, 35	18:7–16	6
16:7	4, 34, 103, 238	18:8	59, 60, 105, 198
16:7–9	2, 62	18:9–11	13, 18
16:7–18	27, 199	18:12	18
16:8	35, 90	18:13	19, 38, 51, 61
16:9	35, 68	18:13–16	19, 20, 27
16:10–13	4	18:13–37	105
16:10–16	97, 109	18:13–19:37	7
16:10–18	16, 17, 35	18:13–20:19	19, 200

2 Kings (cont.)	
18:13–21:21	38
18:14	90
18:14–16	19, 24, 39, 199
18:17	86
18:17–19:13	105
18:17–19:34	63
18:17–19:37	20, 39
18:17–20:19	27, 51, 61
18:18	96, 98
18:19–21	6
18:19–25	20
18:19–36	6
18:22	30
18:28–32	20
18:28–35	23
18:29–30	23
18:33–35	57
19:1–7	6, 20, 117
19:1–34	39
19:2	96, 98
19:7	106
19:8–9	20
19:9	106
19:9–36	22, 24
19:14	39
19:18	86
19:18–19	7
19:20–33	117
19:20–34	7, 23
19:34–35	30
19:35	68
19:35–38	106
19:36–37	20
20:1–7	30
20:1–11	7, 25, 39
20:1–19	117
20:12–18	40
20:12–19	8, 25, 40, 105
20:13	40
20:17	30, 130
20:20	8, 17, 40, 105
20:20–21	17, 19, 40
21	8, 27, 31, 42, 107
21:1	15
21:1–9	41
21:1–18	26, 107
21:2	16
21:3	13, 28
21:3–18	109
21:5	109
21:6	13, 16, 28, 109
21:7	109
21:10–15	8, 30, 41
21:13	28, 29, 30
21:16	8, 30, 107
21:17–18	42
21:19	15, 28
21:19–24	8
21:19–26	27, 43
21:21–23	29
21:23–24	27, 107
21:24	94
22:8	137
23:4	26, 225
23:4–6	42
23:5	18, 109, 110
23:6	26
23:8	26
23:11	53, 109, 110
23:12	26, 42, 110
23:22	36
23:26	42
24:3	42
24:4	30
24:13	26

1 Chronicles	
4:34–43	105
15:22	113
15:27	113
23–26	38

2 Chronicles	
6:37–38	34
7:14	37
8:14	38
9:29	34
12:15	34
13:22	34

INDEX OF BIBLICAL REFERENCES

15:1	34	29:1	32
18–20	200	29:1–2	35
19:4–11	99	29:2	32
19:8	184	29:3–17	96
19:11	184	29:3–36	35
20:13–17	113	29:3–31:21	35
21:15	106	29:3–32:31	32
21:20	35	29:6–11	36
24:2	32	29:12–14	36
24:25	35	29:12–15	35
25:2	32	29:16	38
26:2	53	29:25–30	35
26:4	33	29:30	98
26:16–20	32	29:34–35	35
26:21	3, 94	29:35	5
26:23	35	30	35, 36, 37
27–33	**31–45**, 67	30:1	44
27:1	32	30:3	36
27:2	32	30:5	36, 44
27:3–4	3, 33, 43	30:6	98
27:3–5	15	30:6–9	36
27:3–6	32	30:10–11	36
27:5	33	30:16	36
27:6	33, 45	30:17	36
27:7–9	32	30:18	36, 37
28:1	32, 33	30:21–22	36
28:1–4	3, 32, 33	30:25	36
28:5–8	3, 33, 45	30:26	6, 44
28:5–25	32	31:1	35, 38, 44
28:7	43, 98	31:2	36
28:9–15	34, 200	31:2–19	38, 97
28:12–15	34, 43	31:2–31	35
28:15	4	31:3	38
28:16–19	34	31:5	38
28:17	34	31:12–19	36
28:17–18	4	31:20–21	38
28:19	45	32	38, 45
28:20	35	32:1–8	38
28:21	35	32:1–23	7, 35, 105
28:22–25	35	32:2–5	43, 60, 105
28:23–25	5	32:2–8	38
28:26–27	32, 35	32:3	98
28:27	5	32:3–4	40
29–31	5, 38	32:3–5	7
29–32	35, 211	32:5–6	43

2 Chronicles (cont.)		12:44–47	38
32:7–8	7, 39	13:10–13	38
32:9–23	39		
32:17	7, 39	Esther	
32:20	39	6:1	98
32:23	38		
32:24	39	Job	
32:24–26	35	12:12	141
32:24–29	7	15:10	141
32:25	40, 238		
32:27–29	40	Psalms	
32:28	86, 105	15	186
32:30	8, 40, 43	18	151
32:31	35, 40	24	186
32:32–33	32, 40	44	65
33:1	32	44:2	153
33:1–9	41	45:2	96
33:1–20	8	46	247
33:2	32	48	247
33:3–17	32	49:5	144
33:6	33	72	65
33:10	41	76	247
33:11	68, 73	78:2	144
33:11–13	41, 107	78:2–6	153
33:14	42, 43	80:2	228
33:14–16	181	80:2–3	228
33:14–17	42	80:4–8	228
33:15–17	42	80:5	228
33:18–20	32, 42	80:9	228
33:21	32	80:10–12	228
33:21–25	8, 43	80:15	228
33:22–23	32	80:17	228
33:24–25	32, 107	80:19	228
33:25	94	81:5–6	228
34:6–7	38	81:6	228
		81:6–8	228
Ezra		81:8	228
4:2	2	81:9	228
4:9–10	2	81:9–10	228
8:33	110	81:11	228
13	113	81:12	228
		81:12–14	228
Nehemiah		81:14	228
2:19	33	81:15–16	228
6:7	113	103	186

INDEX OF BIBLICAL REFERENCES

145	186	16:1–4	259
		16:6–7	260
Proverbs		16:12	257, 260
1–9	143, 149, 210	17:5	259, 260, 261
1:1	210	17:8	260
1:2–5	143	17:13	147
1:6	143	17:15	258, 260
4:24	146	17:18	211
6:1–5	211	17:19	145, 146
6:5–11	148	17:23	260
6:6	148	17:26	260
7:7–23	148	18:5	147, 260
10–22	135, 260	18:8	212
10:1	210	18:10	146
10:1–22:6	214	18:16	260
10:1–22:16	210, 211, 212, 215	18:23	96
10:2–3	148	19:2	211
10:3	261	19:17	260, 261
10:4	260	19:24	147
10:4–5	211	20:13	260
11:1	258	20:16	211
11:9–12	148	20:17	148
11:15	211	20:18	257
11:18	146	20:21	211
11:24	260	20:23	258
11:31	147	21:3	260
12:1	145	21:5	211, 260
12:9	147	21:17	260
12:9–11	211	22:2	261
13:1	96	22:7	96, 231
13:3	146	22:8	135
13:11	211	22:12	260
13:18	260	22:16	161
13:21	147	22:17	96, 210
13:23	211	22:17–23:11	143, 210
13:25	260	22:17–24:22	211, 260
14:4	211	22:22	161, 258
14:11	147	22:22–23	210, 260
14:15	147	22:23	260
14:21	260	22:26–27	211
14:31	161, 260, 261	22:28	260
15:5	96	23:4–5	260
15:8–9	260	23:10	260
15:25	261	23:10–11	210
15:27	145	23:19	260

Proverbs (cont.)

23:31	148	28:6–11	213
24:22	210	28:8	211, 260, 261
24:23	96, 210	28:14	147
24:30	260	28:16	260
24:30–34	148	28:19	211, 260
25	213, 214	28:20	211
25–27	212, 213	28:22	211, 260
25–29	10, 65, 210, 211, 212, 213, 215, 258, 260	28:27	260
		29:4	260
		29:7	260, 261
25:1	10, 96, 210, 213, 214	29:13	260, 261
25:2–7	212	29:14	257, 260
25:2–27	212	29:20	211
25:4	258	29:26	96
25:5	257	30:1	210
25:6–7	96, 148	30:15	212
25:11–22	213	30:15–16	148
25:16–17	213	30:15–33	148
25:18–19	213	30:17–20	213
25:19	213	30:18	212
25:20	213	30:18–20	148
25:21–22	261	30:29	212
25:23–28	213	31:1	210
26	213	31:6–7	235
26:1–3	213		
26:1–12	212	*Isaiah*	**49–64, 167–75**
26:5	258	1	9
26:7–10	148	1–6	50
26:12	258	1–12	9, 117
26:13–16	212	1–23	214
26:15	147	1–27	50
26:16	258	1–33	50
26:17–28	212	1–39	50, 51, 127, 128, 129, 247
26:20–21	213	1:1	9, 40, 52
26:22	212, 213	1:1–20	50
26:23	213	1:2–3	241
26:24–25	213	1:4–8	63
27	213	1:4–9	52
27:1–12	212	1:7	90
27:13	211	1:10	98
27:19	146	1:10–17	230, 241
27:23–27	211, 212, 213	1:11–17	229
28–29	213, 261	1:16–17	131, 235, 241
28:3	161, 260, 261	1:17	64, 234
28:6	260	1:18–20	131, 132, 241

INDEX OF BIBLICAL REFERENCES

1:19–20	129	5:7	99, 233, 234
1:21	234	5:8	91, 92, 232
1:21–26	246, 248	5:8–10	92, 118, 234
1:21–28	234, 241	5:8–13	239
1:23	99, 258	5:8–24	57, 64
1:25	258	5:9	91
1:25–26	128	5:10–11	57
1:26	234	5:11–12	234
1:26–27	265	5:13	53
1:27–28	129	5:21	141, 212, 258
1:29	229	5:23	99, 232, 234, 258
2–5	9	5:25–29	235, 245
2–11	214	5:25–30	218
2:1–4	128, 247, 248	5:26–28	53
2:1–14:27	63	6	9, 50, 113, 218, 229
2:2–4	151, 248	6–12	9
2:2–5	53	6:1	117
2:6–8	52, 53	6:1–8	153
2:6–19	235	6:1–8:18	54
2:6–22	50, 52	6:8	217
2:7–17	52, 241	6:9–10	131, 241, 242, 243
2:8	225, 229	6:11	241, 245
2:10	53, 131	6:12	53
2:12–17	53	6:13	249
2:16	53	6:18	153
2:19–20	129	6:28–30	154
2:20	229	7	4, 53, 60, 117
3:1–12	53	7–14	50
3:1–24	117	7:1	53, 131
3:3	141	7:1–9	103, 237
3:6–7	98	7:1–17	54, 127
3:10–11	52	7:1–8:18	53
3:13–15	64, 234	7:1–9:6	53
3:14	232	7:2–9	243
3:14–15	232	7:2–17	54
3:16–24	53, 64, 234	7:2–20	54
3:16–26	235	7:3	117
3:18	129	7:4	237
4:2–6	52, 128	7:4–9	250
4:3	249	7:5–17	62
4:3–6	247	7:6	62, 103, 117
4:4	234	7:9	223
5	50, 57	7:14	249, 265
5:1–4	235	7:14–16	4
5:1–7	241	7:17	53

Isaiah (cont.)

7:17–18	129	10:2	95, 234
7:18–25	55	10:5–15	6, 57, 64
7:20	53	10:6	63
7:22	54	10:12	129
8	50, 53	10:15–19	63
8–9	247	10:20–21	128, 249
8:1	96, 153	10:20–23	52
8:1–2	117, 153	10:24–27	52, 129
8:1–4	4, 55, 62, 116, 128, 247	10:27	129
8:1–8	54	10:27–32	57, 58
8:1–14	2	10:27–34	248
8:2	117	10:27–12:6	50
8:3	117	10:28–32	118
8:4	63	10:33–34	52
8:5–8	55, 125, 126	11:1–5	95
8:6–7	53	11:1–9	249
8:9	54	11:1–9:10	128
8:9–10	55, 129, 248	11:4	95
8:11	54	11:6–9	52
8:11–15	55	11:10	128, 129
8:12	62	11:10–16	52
8:13	235	11:11–16	128
8:16	114, 150, 153	11:12–16	53
8:16–18	55, 62, 117	12	52
8:17	243	12:1	129
8:18	229	13	50
8:19–23	55	13–23	9, 51, 58
8:21–22	55	13:1	51
8:21–9:7	50	13:1–22	51
8:23–9:6	54, 55	14:1–2	128
9:1–6	56, 128, 249, 257, 265	14:1–27	50
9:5	257	14:3–4	129
9:5–6	250, 260	14:4–20	58
9:6	234	14:20–21	58
9:7–11	125	14:24–26	63
9:7–20	218, 235, 245	14:24–27	51, 58, 223, 248
9:7–10:4	56, 57, 63	14:28–32	9, 50, 51, 58, 59, 103, 248
9:8–11	56	14:29–32	237
9:12–16	57	14:32	247, 248
9:17–20	57	15–16	50
10	244	15–33	50
10:1	153	15:1	51
10:1–3	64	15:1–16:14	51, 151
10:1–4	57, 232	16:1	128
		16:4–5	128

16:13–14	52	22:15–25	51, 60
17	51	22:20–23	60
17:1–6	51, 52, 58, 59, 62	22:24–25	52
17:7–8	128	22:24–36	60
17:10	229	23	51
17:12–14	59, 63, 129, 247, 248	23:1	51
18	50, 51, 58, 59, 62	23:1–14	51, 60
18:1–6	237	23:15	129
18:1–19:15	51	23:15–18	52, 60
18:3	59	24–27	9, 51, 60, 214, 247
18:7	59, 128	27:8–13	53
18:48	226	28–31	61
19	50, 51, 59	28–32	214
19:1	225	28–33	9, 50, 51, 60, 214
19:1–4	59	28:1–4	63
19:1–15	52	28:1–6	9
19:3	225	28:1–13	60
19:11–13	57	28:5	249
19:11–14	59	28:5–6	52
19:11–15	212	28:7–13	97, 113
19:14	141	28:9	117
19:16	129	28:12	131
19:16–25	51, 52	28:14–22	61, 62, 245
19:19–25	128	28:14–29	212
20	9, 51, 58, 60, 62, 105	28:16	223
20–22	50, 51	28:16–17	248
20:1–6	237	28:17	234
21	51	28:17–22	248
21:1	51	28:21	63, 223, 226
21:1–17	51	28:22	131, 241
21:11	51	28:23–29	63
21:13	51	29:1–4	62, 241, 245, 248
21:16–17	52	29:1–8	61, 248
22:1–9	51	29:5–7	61
22:1–14	51, 60, 63, 241	29:5–8	63, 129
22:1–19	58	29:9–10	131, 241, 242
22:3	98	29:13–14	61
22:8–11	63	29:13–16	212
22:9–11	38, 43, 105	29:14	212, 223
22:12–13	63	29:15–16	61, 62
22:13	229	29:17–21	128
22:15	98	29:17–24	52
22:15–16	117	29:22–24	128
22:15–19	60	30:1–2	212
22:15–23	98	30:1–5	61

Isaiah (cont.)

30:1–6	9	38:1–8	25
30:1–7	6, 62, 237	38:5–8	128
30:6–7	61	38:6	7
30:8	114, 150, 153	38:9–20	7, 19, 25
30:8–9	154	38:19	153
30:8–14	61	38:22	25
30:12–14	126	38–39	50, 51, 117
30:15	63, 131	39	8
30:15–17	61	39:1–8	237
30:16	63	39:6	130
30:18–26	52, 128	40–55	128
30:27–33	61, 63, 248	40–66	50, 51, 214
31:1–3	6, 9, 61, 62, 105	40:20	141
31:1–9	248	43:10–11	23
31:2	218	44:6–8	23
31:3	39	44:24	23
31:4	248	45:5–7	23
31:4–5	61, 247	51:1–2	209
31:4–9	248	54	54
31:5	61, 63	56–66	128
31:8–9	61, 63		
32:1–5	128	*Jeremiah*	
32:6–8	52	1	113, 218
32:9–14	61	2:8	141
33	52	5:10–14	126
33:1–16	129	7:16–20	126
33:14–16	129	7:18	109, 110
34	9	7:31	33
34–35	50, 51, 129, 214, 247	8:8	96, 141
35	10	8:8–12	141
36–37	7, 50, 51, 61, 63, 105, 237	15:4	41, 42
36–38	127	17:5	39
36–39	19, 51, 61, 117, 214	18:18	96, 141
36:1	19	19:13	110
36:2–37:13	105	20:1	110
36:3	60, 96	23:9–24	113
36:5	257	23:11	97
36:15	128	26:17–19	118
36:22	96	26:18	179, 243
37:1–7	117	28	113
37:2	96	30:2	150
37:5–7	128	32:29	110
37:21–35	117	35:4	113
37:30–32	128	36	153
		36:2	150

37–38	24	4:4–10	97
44:15–19	109	4:6	222, 227
44:19	110	4:7–8	222
48:29–39	151	4:8	227
49:7–22	151	4:11–12	222
51:60	153	4:12	226, 252
		4:13	252
Ezekiel		4:15	9, 128, 131
2:9–10	153	5:1–2	46, 103
7:26	141	5:3–4	46
17:2	144	5:4	222
24:3	144	5:5	9
27:8	141	5:5–7	46
33:24	209	5:8–9	46
43:11–12	153	5:8–11	116
		5:8–6:11	46
Hosea	**45–49, 161–67**	5:8–7:16	46
1	116, 117, 129	5:10	46, 252
1–3	9	5:12–14	46
1:1	9, 46, 115	5:13	46
1:2	116	5:14	244
1:2–8	116	5:15	131
1:2–9	48, 240	5:15–6:6	47
1:4	46	6:2	212
1:7	9, 128	6:3	222
2:1–3	128	6:6	131, 222, 227, 230, 263
2:4	131, 221	6:7	222, 223
2:4–7	48	6:7–10	47
2:4–17	247	6:11	9, 128
2:4–13:15	214	7:3–7	47, 236
2:5–12	227	7:5	47
2:7–9	126	7:8–12	9, 47
2:10–15	48	7:11	103
2:16–17	223	7:14	252
2:16–22	240	7:16	46
2:16–25	116, 128, 130	8:1	222
2:17–25	247	8:4	46, 192, 236, 252
2:22	222	8:4–5	251
2:23	221	8:5	131
3	9, 116, 129	8:5–6	225
3:1	221	8:7–10	47
3:1–5	128	8:10	192
3:5	222, 246	8:11	252
4:1	222	8:12	153, 222
4:4	192	8:13	230

Hosea (cont.)		14:2-9	128
9-12	116	14:4	53
9:7	218	14:5	221
9:10	223	14:5-8	128
9:11-14	48, 115		
9:15	236	Amos	**154-61**
10:1	252	1-2	155, 157, 160, 161, 212
10:1-2	225	1-4	159
10:1-8	48	1-6	156, 159
10:3	46	1:1	50, 56, 114, 157, 158
10:3-4	222	1:1-2	156
10:4	236	1:1-7:9	155
10:5-8	225	1:1-9:6	158
10:11	209	1:1-9:12	159
10:12	129, 132, 221, 222	1:2	156, 157, 218
10:12-13	131	1:3-5	156
10:15	46	1:3-2:3	252
10:24	98	1:3-2:8	258
10:25	39	1:3-2:16	159, 240
11:1	222	1:6-8	56
11:1-4	220	1:6-12	156
11:2	252	1:9-12	155, 156, 157, 158
11:5-6	47, 103, 115	1:13-15	156
11:8-9	128, 130, 247	2:1-3	156
11:10-11	128	2:4-5	155, 156, 157, 158
12	48, 209	2:6	95, 161, 231, 236, 252
12:1	128	2:6-7	232, 258
12:1-2	9	2:6-8	156
12:2	47, 236	2:7	95, 158, 161, 232, 252
12:3	9	2:8	100, 231, 252
12:4-5	209	2:9	245
12:7	129, 131, 132	2:9-11	156
12:8	252	2:10	156
12:10	129, 220, 223, 251	2:10-11	220
12:14	222	2:10-12	157
13	48	2:11-12	156
13:2	226, 251, 252	2:12	156
13:4	131, 220, 251	2:13-14	161
13:4-5	223	2:13-16	156, 157, 236, 240
13:8	125	2:15	156
13:10	236	2:15-16	161
13:10-11	48, 252	3-6	155, 156, 157, 160
13:11	192, 236	3:1	156, 157, 220
13:15	221	3:1-2	158, 220
14:2-3	131	3:2	220

INDEX OF BIBLICAL REFERENCES

Reference	Pages
3:3–8	158
3:7	156, 157
3:8	218, 220
3:9	115
3:9–10	236
3:9–11	161
3:9–4:3	158, 159
3:10	232
3:11	236, 240
3:12	160, 161, 239, 240
3:13	158
3:13–14	229
3:14	157, 158, 231
3:15	161, 240
4:1	95, 115, 231, 232
4:1–3	126, 158, 161, 231, 240
4:1–13	158
4:2	130
4:4–5	131, 158, 159, 161, 229, 231, 252
4:4–12	240
4:5	229
4:6–12	158
4:6–13	157
4:7	156
4:12	159
4:13	155, 156
5–9	159
5:1	95
5:1–2	161
5:1–9:10	159
5:2–3	240
5:2–6:14	159
5:3	160, 161, 236
5:4–5	158, 159, 161, 229, 231, 247, 249, 252
5:4–6	129, 131, 132
5:5	110, 157, 240
5:6	156, 157, 161
5:7	161, 231
5:8	156
5:8–9	155, 156, 157
5:9–17	158
5:10	99, 161, 232, 240
5:10–12	252
5:11	161, 231, 232
5:11–12	231
5:12	99, 161, 232, 236
5:13	156
5:13–15	157
5:14–15	129, 131, 132, 156, 161, 252
5:15	99, 246, 249, 265
5:16–17	161, 240
5:18	240, 258
5:18–20	239
5:18–27	158
5:21	240
5:21–22	161
5:21–24	158, 228, 229, 231, 252
5:21–27	230
5:22	157
5:23–24	161, 229
5:24	131, 231
5:25	156
5:25–26	157
5:26	109, 156, 229
5:27	161, 240
6:1	115, 156, 161, 231, 258
6:1–3	161
6:1–14	158
6:2	156, 157, 161
6:4	161
6:4–7	231
6:5	157
6:6	157, 161
6:7	161, 240
6:8	158, 231, 240
6:11	158, 240
6:11–12	161
6:12	231
6:13–14	240
6:14	156
7	114
7–9	155, 159, 160
7:1	218
7:1–3	239
7:1–6	160, 212
7:1–8	157
7:1–9	156
7:1–17	160

Amos (cont.)		9:8–10	128, 129, 158, 249
7:1–8:3	158, 159	9:9–10	156
7:1–9:4	159	9:11	159
7:2	209	9:11–12	128
7:4	218	9:11–15	155, 156, 157, 246
7:4–6	239	9:13	130
7:7	218	9:13–15	128, 159
7:7–8	239		
7:7–9:10	160	Obadiah	
7:9	156, 157, 240	1–9	151
7:10	114		
7:10–11	115	Micah	**64–65, 175–79**
7:10–17	155, 156, 157, 160, 161	1–3	214
7:13	97	1:2–7	64, 118
7:14	114, 115	1:5	233
7:15	113, 114, 218	1:6–7	118
7:16	157	1:8–16	64, 118
7:16–17	124	1:10–15	118
8–9	155	2:1–3	118
8:1–2	157, 239	2:1–4	126, 129
8:1–3	156, 240	2:1–5	65, 91, 92, 234, 239
8:2	212, 239	2:1–11	118
8:3	114, 156, 157	2:2	232
8:4	158, 229	2:4	129
8:4–6	258	2:5	233
8:4–7	159, 161	2:12–13	128
8:4–14	156, 157, 158	3:1	98, 99, 209, 233
8:5	231, 252	3:1–4	126
8:5–6	91	3:1–12	65
8:6	95, 252	3:5	113
8:7	158	3:5–8	219
8:8	156	3:8	218
8:11	130	3:9	98, 99, 258
8:11–14	156	3:9–11	234
8:14	110, 157	3:9–12	118, 126
9:1	240	3:10	233
9:1–4	156, 157	3:11	97, 219, 232, 258
9:1–14	239	3:12	243
9:5–6	155, 156, 157	4–5	128
9:6	156	4:1–3	151, 247
9:7	156, 220, 244	4:1–4	128
9:7–10	157, 159	5:1–3	128
9:7–15	158	5:1–5	250
9:8	156, 157, 249	5:9–14	53
9:8–9	246	6:6–7	229

6:8	220, 229, 233	Zechariah	
6:9–15	239	7:10	235
6:9–16	65		
7:7–20	128	Sirach	
		51:23	142
Nahum	**180–82**	51:29	142
1:10–11	226		
1:14	226	Matthew	
2:2–3	226	9:13	263
3:8–10	107		
		Ephesians	
Habakkuk		5:22–33	263
2:2	153		
		Hebrews	
Zephaniah		11:37	68
1:4	110		
Haggai			
2:11–13	97		

www.ingramcontent.com/pod-product-compliance
Lightning Source LLC
Chambersburg PA
CBHW032001220426

43664CB00005B/104